CITIZENS AND POLITICS

*Samuel J. Eldersveld
and Bashiruddin Ahmed*

CITIZENS AND POLITICS
Mass Political Behavior in India

THE UNIVERSITY OF CHICAGO PRESS
Chicago and London

SAMUEL J. ELDERSVELD is professor of political science at the University of Michigan. He is the author of *Political Parties: A Behavioral Analysis,* which won the Woodrow Wilson Award for the best book in political science in 1964.
BASHIRUDDIN AHMED is at the Centre for the Study of Developing Societies in Delhi, India, and is coauthor of *Caste, Race, and Politics: A Comparative Study of India and the United States.*

THE UNIVERSITY OF CHICAGO PRESS, CHICAGO 60637
THE UNIVERSITY OF CHICAGO PRESS, LTD., LONDON

© 1978 by The University of Chicago
All rights reserved. Published 1978
Printed in the United States of America
83 82 81 80 79 78   9 8 7 6 5 4 3 2 1

LIBRARY OF CONGRESS CATALOGING IN PUBLICATION DATA

Eldersveld, Samuel James.
  Citizens and politics.

  Includes bibliographical references and index.
    1. India—Politics and government—1947–
  2. Political participation—India. I. Ahmed, Bashiruddin, joint author. II. Title.
  JQ298.A1E48   320.9'54'04   77–21395
  ISBN 0-226-20280-1

To Lucy and Sam and Saleha
and
To the many young Indian students who walked the length and breadth of India, who helped us ask the right questions, and who faithfully recorded the answers

Contents

Preface

T HIS IS A STUDY OF THE INDIAN CITIZEN'S INVOLVEMENT IN THE DEM-
ocratic political process before the June 1975 Emergency. It is based on
national surveys of citizen attitudes and participation at the time of the
1967 and 1971 national elections. The major question we pose is, To what
extent has the Indian public accepted the norms of political democracy and
participated meaningfully in the democratic system? And, consequently,
what is the character of Indian political development at the mass level? In
exploring this problem we use a theoretical model of Indian political
development to interpret the data, leading to system-level generalizations
while describing individual-level relationships. Throughout we attempt to
evaluate the involvement of Indian citizens by comparing their involvement to that of citizens in the United States and other countries for which
national survey data are available. As such, our mode of analysis is
empirical, longitudinal, and comparative, and our contribution, we hope,
is system-theoretical. The unique data presented here, for one slice of
political time in India, 1967–71, are directly relevant for describing and
explaining the nature and extent of political development at that time. In
addition, these data provide a base for speculation, for understanding the
1975 crisis and possible future developments.

The events of June 1975 leading to the declaration of an emergency in
India have produced concern and shock, both sympathetic and critical,
throughout the world. From Independence in 1947 to the crisis of 1975 the
Indian system evolved as a free and open parliamentary democracy based
on massive citizen involvement. In the course of twenty-eight years the
apolitical, mainly illiterate, poor, rural Indian subject had become a
politicized citizen who was significantly committed to democratic norms
and who participated in democratic practices. India had become one of the
leading democratic political societies of the world. There are those today
who see the recent events as only a transitional phase leading to a modified
democratic system; there are others, however, who see these events as
having vital consequences and costs for Indian democracy, threatening the
viability of the democratic Indian polity itself. Scholars and supporters of
India will wait anxiously and impatiently for the return to democratic
practice. Here we wish to empirically demonstrate the character, accom-

plishments, and potential of that democracy at the level of mass beliefs and behaviors prior to the onset of the present crisis, to document what the Indian democratic system has been, and what it still can be.

This is the first serious empirical effort to study mass political behavior in India with national surveys. The development of a national survey research capability for the study of politics in India took place over a seven-year period, from 1964 to 1971. The idea for such a study was generated in 1964 when we met in Delhi and began to collaborate in our scientific study of mass politics. In 1965 our theories and research strategies were first put to the test in the study of the Kerala state election of that year. We mobilized a dedicated group of young interviewers in Trivandrum through the auspices of Sukamaran Nayar and the political science department of the University of Kerala. After that preliminary test of our method and theory, we laid plans for the national survey at the time of the 1967 Indian general election. That study was done in ten languages and in most of the Indian states. This unique project required the recruitment, training, and deployment of an expert and linguistically diverse set of interviewers (and later, coders). A similar research effort was mounted by the Centre at the time of the 1971 election to the Parliament. The data from these two studies are the basis for the analysis presented here. Our initial analysis utilizes the 1967 cross-sectional data. After the 1971 survey data became available, we placed those findings alongside the 1967 data, where feasible, in order to demonstrate the stability or change in the public's orientations and behavior. In both of these studies our vantage point was that of the Indian citizen, in 1967 and 1971, just after he went to the polls to vote.

There are many to whom we owe a great deal in the furtherance of this research. Our greatest debt is to Rajni Kothari, who was as involved in the mundane tasks of raising funds and organizing the field work as he was in articulating and shaping the empirical and theoretical concerns of the election surveys. His understanding of Indian politics indeed provided the basic framework for all the empirical work done at the Delhi Centre. But for him none of the three election studies reported here would have been possible. We likewise owe a considerable debt to our colleagues at the Centre, particularly Dhiru Sheth, Ashish Nandy, and Ramashray Roy, who all helped in great measure in both designing and carrying out the two national studies. Their skill and determination went a long way in making an otherwise difficult task relatively easy. Dwaine Marvick of UCLA participated in all phases of the design of the 1967 study and contributed greatly in the subsequent analysis of the data. Richard Park was an intellectual stimulus to us at several stages of the project. Many others, Indians and Americans, provided insights and suggestions over the last ten years. Gopal Krishna of the Delhi Centre gave us wise counsel and also commented on parts of the manuscript. Douglas Madsen's doctoral dissertation was extremely useful for our analysis and is used or referred to at various points in the book.

The project was funded initially from Ford Foundation grants to the University of Michigan and to UCLA, to which funds from the Centre for the Study of Developing Societies were added for conducting the field work in India. Earlier, in 1965, the Rockefeller Foundation made a grant to help finance the pilot study in Kerala. The subsequent study in 1971 was financed entirely by the Indian Council of Social Science Research, the premier body for supporting Indian and comparative studies undertaken by Indian scholars. The Indian study of 1967 was one in a series of national studies of "Parties and Representation" completed under the basic Ford grant to the University of Michigan.

The first author is grateful to the Netherlands Institute for Advanced Study in the Humanities and Social Sciences for the opportunity to work on the manuscript in both 1973 and 1976, and for the secretarial assistance provided.

We are extremely grateful to the many political and governmental leaders at the national, state, and local level in India who facilitated our research and provided us with the necessary information to select our sample and carry out our interviewing. Without the cooperation of these officials this research could not have been accomplished. We also wish to thank the research assistants in India and the United States who helped us with the innumerable details of planning the research, coding the interviews, and carrying out the analysis. In India we are particularly mindful of the work of Shankar Bose and V.B. Singh, both of the Centre for the Study of Developing Societies. They helped greatly in the analysis of the 1971 data, which was done exclusively in India at the Centre. In the United States the assistance of four persons stands out: Douglas Madsen of UCLA (who subsequently wrote his doctoral dissertation based on these data); Andrew Cowart, who has his Ph.D. from the University of Michigan; Robert Friedrich, who is completing his doctorate at Michigan; and Joanne Banthin Selzer, who participated in the early stages of the analysis while a doctoral student at Michigan.

Finally, we wish to express our appreciation to the wonderful teams of interviewers and coders who began this work in Trivandrum in February 1965 and who completed it in the summer of 1971; we have never known a more devoted group of young men and women. Their commitment made this unique scientific study of Indian political life possible. We owe a special debt of gratitude to the secretaries of both the Centre for the Study of Developing Societies, particularly Ava Khullar, and the University of

Michigan department of political science, particularly Sandra Fine, Lili Kivisto, and Judith Kormos, as well as Lucy E. Murphy and Lousje V. Kuyck, who typed and retyped this manuscript at various stages.

The analysis presented in this book combines data from three studies: Kerala, 1965; all-India, 1967; and all-India, 1971. The major writing was done after the 1967 national study and thus the discussion rests heavily on those data. After the 1971 study was completed, we decided to incorporate some of the findings emerging out of the work done at the Centre in Delhi. This led to introductory sections on "electoral change," "party loyalty trends," and "Indian political culture" which use both 1967 and 1971 studies. The last two chapters also seek to assess the direction of Indian political development by utilizing findings from both national studies.

The aim of our study is two-fold: (1) to understand mass political behavior in India and thereby to begin to comprehend the meaning of citizen political life in this complex political system, and (2) to look at Indian behavior comparatively—to discover uniformities and differences in India compared to Western societies like the United States and Britain, for whom we have considerably similar data. While we believe that it is extremely worthwhile to study a system *qua* system in order to understand it in all its richness and uniqueness, we also are driven to test our theories of political behavior, to demonstrate their generality and utility. Without cross-national analysis we cannot defend the generality of our theories, we cannot really explicate the forces which determine human political behavior, nor demonstrate which human political behavior is significant across time and space. We hope, therefore, that our efforts to place Indian empirical discoveries in a comparative context will be enlightening and will give many scholars and practical men of affairs, both Western and non-Western, pause for contemplation.

SAMUEL J. ELDERSVELD
BASHIRUDDIN AHMED
September 1976

Part One

THE RESEARCH AND THEORETICAL CONTEXT FOR THE STUDY

ONE ·
Theoretical Foundations for Empirical Research on Indian Politics

I NDIA, A SOCIETY IN TRANSFORMATION, IS NO DOUBT ONE OF THE
most difficult systems to observe confidently and to analyze systematically. This is not only because of its size and geographical complexity, and
the rich diversity of its culture and historical evolution, manifest in different patterns of political and social traditions, but also because its leaders
and citizens are living in an incredible period of rapid change and
development. To study democratic institutions and behavior in India one
must, above all, attempt to keep in mind that this diverse and complex
system was until recently "predemocratic" and "traditional." Since 1947
it has revealed great momentum for change and great potential for conflict.

The politicization of Indian citizens and their socialization to democratic
values and political involvement, the focus of our inquiry here, has primarily occurred in the past twenty-five to thirty years, since Independence. Up
to Independence in 1947 the Indian masses were largely left untouched by
the British transference to India of parliamentary democratic institutions
and practices. The elites were certainly socialized to democratic norms in
the period preceding Independence, and the Congress movement was a
vital force to this end. But the penetration of this to the mass level was
limited.[1] There is some controversy among Indian scholars on this matter,
however. One can indeed argue that the liberal democratic tradition as
introduced by the British led to participation by Indians in legislative
institutions, voting for local legislative councils and permission for Indians
to compete for appointments to the Indian civil service. But these opportunities for democratic learning through such democratic institutions, insofar as they were at all successful, were limited to a small number of
Indian elites prior to 1947. Few Indians actually were admitted into the
civil service, and the voting was restricted to an infinitesimally small
fraction of the adult public. The "rich experience" of democracy under the
British certainly had no depth in the population and did not penetrate into
the countryside at all. "Institutionalization," in the sense of the creation
and dissemination of democratic norms, linked to democratic institutions,
practices, and functions, did not occur except among the small westernized
Indian elites. And the Congress movement, while important for mobilizing

opposition to the British, did not communicate such norms to the masses. As Hardgrove says:

> The nationalist movement, even in penetrating the villages, had limited impact. Those who were mobilized in the rural areas were far more likely to be the fairly prosperous peasant than the landless laborers. The mobilization of the still largely inert Indian masses to political consciousness and participation would remain the developmental task of India's leaders in the years after Independence.[2]

It was after the historic events of 1947, at the time of the partition and the creation of a new Indian state, that the gradual process of the involvement of the masses in the new democracy occurred. The post-Independence Indian elites, led by Nehru, established an open democracy, granted the vote to all adults of age twenty-one and over, encouraged opposition political parties, and established popularly elected legislative assemblies at national, state, and district levels. Eventually the concept of local self-government was extended through the panchayat system to the village level. Thus, the norms and institutions for a liberal democratic system were created in India, and transmitted to the public. Gradually the public responded to these opportunities. The percentages of voter turnout in the first four national elections, for example, attest to this response: in 1952, 46 percent; 1957, 47 percent; 1962, 56 percent; 1967, 61 percent.[3] We shall provide much more information in depth on the extent of the Indian public's involvement with this new democratic system. Many observers have discussed this extension of the liberal democratic norm to the rural hinterland of India replacing, as Morris-Jones put it, the educated middle-class elites of the nationalist movement with "the new politics of bread and butter" in which the illiterate, poor, and nonwesternized elites and masses began to assume a more significant and predominant role.[4]

One must be cautious, of course, in interpreting the penetration of democratic norm and practice from 1947 to 1975. There can be no doubt that the public responded to democratic opportunities by participating at election time and in many other ways in the political arena. There can be no doubt that the Congress party as well as the opposition parties after 1947 organized more extensively below the district towns (which had been their major organizational arena prior to 1947) and developed mobilization tactics at the village level. But democratic institutions were in their infancy, and the involvement of the public and the meaning of this for their lives was only gradually learned. As a consequence the fragility of the system as a democracy was continuously apparent. There was much political conflict, many riots, periodic turmoil, threats of secession. Scholars studying intranational violence across nations have placed India rather high on indexes of turmoil, domestic conflict, and riots. In one such study covering the period 1948 to 1967, India was placed second in internal riots.[5] One could indeed wonder, as India moved from crisis to crisis, whether "institutionalization" and effective socialization to democratic norms actually was occurring.[6]

This is a question one should constantly keep in mind in the analysis of India's political development—whether democratic norms and practice have actually penetrated to the Indian masses. It is now only thirty years since Independence, and one should not expect the complete and thorough transference and learning of democratic experience by Indian elites, activists, and citizens. Nevertheless, the Indian system remained a unified and dynamic democracy up to 1975 and the evidence indicates widespread acceptance of, and participation in, modern democratic processes by a public a generation ago committed to traditional, hierarchical, authoritarian political relationships. From 1947 to 1975 India, in contrast to its neighbors such as Pakistan and Burma, produced an open democracy that the public engaged in freely and with great interest.

There are four particularly remarkable facets to India's achievement, facets of Indian development which set the stage for the inquiry presented here. First, the ability of Indian elites and citizens to move toward an integrated polity in the face of great social and regional diversity and dissidence. There were those who had long ago predicted the breakup of the Indian nation because of its presumed incapacity to cope with separatist and fragmentation tendencies. Today, despite such predictions, and despite the continuance of protest, such centrifugal political forces have subsided. Second, there emerged in India a mass-based set of political parties with well-developed structures and mobilization techniques. This transpired in a society which traditionally emphasized nonconflictual, hierarchical authority patterns and the consensus of social and political groups.

Third, although Indian citizens were traditionally immersed in norms emphasizing that they were passive actors in the system, by 1975 many were politically involved. Different paths to politics have been utilized to lead to this involvement, but it occurred through the opportunities provided by the new democratic institutions. And finally, the fact that all these developments are occurring in the villages, far from the westernized centers of power in the cities, despite the parochialism and caste-oriented character of this village society, suggests that a mass, rural-based, political culture has come into existence in a very short span of time. This is nothing short of remarkable given their heritage of limited political involvement, their general illiteracy, and their historical socialization to a self-image of no political competence or efficacy. Both parties and elections have played a major role in the making of this new mass political culture. Accepting the

5

logic of an open, competitive system, the parties reached out from the urban political centers to the rural periphery in search of electoral support. In the process they politicized the masses and extended the boundaries of the political community.

"Political development" has occurred in India, in these four critical senses. Citizens have become politically participant, party and electoral institutions have emerged, identification and commitment to national symbols and a national system have occurred, and the polity has expanded to the rural and social periphery. In an institutional and attitudinal sense, at the micro and macro levels, great political change has taken place since Independence. And one senses that this political development has already had significant consequences for social and economic change, and will have an even greater impact in the future.

Controversies persist, however, over the basic character and meaning of Indian political development. This is true both in terms of what type of abstract "model" of development is most relevant to India and what the specific import is of the new patterns of institutional and individual behavior. One can get embroiled in endless disputes over the appropriateness of the conceptualizations of scholars such as Lerner, Deutsch, Eisenstadt, Huntington, and others. What seems clear to the student of the Indian system is that none of these "models" captures the real meaning of political development in India. It is a travesty of knowledge to suggest that India has progressed (or is progressing) neatly from one stage to the next—from tradition, to transition, to modernization. It is also absurd to argue in India's case that social and economic change must precede political development—that without urbanization, improvement in education, a higher GNP, and the growth of the mass media, political maturity is impossible. As Huntington has put it, it is "ridiculous to think of India as politically underdeveloped no matter how low its per capita income or how high its illiteracy rate."[7] Political development has come to India in the absence of the "modernizing" social and economic change expected. Similarly, there has been no neat sequence of change in India from "social frustration," to "political participation," to "political institutionalization," to "political stability." While the debates over relevant models of political development continue, more specific controversies have emerged among Indian scholars, dealing with particular aspects of political change in India. The questions posed lend themselves to empirical analysis. While they deal with both *structural* and *attitudinal* aspects of the system, we will operationalize these concerns here primarily in individual behavioral and attitudinal terms. They can be classified with the following rubrics (with examples of key questions under each rubric):

Controversies concerning the reality *of political development (that is, mass involvement with politics)*. To what extent has the Indian citizen really developed a view of the society which transcends his locality; to what extent has he actually developed a commitment to the Indian society, and its national, as contrasted to local, institutions, processes, and leadership? For example, is there actually effective identification in India with parties at the national level? How "meaningful" is the vote for the Indian citizen—is it the product of "mature" engagement with the system or is it a nondeliberative, even ritualistic act? These concerns blend in with the next rubric.

2. *Controversies concerning the* linkage *of mass political behavior, attitudes, and orientations toward the system.* To what extent is the Indian citizen's political involvement associated with genuine knowledge of and interest in the system, rather than apathy and ignorance? Do "vote banks" still characterize the vote mobilization process, or is the Indian now making decisions by himself, in his own interest, without manipulation by political brokers? Does the individual's participation reflect his group or caste's interests, and if so, is this the result of a sophisticated awareness of the relationship of politics to group interests? Is the Indian citizen now voting after carefully weighing the issue positions of the parties, or is mass voting behavior basically issueless and nonideological?

3. *Controversies concerning the* causes *of mass political involvement.* Here the arguments revolve around what types of factors are related to voting and other political forms of participation: is SES (Social Economic Status) the key to understanding political activism, or are other factors more important, such as caste status, or the type of family in which one is raised, or the type of social environment in which one is brought up (urban or rural, regional area, type of village, and so on), or is it a combination of these variables with certain basic attitudes which then leads to political activity (SES→attitudes→behavior)? How important are political variables—does the political character of the geographical area play a role, or does exposure to the party as an organization during the campaign seem critical, and are contacts with governmental or party officials relevant?

4. *Controversies concerning the* consequences *of political development* (that is, of mass involvement with politics). Does political involvement influence the attitudes and perspectives of the masses toward the system; for example, do they become more knowledgeable, interested, and feel more confident about their role in the system? Extrapolated broadly, does this mean that a new "political culture" has been emerging in India, a new set of beliefs about how the system functions and how it should function? What are the consequences of mass involvement for the party system? Does it make parties more responsive and responsible or less, more competitive-functional, less oligarchic, more populist, more coherent, or

less? Does mass involvement in politics lead to new policy orientations by elites and thus to innovative social and economic policy? In the long run does increased participation lead to citizen satisfaction and system stability or to greater conflict, dissatisfaction, alienation, and eventual instability? These are important queries which should have empirical answers. They have induced a great deal of speculation, as witness, for example, the disagreements among Indianists in interpreting the Indian elections of recent years.[8] They are the key questions which have informed the analysis presented in this book.

A Proposed Theoretical Model

The basic model presented in this book which dominates our analysis proceeds from a different set of assumptions than other approaches and argues for a different sequence in the post-Independence development of the Indian polity. In figure 1 the temporal movement of developmental phenomena is diagrammed. The process of mass socialization and participation in India was highly dependent on the original, purposive decisions of the national elites after 1947. They created the critical institutions for democratic decision making in a moment of high purpose and then educated, persuaded, and mobilized the masses into involvement with these modern structures of government. The elites decided on developmental goals, established the basic institutions (legislatures, the bureaucracy, courts, the party system), and formulated the strategy for mass mobilization. The *values* of these elites at the critical historical juncture of 1947–50, their *visions* of the type of political system they intended to develop, and their *communication* of these values and visions to the masses were the most important initial variables in explaining the unfolding of the Indian system and the public's support for, and participation in, that system. It is the institution building, democratic values, and "risk-taking" orientations of Indian elites which initially explain much more about the evolution of the Indian polity than do the conditions in the social environment. This is not to say that the GNP, education, and improvement in mass communications are, or were, irrelevant. Certainly variations in political involvement by social status levels will appear. But these socioeconomic variables were not the initial factors, nor the primary factors, and by no means the indispensable prerequisities for Indian political development.

The model of development we work with here then rejects social and economic prerequisites as basic determinants. Rejecting such an approach as basically at odds with Indian developmental reality, we bring political variables to the fore. The manner and extent of the Indian citizen's exposure to the new political institutions (the parties, elections, legislatures, political leaders) through the campaigning activities of candidates as

FIG. 1. A suggested model of Indian political development.

	T1 Pre–1947	T2 1947 and Post-Independence	T3 1950–60	T4 1964 to Present
Elites	Traditional institutions and systems of authority	A. Creation of political institutions 1. Parties 2. Parliament-state legislatures 3. Bureaucracy	Innovative policies adopted by government	Mobilization of mass support and identification
Subelites		B. Developed new ideology and system goals C. Strategy for mass participation evolves	Communication of new system norms, goals Expansion of political organization, training of subelites	Strengthening of party leaders and organization
Public	Parochial identities Nonparticipant—subject culture, politically passive Largely ignorant of political processes beyond the local level	D. Public mobilization begins, but still very ignorant and apathetic Public participates in elections and campaigns	Integration of traditional structures with new ones Mass acceptance of system ideology and institutions such as parties and elections	Strong public identification with parties Public becomes interested and sophisticated about politics Greater political activity Sense of political efficacy grows Radical behavior trends increase

During this entire period, the Indian public remained primarily an illiterate, poor, and overwhelmingly rural and caste society.

well as interelection political exposure were the primary stimulants for involvement, reenforced by social group contacts, caste, and other associations. Such exposure led to a gradual awakening of political self-interest. As the parties expanded and deepened their organizational efforts to contact the public, the Indian citizen became more aware of politics and its direct impact on his life, became more knowledgeable about political matters and more attentive to political activities, voted with greater frequency, adopted more definite attitudes toward the solution of India's incredible social and economic problems, developed strong attachments to the political parties, and generally became more sophisticated in evaluations of the performance of political leaders. To a certain extent this also led to system support, but there was a strong element of skepticism about politics, pessimism about the citizen's capacity for efficacy in the system, and an emerging radicalism about political solutions. The eventual "feedback" from this involvement was a higher level of social and economic demands and pressure for more effective and innovative governmental policy. Nevertheless, throughout this developmental process the politicization of the Indian masses was linked to the achievement of a gradual integration of the polity and the acquisition of legitimacy for the Indian democracy. With political conflict and mass involvement came both change and stability, acceptance of democracy and challenge to democracy.

These developments, of course, did not occur simultaneously. The period from 1947 to the first national election in 1952 was the institution-creating period. The public, not yet a political community, slowly was moved from its apathy and ignorance to some familiarity with democratic norms. There was a beginning of interest in politics, little knowledge, and uncertain participation. After 1957 this engagement with politics was deepened. The lower castes, the illiterates, the rural poor gradually were also drawn into contact with the new institutions and became aware of their opportunities for participation. By 1967 the level of commitment to political parties was unusually high, equal to Western societies, and the political activities of Indian citizens attested to their genuine interest in politics.[9] After 1967 the conflicts within the Congress party and the opposition parties and the paradoxical, often contradictory and unreliable behavior of party leaders may have somewhat diminished the commitment to parties. But the level of mass involvement in politics was only accentuated and there was a heightened sense of the possibility of impact. By 1971 this had transformed the public's role in India. "Traditionals" had become politically "modern," while remaining traditional. The less educated and the less affluent in the hinterland were politically engaged to almost as great a degree as the more affluent and educated public in the cities. A new configuration of mass politics had arrived—linking political cognitions, identifications, knowledge, interest, and behavior. Political development in India from 1947 on had, in twenty-five years, changed the political character of India. And this transformation was leaving its imprint not only on the masses and their ideas about politics, but on the elites, their behavior, their policy concerns, and their demands for more effective and redistributive policy outputs. This then is the model which preoccupies our study. While keeping alternative conceptions and propositions in mind, we hope to present evidence to test and validate this model as we explore and analyze in detail the political behavior of Indian citizens in the critical period from 1967 to 1971.

In attempting to apply this model and to answer the basic questions posed by it one should keep in mind what the nature of mass politics in India is, or better, what the different forms of mass politics are in a society undergoing transformation. Simple characterizations cannot interpret satisfactorily the complex and even contradictory nature of the social and political tendencies in such a society. India is a societal composite of several compatible and yet contrasting *images*. There are many patterns of "mass politics" in India. There is, first, the "mass politics of the small group," almost a contradiction in terms. Many Indians are brought into the political arena through their particular group loyalites—local, communal, familial. Their identifications with the primary groups are strong and the political relevance of these groups in the behavior of citizens is great, while they participate at a secondary level in response to the stimuli and appeals of national and local party leaders and candidates. Second, associated with this, Indian mass politics, while appearing "modern" and "developed," must be seen as the "politics of traditional values." The majority of Indians retain traditional beliefs—concerning authority, the nature of leadership, and the role of the individual in the system—while participating in political processes linked to values alien to traditional society. Third, Indian mass politics is "consensus politics." Indians are participating in "modern" types of political combat while disbelieving in conflict, being anxious about strife, and disapproving of the struggle for power. Fourth, Indian mass politics is focused on the "primacy and saliency of party politics." Indians are extremely conscious of the reality of political parties as groups whose actions—through campaigns, elections, and subsequent legislative decisions—change their lives. No other groups have been so politically relevant. Their mass participation is in response to the efforts and appeals of parties, whose actions must be reconsidered and integrated with the small social groups and communal life which commands their daily primary group loyalties. Fifth, Indian mass politics is often "charismatic leadership politics." The great political heroes of pre- and post-

Independence—Gandhi and Nehru most prominently, but a host of special heroes both nationally and at the regional and local level, for special locales and for special constituencies—dominate the political perspectives of Indians. In the last analysis, while the parties are the focus for mass participation, strong and effective leadership is still the public's manifest hope. Sixth, Indian mass politics is both "mobilist" and "populist." The body politic is brought to political involvement at the encouragement and persuasion of the elites, but the potential for reprisal, for "voting the rascals out," while rarely used, is ever present. A 1962 can lead to a 1967 followed by a 1971. It is a public of great loyalty to political leaders and to the system but yet capable of revolt. Seventh, mass politics in India is a mixture of the "politics of dominance" (through the Congress party) and the "politics of fragmentation" (a multiplicity of opposition parties and independent candidates). It is a system where the masses habitually vote in larger numbers for parties and candidates other than the ruling party and yet rarely (until recently) see these opposition leaders secure political power. It is then a system of both continual diffusion of mass opposition and of continual acquiescence in minority control. Finally, Indian mass politics is "fluid coalitional politics" with considerable potential for political realignment, elite turnover, and the social redistribution of power. Sub-group and caste political loyalties are by no means rigid, party control is not disciplined, movements into and out of parties are common, and thus coalitional arrangements are tenuous and continuously recalculated. Indian mass politics is thus both dominated by the Congress party and, on the other hand, in a continual state of flux.

These are the dilemmas and contradictions of political life in India. Mass politics in India, then, is a mosaic of complex, often conflicting patterns, milieus, and system orientations. As a society in transformation, its politically active public functions in an environment both "traditional" and nontraditional, consensual and competitive, parochial and nationalizing, institutionally based and personality oriented, distinctively patterned and fluidly open. It is in this overlapping set of system contexts that Indians act politically. And it is these contexts which are important to us in interpreting their political behavior.

The National Election Studies
Designing and executing a scientific study of elections, difficult in any country, was particularly challenging in India. The conditions under which one must work must be kept in mind. Problems posed by the size of the country and the miltilingual and multicultural character of its population were considerable. In addition, survey research on a national scale was essentially a new field observational technique for Indian political scien-

tists. Above all, one must understand that political campaigns and elections are gigantic events in India, with over a quarter of a billion persons voting in over 250,000 polling stations located in an area of 1.3 million square miles. The elections lasted a week and were supervised by over one and one half million civil servants. There is universal suffrage for all at age twenty-one, and no registration requirement for voting—the government officials, as in the British system, have the responsibility to prepare the electoral rolls for each district. In this complex setting we carried out our national studies in ten languages, selecting a representative sample of 2,000 to 3,000 citizens and 1,000 leaders from all geographical regions and states except those border areas which were inaccessible because of the emergency resulting from the crisis in relations with China.

Despite the difficulties posed by this electoral setting, as well as the problems attending the transference of a research technology from one culture to another, our national surveys were satisfactorily concluded, both in the sense of utilizing scientific procedures from design to analysis, and in the sense of producing reliable and valid data. There have been scholars who have questioned whether this could be done in a country like India, citing the ignorance and nonresponse of illiterate citizens, their lack of comprehension of questions, the impossibility of maintaining an unbiased relationship between interviewer and respondent (for example, because of individual associations under the caste system), the desire of respondents to be courteous to interviewers, the limited cognition of Indian villagers, and the differences in the meaning of words and concepts from one culture to another. The evidence from previous scholars of India concerned with these matters is sparse and contradictory.[10] Our position on these matters, based on our extensive experience in these two national surveys and in smaller studies, is that in principle the problems of survey research are no different in India than elsewhere. Obstacles of a special character do indeed exist in India, but by careful planning, training, and supervision those which might seriously bias the results can be dealt with. Error does occur and must be allowed for in all studies everywhere—sampling error, interviewing error, coding error—but India is basically no different than other countries in this respect.

Indians are no less reliable informants than adults in other societies, nor are they less honest. They are willing to respond with a "don't know" as frequently as an American. On some matters their "cognitive maps" may certainly be more limited, but that is precisely what research seeks to discover. The problem of communicating meanings to them through a set of questions in an interview, meanings which are standardized for all respondents, poses a more difficult problem in India because of language and conceptual equivalence differences. We paid careful attention to this problem in the construction of our questionnaire. Our experience convinces us that equivalence in meanings can be achieved by rigorous work on translations, back-translations, and pretests.

Sampling also poses special problems, but with the use of relatively up-to-date electoral rolls and random probability selection procedures we are confident a representative sample was drawn. Our completion rate was 87 percent, very high for such surveys. A comparison of our sample with census data (see appendix 1) reveals a close correspondence on demographic and social status variables. The correspondence on voting turnout was not as close, a problem confronting surveys in the West also, due to the overreporting of the vote by respondents. These matters are discussed in more detail in appendix 1.

As for the field work itself, special training and precautions were necessary to minimize the bias in the relationship of the interviewer to the respondent, due to differences in social status, and to ensure that objective interviewing occurred. One special problem in India is the invasion of the privacy of the interview, with family members or curious onlookers insisting on being present, or crowding into the interview setting and on occasion attempting to participate. Our interviewers coded the conditions under which each interview took place, therefore permitting us to control for this in our analysis. In 1967 in 36 percent of the cases interviews were conducted without others being present; in 56 percent of the cases others were present but did not interfere. Only in the case of the remaining 8 percent the onlookers intervened despite the interviewers' attempts to prevent them from doing so. The analysis of relationships within the data for the three groups, however, showed that the presence of or intervention by onlookers had no significant impact on their responses. This is not so difficult to understand if one remembers that the reality of the Indian situation is that a preponderant majority of the people live together day in and day out in small villages in which, along with physical proximity, there also exist norms of group solidarity and collective action. If the first makes it difficult for an individual to keep his beliefs, opinions, and activities from the knowledge of others, the second discourages him from even attempting to do so. There is, therefore, very little difference between one's public and private opinions and preferences, and consequently very little hesitation in expressing them in the presence of one's relatives, friends, and neighbors. The presence of others at the time of the interview is perhaps rightly a cause of considerable concern to researchers in other cultures, but in India's villages, where different cultural norms prevail, a similar alteration of interviewing conditions does not produce any serious problems for survey research.

The Indian survey data used in this analysis are from interviews with men only. This is primarily because the 1967 study was basically a male sample, for reasons explained in appendix 1. Although in 1971 we used a properly proportioned male-female sample, we only used the male responses here, for purposes of longitudinal comparison within India. When we place our Indian data side by side with those from other countries, such as the United States and Britain, we also use male data from those studies at the outset of the analysis (in the sections on party identification, political culture, and participation) to indicate the exact cross-national comparisons on the measures used. Male data were not available for all the comparative analyses presented here, however, and the reader should be alert to the fact that in some comparisons the national samples of other countries were both male and female. The tables clearly indicate where this is the case.

Previous research has revealed that male-female differences in "the West" may be fairly large on some measures and negligible on others. In the early U.S. studies the voting participation rate for women was consistently 10 percent below that for men.[11] But the same study noted that "women are as likely to feel strong identification with a political party as men."[12] And, again, in another connection it is concluded that in the United States the "sex composition of the strong and weak identifiers of the two parties does not differ significantly."[13] On certain attitudes to politics, U.S. women were found similar to men. "Sense of citizen duty" was one of these.[14] One of these orientations, sense of political efficacy, did reveal greater differences in the 1950s studies—for example, 35 percent of men were rated high in efficacy but 20 percent of the women scored high.[15] Aside from this finding, which there is some evidence may have changed in recent years, producing much greater similarity in male-female political attitudes and behavior, there are no striking sex differences in "the West" in political beliefs. This suggests that the types of comparative analyses attempted here, in those tables where we are obliged to compare an Indian male sample with "Western" combined samples, may not be very wide of the mark. Male-female differences in India, however, are great (as our study illustrates); but in the West they are far less dramatic.

Our 200 interviewers were carefully recruited and trained. Virtually all were postgraduate students, hired on a full-time basis and trained by the staff of the Centre. The great number of languages used required us to recruit and train regionally, permitting a final testing of the research instrument in the area where the field work was to be done. Teams of interviewers under leaders were assigned to each language area and supervised by regional directors who were permanent members of the Centre's staff. It was a carefully conceived field operation.

In sum we are confident that there was no greater systematic bias in questionnaire construction, in sampling procedure, or in field work than one finds in studies elsewhere. We were aware of the special problems we faced in India and devised approaches to deal with them. In the final analysis the test of any study is the credibility of its findings, the relationships one discovers between variables and the cumulative evidence in the presentation of data that the findings "move together" and "make sense" in the larger theoretical context. To that final test we submit our work. For the first time we have here empirical analysis for India on a national basis of the progress toward political development in India—the nature of the Indian public's involvement with the political system, their psychological orientations to politics, the meaning of "the party" and "the vote" to them, and the impact of the party system on their behavior and orientations. If our findings "move together" to explain these phenomena, that is the test of their validity and reliability.

Frederick Frey recently suggested how in his opinion comparative research should be conducted:

> Probably the ideal method of developing an effective interrogative strategy for a cross-national research project would be to assemble a group of perfectly trained scholars representing all of the nations included in the study, have them come to a full understanding of the purposes of the research, the concepts and hypotheses to be investigated, the main research techniques to be used, and the resources at hand, and tell them to return to their nations and proceed.[16]

Although one may doubt whether there are "perfectly trained scholars" in the West or in India, this research strategy is in essence what we did in our projects. We brought a team of researchers to Delhi, scholars commanding the ten different languages, together designed the project, agreed on a questionnaire, approved a sampling technique, and decided on training and field operational procedures in great detail. These scholars were then put in charge of regional teams and sent into the field. We combined centralized planning with regional linguistic differentiation and adaptation. This, we agree, is the ideal methodology, and our project model approximated it closely.

In the analysis of the data presented here for 1967 and 1971 we utilize a variety of approaches in probing for specific relationships. We differentiate citizens by their social background, including level of education, economic status, caste, urban or rural residence, religion, occupation, age, in order to get some impressions of the political behavior by different types of citizen sectors of Indian society. We carefully explore the citizen's associations and contacts with the party institutions and the depth of his feelings of loyalty to the party group. We are concerned with his attitudes and perceptions of the political system, his contacts with and images of the leadership of that system at the national and local levels, his opinions on the policies of that leadership, and the subjective orientations he has about his place in the Indian political order. Finally, we are above all interested in the extent of his participation in Indian politics and the meaning of this involvement for him and for India.

The data from our interviews, therefore, permit us to explore the ordinary Indian citizens' perceptions of their own political interests, roles, preferences, and behavior as they look toward elites and government officials, toward caste organizations and caste leaders, toward party groups and their activists, toward family and particular social backgrounds, toward the canpaign to which they have just been exposed, toward fellow villagers and neighbors as they are engaged in politics, and toward the political goals, purposes, and policies of the Indian regime—past, present, and future. We hope in the process of our discussions with Indian citizens to understand a little better how integration is being achieved in the face of diversity, how competitive party democracy functions at the citizen level, what the forces are that are at work stimulating public involvement in a traditional culture, and what the nature of the "new" political mass culture is which has begun to permeate rural as well as urban India.

The relevance of our study for understanding the crisis of June 1975 and beyond is not easy to assess. Although our interviewing was last done in 1971, the findings about Indian attitudes and orientations to politics provide a precrisis description of the state of the polity at mass level, the depth and extent of commitment to democracy at that time, and possibly some evidence which might be used in speculations concerning the future resurgence of democratic activity. We will comment on those aspects of our data in more detail in our concluding chapter. In a real sense there are new and interesting social science questions posed here for us. Can we, by social science research, identify the conditions which may eventually trigger disaffection and opposition to a regime? Can we explain on the basis of these types of data what might happen in a society when there is a sharp disjunction in the behavior of political elites and the democratic belief and practice of the masses? Do we have evidence permitting us to speculate on what might transpire when thousands of subelites, who were originally mobilized by a democratic party system and who subsequently developed a personal stake in a party career, are summarily pushed aside under an authoritarian regime? These are certainly key concerns for us to ponder and for which to search our data for answers. They apply perhaps as well to the interruptions of democracy in Greece and the Philippines, to say nothing of earlier or analogous hiatuses of democracy in Germany, Italy, or France. Above all the central question for India today is how complete and profound the democratic socialization process has been up to 1975 and what the capacity is for the Indian public to return to democracy when the current Emergency is modified or lifted? This is the question toward which our data point, but in the absence of postcrisis data our answers can only be tangential and hypothetical. Indians have been living in an open and pluralist society, and their participation in that society was for twenty-five years conceived of and encouraged as part of a power-sharing process. With the Emergency's radical change in this theory of participation, we now must ask how much damage has been done to the commitment of the masses to democracy as well as to the capability of the elites to know about and deal responsively with the needs and desires of the Indian people.

T W O ·
Electoral Change and Stability in India Since 1947

T HE ELECTIONS OF 1967 AND 1971, WHICH ARE THE PRIMARY observation points for our study, were significant decisional episodes in the process of Indian political development. Each of these elections tells us something different about the nature of Indian politics, and yet each reveals considerable continuity in political life in India. In 1967 Indira Gandhi's Congress party suffered a heavy decline in parliamentary strength, barely surviving as the majority party nationally with 55 percent of the parliamentary seats. Observers predicted the end of India's dominance by Congress. Yet in 1971, despite a serious 1969 split in the party, Mrs. Gandhi registered a striking victory, recouping most of her 1967 losses and dominating the national Parliament again with 68 percent (352 out of 518) of the seats in the Lok Sabha. These were "maintaining" and "restoring" elections, and yet they suggested that the system was in a state of crisis with real potential for dramatic change.

If one looks at the patterns of aggregate and total party strength in all five post-Independence elections, from 1952 to 1971, one can see the extent of party continuity and stability (table 2.1). Congress has been supported by over 40 percent of the electorate consistently, but has never been able to secure 50 percent of the vote (unless one adds together the vote of both Congress parties in 1971). Despite the striking comeback of Mrs. Gandhi's wing of the party (Congress-R) in terms of parliamentary seats in 1971, its proportion of the popular vote increased only 3 percent over 1967. And the other parties have fluctuated in strength at or below the 10 percent level. The small "Right" parties, Swatantra and Jan Sangh, did well in 1967, but declined in 1971. The Communists maintained their overall strength in 1971 (divided about equally between the two wings of that party). The Socialists and the Swatantra parties suffered the greatest decline in the 1971 election, but other parties, regional for the most part, increased in 1971. Thus, one notices remarkable stability in major party fortunes over these approximately twenty years of national elections, despite some fluctuations in small party strength. Yet, these aggregate proportions of party strength hide great political ferment.

If we look first at the 1967 national election results we find considerable evidence of change in voting patterns and party strength. The nation seems

19

TABLE 2.1 Basic Patterns of Party Change in India 1952–71: Percent of Total Votes Cast

	1952	1957	1962	1967	1971
Congress	45.0	47.8	44.7	40.8	43.6
Congress (0)	...	...	...	...	10.5
Jan Sangh	3.1	5.9	6.4	9.3	7.5
Swatantra	...	...	8.2	8.6	3.1
Socialists	10.6	10.4	9.5	8.0	3.4
Communists	3.3	8.9	9.9	8.5	9.8
Other parties	22.2	10.8	10.1	9.4	13.6
Independents	15.8	16.2	11.1	14.4	8.6
Actual number of valid votes cast (millions)	106.0	120.5	115.2	146.7	144.4

SOURCE: *Party System and Election Studies* (Centre for the Study of Developing Societies, Occasional Papers, no. 1, 1967), p. 52; R. Chandidas, Ward Morehouse, Leon Clark, Richard Fontera, eds., *India Votes* (Bombay: Popular Prakashan, 1968; New York: Humanities Press, 1968), pp. 256–66; W. H. Morris-Jones, "India Elects for Change—and Stability," *Asian Survey* 11 (1971): 730–31.

to have been in a state of political indecision or transitional realignment. There were those who called it a "deepening political crisis" (*Economic and Political Weekly*) or India's "second revolution" (*The Statesman*). While such evaluations may have been extreme, there was a general feeling among observers that 1967 was an important election. Rajni Kothari said "the 1967 election marked the end of the dominant party system." Yet, he also observed that "Congress emerged from the 1967 elections as the strongest party."[1] Although one could argue that the proportions of the vote by major party did not change very much (table 2.1), these figures mask the evidence of significant political change. There was a 27 percent increase in the actual vote. The number of candidates for the national Parliament reached a high point (2,317) which was 17 percent more than in 1962. There were at least twenty-two separate parties which received votes for the Lok Sabha. The vote for minor parties increased by 18 percent over 1962 while the vote for independent candidates (the number of which almost doubled in 1967 compared to 1962) increased in the aggregate by 65 percent. Further, if one looks at the candidate competition by constituency one notes fewer straight fights and triangular contests in 1967 and more constituencies with several candidates. Actually in 1967 66 percent of the constituencies fielded four or more candidates compared to 58 percent in 1962. There was evidence then of increased candidate and party interest in the election, in the sense of greater involvement of party groups and independent candidates accompanied by no diminution in the pluralization tendencies of the Indian system.

Drastic alterations in the votes cast for the parties occurred in 1967. True, the changes in the party vote for the Lok Sabha were not considerable if one looks only at the differences over time in their percentages of party strength. Congress declined 4 percent, Jan Sangh gained 3 percent, Swatantra held its own, while the Socialists and Communists (combining the votes for both factions in each case) declined slightly (table 2.1). Yet the aggregate vote increases for the parties and independent candidates were considerable:

Congress	over 7½ million
Jan Sangh	over 6 million
Swatantra	almost 3½ million
Socialists	almost 800,000
Communists	over 2 million
Independents	over 8 million
Other, smaller parties	over 2 million

And these vote changes, with their parallel changes in the state assembly elections, resulted in a great reduction in Congress strength in the Parliament and a great loss in Congress dominance in state legislatures. The party chairman, Kamaraj, and many other prominent Congress MPs lost their seats. Congress declined nationally in percentage of seats in the Lok Sabha, from 73.1 percent in 1962 to 54.6 percent in 1967. Its percentage of seats won in state assemblies dropped below 50 percent—to 48.6 percent in 1967 compared to 58.4 percent in 1962 and 68.2 percent in 1952.[2] Congress failed to get a majority in the legislatures of eight states, a startling decline in its legislative and, thus, state governmental control. As Kothari summarized the consequences,

> The results of the 1967 elections were received with a sense of some dramatic change: with considerable dismay in the Congress ranks and with excitement in the ranks of the opposition. The electorate was seen to have brought an end to the era of Congress dominance. A number of non-Congress governments came to power in the States—key Congress leaders—were defeated. The overall consequences of this "debacle" was felt in a series of inputs in the States, a great deal of governmental instability, a much more vocal and assertive Parliament, and a protracted struggle for leadership in the Congress party itself—ending in the split of the party in 1969. The preexisting consensus had been shaken.[3]

The 1971 election produced results equally startling to many observers and again manifested considerable dynamism in Indian electoral politics.

The number of candidates (2,790) increased again, surpassing the 1967 high point by 20 percent. And the number of independents standing for Parliament also increased considerably. Yet, the total vote declined slightly and voting turnout was at a low point—56 percent compared to the 1967 high of 61.3 percent. The results of the election surprised virtually all observers, politicians, newspaper columnists, academic experts, and pollsters.[4] The IIPO's (Indian Institute of Public Opinion's) prediction that Mrs. Gandhi's vote would be 34.7 percent was 9 percent off the mark. Few people expected Congress-R to come anywhere near the 350 seats the party finally won. Even the general secretary of the party expected only 286. "It seems safe to say," remarks Professor W. H. Morris-Jones, "that in none of the preceding Lok Sabha elections had the results been so surprising."[5]

Congress-R, from which a dissident group (Congress-O) had split off in 1969, made a tremendous comeback under Mrs. Gandhi's leadership after the 1967 debacle. Its vote increased by over three million (despite the general decline in turnout), its strength by 3 percent, and its proportion of the seats in Parliament to over two-thirds (from 55 percent after the 1967 election). Congress-O was badly beaten, electing only sixteen candidates and securing only 10.5 percent of the vote. The parties of the "Right" were severely hurt by the changes in voting preferences, and a shift to the "Left" occurred, with the Communist parties increasing their strength to almost 10 percent (from 8.5 percent in 1967). Yet, as Myron Weiner points out, there were six states where non-Congress candidates were supported by a majority of the voters and there was surprising support for regional parties which won 13.2 percent of the vote (an increase over their 10.1 percent in 1967).[6] What is apparent again in 1971 is that the fragmentation and parochialization of the Indian system remains to a large extent. And yet, with a great resurgence of support, Congress-R returned to a relatively dominant position in the system. Considerable changes in voting behavior between 1967 and 1971 were responsible for this landslide to Congress-R and the demise or decline of other parties. How this occurred and what various crosscurrents in mass political behavior and attitudes contributed to these changes is, as Weiner suggests, "a question best . . . left to those who have been studying electoral behavior."[7] To comprehend the nature of the revitalized Congress party, the nature of its appeal, and the strength of its support in relationship to the other parties, as well as the reasons for voting alignments, requires careful analysis using survey data. There are scholars who argue that the Indian voter in 1971 was more conscious of the issues positions of the parties, while others see a change in social cleavage patterns and the polarization of political conflict on new sociological bases;

still others feel that Mrs. Gandhi employed the traditional appeals to caste and ethnic groups using the old symbols to which traditional local elites mobilized votes in the past. These and other theories require testing with our survey data. Above all, it is clear that 1971, like 1967, was a year of great movement and development in the mass base of the Indian party system.

The parties were very active in the 1967 and 1971 campaigns, more active than in many Western societies (table 2.2). As has been reported elsewhere, in 1967 36 percent of the public reported that they had been canvassed by the parties, 71 percent had received handbills, 26 percent had met at least one of the candidates, over 25 percent had attended party or candidate rallies and meetings. It is important to notice that the opposition parties engaged in almost as much canvassing activity as Congress did. Of the eligible electorate who were canvassed, 41 percent were approached by non-Congress parties. And equally significant is the finding that the parties were approaching each other's partisan supporters. Thus 18 percent of those who supported non-Congress parties in 1962 were in 1967 canvassed by Congress, and conversely 14 percent of the 1962 Congress voters were in 1967 canvassed by non-Congress activists. It was a rather competitive campaign, and neither Congress nor its opposition parties were lax in organizational work.[8]

In 1971 there was also a high level of campaign activity. House-to-house canvassing was at a phenomenal high point—45 percent of our sample reporting such exposure (see table 2.2). This would mean that close to 70 million Indians were contacted at their homes by workers for parties and candidates—truly a remarkable fact. Exposure in 1971 to literature distribution was much less and there was a slight decline in attendance at campaign meetings.

Active participation in the campaign was at the same level in 1971 as in 1967. Between 6 and 10 percent engaged in the following types of activities: canvassing, helping to transport voters on election day, joining a party, distributing literature. Also, 5 percent joined demonstrations or processions; 5 percent also organized election meetings. As our subsequent detailed analysis of political involvement will demonstrate, these proportions of activism are in some instances relatively high compared to the United States and Britain. Attending political rallies or campaign meetings is only at the 7 to 8 percent level in the United States and Britain, for example, while in India it was 25 percent in 1967 and 20 percent in 1971. Except for mass media exposure (which is very low in India),[9] the Indian public was both the target of the campaign stimuli of the parties at a high level of frequency and intensity, and the Indian public took active cam-

TABLE 2.2 Basic Data on Political Exposure and Activity in India, 1967 and 1971*

	1967 (%)	1971 (%)
Exposure to campaign activities		
Were canvassed at home	36	45
Received handbills and literature	71	46
Attended campaign rallies	25	20
Engaged in campaign activities		
Was a party member	7	6
Engaged in house-to-house canvassing	8	9
Helped get people to the polling station	6	10
Distributed literature and/or polling cards	6	7
Helped organize election meetings	5	5
Formed processions or demonstrations	5	5
Have at some time contacted a government official	20	26

* Based only on responses of men in our national cross sections in 1967 and 1971.

paign roles with as great frequency as in the West.

Patterns of Party Loyalty and Defection in 1967 and 1971
Political combat was intense in both recent national elections, as evidenced by the number of parties and candidates and the level of campaign activity. The basic question is, What patterns of voting behavior and party affiliation are emerging in India during this period of changing party fortunes and public involvement with politics? Particularly, how stable or variable are voting and party preferences? In an earlier analysis of political behavior at the time of the 1967 election we suggested that there was a relatively high level of consistent party voting and a higher degree of strong party identification than one might have expected to find.[10] Some summary data here for the public in both 1967 and 1971 will indicate the state of party loyalty at two points in time.

On the surface, consistency in voting either for or against the Congress party appears low for the total electorate (table 2.3). It seems that from 35 to 40 percent of Congress and opposition voters in one election were defecting in the next election. Yet comparatively and in the larger perspective, party voting has been maintained at a relatively high level. Indeed, from respondents' reports in 1971 it appears that consistent voting has increased in the most recent period despite the aggregate changes in party fortunes as measured by parliamentary seats or success in state elections. One may be quizzical about the overall figures of 34 percent and 45 percent consistency for 1967–71. Yet this is a sizable "hard core" of consistent

TABLE 2.3 The Magnitude of Consistent and Variable Party Voting

	1962–67	1967–71
1. % of Congress voters in the first election (either 1962 or 1967) supporting Congress in the second election in each two-election sequence	59	61.9
2. % of opposition voters supporting opposition parties in both elections	65.5	53.3
3. % of all eligible voters for 1962–67 or 1967–71 consistently supporting either Congress or opposition parties	34.1	44.8

SOURCE: Based on responses given us by our national samples in 1967 and 1971. Only those eligible by age to vote in both elections (men only) in each sequence are used in the analysis. Measure 2 includes those who voted for an opposition party in each election, that is, against Congress, but not necessarily the *same* opposition party in each election. If the more rigorous requirements were used, the percentage would be much lower, closer to 40 percent. Because opposition parties run in only selected constituencies, however, this is an unrealistic requirement.

voters in the total electorate. And this proportion compares favorably with a 47 percent figure for the United States in the 1948–52 switch in party presidential fortunes. Similarly, a comparable British figure for 1959–64 is 54 percent.[11] The 1964–68 election sequence leading to a party turnover in the American presidency was probably even more dramatic. The Survey Research Center's report described that American election in the following terms:

> Indeed the pattern of concerns ... combined to produce a shift in popular preferences between 1964 and 1968 which was truly massive. It is likely that the proportion of voters casting presidential ballots for the same party in these two successive elections was lower than at any time in recent American history. Among whites who voted in both elections a full third switched their party .... A full 40% of Nixon's votes came from citizens who had supported Lyndon Johnson in 1964! ... the Democratic proportion of the vote across the land dropped a shattering 19 percentage points from more than 61 per cent to less than 43 per cent.[12]

In this context the solidity of the vote for Congress and opposition parties in India seems reassuring from 1962 to the present. If one looks only at the behavior of voters, the record is one of considerable constancy for up to 40 percent of the electorate and up to 60 percent of the regular voters.

25

The actual patterns and magnitudes of the changes in voting behavior in these two-election sequences were very similar. A detailed analysis of 1962–67 vote switching reveals the diverse nature of the changes in party support and documents the way in which this affected the support for Congress in 1967[13] (table 2.4). First one notices that 58 percent of the party defectors from 1962 to 1967 were Congress defectors. The predominant mood among voters was thus anti-Congress. But there was considerable dispersion of preferences among those defecting from Congress, somewhat greater preference for right parties (41 percent) than for Left parties (26 percent). Yet, one notices that the very small parties received a large share of the vote which left Congress (33 percent). On the other hand, rather large proportions of those leaving the other parties actually decided to vote for Congress. This was particularly pronounced among the Left party supporters, 64 percent of whose defectors preferred Congress. Another finding of interest is that Right party supporters of 1962 defected to Left parties in 1967 (27 percent), although the reverse phenomenon did not occur. And, finally, there was a good deal of interchanging among parties at the same point on the party spectrum. Thus, Jan Sangh 1962 supporters often preferred Swatantra in 1967, or vice versa (27 percent of Right defectors exhibited this pattern), while Socialist and Communist switchers also interchanged support with each other in 1967 (28 percent of all Left defectors). This fascinating vote-switching phenomenon in effect protected Congress from a greater upset. But disaffection with Congress, nevertheless, was relatively high.

Another way of imaging these movements of party supporters is to see the direction of voter choices in terms of a spectrum with a Left pole, a Right pole, and Center (table 2.5). This suggests the relative affect of the

TABLE 2.4 Voting Behavior of Party Switchers, 1962–67*

1962–67 Switchers	1967 Vote Preference (%)				
	Congress	Right Parties	Left Parties	Other Parties or Independents	N
All Switchers	16	33	26	25	320
Congress defectors	X	41	26	33	219
Right defectors	32	(27)	27	14	22
Left defectors	64	0	(28)	8	50
Other defectors	38	34	17	11	29

* Based on the Lok Sabha vote in 1962 and 1967, for those eligible to vote in both elections. Percentages in parentheses refer to those switching from one Right party to another Right party, or one Left party to another Left party.

TABLE 2.5 Movement of Voters across the Party Spectrum
(1962–67 Defection Patterns)*

1967 Preferences	1962 Preference and Movement (%)				
	From Center	From Right	From Left	From Other Parties and Independents	Totals
To the Left	16.6	1.6	X	1	19
To the Center	X	3	3	3	9
To the Right	28	X	0	3	31
To other parties and independents	13	.7	.3	.7	15
Total movement, 1962–67	57.6	5.3	3.3	7.7	74

Movement within sectors of the spectrum		
Within Center	23	
Within Left	2	27
Within Right	2	

*For the purposes of this analysis the Center includes PSP, Congress, and DMK; the Right includes Jan Sangh and Swatantra; the Left includes the two Communist parties and SSP.

parties, the limited movement across the spectrum, and the general direction of the electoral change. It is clear that there was a strong centrifugal movement—from the Center to the Right to the Left and to other parties. Over 50 percent of the movement of voters was away from the Center. The movement to the Right was considerably greater than to the Left parties (31 percent compared to 19 percent). There was very little extreme movement, that is from Left to Right, but there was some sizable movement "outside the spectrum," to smaller parties and independents—about 15 percent of the total electoral change.

The movements of voters between 1967 and 1971 differed in certain interesting respects from the earlier period. There was more movement *to* Congress from other parties, and less movement *from* Congress to opposition parties. There was also more mobilization of previous nonvoters by Congress in 1971 compared to the success of opposition parties in this respect. These vote changes can be diagrammed as indicated in figure 2. The movement of voters to the Center, that is, to the Congress party, is obvious. Whereas Congress's relative *loss* to opposition parties was a net 4.4 percent in 1967, it was a net *gain* of 10.5 percent in 1971. Further, Congress's net gain in the ratio of dropouts (nonvoters in 1967) to "newly

FIG. 2. Vote exchanges in recent Indian elections.

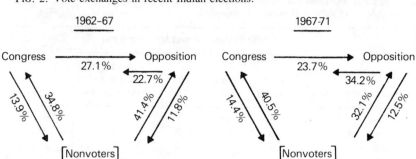

Each percentage is the proportion of the category of electors in the earlier year who defected, dropped out, or became party supporters in the succeeding election.

mobilized'' was about 21 percent in 1967 but 36 percent in 1971. It is clear that (1) there was great movement of the electorate in both election sequences, and (2) that the 1971 election movements benefited Congress while the 1967 movements worked to the disadvantage of Congress. One must be cautious in interpreting the meaning of these movements, particularly as to whether 1971 suggests less "centrifugal" tendencies. Independents and small parties still secured 22 percent of the vote in 1971. But Congress did certainly reestablish itself as the solid center of this fluid party system.

As for changes in party identification, the evidence again suggests stability, but also some evidence of actual and potential change in the attachment to parties. We found in 1967 that 70 percent of our sample "identified" with a party, using a measure similar to that used in the United States. In India we asked, "What parties do you feel close to?" This was followed by the question "Which (of the parties mentioned) do you feel closest to?" Then followed the question "How strongly do you feel (about your party attachment)?" On the basis of this sequence we find a high attachment, with 51 percent feeling strongly identified. In the 1971 study the sequence was different. The questions used were

"Could you tell me the names of the different political parties in the country?"

"Is there any political party you feel close to?" (If yes) "Which is that party?"

"Is your preference for the party very strong or not very strong?"

On the basis of this series we found in our 1971 male sample only 47 percent who were party identifiers, 35 percent strong identifiers. The interesting question is whether there indeed has been a great decline in party loyalty, in a psychological sense, since 1967, or whether these differences are a consequence of a change in the wording of the questions. This is an analysis which we will pursue in detail later.

A comparison of 1967 and 1971 suggests (in the absence of the above detailed analysis) some possible changes as well as some continuities (table 2.6). Indian identifiers are inclined to be "strong" in their self-perceived sense of party attachment. Even with the decline in 1971, 35 percent are "strong," which is identical to the 35 percent previously reported for the United States. (Norway has 25 percent strong, Japan approximately 15 percent, as examples of countries lower in proportions of strong identifiers.) Over 70 percent of those in India who do identify with a party feel a "strong" affiliation—something that is true probably in only one other country, Britain.

TABLE 2.6 Party Identification Comparisons in India: 1967 and 1971
(Male Samples Only)

	1967 (%)	1971 (%)
Total identifying	70	47*
Strong	51	35
Congress		
Identifiers (of total sample)		
Perceiving selves as "close to" Congress	43	35†
Perceiving Congress as the party closest to their position on the question of economic controls	32	36‡
Opposition Party		
Identifiers (of total sample)		
"Close to" Swatantra and Jan Sangh	12.1	2.6
"Close to" Communists (both parties)	4.1	3.3
"Close to" DMK	3.0	2.6
"Close to" SSP and PSP	4.8	.6
Distribution of all		
party identifiers		
"Close to" Congress	61	67
Strong identifiers	73	74

* Based on a somewhat different series of questions than in 1967 (see text).
† 29% Congress (R), 2.9 percent Congress (O), and 3.2 percent Congress (no further information specified).
‡ Actually another 2 percent indicated Congress (O) and 5.1 percent Congress (unspecified).

29

The psychological commitment to the Congress party remains high. It may have declined slightly in 1971, although it is difficult to determine this because of the breakup of the party into two factions. Further tests of this may reveal such a conclusion (of a decline) unwarranted. For example, our identical question on government policy concerning economic controls used in both studies was followed with a question as to "Which party is most likely to do what you want on this issue?" As table 2.6 reveals, similar percentages mentioned Congress both times. About one-third look to Congress for leadership on this issue.

While identification with Congress remains fairly high, our 1971 study suggests considerable fluctuation in loyalty to opposition parties as, indeed, the vote itself revealed. Right parties dropped sharply in 1971, the Socialists almost dropped out of sight, but the Communists and DMK managed to hold their own. On balance, then, the possible aggregate decline in party identification (still to be clarified later with further analysis) and the inconstancy in support for certain opposition parties emerged in 1971 as most evident. The identification with Congress remained stable despite the party disorganization and split.

The relevance of this party identification for the vote in 1971 as in 1967 is also apparent from the data. Party attachment seems to continue to be important as a perspective linked to behavior (table 2.7). The party defection rate is relatively low—only about 25 percent for Congress and also for the opposition. The stability of this finding in two national election studies now suggests that psychological closeness to a party is a meaningful phenomenon in India. The proportion of the total population who have this sense of "closeness" may not be as high as we originally discovered it to be in 1967 (at 50 percent). But it is a significant proportion, even at 35 percent, comparing favorably again with an earlier 46 percent figure for the United States and 53 percent for Britain.[14]

TABLE 2.7 The Linkage of Party Identification and the Vote

	1967	1971
% of Congress identifiers voting for Congress	79	74
% of opposition identifiers voting for an opposition party (not necessarily the same opposition party)	73	73
% of total sample who identify with a party and voted for that party	50	35

If one asks "How loyal are party identifiers in voting for their own party over a two-election span?" the answer is not as impressive, but still suggestive of great loyalty for a large segment of the Indian public—64 percent were loyal during 1962–67 and 48 percent during 1967–71. These are citizens on whom the party can genuinely rely and who constitute the base of electoral support for the system. While actual and potential defection has clearly been evident in recent elections, for Congress as well as for opposition parties, there is a bedrock of party loyalty which is the mark of a mature polity.

If one wishes to characterize the voting behavior of the total Indian electorate over time, in terms of basic patterns of behavior, the two profiles presented in table 2.8 are useful. These reveal the tremendous surge of new voters in 1967 (33 percent) and the decline in the proportion of newly mobilized voters in 1971 (18 percent). The phenomenon of regular voting increased in the period prior to 1971 over the earlier 1962–67 period (45 percent compared to 34 percent). But defection also increased slightly (20

TABLE 2.8 Profiles of the Indian Electorate: Voting Consistency and Irregularity from 1962 to 1971

	1962–67 (%) (N=1,851)	1967–71 (%) (N=1,338)
Regulars		
Voted Congress both elections	26.3	35.2
Voted opposition both elections	7.8	9.6
Defectors		
Congress defectors: left Congress for the opposition	12.1	13.5
Opposition defectors: left the opposition for Congress	2.7	6.1
Dropouts		
Congress dropouts: voted Congress first election, nonvoter the second	6.2	8.1
Opposition dropouts: voted opposition first election, nonvoter the second	1.4	2.2
New entrants		
Congress new voters: nonvoters in the first election, Congress the second	15.1	10.2
Opposition new voters: nonvoters first election, opposition the second	18.0	8.1
Apathetics		
Nonvoters in both elections	10.3	7.0

percent compared to 15 percent). Yet these changes are not sensational, and what is impressive is the appearance at least of stability over time in Indian voting behavior patterns. The data suggest that the level of involvement in voting and of consistent party voting for the total electorate is relatively high and consistency in behavior is on the increase. There remains considerable fluidity in the system, much indecision in partisan commitment, and genuine potential for change in party support. But patterns of behavioral interest and system support obtain despite the fact that Indians have now been exposed to intense election campaigns and heated and divisive party combat.

Prior to 1975, therefore, the evidence from our data document the existence of strong party loyalty for a large segment of the Indian public, considerable consistency in party support, while at the same time revealing the potential for sudden and dramatic shifts and defection in party loyalty. The Indian public by 1975 had come to accept the new party democracy. They were not merely mobilized by it. Yet they also manifested the capacity for defection from parties. It is in this light that recent events certainly may be critical for mass behavior.

Part Two

MASS POLITICAL CULTURE IN INDIA:
SOME EMPIRICAL OBSERVATIONS

THREE

Citizen Orientations toward Politics: India Compared to the West

M UCH HAS BEEN WRITTEN ABOUT INDIAN POLITICAL CULTURE, ITS historical manifestations and its recent transformations. A central argument persists concerning the extent to which "traditional" culture has given way to "modern" culture.[1] Another major argument persists concerning the existence of a gap between elite and mass cultures.[2] We do not intend here to get involved at the abstract theoretical level with these controversies about the content and change in Indian belief systems. Rather we wish, in this brief introduction, to present some summary data on the attitudes of Indians toward their political processes and then look at the theoretical significance of these data. Hopefully this may add to our knowledge of contemporary Indian political "culture."

Gabriel Almond said long ago, "Every political system is embedded in a particular pattern of orientation to political actions."[3] And Sidney Verba has classified these "politically relevant orientations" as being of three types: "cognitive, evaluative, or expressive."[4] To these writers these orientations comprise the "political culture." A society has a set of beliefs and behaviors toward political objects which are learned and shared. Individuals presumably have attitudes and beliefs about the actual nature of political life and the functioning of the system, as well as views about the values and goals they prefer for the political system. In addition, there is presumably an "emotional dimension" in cultural perspectives. These orientations constitute the focus of our presentation.

We present here, then, empirical evidence about the Indian public's beliefs and perceptions about their system and about their own role in that system. In order to understand the Indian public's political actions, as we will analyze them subsequently in this study, it is necessary to comprehend this context of subjective political orientations within which these actions take place. In the process we may be talking about "political culture," although certainly not conceptualized as all other writers have seen Indian culture. The subtle nuances of cultural belief may escape us. Yet, we feel we may be tapping here some of the most important overt manifestations of Indian political cultural development and the manifestations which are meaningful for the Indian citizen as he reacts to the political system or participates in it. This position linking culture to behavior echoes Clifford

Geertz's caveats.[5] Our general theory of Indian political development sees the new Indian leadership after Independence establishing a new "political center," expanding it outward to the periphery of Indian society, mobilizing public support for that new system in a variety of ways, but particularly emphasizing the importance of political participation and voting. The elite emphasized "democratic" and "nationalizing" political norms, beliefs, and values concerning the political system and the individual's place in that system.[6] In the process of doing this, the Indian political elite legitimized change with the symbols of the past. The public thus has been socialized to accept certain ways of viewing politics, which is functional to their involvement in and commitment to the new political institutions and processes established after Independence. Our major query here is, What is the extent of public acceptance of these "democratic" orientations? Is the Indian public cognitively and normatively supportive of the democratic system and the citizen's role in that system? Or is there truly a political cultural chasm between elite expectations and public support?

For the first time in India our national surveys of 1967 and 1971 permit a nationwide empirical exploration of Indian political cultural orientations. We asked our adult samples a variety of questions permitting us to determine, admittedly at a relatively superficial level, the nature of public attitudes toward the political system. These questions were of different types, falling generally into the three classifications used by Verba (although certainly not neatly categorized in mutually exclusive categories):

1. *Cognitive-perceptual questions.* Included here are the individual's knowledge of the system, especially accurate information about elected representatives, caste voting, and so on. In addition, there were questions about what problems confront the country, what the key election issues were, who the leaders in the community were, including a probing of the respondent's awareness of and contact with influential leaders at the local level.

2. *Evaluative-normative questions.* Respondents were asked their view of the party system, the election system (how necessary, how effective in making the government responsive, and so on), what the role of the government should be in dealing with economic (as well as other) problems, and what types of political action (direct and legislative) were proper, how stable government could be achieved, were officials (and Mrs. Gandhi, in particular) doing a good job, and, finally, did the respondent have a feeling of subjective competence or efficacy in acting in the system.

3. *Expressive-affective questions.* A few expressive types of questions were asked, such as the extent of the individual's interest in politics at the local, state, or national level; whether the respondent

cared about the outcome of the election; to what extent there was a feeling of closeness or loyalty to a party; and whether there was faith and confidence in the national and state governments.

These types of questions can help us to a beginning knowledge of Indian political orientations. They will not lead us to any profound knowledge about the Indian's trust or distrust of authority, or to how he perceives his historic, cultural identity (nativist, modernist, Gandhian, or what, using Nandy's terms). But they can suggest Indian public receptivity, at the surface level, of certain salient political orientations alleged to be important for public participation in a democratic polity.[7]

In a very useful previous empirical study in two cities in Tamil Nadu and Madhya Pradesh, Peter Mayer tested certain propositions about support for democracy at the mass level and found no evidence of antidemocratic orientations, thus challenging the views of writers such as Weiner and Morris-Jones. He calls for more empirical research, on village India particularly, concluding that "the study of Indian politics has come to the stage where propositions about attitudes and beliefs must be tested empirically rather than inductively."[8] It is at this point that our data take up where Mayer left off, hopefully contributing also to the knowledge needed to resolve these controversies.

We can begin with a look at *cognitive* orientations toward politics, asking what the level of mental awareness is about political matters and what perceptual maps appear to obtain at the mass level. The data are derived from both the 1967 and 1971 studies, in some cases identical questions being asked, while other questions were asked in one year only. A variety of impressions emerge from these data, covering different aspects of the individual's images of the polity.[9]

Indians seem to be a fairly "knowledgeable" citizenry when it comes to politics (table 3.1). Close to or more than a majority can correctly identify political candidates and election winners. Their knowledge of candidacies at the state level, because of the salience of politics at that level, is greater than at the national level. In the 1971 study respondents were asked to name as many parties as they could. Only 32 percent mentioned none, and 20 percent mentioned four or more. The awareness of caste voting patterns is also quite high. Over 60 percent in each year knew how their own caste had voted, and over 40 percent were also aware of the behavior of other castes, and, further, could link a specific party to caste. Issue and problem awareness is remarkably high. It is particularly notable that over 50 percent of our mass sample ventured to identify a specific party as linked to issue positions—as "most likely to do what you want on this issue (of governmental control of the economy)."

TABLE 3.1 Cognitive Orientations toward Politics in India*

	1967 (%)	1971 (%)
Knowledge of candidates		
Correct knowledge of winner in parliamentary constituency	50	67
Knew 2 or more candidates for the state assembly in respondent's district	69	. . .
Knowledge of parties		
Could name a political party	. . .	68
Could name 3 or more parties	. . .	31
Could name the party of the prime minister	. . .	62
Could name the party of the state's chief minister	. . .	38
Perception of caste and politics		
Knew how own caste voted	68	63
Knew how other castes voted	44	. . .
Perceived a link between own caste and a specific party	47	. . .
Issue and problem awareness		
Mentioned at least one problem "facing the country"	88	82
Had an opinion on the issue of governmental control over the economy	82	78
Linked own issue position (on the economic controls issue) to a specific party	53	51

* Where the data are missing, either the question was not asked or not asked (or coded) in such a way as to make a defensible comparison possible. Based on men only.

The high level of cognitive sophistication about politics seems stable from 1967 to 1971. Obviously we did not probe into many cognitive aspects of citizen orientations toward the political system—only selected perceptions preoccupied us and many types of actors and certain arenas of the Indian system were not looked at. Nevertheless, using two different observational time-points, we can verify for the specific cognitions we did probe that there was continuity in the high level of awareness we discovered in 1967. There is no significant variation in these measures over time for these two national cross sections, with the possible exception of increased knowledge in 1971 of successful constituency candidates.

From a comparative perspective, the Indian public's cognitive awareness seems high. There are unfortunately very few occasions when equivalent questions are used in other national studies. The ability of the public to identify its constituency representative in the national legislature is one possible comparison. In India 50 percent were able in 1967 to provide some identification (by party or person's name), and 67 percent in 1971. In the United States in 1967 a study revealed that 40 percent could identify their congressman by name. In Britain in 1963, 51 percent could do the same for their MP. The Indian test of level of knowledge was less rigorous in this comparison.[10] The low level of knowledge of the American public of its candidates for office, compared to expectations, has been commented on often. An earlier report of the 1958 election revealed that 59 percent of those respondents living in congressional districts where the election was contested had read or heard nothing about the candidates.[11] A higher level of information is reported by Verba for U.S. senatorial incumbents—58 percent of the public could name at least one such incumbent in their state. Also the British study reports a higher ability to remember the MP's name in 1964 than in 1963.[12] On balance, however, the extent of the Indian public's cognitive engagement with politics, by this one test at least, seems relatively convincing. Western publics are not necessarily more knowledgeable about politics than are Indians. It would be interesting to see directly comparable data on other cognitive measures, such as the capacity of other publics to link parties and issues, on which Indians do well, as they do in linking caste and party. On the latter, any approach to comparison is probably impossible, but as to the former linkage, the cognitive finding here is impressive.

Turning to *evaluative* orientations, certain very special aspects of Indian political culture emerge from our data. First, one notices there is strong support for the institutions of parties and elections, although somewhat of a decline in such support is noticeable in 1971 (table 3.2). Two-thirds or more were supportive in 1967, but in 1971 this dropped to 42 percent (parties) and 51 percent (elections). Yet only a small minority are clearly negative as to the role of these subsystems. (A fourth or more were undecided in 1971.) Further, on another question concerning the necessity of parties, only 13 percent (in 1967) and 18 percent (in 1971) say parties are unnecessary, although 70 percent feel party conflict may be harmful to the system.

These fluctuations in public support for parties and elections are not uncommon, in the West or in India. For example, the identical question on the function of parties was used by Butler and Stokes in the British surveys of 1963 and 1966, with these strikingly different results: 24 percent replied "not much" in 1963 and 46 percent in 1964.[13] Approximately 50 percent in both surveys felt parties were important in this respect. Similarly it is interesting to note in the past year or so the decline in political trust in electoral institutions in the United States. Data from the Center for Political Studies for 1972 and 1973 at the University of Michigan document this change. Whereas in November 1972, 56 percent felt that elections make the government "pay attention a good deal," only 33 percent felt that way in November 1973.[14] Recently in the United States there has been a sharp decrease in faith in democratic institutions. In this context of change in public support, and relatively low levels of such support, for parties and elections in the West, the Indian commitment to these democratic institutions is comparatively strong.

TABLE 3.2 Evaluative Orientations toward the Party and Election Systems in India

	1967 (%)	1971 (%)
"How much do political parties make government pay attention to the people?"		
A good deal	31	15
Somewhat	35	27
Not much (not at all)	19	30
Don't know	14	28
"How much does having elections from time to time make the government pay attention to the people?"		
A good deal	42	25
Somewhat	31	26
Not much	15	24
Don't know	11	25

Attitudes concerning the role of government in India emphasize approval of affirmative governmental action but also, at least in the 1971 survey, considerable support for direct mass action (table 3.3). This development, on which we have no earlier base data, may be very significant. The strong mass support for intervention by the government in the economy has been accepted for a long time. We find corroboration for this in both 1967 and 1971, although there may in fact be a larger minority not completely committed to governmental control of the economy than was expected. Nevertheless close to 50 percent of all men support regulative socialism as far as business and agriculture is concerned, 83 percent of those who knew anything about the bank nationalization approved it, and 76 percent wanted egalitarian redistribution of land and property. These are high proportions. Added to this now is the relatively large proportion who approve of strikes, demonstrations, gheraoes (the action technique of surrounding a political

TABLE 3.3 Evaluative Orientations in India toward Government's Role

	1967 (%)	1971 (%)
Government should legislate (some) controls over trade, industry, and agriculture		
Yes	41	48
Don't know	18	22
No controls or less controls	32	27
Proper for the government to nationalize the banks (52% uninformed)		
Those who had heard of this matter who approved	...	83
Government should pass legislation to limit ownership of land and property		
Yes		76
Don't know		9
Extent of satisfaction with the performance of government officials		
Satisfied with national officials	43	...
Satisfied with local officials	40	...
Feels Mrs. Gandhi is doing a "fair" or "good" job	...	75
Propriety of direct political action		
Strikes, demonstrations, gheraoes are a proper way to make those in authority pay attention to the grievances and demands of the people		
Yes	...	32
Don't know	...	21
Poor people with no land and property should occupy a part of the land and property of those who have a large amount		
Approves	...	48
Disapproves	...	˙46
Don't know	...	5

figure and holding him prisoner until he agrees to act in a certain way, to resign, and so on), and those who believe poor people should occupy land. These proportions favoring direct mass action are in the neighborhood of a third to a half. They document that Indians live in a political environment which both actually and politically is anything but passive. There is great pressure for governmental or mass action to redress grievances and to resolve people's needs. In this context the study of Indian political participation takes on a new meaning.[15]

Evaluations about one's own role in the Indian system reveal a high level of consistent pessimism. This appears to be on the decline somewhat in 1971, however. On the three most standard efficacy items (table 3.4), there are far fewer persons giving the inefficacious response in 1971. Thus, while 79 percent felt in 1967 that people they elected did not care about the ordinary citizen's ideas, in 1971 this was only 60 percent. Nevertheless, the low level of efficacy in 1967, and on some items in 1971 also, is quite pronounced. Few Indians appear to have a consistently strong sense of subjective political competence. And as Edward Shils has said, this is to be expected in a society hierarchized as India has been historically, with traditional respect for authority, and with social-religious cultural expectations playing down the political role of the individual. We will return to these matters later.

TABLE 3.4 Political Efficacy Orientations of Indians*

	1967	1971
Elected representatives don't care what people like me think	79	60
Sometimes politics and government seem so complicated that a person like me can't really understand what is going on	80	57
People like me don't have any say about what the government does	70	37

* The phrasing in the two studies varied. The 1967 study used the standard ISR version with agree-disagree options. The 1971 language differed in the way each item was introduced, with the phrase "Would you say that...." Values given here are percent agreeing with the statement.

The level of political efficacy in India is comparatively low in relation to the United States, but not consistently low in relation to other countries. Douglas Madsen, who has done an authoritative study of efficacy in India, assembled comparative data which illustrate these differences. We present an example of the distributions by country on one efficacy item in table 3.5.

It is surprising to find that in 1971 the level of political efficacy in India was similar to that in Britain, the Netherlands, and Canada, and, above all, higher than that in West Germany. On this type of measure the United States stood out in earlier studies, but had declined considerably by 1974.[16] But in other democracies usually much less than 50 percent of the citizens indicate this feeling. Italy and Mexico, according to the Almond-Verba

TABLE 3.5 Comparative Levels of the Sense of Political Efficacy

	"People Like Me Don't Have Any Say about What the Government Does" % Disagreeing (% Efficacious)	Year of Study
United States	72 (57)	1960 (1974)
Canada	47	1965
Netherlands	40	1969
United Kingdom	39	1959
India	39 (22)	1971 (1967)
Japan	26	1967
West Germany	25	1959
Mexico	21	1959
Italy	14	1959

SOURCE: See Douglas Madsen, "The Sense of Political Efficacy in India: An Exploration in Political Psychology" (Ph.D. diss., UCLA, 1973), pp.117–20. The Indian data, one must remember, are based on male responses only. The 1974 U.S. data come from Warren Miller and Teresa Levitin, *Leadership and Change* (Cambridge, Mass.: Winthrop Publishers, 1976), p. 228. Earlier research indicates that the male proportion for the United States is about 5 to 7 percent higher.

study, are particularly low. In this comparative array, however, India emerges, at least in 1971 (the 1967 figures are lower) as reasonably high in efficacy. It is almost as if Indian citizens, after twenty-five years of exposure to and experience with democratic processes, are rejecting their traditional self-perceptions as "subjects" of political authority and are seeing themselves as potentially influential participants in the political order. At least about 40 percent of the 1971 electorate convey that impression.

A third type of orientation concerns the extent of "attention" to political matters, similar to what others have called *"expressive"* orientations (table 3.6). Here we are dealing with the degree of interest and concern about politics. Indians rank behind Americans and British in their own expressed interest. By their own admission only a third to two-fifths admit a high attention level, while approximately two-thirds or more in Britain and the United States claim to be concerned and attentive. How important and relevant these differentials are is not clear. Certainly they do not appear to lead to higher levels of political participation in the West, nor to higher levels of political knowledge, as we have already shown. These matters will be explored more thoroughly later when we look at the relationship between psychological orientations to political behavior. Here we only note that there are differences in the proportions of the population professing an interest in politics, with India revealing a smaller proportion than the United States and Britian.

TABLE 3.6 Attention and Commitment to Parties and Politics in Three Countries (Men Only)

	India (%) 1967	India (%) 1971	Britain (%)	U.S. (%)
General interest in politics	35	38	68	94
Interest in the campaign	32	37	76	73
Personally care about the election outcome	40	52	71	66

SOURCE: Based on our special analysis of men in the 1963 or 1964 British studies. The male American data are for 1956 and 1960. See also Angus Campbell, Gerald Gurin, and Warren Miller, *The Voter Decides* (Evanston, Ill.: Row, Peterson & Co., 1954), pp. 34, 36.

One final type of orientation to politics which emerges from our Indian analysis is what we call the "conformity orientation to politics." We asked our respondents how the people in their village voted—and *whether it was important* to them to vote the way the others voted. Similarly, we asked them how their caste or religious group voted, and *whether it was important* to vote congruent with other caste members. And, third, the same series of questions was used for family members. Here are images of the individual as he sees his political behavior in three social group contexts. Our findings are interesting but they have to be interpreted cautiously. In 1971 we found that just over 50 percent felt that it was important to vote the way their caste and village voted, and 65 percent felt that it was important to have family uniformity in voting. Although there is a suggestion here of considerable social conformity orientations, in an "empirical-analytical" sense this may not actually be the case. An earlier study of the relationship of caste to politics underscores this warning.[17] For one thing we find only a minority of our respondents in both years perceiving their caste as voting for a single party—24 percent in 1967 and 36 percent in 1971. Further, the socioeconomic heterogeneity of castes is considerable. In addition, only a minority of our respondents knew what the caste leader's party preference was and agreed with it—35 percent in 1967 and 25 percent in 1971. Thus, in reality the amount of conformity behavior must be much lower than these cultural expectations would suggest. One should not overdo, therefore, the interpretation that political behavior is highly conformist.

We can conclude this discussion of "cultural" orientations of Indians with a few general observations. On balance there is strong evidence from these data that a large proportion of the Indian public are cognitively aware of politics, support parties and the election system, and demonstrate considerable personal "psychological involvement" with that system, while feeling pessimistic about their capacity as individuals to be effective in that system. This emergence of a "modern" set of political system orientations and attitudes, what might be called the new "competitive party democracy political culture," may be the most significant aspect of Indian political development. This is related to a key concern which developmental theorists of India have speculated about. Is there a mass culture emerging? What is its content? Has it permeated throughout the society? Or are there different mass cultures—does it vary by region and individual states? Is there one for urban India and one for rural India, or one for the educated and one for illiterates? And a related basic query is, To what extent does this new mass culture resemble the structure of political orientations of the masses in industrialized Western societies? This question, in turn, is related to the stage of political development in India. Is there an association between a certain *level* of social and economic development, on the one hand, and political development on the other? If India is already, in 1967 and 1971, manifesting the characteristics of presumably more "modern" westernized systems, the antecedent irrelevance of the requisite social and economic development becomes apparent. It becomes difficult to argue then that a certain level of literacy, urbanization, economic productivity, as well as other socioeconomic progress, is necessary before political development can occur. Further, and perhaps more important, if India has already developed politically in the sense of achieving a high level of public acceptance and support for such processes and institutions as competitive elections, a democratic party system, combative campaigns, and political elites struggling for governmental power, this new culture will no doubt have a profound effect on the behavior of elites and masses and greatly influence the agenda of Indian politics, its decisional process, and its policy outcomes. Clearly, if once again given the opportunity to express its "new" political cultural predispositions, the Indian public will do so, in a variety of types of involvement, in the process demonstrating its commitment to democratic practice.

FOUR·

How Many Indian Cultures? Urban-Rural, Generational, and Party Differences in Orientations to Politics

I N EXAMINING THE NATURE AND REALITY OF THIS "NEW" MASS political culture in India, one must confront the question of whether this culture is one system or pattern or fragmented into several subcultures. One of the recurring questions about Indian society, to begin with, has been whether there are two cultures—one urban and one in the villages. Certain scholars have strongly suggested this. Our concern here is whether our data support this expectation.

If we partition our sample so that we isolate the nonmobile villagers (those who were born in and have never left their village) and compare them with the urban population, we can discern whether there are distinct patterns (table 4.1). What is immediately clear from such data is that the attitudes toward politics for the urban and rural populations are remarkably similar, on a national sample basis. If one compares the total urban with the total "nonmobile rural" population, the size of the percentage differences in table 4.1 are small. Thus, 61 percent of the nonmobile villagers feel parties are responsible for making government "pay attention" to the people, while 70 percent of the urban population take this position. These are, incidentally, strikingly high proportions. In response to some of our other questions about the party system, the attitudes were not as "modern" (for example, only a minority approve party and group conflict).[1] Nevertheless, the point here is that the extent of the differences is small between urban and rural sectors. On party identification, 53 percent of the nonmobile villagers are "strong" compared to 51 percent for the urban sample. One of the largest differences we discovered was in candidate knowledge—46 percent of the rural compared to 62 percent of the urban group having a high level of information about local candidates (less than 20 percent of the villagers and less than 10 percent of the city dwellers had no knowledge of any candidate).

On balance, it appears that "modern" orientations to politics are only slightly less evident in the peasant culture than in the urban culture. And this is true of the "active political minority" in rural areas as well. This sizable group (12 percent) is overwhelmingly "modern" in its attitudes toward the role of parties in the political system, in level of general political interest, in candidate knowledge, and in party identification. They

TABLE 4.1 Does India Have Two Political Cultures—Urban and Village?*

	Nonmobile Villagers (%)		Urban Population (%)	
System Orientations	Total Group (N=781)	Most Active Political Minority (N=91)	Total Group (N=222)	Most Active Political Minority (N=30)
"Modern" attitudes				
Parties help make government responsive				
A good deal	27 ⎫ 61	41 ⎫ 81	35 ⎫ 70	37 ⎫ 74
Somewhat	34 ⎭	40 ⎭	35 ⎭	37 ⎭
General interest in politics				
Great interest	10 ⎫ 29	25 ⎫ 62	13 ⎫ 32	23 ⎫ 63
Some interest	19 ⎭	37 ⎭	19 ⎭	40 ⎭
Knows 2 or more candidates for assembly	46	75	62	83
Strong party identification	53	78	51	83
"Traditional" attitudes				
Favors a ban on cow slaughter	76	69	58	53
Feels MPs and MLAs should work for caste interests	47	44	41	43
Sense of political efficacy: "people like me don't have any say about what the government does"	70	60	67	70

* Based on 1967 data from a sample of men who were eligible to vote from 1957 to 1967.

are only very slightly less "modern" than urban dwellers. If we conceive of these people as "opinion leaders" or, as Kothari calls them, "linkmen" in village communities in which party politics is very salient, we can well speculate on the long-range significance of this cadre of activists for politics in the countryside. Thus, 81 percent feel parties are important intermediaries, 75 percent are knowledgeable, and 78 percent are strong party identifiers. These are the orientations of a rapidly developing, if not developed, "modern" political culture.

That "traditional" orientations toward politics still persist side by side with presumably "modern" ones, is clear also from the last section of table 4.1. On a key issue such as banning cow slaughter, which was important in the 1967 campaign, the nonmobile rural population is conservative (76 percent favor a ban), but then so is the urban population, only slightly less so (58 percent). Both urban and rural citizens overwhelmingly oppose the idea of a party struggle (82 percent and 72 percent, respectively), revealing the persistence of a traditional norm of harmony in social relationships. They oppose such political conflict, even though they are now a part of that struggle as voters and activists. There is, surprisingly perhaps, less norma- tive support for the idea that caste interests should predominate than one might have thought (only slightly more than 40 percent are "caste priority conscious"), and again there are no differences between the villager and the urbanite. And on sense of political efficacy, the degree of pessimism about one's own role in the system pervaded countryside and city alike in 1967. In short, there is much so-called traditionalism in political views in India, among the same populations that exhibit "modern" orientations. But the urban pattern does not differ markedly from the rural pattern. Rather than two distinct political cultures, one urban and one village, India reveals a remarkable homogeneity in political cultural development by 1967.

Evidences of differences by age cohorts and by generation are also not striking. Our data for 1967 do not reveal great variations in attitudes by life cycle or by the historical circumstances under which citizens came to political adulthood. It is true that those who most recently have come of political age were socialized to politics earlier in their lives (up to 25 percent by age fifteen compared to only 6 percent of those who came to adulthood prior to Independence). And they are less likely to be illiterates (40 percent of the younger age category compared to 62 percent of the oldest group). But aside from small differences in level of political interest (42 percent for the young compared to 30 percent for the older), and the greater self-perception by the younger citizens of being open to "new ideas," there are no striking differences by age categories, and particularly no evidence that young Indians are greatly different from those who are older. One possible exception to that is noted below. All groups are inclined to be party identifiers, to support on balance (at the 49 to 59 percent level) a competitive party system, and split close to 50 percent in support of the election system. At the same time, all these generational categories in 1967 were very "traditional"—on the cow slaughter issue (80 percent against) and on their sense of political efficacy (80 percent pessimistic).

There is a possibly significant tendency, observable in our data, that those who came to political adulthood in the period immediately before Independence show a consistent pattern of "modern" attitudes, slightly more "modern" than those preceding them generationally (see fig. 3). This "Independence generation" (coming of political age just before 1947) revealed levels of political knowledge, political interest, support for the party and election system, and party identification which were greater than the previous "generation" (coming of political age ten years or more before Independence), and which usually were not superseded by subsequent "generations." In short while the younger age cohort is more "modern" in dress, earlier socialized to politics, more educated, and sees itself as more "innovative," its degree of support for the system and its culture orientations toward politics is basically no different from that of the citizens who came to political maturity in close proximity to Independence. Although the evidence is not overwhelming on this point, it is there and

FIG. 3. Changes in political culture orientations in 1967, by the time of arrival at political adulthood.

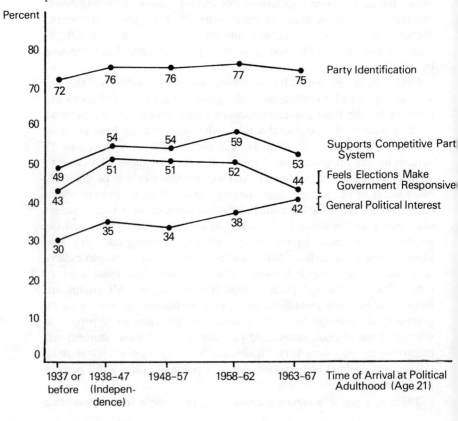

suggests that Independence may have had an impact on molding Indian political culture. What has replaced that historic experience in the lives of those coming of age since Independence has been the continuous exposure to elites and institutions which communicated these Independence cultural values, reenforced more and more by greater and earlier socialization in the family.

A basic type of cultural cleavage to explore concerns the political party subcultures. Do party support groups differ radically in their orientations toward the system? Again we can attempt to get some perspective on cultural change by comparing the support cadres of the newer political parties with those of Congress. And there is very little indication that this factor—the recency of origin of a party—is discriminating. The Swatantra and DMK identifiers are not consistently different from the supporters of other parties. This is not to say that differences do not exist, because they do, and it is rather interesting to speculate on the meaning of these differences. Congress loyalists are most supportive of the party system (94 percent feel parties make government "pay attention" to people); Swatantra loyalists are the least supportive (68 percent)—a sizable 26 percent difference. But the partisans of the most recently established DMK are also very supportive of the party system (91 percent). The Communists and Socialists are supportive at the 75 percent level, Jan Sangh at 87 percent. The reason for these differences is by no means clear. What is perhaps remarkable is that the identifiers of these small parties, whose strength by 1967 was each below 10 percent of the electorate and whose prospects for increasing this percentage much were improbable, were nevertheless supportive of the party system.

A comparison of 1971 and 1967 orientations toward the party system reveals a considerable fluctuation in support. The following data will illustrate this:

	Strong Identifiers of the Party Who Feel Parties Make Government Pay Attention to the People (%)	
	1967	1971
Congress	94	55
DMK	91	78
Communists	75	66

What this decline is attributable to is difficult to say without a careful analysis. One theory that could be advanced, however, is that the split in the Congress party—coupled with Mrs. Gandhi's attack in 1971 on the older politicians who made it difficult, she said, for her to provide leadership—may be reflected in these figures. Another theory which might have credibility is that continuing dissatisfaction with one's own financial situation (close to 60 percent in both 1967 and 1971 were not satisfied), plus the appearance in 1971 of support for direct political action by at least a third of the population, may have contributed to a decline in support for parties. We will examine these and other hypotheses more carefully in a later analysis.

These party identifiers were also not very parochial in their orientations, except perhaps for the DMK whose success was due at least partially to regional and local appeals. Nor were these partisans very "authoritarian" in their views, the two extreme Left and Right parties, the Communists (32 percent favoring strong leaders) and Jan Sangh (25 percent favoring strong leaders), having the largest proportions of "authoritarians."

It may be significant that the older, established parties—Congress, the Communists, and the Socialists—have the highest proportion of partisans with a sense of political efficacy. The contrast between Congress and the Communists, on the one hand, with 33 to 42 percent feeling personally efficacious, and, on the other hand, the two newest parties—Swatantra and DMK—with only 13 percent and 14 percent feeling efficacious, may well reflect the influence on these supporters of experiences of relative effectiveness of their parties on the system over time.

Although there are differences in the cultural orientations of the supporters of the parties, they do not suggest any deep cultural cleavages. There is relatively high support for the party, and election, systems. There are, as in the rest of the sample, low levels of feelings of confidence in one's own capacity to influence the political order, but antisystem cultural orientations are not manifest in these data. The Communists are, for example, relatively high in system support and sense of efficacy. They may be critical of the regime and its officials and policies, but this is also true of all other parties except Congress. They do not, however, reject the emerging political culture.

Therefore, our analysis of political attitudes and cultural orientations reveals that there is much greater homogeneity than might be expected. We have looked here at urban-rural differences, generational differences, and differences by party support groups. There are some interesting discoveries in these data, interesting differences on particular items for particular subgroups. And tendencies are found in the data. Nonmobile peasants in the villages tend to be less knowledgeable about politics and somewhat more "traditional." Those age groups coming to political maturity at Independence in 1947 display a consistent increment in "modern" orientations. Supporters of the more established parties are inclined to have a higher sense of political efficacy. But after inspecting all these data, what strikes one is the remarkable similarity in cultural perspectives for all sectors of the population. It is basically a population which supports democratic parties and electoral institutions, which is developing knowledge about and interest in the system, while retaining a clear feeling of skepticism about the citizen's role in the system and is strongly "traditional" in orientations. It is this convergence of traditional and modern cultural inclinations which stands out in our data.

Specific findings in this chapter may be interpreted as particularly significant in the light of the 1975 developments. The extremely high proportion of Indians who dislike party conflict, the low levels of political efficacy except among the activists of the older and established parties, and the decline in support for the party system between 1967 and 1971 may help us understand *both* opposition to the regime by certain party activists as well as a temporary tolerance for nonconflictual politics. For that very large segment of the urban and rural Indian population who are interested and supportive of the party and election system, who identify with it, and who favor a plural party system, it is hard to conceive of that public permanently relapsing into the quiescence of the noncompetitive one-party state.

FIVE.

Cultural Differences and Uniformities by States

T HE REGIONAL DIVERSITY OF INDIA HAS BEEN OBSERVED BY MANY scholars, leading one to expect great variations in the acceptance of political cultural norms. And yet, as Kothari has said, "the essential identity of India has not been political but cultural."[1] Even though government was not the unifier historically, presumably the "wide diffusion of the cultural symbols" also included the diffusion of political cultural norms. The extent to which this is so can be explored with our data. We will rely here primarily on the 1971 study data since the state samples were drawn in such a way as to be directly representative of each state's electorate. Yet, because the states vary greatly in size, our presentation rests on far fewer cases in some states (as, for example, Haryana with 41 interviews) than in others (as Uttar Pradesh with 369).

One should note at the outset that Indian states revealed a considerable range from 1952 to 1971 in the level of voter turnout (table 5.1). Madras was consistently over 70 percent in recent elections. The same was true of Kerala and other states, such as Maharashtra, Punjab, and Haryana. On the other hand, five states were consistently low in turnout: Rajasthan, U.P., M.P., Bihar, and Orissa. The last of these has had an extremely low record, although in 1967 and 1971 it increased dramatically. This suggests that there may indeed be state-by-state differences in public support for parties and elections.[2]

If we look at the distributions of our responses by states we do find that the range in public attitudinal support for parties and elections is considerable (table 5.2). On two of our questions, whether parties (or elections) tend to make government "pay attention to what the people think," the states reveal consistent differences, and rank very similarly. States like Madras (Tamil Nadu), Punjab, Kerala, Maharashtra, and Haryana are high on both measures. Some states, such as Gujarat and Rajasthan, are high on one measure but low on another. At the lowest level of support is Orissa and following closely is Bihar. The range in support percentages is 39 percent on elections and 54 percent on the parties question. These are sizable differences, higher than the ranges in turnout in table 5.1.

Turning to state differences in strength of party identification (table 5.3), we see yet another rank ordering of states. Kerala, the Punjab, and Gujarat

TABLE 5.1 Differences (Percents) in Voter Turnout by States in the Elections of 1962, 1967, and 1971 (Average of Turnout for All Constituencies)

	1962	1967	1971	1952–71 Average	Our Sample Con- stituencies Average (1967)
Kerala	68.9	72.8	64	70	71.4
Punjab	65.2	67.9	59	59	70.2
Madras	64.2	74.3	69	72	72.2
Andhra Pradesh	62.6	65.3	58	59	64.5
Maharashtra	60.6	69.7	58	60	64.4
Haryana	57.2	61.2	63	64	60.9
Mysore	53.8	63.5	55	55	67.5
Gujarat	56.4	60.3	53	56	63.4
West Bengal	55.6	60.4	59	63	62.3
Rajasthan	50.2	55.7	52	54	57.0
Uttar Pradesh	49.5	51.7	45	46	52.2
Bihar	45.0	48.7	48	49	52.1
Madhya Pradesh	42.3	50.3	45	48	50.9
Orissa	23.2	40.3	41	43	38.8
Range	45.7	34.0	29	29	33.4

SOURCE: These are official election statistics (col. 1–4). Data in columns 1 and 2 are from Chandidas et al., eds., *India Votes*, pp. 362–643; column 3 from Election Commission of India, *Report on the Fifth General Election to the House of the People of India*, 1973, pp. 179–82; column 4 from Norman D. Palmer, *Elections and Political Development: The South Asian Experience* (Durham, N.C.: Duke University, 1975), p. 74.

now are quite low (35 percent and less are strong identifiers), while Bihar and Andhra are relatively high. Tamil Nadu, Maharashtra, and Haryana appear consistently high in commitment to parties and Orissa remains very low. There seem to be some continuities, therefore, and also some important deviations. This suggests that these dimensions of system orientations are discrete and states may be high in support of parties as responsibility mechanisms but low in party identification (Punjab and Kerala, for example), or low in support of parties as instruments of making government responsive but high in party identification (Bihar, for example). In these states the publics' orientations are not convergent, while in other states (as Orissa, Tamil Nadu, and Maharashtra) these orientations do converge.

If we group states by their level of support for parties and elections (as making government responsive) and then look at state averages on other

53

TABLE 5.2 Variations by States in Support for the Party and Elections Systems (1971)*

	Support Parties: Feel They Make Government Responsive (%)	Support Elections: Feel They Make Government Responsive (%)	N
States highest in support			
Kerala	71	68	59
Tamil Nadu (Madras)	61	63	156
Maharashtra	60	68	148
Haryana	54	73	41
Punjab	51	75	55
States medium in support			
Gujarat	42	59	82
Andhra Pradesh	42	51	195
West Bengal	40	42	196
U.P.	40	55	389
States lowest in support			
Mysore	37	38	108
Rajasthan	34	58	79
Madhya Pradesh	33	38	159
Bihar	22	33	221
Orissa	17	29	102
Range in support percentages	54	39	

* Columns 1 and 2 are percentages who say parties or elections are a "good deal" or "somewhat" responsive.

responses, we see some evidence of differences (table 5.4). The high support cluster of states is considerably higher in mean voter turnout (65 percent compared to 49 percent) and to some extent in sense of political efficacy. Similar differences on party identification and general political interest also exist.

If we group states by their level of turnout since 1952, using official statistics (table 5.5), we find considerable linkage to other political orientations. High turnout states are consistently more supportive of parties and the election system— a 25 to 30 percent difference compared to states low in turnout. There is a slight association with party identification but none actually with general political interest. This suggests that the following orientations may be linked together: support for parties, support for elections, possibly strong party loyalty, and voter turnout. Also suggested is that party identification and extent of political interest are not necessarily linked to turnout. Orissa, for example, with the lowest average turnout,

TABLE 5.3 Variations in Party Identification by State (1971)

States, Ranked by Party Identification Strength	Strong Identification (%)	No Party Identification (%)
Maharashtra	53	41
Andhra Pradesh	52	39
Tamil Nadu	46	37
Haryana	44	51
Bihar	39	59
U.P.	39	55
Punjab	35	56
Rajasthan	35	62
Mysore	32	64
Madhya Pradesh	26	64
Kerala	22	41
West Bengal	22	54
Orissa	21	62
Gujarat	20	71
Range	33	34

had a high level of general political interest (60 percent) in our 1971 study.

To rank order all states on these measures we computed basic support scores (table 5.6). The rank order for states, by proportions supporting the system in 1971, is quite interesting, ranging from Tamil Nadu (61 percent) to Orissa (25 percent). What is striking is the consistently high level of support for the system in Madras/Tamil Nadu, Punjab, Kerala, and Maharashtra. Equally striking is the consistently low level of support in Mysore, Madhya Pradesh, Bihar, and Orissa. There seems to be some uniformity over time in the level of popular support for the party and election systems.

Is there adequate support for the system in these attitudinal distributions for one to argue that India now has a "political culture" in all states? And is it an integrated "culture" or only composed of random types of support, or found only in certain "pockets" of the population? From the evidence presented in this section it is clear that there are several states where the level of support for the party and election system was minimal in 1971. From three to five states, depending on one's criteria, are notably lacking in public support. When one asks more specifically, as we did in 1967, whether the respondent approves of a one-party system, or a system with two or more parties, consensus is particularly low in some states. States like U.P., Madhya Pradesh, Bihar, and Orissa have publics which reveal majority disagreement with the idea of a plural, competitive party system. Further, there is a great variation in the proportions of state populations

TABLE 5.4 "Political Cultural Types" of States and Linkage to Other Variables* (1971)

States and Types	Mean Score on Support Index (%)	Mean Party Identification (% Strong)	Average Turnout (%) 1952–71	General Political Interest (%)	Political Efficacy (%)
States high in support of party and elections (Kerala, Tamil Nadu, Maharashtra, Haryana, Punjab)	64	40	65	44	37
States mixed or moderate in support (Gujarat, Andhra, West Bengal, U.P., Rajasthan	46	34	56	35	25
States low in support (Mysore, U.P., Bihar, Orissa)	31	29.5	49	33.5	28.5

* These percentages are based on the averages for the states in each group. The efficacy item used here is "Sometimes politics and government seem so complicated a person like me can't really understand what is going on." The index is based on the questions asking separately whether parties and elections make government "pay attention." General political interest is used here and the proportions include those with a "great deal" or "some" interest.

strongly identifying with parties—states like Gujarat, West Bengal, Kerala, Madhya Pradesh, and Orissa were particularly low in strong party identification in 1971. The low level of party identification probably is related to special conditions in the party life of these states, particularly the breakdown in the organizational strength and elite support for Congress party and the divisiveness and strife in party politics.

Our correlational analysis based on *individual response data* in 1967 corroborates certain of our expectations, some to a great extent (table 5.7). Those respondents who support the party system clearly are inclined to support the election system (correlation of .52). Those who have general interest in politics are often also those who have an interest in the campaign (.59). The other correlations are not as striking, although *positive associations are found for all our respondents between party identification and political participation (.21) as well as campaign interest (.24)*, but the correlations are small. Also a positive correlation emerges between politi-

TABLE 5.5 The Linkage by level of Voting Turnout (by States)
and Other System Support Variables*

Classification of States by Voting Turnout Levels 1952–71 Averages	% Supportive of Elections 1971	% Supportive of Parties 1971	% with Strong Party Identification 1971	% with General Interest in Politics 1971
States high in turnout (Madras, Kerala, Maharashtra, Haryana, West Bengal) *Average turnout 66%*	63	57	37	45
States medium in turnout (Gujarat, Mysore, Rajasthan, Andhra, Punjab) *Average turnout 57%*	56	41	35	32
States low in turnout (Uttar Pradesh, Madhya, Bihar, Orissa) *Average turnout 46.5%*	39	28	31	36

* These percentages are averages of the states in each group.

TABLE 5.6 Rank Order of States in Consistency of Orientations Supportive of the System*

	Average Percentages of Samples Supporting Parties and Election Systems, 1971
Madras/Tamil Nadu	61
Maharashtra	60
Haryana	59
Kerala	58
Punjab	55
Andhra Pradesh	51
Rajasthan	45
U.P.	45
Gujarat	44
West Bengal	42
Mysore/Karnataka	41
Madhya Pradesh	36
Bihar	36
Orissa	25

* These average support scores are based on four items: (1) support for elections as making the government responsive, (2) support for parties as making the government responsive, (3) strong party identification, and (4) average voting turnout (official statistics).

TABLE 5.7 Correlations of Political Orientations for Individuals, by States (Male Respondents, 1967)

	Support for Parties with Support for Elections	Campaign Interest and General Political Interest	Party Identification and Campaign Interest	Political Participation and Support for Political Parties
All respondents	.52	.59	.24	.16
Respondents by states				
Kerala	.33	.40	.68	.18
Uttar Pradesh	.57	.59	.14	.17
Madhya Pradesh	.49	.51	.27	−.05
West Bengal	.12	.60	.47	.23
Andhra Pradesh	.63	.52	.14	.11
Rajasthan	.63	.72	.33	.31
Bihar	.49	.49	.11	.12
Madras/Tamil Nadu	.37	.62	.43	.05
Orissa	.23	.62	.42	.21
Punjab	.88	.72	.35	.20
Haryana	.55	.72	.33	.15
Mysore	.58	.56	.27	.00
Maharashtra	.63	.67	.18	.16
Gujarat	.30	.53	.25	.21

cal participation and attitudinal support for parties (.16), but it is also low. Further, the variations by states are considerable. Nevertheless, there is evidence here that some of these attitudinal-cultural orientations toward politics do cohere and that there may be the beginning of an integrated political culture.[3] One final set of data suggests differing and pervasive cultural patterns, by states. All levels of education in a given state seem to reflect strong or weak support for parties and elections (table 5.8). In states where support for parties and elections is high, illiterates manifest this support at *relatively* high levels, although not as high as for those with more education. Where support is weak, those with education reveal low levels of support, as do the illiterates. This is an important observation to take note of for it suggests that there may indeed be a pervasive culture for a state, and that cultural norms about the system are communicated at all levels of society. It is not as though the educated elite are very supportive of the system throughout India, and the illiterates throughout India equally alienated. Rather, the degree of acceptance of political system norms seems dependent in part on geography, region, and state. Thus, we find in table 5.8, for example, that in Madras/Tamil Nadu, where there is high

TABLE 5.8 Contrasting Levels of Party System Support in 1971:
For Illiterates and the Educated

Classification Based on Index of Party and Election System Support	Respondents Who Felt Parties Made Governments Responsive (%)	
	Illiterates	Some or Much Education
States highest in system support (Kerala, Tamil Nadu, Maharashtra, Haryana, Punjab)	37	75
States medium in support (Gujarat, Andhra, West Bengal, U.P.)	25	52
States lowest in support (Mysore, Rajasthan, M.P., Bihar, Orissa)	17	39

support for the party and election system, 40 percent of the illiterates feel the party system is responsive (as do 74 percent of the more educated). But in Bihar, *both* the illiterates *and* educated are much more negative (only 14 percent and 30 percent, respectively, feel parties make government responsive). Educated citizens tend to be more supportive, although the data are not completely consistent on this point. What is fairly consistent is that where one finds illiterates most supportive, one finds educated people supportive; where illiterates are negative or alienated, the same basic orientation exists for educated people.

What emerges from these data on the political cultures of Indian states are the following major observations: First, there is a fairly high level of system support in a cluster of five to eight states, particularly in public support for parties and elections, although the variations in support are considerable. On other cultural orientations, such as level of political interest, party identification, and political efficacy, the evidence is less strong and more varied. Second, the evidence points to the existence of some "structuring" or "consistency" in cultural orientations for the individual. On some of these orientations the correlations are very high. Thus, we found an .86 correlation between support for the party system and the support for the election system. On the others they are low, particularly in the association of party identification with party support and in the relationship of political interest to other orientations. Nevertheless, given the expectation that some citizen orientations are unlikely to be consistent or structured, finding this level of "constraint" for India is significant. Finally, we have discovered in this state-by-state analysis some evidence that illiterates in some states may have different orientations than in other states, and the same is true of those with an education. Penetration and assimilation of cultural norms thus does not appear to be a social status phenomenon, happening to certain sectors of the population and not to others, but rather it appears to occur with some uniformity of incidence in the society. This attests to the meaning and reality of political culture for India. There is such a reality as a cultural environment; its linkage to political behavior requires examination.

S I X ·

The Role of Parties in Mobilizing Support
for the Emerging Political Culture

I MPLICIT IN MUCH OF WHAT WE HAVE SAID THUS FAR IS THAT TREMEN-
dous political change has occurred in India since 1947, that this has
penetrated to the periphery of the society, that above all this has not been
merely a change in voting behavior and party preferences, but rather that a
fundamental change in the public's orientations toward politics has
transpired, and that exposure to the "new" political institutions and pressures of political parties, elections, and campaigns have been largely
responsible for this political cultural transformation. We would now like to
demonstrate the nature and consequences of this mobilization process.

We can begin with the relevance of party exposure, both for citizen
interest in politics and for attitudes revealing political system support. This
can be dramatically seen if we divide our sample by extent of each
respondent's exposure to the parties in the 1967 campaign. A fourth of our
sample were out of contact completely, 30 percent minimally exposed, and
slightly less than half considerably exposed. As exposure to the campaign
increases there is a striking increase in political interest (both general and
campaign interest), in support for the party system, and there is a tendency
to feel a sense of political efficacy (table 6.1). The differences are great. Of
those not exposed to the campaign only 14 percent are interested in
politics, while 76 percent of those most exposed are interested. The other
findings are similar. One notes, however, that even 40 percent of those not
exposed do support the party system, a gratifying discovery. These results
only set the stage for further analysis. By themselves they prove little, and
may be tautological—interested people are the ones exposed, and vice
versa. Although this is too glib a reaction to even these data, further
analysis is necessary to demonstrate the importance of the party system and
the campaign for socializing the public to acceptance of politics and party
institutions.

It is instructive in this connection to look carefully at the "new entrants"
into the system. What we mean here is that group of citizens who previously did not participate through voting and who at the time of our study
voted for the first time. If we compare these new entrants with those who
are perennial nonparticipants, some interesting differences in characteristics and orientations emerge. Our data indicate that the new entrants

TABLE 6.1 The Relationship of Party and Campaign Exposure to
Orientations to Politics (Total Male Sample, 1967)

	Campaign Exposure Score (%)				
	0	1	2	3	4
Interested in politics generally	14	24	39	54	76
Interested in 1967 campaign	11	20	38	51	83
Supports party system as necessary and making government responsive	40	54	62	74	72
Prefers plural party system over a one-party system	36	45	51	62	70
Sense of political efficacy (highest two scores)	7	7	12	14	19
N	468	568	475	314	148

were more exposed to party campaign efforts (24 percent were highly exposed, compared to 10 percent of the perennial nonvoters). Political party and caste leaders were also in more contact with the entrants. The new voters also were much better informed about politics. Over 60 percent could identify at least one candidate while this was true of only one-third of the perennial nonparticipants.

If we now turn to their orientations to the political system, we see some consistent differences between these newly mobilized voters in 1967 and other categories of respondents (table 6.2). They are inclined to be more interested in politics generally and to believe in the party and elections system. Although one must note that a majority of Indians do support these subsystems, there is overwhelming support for the system among those who became voters for the first time in 1967. This has significance for the argument that the political development process is socializing the public to greater support for the democratic competitive system. It also suggests, but only suggests and does not prove, the relevance of parties for expansion of public support for the system.

This relevance is dramatically evident when we determine the exposure to the parties during the campaign for each respondent and then look at the respondents' orientations by exposure level. The results are striking. In table 6.3, one can see that those not exposed to the party effort, for all mobilization and participation types, are much less interested in politics. There is almost a 60 percent differential for the new voters. But even for

TABLE 6.2 Selected Orientations to Politics for Newly Mobilized Voters, Regular Voters, and Other Types of Citizens

	Newly Mobilized (%)	Regular Voters (%)		Irregular Voters (%) 1952–67	Dropouts Were Non-voters in 1967 (%)	Perennial Nonvoters (%)
		Since 1962	Since 1967			
Interested in politics generally ("some" or "great" interest)	41	40	38	30	27	24
Believes parties are necessary and make government responsive	72	71	64	54	60	55
Believes elections are necessary and make government responsive	80	78	74	67	71	68

TABLE 6.3 Differences in Level of Political Interest for Mobilized Subgroups*

	Exposed to Parties and Campaign (%)		Not Exposed to Parties and Campaign (%)	
Newly mobilized in 1967				
Not eligible before; voted first in 1967	73	(41)	17	(42)
Eligible but nonvoters before	57	(61)	18	(38)
Dropouts				
Participated previously but were nonvoters in 1967	69	(16)	12	(34)
Consistent nonparticipants	57	(14)	10	(62)
Total sample	41	(1,480)	16	(432)

* The N for each subcategory is in parenthesis. Each percentage is the proportion of the mobilization and exposure subgroup who had "some" or "great" interest in politics generally.

the nonparticipants party exposure was clearly linked to interest—a 47 percent differential.

We can refine this analysis by using our campaign exposure index. Each respondent was given a score (based on being exposed to house-to-house canvassing, attending party rallies, receiving party literature or handouts, and meeting candidates). The relationship between the amount of exposure and orientation to politics can then be seen. It is clear that the degree of exposure "results" progressively in greater proportions of the population demonstrating orientations supportive of the system. Thus, in table 6.4, for example, among nonparticipants not exposed to parties the level of belief in parties is below the 40 percent level. It increases to 88 percent with high exposure to the parties. While the newly mobilized (that is, new voters in 1967) begin with more support for the system (from 50 to 60 percent), party exposure for them also is relevant to increased support. The influence on them of the campaign activity of the party is still considerable, although the threshold of their initial commitment to the system is higher than that of the chronic nonvoter.

TABLE 6.4 Support for the Party System for Mobilized Subgroups by Degree of Campaign Exposure*

	Campaign Exposure Score (%)			
	0	1	2	3 or 4
New entrants				
Not eligible before; voted first in 1967	50	63	73	78
Eligible but nonvoters before	61	55	75	74
Nonparticipants				
Dropouts in 1967	30	56	74	75
Perennial nonvoters	39	48	41	88
Total sample	40	54	62	73

* Based on a party support index using questions concerning the necessity of parties and whether they make government pay attention "a good deal" or "somewhat."

What type of party system do Indians prefer—a one-party system or a system which is plural and competitive? Our 1967 study revealed that our total sample was split on this question—42 percent desiring a one-party system, 49 percent a plural system, and 9 percent having no opinion. The question here is whether actual exposure of citizens to parties results in disillusionment or greater support for the plural, competitive system. Our data suggest that the latter is the case, for all categories of participants (table 6.5). The perennial nonvoters particularly are less in favor of the one-party system as they are exposed to parties—a 50 percent decline from those with no exposure (42 percent favoring a one-party system) to those with exposure (only 21 percent approving a one-party system). This leads to optimistic projections for the Indian system, indicating that among those potentially capable of being mobilized for involvement there is already a basic support for a competitive party system. Withdrawal from participation and nonvoting has not meant a simultaneous hostility for a plural system for them, if they have been exposed to the campaign.

TABLE 6.5 Extent of Preference for One-Party System for New Voters and Nonparticipants by Campaign Exposure*

	Campaign Exposure Score (%)			
	0	1	2	3 or 4
New entrants in 1967				
Not eligible before; voted first in 1967	45	43	43	29
Eligible but nonvoters before	47	43	35	25
Nonparticipants				
Dropouts in 1967	56	67	63	31
Perennial nonvoters	42	43	36	21
Total sample	46	46	42	34

* Each percentage is the proportion in each subcategory who said they preferred a system with one party over a plural (two or more) party system.

The role of education as a factor in producing interest in politics and support for the system is important. If we look at the straight distribution by education level, it is clear that there are considerable differences in levels of system engagement for illiterates compared to those with more education (table 6.6). The illiterates are minimally interested in politics (29 percent) while the upper educated are more inclined to be interested (78 percent). The illiterates, similarly, are less convinced of the value of the party system.

If we look at the degree of exposure to the parties, however, for these education groups we can see the impact and relevance of the party activity for cultural orientations (table 6.7). The increase is not extreme, but it is consistent. There is a regular increase in supportive attitudes for parties as respondents are exposed to parties during the campaign—an increase in

TABLE 6.6 Education Level and Political Orientation

	% Illiterates (N=908)	% Some Primary (N=370)	% Primary Plus Middle (N=402)	% High School and College (N=200)
High in level of political interest	7	15	17	22
Has some political interest	22	40	49	56
Support for parties Feels they are necessary and make government responsive				
"A good deal"	29	28	40	51
"Somewhat"	34	39	37	35
Prefers plural party to a one-party system	42	52	64	86

TABLE 6.7 Combined Effect of Education and Party Exposure on Supportive Attitudes toward the Party System*

	Campaign Exposure Score (%)				
	0 (N=174)	1 (N=244)	2 (N=173)	3 (N=92)	4 (N=26)
Illiterates	26	27	30	32	35
Some primary	22	30	21	37	34
Primary plus middle school	26	34	40	47	50
High school plus college	45	46	44	55	60

* Each percentage is the proportion of each subgroup (education and exposure subgroup) who felt parties were necessary and make government pay attention to people "a good deal." Those who said "somewhat" but not "a good deal" were excluded here.

support of 9 percent for illiterates, 12 percent for those with more primary education, and 14 to 15 percent for those with higher education. Party exposure, therefore, can make a difference in affect toward the party system. Citizens in India respond less negatively at all educational levels when they come into contact with parties.

Another type of political exposure occurs in the family. This was not high in India in our 1967 data, only 14 percent of our sample indicating that their father was interested in politics while they were growing up. (The proportion was 17 percent in 1971.) There is evidence that such family influence is related to support for the party system. Our analysis reveals that 36 percent of those exposed to politics in the family strongly supported the party system and only 20 percent were weak supporters; only 23 percent of those not thus socialized were very supportive and 33 percent were weak in support. The differences are not extreme, but suggestive.

For previous and chronic nonvoters, family socialization again seems particularly relevant. If we combine family socialization and campaign exposure, we see their individual and concerted relevance to system support clearly (table 6.8). For the newly mobilized voters the key contrast is between those not exposed at all, in family or in the campaign (29 percent of whom were supportive) and those exposed through both family and party (64 percent of whom were supportive). It appears that the impact of party exposure is weightier than that of the family, but both influences are certainly relevant.

TABLE 6.8 Combined Effect of Family Socialization and Campaign Exposure on Attitudes toward Parties (% Feeling Parties Are Necessary, and Make Government Responsive "a Good Deal")

	Campaign Exposure (%)	
	None or Little	Some or Much
All respondents		
Socialized in family	29	44
Not socialized	29	36
New voters in 1967*		
Socialized in family	35	64
Not socialized	29	45

* Based only on those who became eligible to vote in 1967 and did vote.

What is particularly striking in these data (table 6.8) is the relevance which party exposure had for new voters in 1967. Those participating for the first time were much more likely to be strong supporters of the party system if they had had contact with the party, *whether socialized in the family to politics or not* (64 percent compared to 35 percent). Equally significant, however, is that a large minority of those *not exposed* to party system stimuli were convinced that the party system was necessary and effective. For certain critical cultural orientations about politics there is strong evidence here that processes of political mobilization, communication, exposure, and socialization have been at work in Indian society and are productive of citizen support for the system. This is

67

much more so for certain orientations than for others. Thus, we found that for the sense of political efficacy in India the socialization and exposure processes have had some, but minimal, impact. Among our new voters in 1967, for example, the contrast is between those with no exposure to parties (9 percent of whom were high on our efficacy index) and those with much exposure to parties (24 percent of whom were high in efficacy). For basic orientations concerning interest in politics, support for the party system (and particularly the competitive party system), and belief in the election system, exposure to parties is strikingly linked to support. True, up to a third of those highly exposed to the party system still prefer a noncompetitive system, but this is far fewer than those not thus exposed. Regular participants, supporters of non-Congress parties as well as Congress supporters, particularly if exposed to the system, see parties as important links in the system. But what stands out in these data is that even political nonparticipants, if they have been exposed to the parties and to campaigns, are much more likely to be attitudinally committed to the system.

We can assess the relevance of environment with even more decentralized control by looking at the 188 polling stations in which the respondents lived. If we select the extremes in polling station environment—those in which a sizable number of respondents were highly exposed to parties and those in which none were highly exposed, we see important differences in the level of political sophistication and party support. The following quick summary using 1967 data documents the point:

Polling Stations	% of All Respondents High on Exposure (in top Two Categories of Exposure)	% High in Support for Party System	% Having a Sense of Political Efficacy	% High in Candidate Awareness
Highest in campaign exposure—over 40% of respondents highly exposed (31 stations)	53	37	46	63
Lowest in campaign exposure—no respondents highly exposed (30 stations)	0	31	28	24

Clearly the type of party exposure environment in which a person lives is associated with "developed" political orientations. If one lives in an area or neighborhood or village where the parties seem to be active, this environment leads to a tremendous increase in candidate familiarity and political efficacy and a modest increment in support for the party system. This attests again to the impact of environmental conditions on political involvement.

If political development means the acquisition of new cultural orientations—new awarenesses of and belief in new institutions and processes, such as parties and elections, then clearly such development has occurred in India, greatly spurred on and influenced by the exposure of citizens to the activities of the parties. This may well be the most central reality of Indian development.

Part Three

PARTY IDENTIFICATION IN INDIA
IN COMPARATIVE PERSPECTIVE

The Meaning of "Party" for the Indian Citizen: Theories and a Suggested Analytical Model

T HE COMMITMENT OF CITIZENS TO POLITICAL PARTIES IS PRESUMABLY vital for the maintenance of stable democracies. Whether as organizational apparatus, ideological tendency, leadership system, or symbol, the parties must engross the attention of large segments of the population and enlist their loyalties if party democracies are to survive. This has been the essence of the study of "party identification" in the West, where this phenomenon has become one of the keys for understanding political behavior. In the United States and western Europe the concept of party identification has been operationalized to mean psychological attachment to a political party, variously referred to as a feeling of belonging, affiliation, and loyalty. It is presumably the depth of this commitment, its extensiveness in the population, its reliability over time, and its consistent linkage to other citizen attitudes and behavior which help determine the character and viability of the modern democratic polity.

In India, too, scholars have been recognizing, in the absence of clear empirical support, the probable importance for the system of strong attachments to political parties, both in helping to maintain democracy after Independence in 1947, and in explaining the changes occurring in the system leading up to the 1967 election. Thus, Rajni Kothari, while noting the "crystallization of allegiances" even before Independence, and the downward communication of political affiliation after Independence, notes with reference to 1967 that the "enormous shifting of political loyalties at the state level ... brought out a major weakness of the Congress organization, its lack of sufficient institutionalization."[1] He noted then that the need of Congress was for "building strong party identities among lay supporters which would cut across more traditional loyalties."[2] In a later analysis, in a discussion of political development trends in India after 1967, he advances the following theoretical argument:

> The voter has started playing a relatively direct and independent role—not just being "mobilized" by party organizational elites and "vote banks" but exercising his own judgment—making his own partisan commitments and allegiances—effective in the votes that different parties mobilize, and making these commitments a basis for stable orientations to the political system.[3]

Similarly Gopal Krishna has argued that elections have an integrative and legitimation function, and that the displacement of traditional identities with new ones is part of this functional development.[4] And Dhiru Sheth, in a recent analysis of partisanship based on the 1967 election data, links the emergence of "strong" partisanship to five different aspects or meanings of political development.[5] His is the only article explicitly presenting Indian data on this matter. An earlier article by Eldersveld presented some preliminary findings on party loyalty and defection in 1967.[6]

Certainly, viewed strictly from the Indian perspective alone, there are some interesting and basic questions to pose in the study of party identification. Does identifying with a party seem to be generally meaningful to Indians or only to certain more "westernized" sectors of the population? Has the concept penetrated throughout the society? Since time is necessary for the crystallization of such loyalties, is there evidence of temporal continuity and stability since 1947? How do party identifications interact with more traditional group loyalties—do they have a crosscutting relationship or do they substitute for tradition? What is the origin of such party identities and what is the role of the family in socialization—is generational transmission already apparent in India? Is Kothari's theoretical position that it is not group conformity which is determinative in the forming of party allegiances but rather individual initiative and deliberation supported by the empirical evidence available? How are party identifications in India linked to other attitudes, orientations, and behavior? Does "party" have a content or image for the Indian citizen? Is identification congruent with other attitudes toward the political system, and are these supportive or alienative attitudes? And what is the linkage to voting behavior and other forms of political participation—consistent and supportive, or not? In sum, what is the evidence that party identification is linked to, relevant for, meaningful involvement of citizens with the system, and functional to the competitive party system and the development of an integrated polity? This in a sense is the fundamental question at issue when we examine the meaning and role of party in the Indian polity from the public's perspective.

Although there are ambivalences in Indian political development and in the contemporary political scene in India, one would expect to find the emergence of important patterns of party loyalty and commitment there in the study of political behavior. For the less literate and less involved sectors of the population one might expect party identification to be more symbolic and ritualistic than in the West, although one should be cautious on this given the unthinking and automatic identification behavior of many people in the West. Although social conformity may induce party identification in special ways in India, due to its special social status system, the extent of social conformity may be no greater than in other countries. There is one important system difference, however. India's competitive party system has had a brief history, only since 1947, although the dominant party, Congress, had its origins before 1900. One would expect a shorter time period for political socialization and for familial transmission of political orientations, such as party identification. The Indian citizen has been exposed to a party system for such a short time that one might not expect the crystallization and reenforcement of strong party loyalties, particularly in those younger sectors of the population which are predisposed to be non-Congress.

One might argue, then, that stable, reliable, meaningful party identification could not develop in India in such a short time. There are certain counterbalancing factors, however. The very newness of competitive politics has made parties and all that is associated with them very salient to the majority of Indians. In addition, the parties have been "populist" and mobilization-conscious in their relations to the public, educating and enlisting support. Caste groups have become aware of the importance of political power, and the relevance of parties and elections and votes. And the individual citizen has become aware of parties as institutions which affect him and through which he can work. In brief, one might theorize there has been a relatively fast politicization process in India. The Indian citizen is learning fast. Politics is close to him, exciting, important. He notes the prestige of the party leader, local as well as national. He notes the large number of candidates competing for public office, getting larger with each election. He notes the seriousness, as well as the bitterness, of party conflict. He notes the policy outcomes of party action.

In this context of rapid politicization one might well expect, in a society whose elites constantly compete for power and who exhort the public to be participant, a relatively fast crystallization of party loyalties. Local and regional localities enhance this. Social networks reenforce it. The pluralization of the opposition to Congress is true nationally, but at the local and regional level party continuity has been relatively high. Although one should certainly not expect as stable a pattern or as much historical habituation to a party system concept in India, say, as in the United States, yet the strengthening of party ties for large numbers of citizens is not an unreal expectation in contemporary India. Congress party dominance, plus rapid politicization, and the development of a truly competitive party system whose leaders have been public-oriented after Independence, may well have converged to generate party identifications which already are providing stability to the society. India may go through successive periods and types of party crisis, as have Western democracies, but we would argue that the foundation for an enduring system of party identifications has already been laid and built on. It is in this theoretical perspective that our Indian data on party identification should be interpreted.

We are particularly interested in a careful analysis of the meaning of "party" in India, partly because the student of developing societies might suspect, and might argue, that much of the partisan loyalty and attachment in such a developing democracy must be ritualistic, symbolic, and/or the product of group or social pressures and sanctions and thus really incom- prehensible to the ordinary, illiterate Indian peasant. Party identification behavior may not actually vary much in these respects from such behavior in the West, much of which is often hypothesized as habitual, automatic, "traditional," and socially conformist. Nevertheless, in a "developing" society where the role of the party system is considered to be functionally central to change, we must inquire as to the cognitions of citizens about the party system and the consistency of such images with party identification. What is the evidence that Indian citizens, particularly those who identify with the parties in that system, have a meaningful attachment to party? It seems to us there are five types of cognitive linkages which must be explored concerning the relationship of party identification and the citi- zen's attitude and value involvement with the system. These at least are "capabilities" which one might expect and which should be explored empirically. In ideal model terms, we would expect, on the part of iden- tifiers with parties, (1) at least a minimal support for a system role for parties; (2) some awareness of the differences between the parties on some relevant dimensions; (3) perceptual, if not actual, consistency between one's own issue positions and those of the preferred party; (4) ability to provide some rudimentary ordering or "spacing" of parties in the party system; (5) congruence of identification with level of political interest, knowledge about politics, and feelings of personal optimism about work- ing within the system, particularly the party and election systems.

These five desiderata can be viewed as progressively more rigorous requirements for an idealized "mature" polity. They are presumably as relevant for Western societies as for India. If party identification is to be used as a datum signifying a meaningful engagement of the individual with the political system, the suggestion here is that we might expect his attachment to a party to be accompanied by a capacity to think intelligently about the party system, the relation of the parties in that system, and his own relation to the parties in that system. His mere psychological response that "I am close to the Congress party" or "I consider myself to be a Democrat" is not enough for party identifications to be considered relevant or sufficient evidence about the maturity or development of a political system. "Party," if meaningful for the modern citizen, and "party iden- tification," if it is to be analytically useful as a handle for the study of development, should be associated with some capacity for discriminating thinking about oneself in relation to the "parties in the system."

Perhaps we can diagram the analytical relationships on which we need data as shown in figure 4. We shall be analyzing these relationships and applying this model in subsequent chapters of this party identification section.

FIG. 4. A model of the citizen's orientations to parties and the political system.

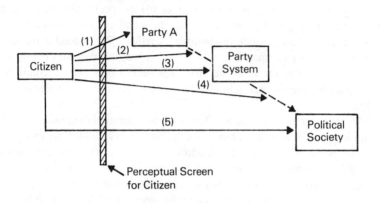

The meaning of these relationships is as follows: (1) the psychological relationship of the individual to his party—party identification; (2) the citizen's perception of his party's position in the party system, which includes (*a*) his awareness that there are differences among the parties on some dimensions and (*b*) his ability to "space" the parties on some dimensions; (3) the citizen's perception of his own relationship to the party system, particularly his demonstration of congruence between his own issue positions and those of his party; alternatively, he may demonstrate congruence between his own location in party space and that of his party and other parties; (4) the citizen's belief orientation toward the role of parties and the party system in the society, including the extent of his confidence in being able to work effectively through the party system; (5) the citizen's interest in, knowledge about, feelings of involvement with, and ability to work in the political system.

Our interest here is primarily to present the Indian data on party identification in a comparative context and to interpret the meaning of our data comparatively, rather than to analyze the Indian system exclusively. Considerable research has been done on party affiliation in the United States, France, Norway, and England: limited explorations have been attempted in a few other countries. We wish to place the Indian findings alongside those from those countries and observe the cross-national uniformities or contrasts. In a sense the question posed is whether the concept "party identification," defined and researched initially in Western democracies, has utility and meaning in a quite different "developing" society such as India. Further, a very important query is whether the findings on party identification in India support the theory of party identification which has been emerging in the West. Where the findings are similar to other countries, *and* where the findings differ, are they explicable in terms of the available body of theory? Above all, are these differences and similarities explicable in systemic terms? Are systemic variables relevant, and what system variables are relevant? Is (1) the developmental stage of a system a relevant variable, or (2) its type of party system, or (3) its election system, or (4) its special historical pattern of politics, or (5) particular features of its social system, or other types of systemic variables which distinguish societies? This indeed is the most fruitful query for comparative analysis. Can we observe, and eventually measure precisely, the relevance (or irrelevance) of systemic conditions for explaining the differential patterns of party identification in democratic polities?

The preferences of scholars differ as to the operationalization of "party identification." For some it has an exclusively psychological meaning; for others a behavioral component is added.[7] In the former sense the respondent's identification is determined by questions which reveal his self-perception, his own choice of party, followed subsequently by a question or questions which seek to determine the intensity of his commitment to party. In the analysis presented here we will employ the psychological self-perception approach only, even though conceptually this may not be most valid for India. It permits the greatest possibility for comparing Indian political behavior with that in other societies where party identification data are available. Although this operationalization has limitations, it has the virtue of being the one, simple measure of party allegiance or acceptance, combining cognitive awareness of party (or parties) and specific self-location in the party system, as well as affirmative admission of some type of adherence to a group called a party. The particular questions used to elicit the responses vary from one society to another. In India the adaptation most successful was "What party do you feel closest to?", while in the United States the most regularly used question has been "What do you consider yourself to be—a Republican, Democrat, Independent, or what?" Other variants have been used elsewhere. Restricting our conceptualization to the psychological components gives us the purest observation yet at hand of one critical phenomenon of any society, and one particularly important in the study of India. It is an observation about the citizen's affirmation of self-perceived linkage to the system, whatever the content, affective or evaluative, of that linkage may be, and whatever the consequences for his voting or other behavior may be. Though perhaps a fragile test, it is an index of his involvement with the ongoing party system.

Note

The above, of course, was written before the 1975 events. While one could properly argue the saliency and relevance of party politics for the Indian citizen prior to that date, the "interruption" of the system in 1975 could have serious consequences. Our analysis here will be valuable to indicate the extent and pattern of the Indian citizen's identification with his system, establishing thereby the "level" which the system had achieved before the developments of 1975 and subsequently.

Dimensions and Social Bases of Party Loyalty in India[1]

The Magnitude of Party Identification: India Compared to the West

BASED ON PRE-1975 EVIDENCE, INDIAN ADULTS ARE NO MORE RE-luctant than those in other societies to indicate a party choice when asked to do so. As table 8.1 indicates, the 70 percent proportion identifying with a party in 1967 is close to or above that in the United States, below the British figure of 80 percent or more, and above the earlier French low of 45 percent. And a strikingly high proportion in India consider themselves "strong" partisans, close to those who are "very strong" in Britain.[2]

TABLE 8.1 The Extent of Party Identification in India and Some Western Systems*

	Total % Identifying	% Strong	% Weak
Men only			
India (1967)	70	51	19
United States (1956)	73	36	37
United States (1972)	60	25	35
Britain (1963)	81	41	40
Britain (1964)	88	47	41
Total sample			
Norway (1957)	66		
France (1958)	45		
France (1967)	65		
Italy (1968)	75		

SOURCE: Samuel Barnes and Roy Pierce, "Public Opinion and Political Preferences in France and Italy," *Midwest Journal of Political Science* 15 (1971): 645 n. The sources for the data for other countries are from the publications previously cited.
* In the British studies the labels were "very strong" and "fairly strong." In the French and Italian studies the definition of identifiers was very loose.

On other measures of partisanship Indians appear to demonstrate as much "consistency" in party support as do citizens in other countries (table 8.2). It is interesting to note that approximately one-half of the electorate in India, 60 percent in the United States, and over 75 percent in Britain are consistent and stable in the sense that they identify with *and*

TABLE 8.2 Comparative Partisanship Measures: India, United States, Britain*

Measure	India (%)	United States (%)	Britain (%)
1. Consistent party voting in 2 elections over time	34	47	54
2. Consistent party voting in national plus state or local election (same election year)	63	61	...
3. % of sample identifying with and voting for the same party	50	60	77
4. % of identifiers voting for own party	70	82	83

* Measures 1 and 2 are based on the total sample in the U.S. and British studies. Measures 3 and 4 are based on men only for all countries. Except for measure 4, each percentage is a proportion of the national sample. The basis for the data, aside from India, are recalculations of the data of the 1956 U.S. and the 1964 British studies.

vote for the same party. Indians are also apparently less consistent in voting over a two-election period, but more consistent than the U.S. voters in "vertical" voting behavior. Identifiers in India in 1967 revealed a high level of voting consistency—70 percent compared to 82 percent in the United States in 1956. The British seemed to be at the same level as American voters in these early years. (However, in some recent studies the level of such consistency has dropped considerably in the United States.)

What these data suggest is that not only is the partisanship of the population high in India, but the defection rate by partisans is relatively low. This can be expressed as the difference between the proportion who identify with a party and the proportion who identify and vote for their party. This is a 20 percent "defection proportion" in India (measurement 3 in table 8.2 compared to table 8.1 percentages), 13 percent in the United States, and 11 percent for Britain. Except in consistency in party voting, then, on which India is low, the evidence points to a high level of party awareness, affiliation, and, in a narrow sense, perhaps commitment.

Patterns of Socialization to Party Identification: The Role of the Family
The role of the family in developing and maintaining partisan orientations is considered important in the West. Studies have often asked whether the respondent can recall father's, mother's, and other relatives' party affiliation, as well as other aspects of family political behavior, and have noted the close congruence of such perceived family party choice and subsequent party choice of offspring. Great differences have been discovered in the West, however, in this phenomenon. In an early study Converse and

Dupeux uncovered the striking finding that in France only 25 percent of the public could recall their father's party identification, compared to 76 percent normally in the United States (table 8.3). The proportion in India is even lower than in France—only 11 percent in our national study and only 17 percent in a 1965 sample survey in Kerala. (The figures are slightly higher if the ability of respondents to recall the party identification of other relatives is included.)

TABLE 8.3 Recall of Family Partisan Orientations in Relation to Respondent's Own Party Identification: Comparisons for Five Nations

	Can Recall Father's Party Identification (%)	% Identifiers among Those Who Can Recall Father's Party	% Identifiers among Those Who Cannot Recall Father's Party
United States	76 (90)	82	51
France	25	79	48
England	79 (82)	90	89.5
Japan	43	88	65
Kerala	17	82	62
India*	11	85	74

SOURCE: Japan: Akira Kubota and Robert Ward, "Family Influence and Political Socialization in Japan," *Comparative Political Studies* 3 (1970):164. Sources previously referred to were used for the other studies. For the British data, see David Butler and Donald Stokes, *Political Change in Britain* (New York: St. Martin, 1971), questionnaire, p. 470 and table, p. 53. The figures in parentheses are for the men in the samples; the Indian data, as indicated previously, are based only on the male sample.
* The Indian percentages are higher than the 70 percent party identification noted in table 8.1 because of the nonascertained category which had to be excluded from this calculation.

Cross-national behavior is similar among those who can recall their father's politics—they are usually more able to state their own party identifications—and India is no exception to this. The difference in India, however (between 85 percent and 74 percent), is small compared to the United States. The fact that their father was not interested in politics or affiliated with a party (for many the only possible political identification of their father could have been the Congress movement before 1947) is clearly not closely linked to whether the Indian citizen affiliates with a party today. Although this might suggest the irrelevance of early family political socialization for Indians, one should be cautious about such a generalization in the absence of more data. At this point it is important to observe that only a tenth of the Indian electorate had some prolonged exposure to partisanship in the family when they were growing up.

For those who have been exposed to party politics in the Indian family, there is already evidence of strong generational continuity (table 8.4). In

TABLE 8.4 Family Continuity in Party Identification in India*

Party of Family Socialization	India National (1967)			Kerala (1965)		
	% Identifying with Father's Party	% Identifying with Other Party	% with No Party Identification	% Identifying with Father's Party	% Identifying with Other Party	% with No Party Identification
Congress	64	26	10	69	14	17
Non-Congress	71	24	5	42	36	22
Communist				41	44	15
Other party				43	24	33

* There were too few cases in the national study for analysis of specific party choice continuity for non-Congress parties. In Kerala this was possible for the Communists. The percentages cumulate across to 100 percent.

both our 1965 Kerala study and the 1967 national study we find close to two-thirds of our samples supporting Congress if they recall that their fathers did. In 1967 those who recalled that their fathers supported a specific non-Congress party demonstrated even greater continuity from father to child in party identification. This was not so in our Kerala finding. There was considerably more Congress generational support than for the Communists and other opposition parties. Above all, if a citizen in India was exposed to a party-oriented father he was very likely to manifest some party affiliation. In the 1967 study, only 10 percent or less rejected party affiliation if socialized in the family. The transmission of party loyalties by the family seems already to be an important developing facet of Indian political life. It is clear that the next generation in India should exhibit this pattern to a much greater extent.[3] As table 8.5 reveals, exposure to politics in the family is associated with a stronger commitment to party. Indeed, India's public seems to be particularly responsive to a family interest in politics. Whereas in the United States only 45 percent of those whose families are politically interested manifested strong party identifications, the figure was 66 percent in India. This again attests to the eventual utility and developmental meaning of the family in Indian partisan politics. Today the proportion of the electorate identifying with Indian parties who came from politically interested families is low—20 percent, compared to the American proportion—50 percent. But this gap will become smaller as India's polity is expanded and as the family continues to take a greater and more active interest in politics.

Patterns of Socialization to Party Identification: Age Differences
The recency of independence and, therefore, of the involvement of Indian

TABLE 8.5 Relation between Family Interest in Politics and Offspring's Strength
of Party Identification

	Strong Party Identifiers (%)	Weak Party Identifiers (%)	Non-identifiers (%)	Identify with Indepen-dents Only (%)	N
Family interest in politics					
India	66	16	17	3	313
United States	45	39	16	...	662
Family not interested in politics					
India	54	19	24	3	1,385
United States	35	42	23	...	694

SOURCE: The U.S. data are taken from Angus Campbell, Philip Converse, Warren Miller, and Donald Stokes, *The American Voter* (New York: John Wiley & Sons, 1960), p. 147, table 7.1. They are 1958 data, recalculated for use here. The term used in the American question was not "interest" but "actively concerned."

adults with competitive, partisan politics is a distinctive system-historical attribute of a developing society like India. One would expect that this fact would be reflected in the patterns of family political socialization, as noted above, as well as in the age at which Indians were exposed to politics and first developed their party identifications. So far as age of "awareness of politics and parties" is concerned, Indians appear to be much later in their political education than in Western democracies. Whereas almost 50 percent of youths by the age of ten had developed party identifications in the West, according to previous studies, less than 3 percent had done so in India. And in India only 12 percent in the age bracket of eleven to fifteen years had become aware, and only 26 percent of the age bracket sixteen to twenty. These are strikingly different findings from those in Western societies, where certainly by age twenty over 60 percent had developed party identifications.[4]

If one looks at the Indian data *by the present age* of the respondent who is giving us the recall data referred to above, one sees a changing picture for India, however. Controlling for present age as we do in table 8.6, one sees that the younger sectors of the Indian population are beginning to conform to the expectations of a society which has a longer history of party politics. The younger cohort, age twenty-one to twenty-five, is now reveal-ing almost as high a proportion (60 percent) who were socialized relatively early to parties as is the case for Western democracies. There is still little

TABLE 8.6 Age of Socialization to Politics for Five Age Cohorts in India

Age When "First Aware of Politics and Parties"	Present Age of Respondent (%)				
	21–25	26–30	31–40	41–50	51+
Up to age 10	4 ⎫	2 ⎫	2 ⎫	1 ⎫	1 ⎫
11 to 15	18 ⎬ 60	14 ⎬ 53	10 ⎬ 42	6 ⎬ 25	3 ⎬ 17
16 to 20	38 ⎭	37 ⎭	30 ⎭	18 ⎭	13 ⎭
Over 20	25	33	46	58	61
Not socialized— has no interest	15	14	12	17	22
N	318	308	510	333	381

evidence that Indians are involved with politics at all before the age of ten, but large proportions are involved before age twenty. The age period sixteen to twenty seems to be critical. It is the older citizens, however, who are behaving from a frame of reference, in terms of socialization, which is quite different from the West. The great majority of those over forty indicate that their political learning took place much later in life than is true in the West. Whether this makes for more or less stability or maturity in partisan identifications is an interesting question we can attempt to answer later.

In the West studies have discovered larger proportions of party identifiers, and of strong identifiers, in the upper age brackets. This has raised the question of whether strong party commitment is a consequence of growing older or of length of political socialization, or of generational differences, or other factors. If the Indian case is presented, it seems clear that older citizens are not necessarily more committed to parties. Early socialization is suggested as the more critical variable. Table 8.7 shows a monotonic increase in party identification for the United States and England from the lower age groups to the higher. In India, however, the proportion of strong identifiers, and of all identifiers, is pretty constant for the age levels, with the lowest age cohort of twenty-one to twenty-five having the largest percentage of identifiers. India's older citizens thus appear to be no more committed to parties, and possibly less, than the younger citizens. This marks an important difference between India and the West.

Further support for the early socialization hypothesis as a theory of age differentials in party identification is provided by our Indian data. If we look at the proportions of strong party identifiers today by age of "first becoming aware of politics and parties" we find small but suggestive differences. Those recalling an early exposure to politics (up to age twenty)

TABLE 8.7 Age and Party Identification: Cross-national Comparisons

	Age Categories (%)				
	21–25	26–30	31–40	41–50	50+
India					
Strong identifiers	52	48	50	48	45
All identifiers	70	63	66	65	63
United States					
Strong identifiers	24	27	31	35	44
All identifiers	69	74	77	78	82
England					
"Very or "fairly					
strong" identifiers	58	62	65	73	74

SOURCE: For U.S. data see *The American Voter,* p. 162. Data based on samples from seven national studies, 1952–57, recalculated for our purposes. Age categories almost but not quite equivalent. British data from Butler and Stokes, p. 55.

are somewhat more likely to be strong identifiers (56 percent), than those socialized between twenty and twenty-five (48 percent strong identifiers). If we control for present age, we get basically the same pattern. The differences are not great, but those socialized later in life are less inclined to be strong identifiers.

The role of the Independence movement in socialization lingers on today. When asked to recall political events which influenced their awareness of politics, about 15 percent of the respondents referred to the struggle for independence, and 52 percent of these were Congress identifiers. This contrasts with 41 percent Congress identification among the youngest age group in the electorate, those between age twenty-one and twenty-five. Indeed, the interesting phenomenon of the "younging" of the opposition has been occurring in India as the nation puts more time between the present and Independence. Congress identifiers are older (70 percent over age thirty, compared to 53 percent of the Communists and 60 percent of Jan Sangh). They were also socialized at a later age. The new generation of the opposition to Congress is considerably younger and was socialized at an earlier age. Almost 60 percent of the strong Communist and Jan Sangh supporters were exposed to politics in the family while they were growing up, compared to only a third of the Congress supporters. If the development of party identification at an early age signifies a tendency to party loyalty and habitual party support, then there is evidence here that the non-Congress opposition parties may be on the way to becoming well entrenched.

The question of familial transmission of, and intergenerational agreement in party identification thus becomes very important. What do the data show in India in comparison to the West? In the United States 56 percent of those who recall their parents' party affiliation identified with the same party. In Britain and India it was 60 percent.[5] The extent of parent-offspring agreement is remarkably similar for all three countries. Of course one must remember immediately that over 75 percent can recall a parent's party identification in the United States and Britain, whereas fewer than 20 percent can in India. Nevertheless, where recall is possible, or when socialization occurs, the impact on offspring is just as relevant and strong for as large a proportion of those socialized in India as in the West.

The variations by age cohorts on family-offspring agreement is quite interesting. Both the youngest and oldest members of the electorate reveal the greatest intergenerational congruence in party identification. Note the following distributions:

Age Group	% Parent-Offspring Congruence in Party Identification in India
21–25	75
26–30	63
31–40	44
41–50	45
50+	71

Thus those socialized under the influence of the Congress movement and those who became aware of party politics most recently reveal the greatest amount of familial transmission. The influence of the family for those in the middle-aged brackets was either less powerful or else the rebellion of offspring has been more intense. Somewhat in contrast to findings from socialization studies in the West, India reveals then that the young members of the electorate have been socialized to a greater extent, have developed somewhat stronger party identifications than older citizens, and are adhering significantly to the party affiliation of their fathers.[6] Though very small proportions are socialized in the Indian family, its impact is not to be ignored, now and certainly in the future.

Evidence of the Temporal Stability of Party Identification
Party identification analysis is especially useful to explicate the stability of the individual's involvement with the system and the extent to which the partisan nature of the polity has expanded toward the social periphery. Where party identification is unstable, confined to only limited and special sections of the public, manifested asymmetrically in relation to the parties in the party system, one could say that this may be evidence of, at the least, partial and incomplete system integration and, at the worst, perhaps a

party system "identity crisis." Where party identification stability over time is found, where penetration of party commitment at all levels and in all major public sectors is occurring, one can interpret the system as more apparently in equilibrium and, in this one sense at least, giving some appearance of being integrated.

In our analysis so far, considerable evidence emerged suggesting that since 1947 Indians have in the aggregate developed strong party attachments, almost equal proportionately to Western countries. Seventy percent of the Indians after all do identify with the parties, and even though this is not closely associated with parental political socialization, since only about 10 percent can recall parents or relatives who were partisan, there is some implicit suggestion in the data that party attachment persists and is not quixotic. In the analysis presented in the next two chapters we wish to pursue further the question of the stability or durability and pervasiveness of the phenomenon of party identification in India.

One test of the meaningfulness of party attachments is obviously temporal consistency in commitment to parties and in voting behavior. Despite considerable change in Congress party fortunes in the period from 1962 to 1967 in both the national and state electoral contexts (and a strong Congress victory again in 1971), leading one to expect evidence of instability in partisan attachments, India reveals strong signs of affiliation consistency. Of the total sample in our 1967 study, 15 percent were defectors from one party to another, with approximately 12 percent shifting *from* Congress and 3 percent shifting *to* Congress. Combined with other shifts within the electorate (including the decisions among new voters and the behavior of the "dropouts," that is, 1962 voters who stayed home in 1967) the net result was only a loss of about 4 percent in the actual vote for the Congress party, despite heavy losses for Congress in Parliament (from 73 to 54.6 percent of the seats).[7] What is perhaps particularly interesting in this analysis is that the proportions of defection are lowest among the younger age groups—12 percent for the age group twenty-six to thirty compared to 19 percent for the age group fifty-one to sixty.

Turning from voting behavior to party identification, we find again that India already demonstrates considerable regularity in the public's partisan attitudes. Table 8.8 presents some comparable data for India and the United States. The remarkable similarity in the proportions of identifiers who claim they have remained constant in their party commitments—at the 80 percent level in both countries—is the most important datum here. If one can believe the respondents, there is a majority with strong self-images of partisan commitment in both countries.[8] When asked to project this loyalty into the future, 67 percent of our Indian respondents tell us their intentions are to remain loyal (73 percent of Congress). The defection

TABLE 8.8 Party Affiliation Stability in India and the United States

	India (%)	United States (%)
Nonidentifiers	30	24
Identifiers	70	76
Identified with another party earlier (% of all identifiers)	17	19
Never identified with another party (% of all identifiers)	83	81
% of total sample who were identifiers and did not change party identification	60	66

SOURCE: Indian data based on 1967 study, U.S. data derived from the 1956 study. See *The American Voter,* p. 148, table 7.2, which was recalculated for this purpose. The U.S. figures are based on an N of 1,669 which did not include the nonvoters. The question used was, "Was there ever a time in the past when you felt closest to another party, as opposed to (your present) party?"

potential of Congress voters is lower than for the non-Congress partisans—27 percent compared to 40 percent. This is primarily due to uncertainty, however. The percentage who definitely assert a determination to vote for other parties is close to 6 percent for all voters.

The Social Penetration of Party Identification

A key question, as suggested in the discussion of partisanship patterns for age groups, is whether the concept of party identification, apparently so important to the development of party systems in the West, has taken hold throughout Indian society. Is it prevalent only in the more "westernized sectors" of the population, or has psychological attachment to party permeated the more traditional, remote, and less developed sectors of the system? This is a concern which is rarely voiced in Western studies. Converse and Dupeux, it is true, noted the "widespread absence of party loyalties" in France and suggested that this was related to "French political turbulence."[9] But data were not presented on the extent of party loyalty by population subgroups. Even though other scholars have not been preoccupied with the penetration question, data have been reported for the United States and Norway, on the relationship of party identification to demographic and social differences in the population, making some comparisons possible with the Indian data. Table 8.9 presents one such comparison, by education level. The interesting difference by country is not the total proportion of identifiers, since this is at the 65 to 70 percent level or above in all three countries, except in the "high school" and "gymnasium" sectors of Norway where it declines to 55 percent. Rather, it is the

TABLE 8.9 Educational Differences in Party Identification: India, United States, and Norway

	All Identifiers	Strong Identifiers	Nonidentifiers (Independents, Apolitical, etc.)	N
India				
Illiterates	74	54	26	925
Some education	76	57	24	321
Primary, plus some middle	81	64	19	282
High school	65	46	35	70
College	71	37	29	73
United States				
Grade school	74	36	26	416
High school	75	34	25	517
College	70	31	30	202
Norway				
Elementary	68	26	32	428
Elementary & vocational	66	24	34	213
Continuation	69	24	31	208
High school	69	21	45	131
Gymnasium	55	33	45	36

SOURCE: India, National Study of 1967: United States, Angus Campbell and Homer Cooper, *Group Differences in Attitudes and Votes* (Ann Arbor: Institute for Social Research, University of Michigan, 1956), p. 49; Norway, Henry Valen and Daniel Katz, *Political Parties in Norway* (Oslo: Universitet, 1967), p. 213.

high proportions of *strong* identifiers in India, *particularly at the lower educational levels.* Illiterates and those with only a minimal education are strongly committed to parties, it appears—54 to 64 percent—while in the United States and Norway the proportion is much lower—24 to 36 percent.[10] Thus, where one might have suspected that the feeling of "party" might not have entered the consciousness and lives of Indians, that is, at the lowest social status levels, one finds the reverse to be true. The illiterates are the most strongly loyal to parties in India. It is at the college level in all three societies where the proportions are lower and almost identical—approximately one-third are strong identifiers. It should be noted also that a country like Norway, presumably with a viable party system, has relatively high proportions of nonpartisan or nonpolitical persons at the upper educational levels—45 percent—and that the Indian proportions of identifiers are similar to those in the United States.

There seems to be a "Western norm," then, of one-fourth to one-third of electorates manifesting strong party identification, and perhaps a similar range revealing no interest in partisan affiliations. There are variations by social groups within countries, but it is not great. Farmers in Norway are at the 34 percent level of strong identification, compared to businessmen who are at the 18 percent level. The proportions for groups in the United States distinguished by religion, race, residence, and occupation are remarkably close to the 30 percent level of strong identification. Blacks, at least in earlier studies, seemed to be somewhat more apolitical or nonpartisan, as did the unskilled and unemployed—but the proportions were still close to one-third. This is the comparative backdrop against which to evaluate the extent of penetration of the party identification concept in India.

Another test of the penetration of party identification in India is provided by looking at residence and mobility patterns. The proportion of strong identification holds up even among those persons who have remained in the village all their lives (57 percent), compared to those who have been exposed to the more "modern" influences of the city (49 percent). There is only a 4 percent difference in strong identification between the nonmobile village residents and the mobile citizens. No more than 25 percent of nonmobile villagers are nonidentifiers. Similarly, although there are differences in the proportion of strong identifiers among religious groups—varying from the 45 percent for the Sikhs in our sample to the 65 percent of the Muslims, compared to 55 percent of the Hindus and Christians—it seems clear that the phenomenon of party identification has taken hold among all religions in India.

One might even suggest that those sectors of the Indian population which are most "traditional" or least "modernized" manifest the highest levels of party identification strength. The evidence for this is not overwhelming, but it does exist. Thus the Muslims are very high relatively in percentage of identifiers (65 percent), as are those who have always lived in the village (58 percent). In another analysis we made, we classified families as to how family voting decisions were made—whether by each individual or by the head of the household. We found that where the head of the household decides for all the others (as reported by those we interviewed) our respondents in such a family situation were more likely to have strong party identifications—60 percent compared to 53 percent for those who were permitted to make their own decisions. And in a further analysis of our respondents' awareness of caste (based on a variety of questions concerning the way his and other castes voted, his knowledge of the caste of his parliamentary representatives) we have the following very interesting distribution:

	Strong Identifiers (%)	Non-identifiers (%)	N
Not aware of caste	38	38	164
Some awareness of caste	47	33	387
Aware of caste and caste quite important	57	24	557
Aware of caste and caste very important	67	17	605

Those who were the most aware of caste and the most caste-conscious revealed the highest proportion of strong party identification—67 percent. This was 29 percent higher than those for whom caste was not salient. This is a significant finding and provides some evidence that the party as the modern institution has combined with the traditional caste institution as the media or instruments for involving the Indian public with politics. Party has not displaced caste, and caste is not an obstacle to acceptance of party. Indians can identify psychologically with both effectively. Here then is empirical evidence not that caste is obsolete or dysfunctional, nor that party and caste conflict, but rather that party and caste may be working together in India to function meaningfully in the politicization of the society, in the involvement of Indian masses with the political system, and in the expansion of the polity into the most "traditional" sectors of the population. Perhaps these data document the basis position of the Rudolphs in their stimulating book on India, in which they emphasize "the persistence of caste communities in contemporary Indian politics . . . . Paracommunities, associations combining traditional and modern features, are not merely transitional phenomena but a persistent feature of modernity."[11] This analysis also provides the empirical support for Rajni Kothari's theoretical insight about the linkage of party politics to castes:

> The Indian approach to development may be characterized as one in which the exposure to modernity led to a renewed awareness and quickening of traditional identity, its reinterpretation and rejuvenation, and its consolidation in the framework of new institutions and ideas . . . . The process of politics is one of identifying and manipulating existing structures in order to mobilize support and consolidate positions. Where the caste structure provides one of the most important organizational clusters in which the population is found to live, politics must strive to organize through such a structure. The alleged casteism in politics is thus no more and no less than *politicization of caste.*[12]

Concluding Observations

The capacity of citizens to think in terms of political parties and to demonstrate some loyalty to them is, we assume, a test of a maturing polity. In our analysis of Indian party identification we looked at the overall dimensions of the phenomenon in India in comparison to Western societies, as well as the patterns of socialization in the family and the generational differences. Considerable evidence emerged suggesting that, since 1947, Indians have developed strong party attachments, almost equal proportionately to Western nations. Seventy percent of the Indians, after all, do identify with political parties; and even though this is not closely associated to parental political socialization—since only about 10 percent can recall parents or relatives who were partisan—there is clear evidence in the data that party attachment persists and is not quixotic. The large proportion (51 percent) in India who are "strong" identifiers is a significant finding. Also significant is the finding that the youngest members of the Indian electorate are being socialized to politics at an earlier age (60 percent before age twenty for those in the twenty-one to twenty-five age group compared to 17 percent in the fifty-one and over age group) and have stronger party attachments. All of this suggests that despite the short life of the Indian party system, the great majority of Indians have no difficulty expressing an identification with it and the system has encouraged or facilitated an infrastructure to support such loyalties. Already we see evidence of temporal stability in our 1967 national study, dramatically noticeable of course in the solidity of the Congress vote, but also evident in the low defection rates of identifiers. Finally, although one might expect in India much more commitment to parties in certain "modern" or "westernized" or "urban" social sectors, we find no such asymmetry. Party identification has penetrated to all social sectors, particularly to the nonmobile peasants in the villages. Indeed it appears that the most traditional groups or population categories reveal the greatest penetration.[13]

Stability, penetration, depth, and breadth—these are the characteristics of the developing patterns of Indian partisanship. Our data suggest that the Indian citizen has an awareness of his party system and interacts meaningfully in a psychological sense with it. The patterns of partisanship revealed here indicate both system change since 1947 and system integration. Parties and elections are salient democratic phenomena for Indian citizens with which they have learned to become involved. Our analysis suggests that in the almost three decades since 1947, in terms of citizen identifications the Indian system has developed durable party commitments in the face of crisis. The consequences of the "interruption" of party activity in 1975 under the Emergency could be serious and could lead to a regression in the strength of such commitments.

93

NINE

Cognitions of the Indian Party System by Party Identifiers

Images and Beliefs about the Party Process

ANALYSIS OF THE MEANING OF "PARTY" TO CITIZENS OF MODERN states has generally not been pursued.[1] We have been content to accept a shorthand expression of "closeness" to party, or "support" for party, or other simple affiliative language as sufficient. This leaves open the big question—what does a "party identifier" mean substantively when he tells us that he perceives himself as a partisan? What is the content of his thinking, his substantive "frame of reference"? Unless such content is provided, demonstrating some cognitive meaning and, hopefully, consistency among partisans, it might be argued that knowledge of the party identification of a person may be of little use as a datum in explicating his orientation to the political order, useful as such data may be aggregatively in plotting party systemic changes over time.

In chapter 7 we outlined a model of the "cognitive linkages" which are basic for understanding the meaning of party to the ordinary citizen. We here will explore one of these linkages—the relationship of party identification to belief in the idea of a party system.

The data available for different countries suggest some striking incongruities and possible inconsistencies in public attitudes toward parties. Consider these findings for the United States: 68 percent feel that democracy needs strong competitive parties, but 54 percent feel the parties do more to confuse the issues than to clarify them, and 53 percent feel that government would function more efficiently without the conflicts of parties.[2]

Or, from a study of the political socialization of fourteen- to fifteen-year-olds in England: 51 percent agree that democracy works best where political parties compete strongly, but only 30 percent believe that party conflicts "help the country more than hurt it."[3] It is interesting also to note in a Detroit study that while 70 percent expressed strong support for the party system, only 10 percent would be willing to work through parties in order to get things done in the community and only 13 percent would encourage their sons to go into politics.[4] In an earlier study in Detroit, while 71 percent approved the party system, over 60 percent also approved the nonpartisan system.[5] It is against this backdrop that the Indian findings concerning party support should be interpreted. We, too, find apparently contradictory findings for India in our 1967 study, such as these: 77 percent feel that political parties are necessary, but only 48 percent feel that more than one party is necessary, and 41 percent would prefer only one party, and 71 percent oppose party conflicts.

As in other countries, the Indian public accepts the basic idea of a party system, but is concerned about the party struggle for power. The cultural norm of political agreement and consensus is pervasive. Only 15 percent can see their way to approving party conflict, compared to perhaps 35 percent in the United States.[6] The legitimacy of political controversy and dissensus is less accepted in India, no doubt, but the differences are certainly not extreme in comparison to the West. On the basis of the sparse data available, we can say that in the United States and Britain the majority do not approve of party conflict either.

One direct comparison of attitudes toward parties which is possible from available analysis is with Britain.[7] This concerns the virtually identical query as to whether the parties are perceived as "making the government pay attention to the people." Such a comparison for 1966–67 reveals that there seems to be more faith in parties in India than in Britain. The level of cynicism and uncertainty was over 50 percent in 1966 for the British public, but below 40 percent for the Indian public. On balance, then, it would seem that the Indian masses in 1967 exhibited both great support for parties and considerable concern about both the number of parties and the effects of the party struggle. And these incongruencies seem similar to those in other countries, if not as extreme.

A four-nation study, reported by Dennis, based on responses of youngsters ranging in age from eight to sixteen, revealed considerable incidence of "antidemocratic response" toward the party systems on certain items in certain countries. One item evoking a high percentage of negative responses in all countries except the United States was, "The conflicts among political parties hurt our country more than they help it." At the older age levels (fourteen to sixteen years) in these studies the proportions agreeing to this item were 61 percent Germany, 54 percent Italy, 47 percent Britain, and 8 percent United States.[8] Our Indian study had a similar item: "It is not desirable to have political parties struggling with each other." Our youngest age cohort, age twenty-one to twenty-five, was overwhelmingly in agreement on this issue, 71 percent supporting it and only 16 percent disagreeing. On the other hand, 82 percent of this young Indian age cohort felt parties are necessary and 65 percent felt parties make the government responsive to the people. The Indian study then corroborates the finding that young people, like their parents, feel democracy needs parties, but that party conflict is destructive.

Our major theoretical interest here is whether strength of party identification in India is linked to attitudes toward parties and the party system in such a way as to suggest that party attachment has some meaningful content. Although there is some evidence in support of this, on balance it is ambivalent. Strong identifiers in India are indeed somewhat more likely to be supportive of parties than weak identifiers, but ironically the nonidentifiers are as supportive as the strong identifiers. In other questions, asked to explore respondents' attitudes to parties, we found essentially the same relative distributions. Thus, approximately three out of four strong identifiers oppose party conflict, which is identical to the percentage for weak identifiers, and actually slightly larger than the percentage for those not affiliating with parties. Further, when we asked whether the respondent would consider joining a political party, 15 percent of the strong identifiers replied affirmatively (and 9 percent were already members), compared to 7 percent of the weak identifiers (5 percent of whom were party members). The desire to be active through parties is thus slightly increased in relation to party identification strength, but not significantly.

In this respect India apparently is no different than the United States. Dennis' findings suggest that only 40 percent of the strong identifiers are very supportive of parties, similar to the 37 percent in India, and that strong party identification is associated only slightly more than weak identification with attitudinal party support. In both countries many citizens are strong party identifiers but have serious reservations about party organizations as they function in the society. Perhaps the most important finding in both countries is that only a relatively small minority of identifiers are hostile to parties. In India this is particularly low, for *all* citizens, however, not merely for *strong* identifiers—only 13 percent of all respondents feel parties are unnecessary.

On the strength of the evidence available from comparative data there is no basis for concluding that in India, or any other country, people who identify with political parties are more inclined than nonidentifiers or independents to feel that political parties are necessary for the country, responsive to public demands, or important for effective government. In India as well as in Western democracies, large majorities are generally committed to the idea that political parties have a role to play, and large majorities also fear the consequences of party conflict. But a psychological attachment to party is not linked more strongly to a belief in party government and the party process.

Perceptions of Party Differences
Do party identifiers see differences among parties more frequently than nonidentifiers, and is strength of identification related to such awareness? This is the second requirement our model specifies if party identification is

to have relevancy for deliberate political behavior. Societies differ radically in the public's consciousness of party differences. As Valen and Katz have demonstrated in their Norwegian study, a society with a "class-distinct" party system, whose parties take strong ideological positions and devote energy to communicating these positions through a party press, can have an electorate very aware of distinctive party issue orientations.[9] The comparative data in table 9.1 show the striking contrasts between Norway and other countries. Norway's public sees "big differences" among its five major parties, but only a minority see important differences in Britain, the United States, and India.

TABLE 9.1 Public Perceptions of Party Differences: Four Countries

	India (%) (1967)	United States (%) (1956)	United Kingdom (%) (1963)	Norway (%) (1957)
Parties differ "a good deal," or parties have "big differences" or "important differences"	29	12	36	71
No differences among parties	41	40		11
Don't know whether differences exist among parties	29	8	10	8
Some differences	...	30	20	10
Not much difference	...	10	34	...

SOURCE: India data from the 1967 national study; U.S. data from Angus Campbell, Philip Converse, Warren E. Miller, and Donald Stokes, *Elections and the Political Order* (New York: John Wiley & Sons, 1966), pp. 257–59, partially recalculated; Norway, ibid., recomputed; Britain, Butler and Stokes, *Political Change in Britain,* p. 466. See also the discussion in *The American Voter,* chapter 10, p. 249; also M. K. Jennings and L. H. Zeigler, eds., *The Electoral Process,* chapter 8; *The Voter Decides,* pp. 38, 125–29. Also see Butler and Stokes (pp. 482, 496) for the proportions for 1964–66.

Admittedly the proportions who see differences will vary, depending on the election campaign and how one conceptualizes the perception of party differences and interprets responses. In the 1952 American study 21 percent are reported as seeing a "good deal of difference," higher than reported in 1956. However, in the 1956 analysis, if perceptions of differences in group-oriented terms (42 percent) are combined with perception in issue-oriented terms (12 percent), one would get a higher percentage than is used in table 9.1. In the British studies one notes also that the proportion of the adults seeing a "good deal of difference" between the parties varies from 1963 to 1966, 36 to 42 percent, depending on the election.

Despite such within-country variations over time the comparative findings remain clear. Norway stands in sharp contrast to India, and also to Great Britain and the United States. Less than one-third in India see the parties as differing greatly, which is similar to Britain, and a larger percentage than the United States (depending on what interpretation and election year you use). To put the findings a different way, the following proportions of the public see no differences or "not much difference": India, 41 percent; United States, 50 percent; Britain, 34 percent; Norway, 11 percent. Parties in Norway are seen as in ideological conflict. India seems to fall into the opposite political pattern—the pattern of minimal party conflict and muted ideological party politics.

Whether party identification leads to or is linked to a sharper awareness of party differences is the basic query here. As table 9.2 reveals, the differences by country are considerable. In all three countries for which data were available, identifiers were likely to see big differences between the parties. But the differences reported for Norway are striking, while for the United States and India they are much less so.[10] And in India strength of identification is not related to a sharper awareness of party differences. In the United States the level of awareness of "big differences" between the parties is extremely low—16 percent for strong identifiers, compared to 36 percent for India, and 85 percent for Norway. The observations one is forced to make, therefore, as to India are as follows: (1) the capacity of identifiers to see important differences is moderately in evidence, and much greater than at least in one Western society; (2) strength of party commitment does not enhance this capacity in India. One must remember, of course, that in India and the United States there were only slight differences in the perceptions of strong and weak identifiers.

The content of the public's images of parties in India is difficult to generalize about, as it is in the West. In our interviews we included a series of open-ended questions encouraging respondents to tell us the strong points and weak points, the advantages and disadvantages, and the nature of the differences they saw in their own party and other parties. Elaborate coding operations reduced these responses to a lengthy set of categories, similar to those used in the U.S. study of 1956.[11] A careful analysis of these suggests the distributions found in table 9.3. These comparisons are to be used with caution and not dogmatically. They are rough and exploratory. They probably can be used with greatest confidence "at the extremes," that is, the proportions of the Indian and American publics who are clearly ideological in their thinking about parties. These are at the most 18 percent in India and 12 percent in the United States. In India these are people who reveal a structure of attitudes emphasizing a preoccupation with problems of socialism, free enterprise, secularism, democracy, peace-

TABLE 9.2 Awareness of Party Differences by Strength of Identification: India, United
        States, Norway

	% Strong Identifiers	% Weak Identifiers	% Independents and/or Nonidentifiers
"Big differences" or "important" differences exist between the parties			
Norway	85	60	47
India	36	34	20
United States	16	7	. . .*
No differences exist between the parties			
Norway	2	14	16
India	42	44	44
United States	33	48	. . .*

SOURCE: Norway, see Valen and Katz, p. 206; United States, Angus Campbell
and Henry Valen, "Party Identification in Norway and the United States," *Public
Opinion Quarterly* 25 (winter 1961): 259; India, 1967 study.
  * No data available.

TABLE 9.3 Conceptualization of Party Images on the Basis of Issue Content: India
        and the United States

	India (%) (1967)	USA (%) (1956)
Ideological content		
Strong evidence	5	2.5
Near-ideology	13	9
Group benefits and conflicts	5	42
Current concerns or "nature of the times" with low issue content	8	24
No issue content		
Party or candidate orientation	10	13
Other—or general response	2	
Don't know what differences are, or does not mention anything about party image	57	9.5

ful methods of change, nationalism, and so on. They differ from the small minority (5 percent) for whom caste, religious, language, or class differences are salient when discussing party differences. Then there are a group of citizens (8 percent) who have immediate interests in getting better facilities (roads, buses, seeds, fertilizers, schools, medicines, water, electricity, credit) and who discuss party differences in these terms, or reveal a preoccupation with questions of public administration generally, but who do not really manifest much awareness of issue controversies as such. Another 8 percent talk about the relative merits of party candidates, organization, and strategies and reveal no issue content at all, but do attempt to articulate party differences. Finally over half (57 percent) have no capacity to articulate any image about parties as they differ from each other.

The Indian public is, thus, if one can accept these data as providing a test of the content of public images of parties, as ideological as the American public (18 percent compared to 12 percent), but also much less articulate. Whereas a tenth of the American public has no perception or no capability to state a party image, over 50 percent of the Indian public is incapable of expressing differential party images. Thus far this may be the most striking difference in our data between India and the West. Aside from Norway, which is unique because of its "class-distinct" and "ideology-conscious" system, one does not find (and perhaps it is unrealistic to expect) members of the public in Western or non-Western societies to perceive parties as differing greatly and differing ideologically. It is no doubt, however, a significant commentary on both the American and Indian systems (and certainly others, such as the English, as well) to find so few citizens able to link party differences to basic issue dimensions. One wonders what being "close to" a party means, both for the individual and the system. For very few Americans and Indians is it linked to basic issue controversies. For many Indians, over 50 percent, there seems to be no cognitive awareness of party differences at all.

Congruence of Issue Preferences and Perceived Party Positions
Returning to our basic model, we are now interested in examining the third relationship identified there. In shorthand terms this concerns the matter of issue consistency or "rationality." To what extent in India is party identification linked to perceptual consistency in issue positions, consistency between the individual's position on issues and that of his party (as he perceives that position) as one party in relation to other parties in the party system? Historically this has been the classical, theoretical requirement for deliberative behavior in electoral party democracies.

Many studies of American political behavior have documented the relatively small differences between Democratic and Republican supporters (particularly "weak" supporters) on campaign issues. One direct comparison between the United States and Norway based on 1956–57 data has revealed the striking interparty differences in Norway.[12] Thus, on an issue like tax policy, while the Democratic-Republican difference for strong identifiers was 21 percent, for the five Norwegian parties there was a 47 percent spread. The systems differ radically. The American system manifests issue heterogeneity within its partisan support groups, while the Norwegian system, with parties which are more issue-distinctive, manifests its heterogeneity on issues across the party spectrum. Both systems, however, reveal more interparty issue conflict among strong identifiers than among weak identifiers. Weak Democrats and weak Republicans are very much alike on most issues—if the parties differ at all they do so in the comparison of strong identifiers. While in Norway the average differences among the weak identifiers is less than for strong identifiers, it is still considerable—46 percent compared to 4 percent in the United States. (This, of course, was based on the American studies of elections in the 1950s.)

These sharp contrasts provide a backdrop and focus for the analysis of our Indian data. It is important to note at the outset the "distance" between India partisans on the basic issues confronting the society. One example is afforded by the responses to the question whether "for the progress of the country the government should exercise greater controls over industry, trade, and agriculture than at present, or less controls, or keep them as they are?" As table 9.4 indicates, there are great differences in issue positions among the major Indian parties, ranging from two-thirds or more of the Communists favoring greater economic controls to less than a fifth of the supporters of Jan Sangh and Swatantra. In a sense the Norwegian pattern is seen again here. There is one difference, however. The strong identifiers in India do not necessarily take the most extreme positions. In fact it is the "weak" identifiers among the Communists and Congress who have a higher proportion favoring more controls. On this key issue, then, the greatest extremes are found among the weak identifiers (a range of 72 percent for weak identifiers compared to 49 percent for strong identifiers).

The Indian parties do appear to fall along an ideological Left-Right continuum, much as might be expected. The DMK supporters appear to be to the right of Congress on this issue but not as conservative as Swatantra and Jan Sangh supporters. The gap between the Communists and Socialists is considerable, but the gap between the Socialists and Congress is negligible on the question posed here. Yet, where to place these parties exactly on the Left-Right continuum is difficult to decide. For example, Congress in one sense appears to be slightly right of center and right of the Socialists, with its score (−9) in the second measure used in table 9.4.

TABLE 9.4 Issue Differences of Indian Parties: Government Control of Economy*

	Commu- nists	Social- ists	Congress	DMK	Swatan- tra	Jan Sangh	Non- identifiers
			Identifiers				
% favoring greater controls							
Strong ID	64	42	34	27	19	15	32
Weak ID	86	38	38	†	19	14	
Difference between those favor- ing greater controls and less controls‡							
Strong ID	+40	−6	−9	−30	−55	−50	−16
Weak ID	+79	−5	−3	−35	−51	−58	

* These are percentages of identifiers for each party. In the second analysis here, those indicating an interest in maintaining the same controls or who were ambivalent are excluded from the calculations.

† Too few cases for analysis.

‡ A plus sign means a balance in favor of governmental controls, a minus sign means the opposite.

If we use a different calculation—the percentage of *strong identifiers* who favor *some controls* over the economy—the location of the parties would be as follows:

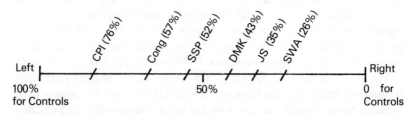

This results in the placement of Swatantra to the right of Jan Sangh, and the Socialists to the right of Congress. The space to the left of the center has three parties, as does the space to the right (although only two are national parties). It suggests considerable distance between the center and the right-wing parties, and considerable distance between the center configuration (Congress, SSP) and the extreme left.

There is considerable "spread," then, in opinion, by party. Voters can be seen as over time occupying naturally any of three "polar positions" on the issue of government control of the economy. Further, many party supporters have issue positions not shared by fellow partisans. The diversity of positions within Congress, the Socialists, and DMK are particularly apparent, while the Communists and the two rightist parties are much more homogeneous.

On two other issues of the 1967 election the Left-Right positioning of partisans is not the same as on the question of controls over the economy. These are the questions of governmental action to ban cow slaughter and of the utility of fasting in order to influence the government's policies. For strong identifiers the following distributions occurred:

	Commu- nists	Social- ists	Con- gress	DMK	Swatan- tra	Jan Sangh	Non- identifiers
Cow slaughter Favoring a ban (%)	59	79	77	62	72	90	67
Fasting Approve of as tech- nique of political in- fluence (%)	49	66	48	60	59	72	42

While Jan Sangh is consistently on the far Right on these questions, and the Communists tend to be at the Left, the other parties do not array themselves on the continuum as one might have expected. There is obviously strong support for what might be construed as the "conservative" position in all parties. Congress is not necessarily "centrist" and the Socialists are more Right than Left. Swatantra's partisans are not liberal, but more so than the Socialists. It is apparent, then, that the ordering of Indian party identifiers on any issue continuum will produce differences depending on the issue, although the extremes in the party system seem fairly stabilized—the Communists and Jan Sangh partisans are relatively consistent as to their places in the party spectrum.

A key question related to the political development of India is whether the Indian public reveals congruences between party identification and the party perceived as closest on a given issue to one's own issue position. After asking the question concerning governmental control of the economy, we asked our respondents to tell us which party would "most likely do what you want on this issue." There is a high correspondence between strong party identification and party-issue preference. Thus, 67 percent of strong Congress identifiers say Congress is closest to what they want done on the regulation of the economy. The strong Swatantra supporters have the same level of congruence—67 percent; for Jan Sangh it is 63 percent, for the Communists 69 percent, for the Socialists 66 percent, and DMK is particularly high with 76 percent. This does not mean, of course, that these respondents understand the party position, nor that their actual position agrees with the actual position of the party leadership. It merely suggests that the *strong* identifiers sense a like-minded issue position for their party. This is not as apparent for *weak* identifiers, less than 50 percent of whom feel their own party is closest to their own attitudes. Weak identifiers are less able to articulate a position or are less informed about the stands of parties. But they also have a greater tendency to opt for other parties on the issue.

A more refined test of issue-party consistency is presented in table 9.5. Here we show the link between *own position* on the issue of governmental economic controls, *party preferred,* and *party identified with*. Particularly significant is the division of opinion among strong identifiers who prefer their own party on the issue. While the division for Swatantra and the Communists is skewed pretty much as would be expected (4 to 1 opposing controls and 3 to 1 favoring controls, respectively), the division for the other parties is much closer. Thus, of the 67 percent of the strong Congress identifiers who prefer their own party, the ratio is only 4 to 3 in favor of controls; for the Socialists it is virtually 1 to 1. This attests then either to much ignorance or misperception of the party's position, or to support for the party despite an awareness that the party's position is really at odds with one's own position. The former interpretation—ignorance or misperception—is probably more tenable, because we specifically asked, "Which party is likely to do *what you want* on this issue" (italics supplied).

The level of party-issue congruence in India is very respectable. We find that 67 percent of those who identify strongly with the five major parties prefer their own party on the economic control issue, as do 42 percent of the weak identifiers. There are obviously a large number of citizens who identify with parties for whom compatibility between self and own party on issues is not salient, relevant, or accurately perceived. Our limited research, but inferential "knowledge" from American and European studies would lead us to believe that the Indian findings should inspire optimism,[13] particularly in a society where exposure to the mass media is minimal and where the public consequently secures its political cues from local leaders. Indeed, to find a developing society with 70 percent of its citizens identifying with parties and over 40 percent of these demonstrating

TABLE 9.5 The Basic Test of Issue-Party Congruence: Linkage of Party Identification with Own Issue Position and Party Preference on the Issue (Issue: Governmental Control of the Economy)

Identifiers	Favor Governmental Controls and Prefer Own Party as Closest on This Issue (%)	Oppose Governmental Controls and See Own Party as Closest on This Issue (%)	N
Congress			
Strong	40	27	627
Weak	30	11	200
Swatantra			
Strong	16	51	68
Weak	17	33	30
Jan Sangh			
Strong	24	39	95
Weak	10	26	42
Communists			
Strong	55	14	51
Weak	48	4	27
Socialists			
Strong	34	32	68
Weak	32	18	22
DMK—all identifiers	30	46	58

issue-party consistency on the key issue of economic controls is evidence of extensive political maturity.

On another type of question which was a key campaign issue in 1967—whether the government should pass a law to ban cow slaughter—the pattern of congruence was similar although not as strong (table 9.6). However, for one party for whom this was a most relevant matter, the Jan Sangh party, the consistency between party identification and the perception of "which party would be most likely to do what you want on this issue" was much higher, particularly for the weak Jan Sangh identifiers. They perceived this issue partisanly more than the economic controls issue, while for the other parties the proportions of strong identifiers who were issue partisans on this issue declined from 10 percent (for Congress and Swatantra) to as much as 20 percent for the Communists. Among weak partisans on the Left there were apparently considerable defections from their party on the cow slaughter issue. There was some movement toward Jan Sangh and Congress by weak identifiers of the Socialist and Communist parties (15 percent of the Communists and 27 percent of the Socialists), but the majority were confused, unable to state a preference, or unwilling to commit themselves. There is no question that Jan Sangh was

TABLE 9.6 Congruence of Party Identification and Party Preference
on the Cow Slaughter Issue

	% of Identifiers Seeing Own Party as Closest on the Issue	
	Strong Identifiers	Weak Identifiers
Congress	56	36.5
Swatantra	56	40
Jan Sangh	78	69
Communists	49	19
Socialists	41	18
DMK	55	*

* Too few cases for analysis.

the preferred party for those defecting on this issue, and that it profited much more from this issue than from the economic controls issue. Thus 6 percent of the Communist strong identifiers preferred Jan Sangh, as did 12 percent of the Socialists and Congress strong identifiers, and 7 percent of Swatantra. Despite this pattern of preference of defectors, however, the level of party identification and issue partisanship congruence for strong identifiers is high.

On balance, this is impressive presumptive evidence of the linkage of party identification to issue perceptions in India. There is no exactly comparative data to look at from the West to place side by side with these data. American and British studies actually suggest less congruence. Studies of multiparty Western systems which are presumably issue-distinctive, however, might reveal greater congruence than revealed here. But none have precisely measured the phenomenon as we have here for India.[14]

Party Defection Patterns and Issue Positions
A detailed analysis of the "defectors" (that is, those respondents who preferred a party other than their own on this issue) strengthens the argument for party-issue perceptual congruence. Table 9.7 presents the relevant data. Explicit, overt defection to another party on an issue (such as the economic controls issue used here) is not great. Only 15 percent of our sample specified another party than their own as closest to their own position on the issue. It is interesting that the defection rate for Congress and Communist identifiers was lowest among the five national party groupings. More instability in opinion was manifest on the extreme Right and the moderate Right and Left.

The important question is, Where did these identifiers go if they left their own party on an issue? One way to conceptualize this problem is to see all

TABLE 9.7 Destination of Identifiers Defecting from their Party on an Issue (Issue: Governmental Control of the Economy)

Identifier Group	% of Total Preferring Another Party*	% of Defectors Who Prefer						% of Defectors Preferring a "Close" Party
		Congress	Swatantra	Jan Sangh	CPI	Socialist	DMK	
Congress	13	X	12	23	10	10	7	29
Swatantra	18	62	X	8	8	15	...	70
Jan Sangh	21	75	5	X	5	5	...	5
Communists	14	38	...	...	X	...	·13	0
Socialists	21	73	...	...	...	X	...	73
DMK	5	†						†
Total	15							33

* Includes those responding "no parties," "independent," "all parties," and so on. Calculations based on the N of those ascertainable and knowledgeable on this question (Congress—578, Swatantra—71, Jan Sangh—95, Communists—57, Socialists—70, DMK—46).

† Too few cases for analysis.

parties on a Left-Right continuum (Communists at the extreme Left, Jan Sangh extreme Right, Congress in the center—as diagrammed earlier), and then to ask whether the movement of identifiers was "understandable" or "rational" in terms of this continuum. Table 9.7 suggests that the movement was more "rational" for some parties than for others. Thus 29 percent of Congress defectors went to "close" parties, that is, parties which presumably are closest to Congress in terms of a Left-Right continuum (Swatantra, Socialists, and DMK), but 33 percent "jumped over" these parties and preferred either the Communists or the Jan Sangh.[15] For these people the expectations we might have, based on a Left-Right continuuum, and on their presumed preference to a proximate party, were not borne out. The heterogeneity of opinion in Congress is dramatized by these data as well as the extremism in political opinion defection possibilities for a small minority of Congress supporters. There is much less actual "irrationality" in the other parties, although the large percentages of Jan Sangh and Communist defectors who prefer Congress to their neighbors in the continuum (Swatantra and the Socialists, respectively) is a significant deviation from rationality expectations (based on our continuum). For all the defectors from own party on the economic controls issue, only 26 percent took what could be called an "extreme" or "irrational" defection position, that is, preferring a party far removed from their own party on an issue. This compares to 33 percent who opted for a party "close" to them, and 41 percent whose party destination was uncertain. This, combined with the small percentage (15 percent) who explicitly preferred another party on the issue, is certainly testimony to the relatively high (and presumably developing) coherence of the Indian party system. The "movement toward the center" and "at the center" stands out in this picture of the defection of identifiers on issues.

There are both centrifugal and centripetal tendencies manifest in the issue preferences of Indian partisans. On balance there seems to be more centripetal movement, toward the center or at the center. This is salutary for party system integration, no doubt.

Summing Up: Party Loyalty and Issue Partisanship
One way of summarizing our findings on issue-partisan congruence for our study in 1967 is as follows (using again the issue of government controls for the economy):

	Total Sample	All Identifiers
% who have a position on the issue and do refer to a party (or independent candidate) as closest to their own position	53	71
% of above who are identifiers and also see their own party as closest	40	60
% who are identifiers with a party, have a position on the issue, see own party as closest to own position, and whose party is actually close on the issue to R's position	25	39

There is strong indication here that for a large proportion of the Indian public there is a coherent relationship to the party system in issue perception terms. Fully 50 percent in our sample demonstrated some minimal level of issue-party involvement. For the identifiers this involvement was considerably more frequent and consistent, as one might hypothesize should be the case. Party identification is clearly linked to partisan issue perceptions in India.

A final comparison with U.S. data as presented in *The American Voter* is interesting. Caution is necessary since the analyses are not absolutely identical. Three conditions for "issue-oriented political behavior" were examined in the American study: expression of an opinion on an issue, perception of what the government is doing on the issue, and the perception of relevant differences in party policy (and the ability to "locate one or the other party as closer to 'own' position"). Americans range from 10 to 30 percent as having no opinion on the sixteen issues used. Another 10 to 30 percent had no opinon as to what the government was doing. And another 20 to 46 percent had no perception of partisan differences. Examples of issues and the percentage of respondents who meet all three conditions in the United States are as follows:

	Has an Opinion (%)	Has Opinion and Knowledge of Government Policy (%)	In Addition, Knows Party Issue Positions (%)
Government aid to education	90	67	27
Leaving electricity, housing to private industry	70	51	22
Segregation of schools	88	54	31
Economic aid to foreign countries	83	67	23

If a fourth condition, that of party identification, was required, the percentages in the second and third columns would be considerably lower. The authors conclude at one point:

> Only 40 to 60 percent of *the "informed" segment* of the population . . . perceive party differences. . . . The discrepancy between those who hold attitudes and those who can relate the content of these attitudes to the differences in party position is substantial. The lesson shows clear that even when "political" attitudes are held, there is no guarantee that *partisan* implications are drawn.[16]

The previous analysis of Indian data demonstrates that the extent of issue partisanship perceptions of the Indian public is by no means low in comparison with that of the American public.

TEN·

"Party Space" and Citizen Images of the Party System

T HE CAPACITY OF THE ORDINARY CITIZENS TO THINK IN TERMS OF "party system" and to locate the parties in such a system may be a significant test of a maturing polity. It is the fourth test in terms of the "model" in chapter 7. We assume in our research that citizens can space parties, for in the questions we ask of them in probing their party identification we use such language as "which party do you feel closest to." This suggests the existence of distance between the respondent and various parties as well as distance, perceptible to ordinary citizens, between the parties. We therefore are interested in what spatial images of the party system citizens have, and we are inclined to expect that some rudimentary spacing capability should be evident for the involved citizen if his party identification, indeed if his basic relationship to the party system, is to be meaningful. One must be careful, of course, not to press this point too far. It is certainly possible for many citizens in Western as well as non-Western societies to be aware of the existence of only one party, the dominant party in their community, and to participate effectively in politics despite such myopia. On the other hand one might well argue that the achievement of a politically integrated polity and the development of an attentive, deliberating public, requires, among other things, a fairly large segment of the citizenry who know of the existence of the major parties, have some minimal or crude vision of the space they occupy, and can articulate some preference distinctions and/or spatial orderings. It is in this sense that the relationship of citizens to parties and elections may be relevant to political "integration," either as index or as prerequisite.

The research on these questions thus far is sparse. Philip Converse's discussion of some early data in this context for France and Finland suggests the complexity of the analysis and the chaotic patterns of individual responses.[1] In their English study, David Butler and Donald Stokes asked their respondents to locate the parties on a series of twelve scales, one of which was "left-wing/right-wing." The results led them to question the validity of such party location efforts for the British public.[2] The study by Samuel Barnes of party space perceptions of Italians in 1968 appears to be more successful, and is a helpful reference for our purposes here.[3] Similarly, a recent application in a study in Germany (Hesse 1970)

110

suggests the usefulness of such analysis.[4] The approaches and methodologies for conceptualizing the problem and for data acquisition vary for these studies. The major alternatives are two—either the specification by respondents of party preference orderings, or the location of parties along a given continuum with some ideological meaning. In the former case the respondent was asked to give his party preferences, in order of priority either from a list of parties, ordered or not ordered on a continuum, or his second, third, or fourth preferences in case his own party did not present a candidate in a given election. In the latter case the respondent was given a list of parties, a diagram of a scale described, such as a Left-Right scale, and asked to locate the parties precisely on the scale. Party names may or may not be provided to the respondent. There are a great many technical questions as well as arguments as to the utility of these spacing strategies, and we suspect that the size of the proportions of the public who can locate parties is related to the nature of the stimuli provided by the investigator. The intellectual exercises required in the different approaches are somewhat different, and the inferences permissible therefore differ. It is one thing to ask respondents to express affect for parties in a ranking system; it is another matter to ask them to know the location of the parties in a system on a substantive dimension which is at least theoretically preference-neutral. Preferences may be implicit, and certainly deduced, in this latter case, particularly since the respondent is also asked to locate himself on the dimension. It is this latter approach which emphasizes cognitive awareness and capacity which is used in our explanatory Indian analysis here of party space perception. We hope it will help us to better explain the public's involvement with the Indian party system as well as to explain certain aspects of Indian political behavior.[5]

In our 1967 Indian study we devised (after much pretesting which revealed that the Left-Right continuum was largely meaningless to most Indians) a "tradition-innovation" party distance scale explained in our interviews as follows:

> One way people think of parties is represented by this picture [Hand card] The party which strongly believes in the maintenance of old traditions and ideas is in the extreme right block of the line, and the party which believes in new ideas and new ways of doing things is in the extreme left block. Now as we move leftwards from the extreme right, we place parties that are less and less traditional and more and more given to new ideas. If you now consider the line as a whole with these two extremes and the blocks in between where would you place these parties?

Then follows six parties with their symbols, randomly presented:

Parties	Symbol
Congress	Bullocks
CPI	Sickle
Jan Sangh	Lamp
SSP	Tree
Swatantra	Star
PSP	Hut

A probe for other parties which the respondent wishes to place on the continuum is also included, followed by "Where would you place yourself on this line?" A seven-point scale was used and the coding references were, "very much new traditions," "somewhat new traditions," "very little new traditions," "50-50," "very little old traditions," "somewhat old traditions," and "very much old traditions." In 1967 this was the only basic scale which we felt made sense to the Indian citizen and in terms of which he could cognize his party system.

The Public's Capability to Think in Terms of Party Space
The overwhelming majority (78 percent) of our Indian respondents were able to place *themselves* on this continuum. Their ability to place the *parties* was considerably lower, however, but high enough to suggest a significant level of party awareness. About 19 percent of our sample could place no party and another 10 percent could place only one party, usually the Congress party. On the other hand, 47 percent were able to place Congress plus two or more parties—30 percent could actually place from five to eight political parties on our continuum. This suggests a high spacing capability and, possibly, "party involvement" for the Indian public. It compares with the 60 percent of Finnish respondents who were able to place parties in that system, or the 76 percent of the Italian respondents who were able to place themselves on a Left-Right continuum in 1968. In England, only 21 percent said they thought in "left-wing/right-wing" terms but 80 percent did place the parties on the continuum.[6] On the basis of the Indian public's responses to our request to them to place themselves and their parties on our contrived continuum, they revealed as great a willingness and interest as has been found in other countries. One contrast with the Italian data should be noted. In India nonidentifiers and independents were almost as able to locate themselves on the scale as were identifiers—at the 70 percent level (as compared to 86 percent for strong identifiers). In Italy, however, only 47 percent of the nonidentifiers located themselves on their Left-Right scale.[7] The uncommitted citizen in India apparently has a much higher than ordinary, or expected, tendency to express his cognition of his personal partisan space location.

The ability of the identifiers to locate their party was, as expected, much greater than for the ordinary citizen (table 10.1). The difference was the smallest for Congress, since 70 percent of the public could place it on our scale. Only 31 percent of the public could place the Socialists (either the SSP or PSP), however, and 42 to 44 percent the other major parties. The weak identifiers were usually capable of placing their parties on the continuum, with the exception of the Communists, whose capability was barely more than 50 percent for some unexplained reason. Comprehension of a party's location in space is greatly enhanced, therefore, for the identifiers, suggesting a strong functional relationship between identification and spatial awareness.

TABLE 10.1 The Ability and Willingness of Indians to Place their Parties in Space*

Party	Total Sample (%)	Strong Identifiers of That Party (%)	Weak Identifiers of That Party (%)
Congress	70	80	71
Communist	43	67	52
Jan Sangh	42	79	74
Swatantra	44	81	77
SSP	34	89	68

* Each proportion is the percent of the relevant category who could place a particular party on our continuum.

The Indian Party Space Patterns

The Indian party system is interesting to study in this connection, in contrast to Western established systems, for at least three reasons. First, it is a relatively new system, as a *system* of parties, having not much more than twenty years existence, and for some parties, such as Swatantra (founded only in 1959) and the rebel Communist and Congress parties, a much shorter life span than twenty years. Second, it has been a fragmented system with many small and regional parties—as many as twenty-five parties have had seats in Parliament. Third, Congress, despite its socialist and secular ideology, is the oldest party (founded in 1885) and the party dominating the scene until 1967. For these reasons a study of the public's images of that system is fascinating. But one's expectations must be conditioned by an awareness of the complexity and recency of that system.

One notes from our data that there is great variation in opinion as to where on our continuum the Indian public places their parties (table 10.2). The public is most split as to where to place Congress and Jan Sangh, dividing 46–49 ("new vs. old") on Jan Sangh and 36–57 on Congress. As we might expect if one views the party system historically, the majority see Congress as the party of "old traditions and ideas," the only party for

113

TABLE 10.2 Locations of Parties by the Indian Public
on the Innovation-Tradition Scale*

	Very New Ideas and Ways (%)	Some- what New (%)	Slight- ly New (%)	Mid- point (%)	Slight- ly Old (%)	Some- what Old (%)	Very Old Tradi- tions and Ideas (%)	N
Communists								
—Left	70	19	0	0	0	4	7	27
Communists	39	22	6	4	4	10	15	857
SSP	29	26	9	7	4	14	10	673
PSP	25	26	8	9	4	14	15	716
Swatantra	30	22	7	8	4	11	28	886
Jan Sangh	22	18	6	5	4	15	30	845
Congress	18	15	3	6	4	18	35	1,419
DMK	69	26	3	1	1	0	0	70

* Those unable to space parties or uncertain of where to place the parties on this scale are excluded from these figures.

which this is so. All the other parties (even Jan Sangh, though narrowly) are seen as locatable at the "new" end of the continuum. These range from the Left Communists and regular Communists, whom 89 percent and 67 percent of the public see as "new," to the two Socialist parties, whom 64 percent and 59 percent see as "new"; almost 59 percent also consider Swatantra "new," while Jan Sangh is considered "new" by 46 percent.

Nevertheless, aside from Congress, and Swatantra possibly, these locations fall sequentially as one would expect them to on a Left-Right ideological scale. (One would expect Congress ideologically to be at the center or left of the center between the PSP and Swatantra on such a scale.) The problem is that all parties, aside from Congress and Jan Sangh, tend to be at the Left end of the scale. Swatantra is at the "new" end of the scale, contrary to some expectations. ("New" for Swatantra undoubtedly means something different than "new" for the Communists.) Jan Sangh is much closer to the center than one might expect. We do not see the great "spread" in party locations which, for example, the Italian data revealed with the Communists at the extreme Left and the Neo-Facists at the extreme Right.[8] Because of the difficulties with the placement of Congress and to some extent Swatantra, therefore, no more than 40 percent of our sample approximates the ideological Left-Right scale expectations in their placement of the parties. Perhaps the fact that 40 percent do meet these expectations given the special character of the Indian system is surprising.

The average location of Indian parties (table 10.3) underscores these observations.

TABLE 10.3 Average Location of Indian Parties

Placement by Total Sample	Scale	Placement by Strong Identifiers*	Placement by Weak Identifiers
	Very "new" 0		
CPI—L (.81)			
	1	DMK (1.1)	(.83)
		CPI (1.1)	(1.75)
		Socialists (1.9)	(2.9)
CPI (2.0)	2		
SSP (2.1)			
Swatantra (2.4)		Swatantra (2.4)	(2.6)
PSP (2.4)			
Jan Sangh (3.2)	3	Jan Sangh (2.9)	(3.0)
Congress (3.6)		Congress (3.5)	(3.1)
	4		
	5		
	6 Very "old"		

* These are placements of their own party by strong and weak identifiers. These are average scale positions for each set of identifiers.

It is interesting that strong identifiers see their party as more "new" than do the weak identifiers or the total sample. The one exception to this again is Congress, whose weak identifiers place the party about at the midpoint in the scale, when one uses averages, while the strong identifiers average out to a slightly "older" location on the scale.

Averages or mean scores, it should be emphasized here, are misleading in actually conveying the mass images of the parties (fig. 5). Although the parties are inclined to cluster between the 2 and 3.5 locations on the scale, the actual distribution of opinion of Indians is quite different—they are not at all inclined to place their parties at the midpoint of this scale. This anticentrism in spacing patterns will be discussed further below.

Party identifiers view their party quite differently than the public does.

FIG. 5. Mean location of self and all major parties for identifiers (by total sample and by each set of identifiers).

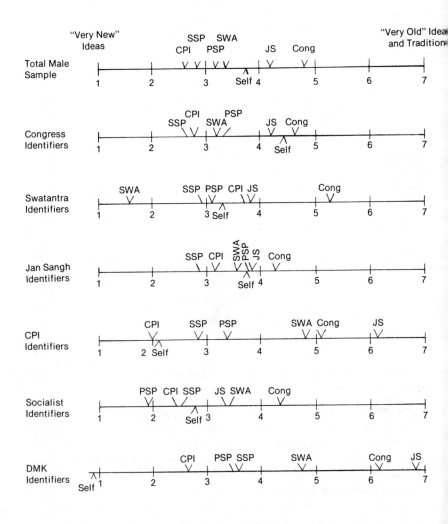

This is dramatically evident in figure 6. Much higher proportions of the identifiers are likely to scale their party as "very new," except for Congress and Jan Sangh. The slope of the curves of the other parties is rather steep on the left, with just a slight rise at the "very old" end of the scale, suggesting a small minority of identifiers who are extremists at that "old" end of the continuum. For Congress and Jan Sangh, however, there is a gentle slope, or no slope, at the "new" end and a sharp upward slope at the "old" end of the scale. These two different curves suggest important differences in spatial images and the dimensions on which they are based. We will attempt to define these differential dimensions later. We can summarize here by noting that the public did not see the Communists, Socialists, and Swatantra as extremely innovative parties to the extent that the identifiers did. While only about one-third of the public saw Swatantra, the SSP, the PSP, and the Communists as very innovative, close to 60 percent of the identifiers of those parties perceived their structure as "very new." This implies that perhaps the party images as they are communicated through the mass media differ from those appearing in party media. Further, the dilemma posed by these differential images is obvious. A party must work to attract new supporters while that party at the same time must act to meet the expectations of loyal supporters and members whose image of the party might differ from the new recruits. These contrasting popular and identifier images do not appear in the same form for Congress and Jan Sangh. There one finds much more *internal* dissensus as to the party image, with a 50-50 or 40-60 split between those seeing the party as "innovative" or "traditional." Theoretically Congress and Jan Sangh have much less agreement among their identifiers internally on party image, and are much less coherent as image structures than the other major parties.

The "Order" and "Meaning" of These Patterns
Having noted on the one hand the willingness of Indians to respond to party space concepts, as well as the differential images of the party system which emerge from their responses, it is natural to ask whether there is order or chaos in these spacing efforts. One might well argue that our respondents were "guessing," as Butler and Stokes argue for the majority of their British samples, or that Indians were not manifesting an informed or sophisticated political insight in their attempts to space their parties.

Inspection of the specific patterns does reveal that close to 100 percent were different for those of our respondents who attempted to place three or more parties. This corresponds to the earlier finding of Converse for Finland and France.[9] Although this suggests a lack of consistency, and considerable idiosyncratic spacing behavior, it does not necessarily permit

117

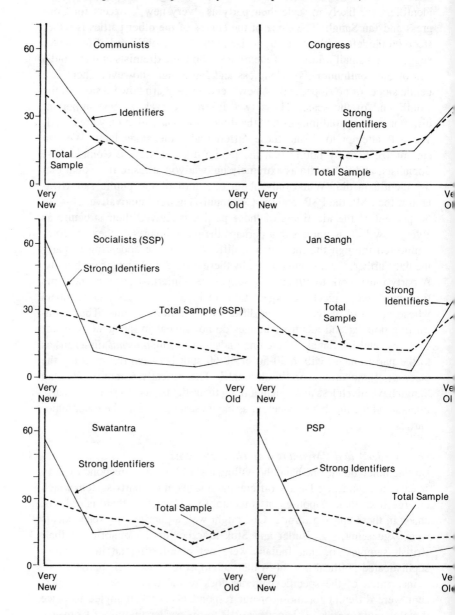

FIG. 6. Images of Indian parties (by total sample and identifiers).

These graphs are based on those who were able to space the parties. For the Communists, all the identifiers were used since there were too few cases of strong identification.

us to interpret the results as "chaotic" or as a matter of "chance." Several different tests are possible which suggest that there are some common patterns in the data, and strong evidence of deliberate, not quixotic, behavior.

One such test used by Converse, derived from Coombs, is the location of presumably "polar objects" in the system. Assuming for the sake of exploratory analysis that ours is a Left-Right ideological continuum, the proper "polar objects" most students of Indian politics would agree are the Communists at the Left and the Jan Sangh at the Right. To what extent do Indians see these parties as polar parties? Among those respondents who space three or more parties, 40 percent "correctly" placed them at the extreme polar positions and another 25 percent "correctly" placed one of these two extreme parties at the polar position.[10] A different test and one more directly comparable to the Converse data is a comparison of self-location on the continuum with that of the farthest party from self, as placed by the respondent. Assuming that the least desired parties are one or the other of the theoretically polar parties mentioned above, and assuming that some preference is implicit in the distance between self and the party placed farthest from self, what findings emerges? For those who place five or more parties, 66 percent place either of the polar parties as farthest removed, and an additional 13 percent place either the Swatantra party or the SSP, which might be considered "near polar" on a Left-Right dimension, as farthest removed from self. This compares very favorably to Converse's Finnish data but is less impressive than the 90 percent French figure.[11] Although there may be more than one dimension involved in this spacing of parties by Indian respondents, these results suggest some "order" in the images which Indians have of their party system. For the 65 percent of our sample who did place more than one party, from 40 to 80 percent had some view of what the polar parties in the system were, depending on how rigorous one's expectations are.

Another test to apply is the "next closest to own party" test. We do not have a preference-ordering question in our Indian study. But our party space continuum is a possible substitute. Assuming again an ideological Left-Right continuum, is the identity of the party located closest to own party the one we would expect (with the Communist at the Left, the Socialists at the moderate Left, and Jan Sangh at the far Right, and Swatantra at the moderate Right)? A special analysis of the identifiers' second "choices" reveals that 59 percent placed their second party according to such expectations, and if the Congress identifiers are excluded (since there is great dissensus among Congress identifiers on party location, and evidence of the irrelevance of ideology in their spacing) the percentage increases to 67 percent. This suggests again that Indian cognitions of their party system are more "ordered" than one might expect from the original inspection of the data.

A final analysis strongly demonstrating that Indian spacing capability is not the product of chance is the relationship between educational level and spacing. These data will be presented in greater detail later. We find a monotonic increase in the ability to locate parties by educational level. Thus 41 percent of illiterates cannot locate the Congress party, but only 5 percent of the college educated cannot; 71 percent of illiterates cannot locate the Communists, but only 17 percent of the college educated cannot. Both educational achievement and political exposure are consistently linked to spacing capability, clearly indicating that party space data for Indians may meaningfully inform us about their cognitions of their system.

The Location of Self in Relation to Party.

Indians generally found no difficulty in placing themselves on our innovation-tradition continuum. Only 22 percent of the sample failed or refused to engage in this exercise. The structure of their self-placements is, however, distinctive—it is almost a perfect U curve, for identifiers, independents, and nonidentifiers. As table 10.4 reveals, the picture is one of 30 percent at both extremes and the balance distributed in decreasing proportions toward the midpoint where there is a slight increase in placement, to 10 percent. The distributions are also slightly skewed to the "new" end of the continuum. This pattern is in marked contrast to the Barnes finding for Italy (1968), for example, where the bulk of the population was found at the Center-Left. The French data (1967) and German data (1970) also are in striking contrast to the Indian data, since all three Western countries show self-location distribution as a bell-shaped curve.[12]

TABLE 10.4 Self-Placement of Indian Citizens on Party Space Continuum*

	Very New Ideas and Ways (%)	Some-what New (%)	Slight-ly New (%)	Mid-point (%)	Slight-ly Old (%)	Some-what Old (%)	Very Old Tradi-tions and Ideas (%)	N
Total sample	31	13	4	11	2	9	30	1,661
Strong identifiers	34	10	3	11	2	7	33	667
Independents	35	10	6	10	3	16	20	39
Nonidentifiers	29	18	4	12	2	12	26	287

* Percent unable to place self is not included. It ranges from 13 to 21 percent.

There is considerable consistency between self-placement and party placement. Of those with a party identification who locate self and own party, 63 percent located themselves identically with party or one space removed; 16 percent six or more spaces removed. The party differences on this comparison are interesting. Congress and Jan Sangh identifiers are inclined to see themselves as more "innovative" than their parties, while the Communists, Socialists, and Swatantra tend to see their parties as somewhat more "innovative" than themselves. The extent of agreement, however, is very high, as table 10.5 indicates. If, in addition, one combines the proportions at either side of the continuum, the evidence of congruence is even greater. Thus, 33 percent of all Congress identifiers see themselves as "new," which is the identical proportion for the location of party. For Jan Sangh the proportions are 47 percent "new" for self and party. For the Communists the proportions are 76 percent and 85 percent; for Socialists the proportions are 61 percent and 72 percent; for Swatantra 51 percent (self) and 77 percent (party), the greatest discrepancy. This indicates that party identifiers are demonstrating great regularity in their political perceptions. Close to 50 percent of the party identifiers reveal perfect accordance between their own locations and that of their party, and 63 percent reveal near-perfect congruence (a location of self only one space removed from own party). This consistency does not vary greatly and regularly by strength of identification. The average consistency between self-placement at the "new" or "old" end of the continuum and their party placements is over 60 percent. While this consistency tends to be higher for strong identifiers, the differences are not great for all parties. For all strong identifiers perfect congruence in location of self and party is 51 percent; for weak identifiers it is 39 percent. Extreme inconsistency in self-party space perceptions is low, highest for weak Congress identifiers and Jan Sangh identifiers, especially strong identifiers. The Communists are most consistent (100 percent congruence in self and party placements). For all identifiers extreme inconsistency is below the 20 percent level.

Since the Communists, Socialists, and Swatantra supporters are themselves at the "innovative" end of the continuum, it is significant to find that those who do locate themselves as "new" are overwhelmingly inclined to place their party to the Left also—100 percent for the Communists, 75 percent for the Socialists, and 89 percent for Swatantra supporters. The proportions of Jan Sangh supporters seeing themselves as "traditional" who also see their party on the Right is 63 percent, and self-party congruent locations on the Left for Jan Sangh are similarly 65 percent. The level of congruent perceptions for Congress supporters on the "innovative" end of the scale is also high, 60 percent, but higher on the "traditional" end of the scale, 77 percent.

121

TABLE 10.5 Similarity of Self Locations and Own Party Locations, by Party Identifiers

	Location as "Very New" (%)		Location as "Very Old" (%)		Actual Congruence between Self and Own Party Locations (%)		
	Self	Own Party	Self	Own Party	Perfect	Perfect and Near-Perfect	N
Congress identifiers	21	17	36	36	46	63	616
Swatantra identifiers	40	56	18	7	43	57	73
Jan Sangh identifiers	38	21	28	34	48	58	104
Socialists (SSP)	43	54	25	14	57	68	70
Communists	47	57	6	7	61	81	14

Do Indian identifiers select the party (as they locate the parties on the continuum) closest to their own location as the party to identify with? This is a final way to state the extent of mutuality in self-party perceptions. Confining our analysis to identifiers who located both self and own party (75 percent of all identifiers), we find the following: 54 percent identified with the party which was located on the identical space as themselves; 9 percent, in addition, identified with a party on an adjacent space *not* occupied by other parties; and 10 percent, in addition, identified with a party on an adjacent space occupied by other party or parties. Thus 63 percent of the identifiers in this analysis met the requirements for consistency in terms of identifying with a party located identically or proximately to self-location, and another 10 percent came close to meeting this requirement. Thus, just over 50 percent of our identifiers demonstrated high ''rationality'' in party space perceptions.

Thus evidence is strong that the capacity of Indian party identifiers to locate self and party in the party system with high consistency is considerable. Consensual perceptions of the spatial locations of their parties do emerge (particularly for the Communists, Socialists, and Swatantra supporters), and this is congruent with spatial locations of self for a majority of party identifiers. That the public's images of the parties often do not converge with identifiers' images poses a special problem for Indian political analysis. But there is clear empirical support in our data for the competence of Indian citizens to think meaningfully and consistently in party system terms.

Characteristics of Indian Images of Their Party System

It should be apparent from the preceding analysis that the way in which Indians visualize their party system spatially is distinctive. And further analysis bears this out. One of the major tendencies is that of seeing the system in "bipolar," if not "bipolarized," terms. By this (bipolarity) is meant the tendency to see parties as distant from each other, not necessarily as distant *and* in conflict, which would define "bipolarized" relations. Our data suggest that Indians generally are not "centrist-oriented" in their image patterns. We have already noted that in self-placements on our continuum we found only 11 percent of our sample placing themselves at midpoint. And Congress party, which we might have expected, ideologically and also in terms of other perceptions, to be located near the midpoint is in fact placed by all but about 15 percent of the respondents outside of the central area of our scale. A special analysis of the exact locations of the parties for those who space two or more parties revealed the following patterns: 14 percent, nonpolar (place all parties at one point on the scale); 86 percent, polar (48 percent extreme bipolar, 14 percent moderate bipolar, and 24 percent tripolar [place parties at center plus both ends]).[13]

The existence of this tendency, or tendencies, is obscured by averages. It can only emerge from a precise inspection of exact locations of parties by respondents. It suggests for India that, while there are multiple images, bipolar images of the system predominate. There is limited evidence that Indians perceive a center (only 24 percent in this analysis do) and considerable evidence that they see parties arrayed on either the Right or Left of our innovation-tradition continuum. Whether this is related to a cultural predisposition, or linked to an awareness of political conflict, polarization, and system dissensus are later questions to investigate. It conceivably could merely be bipolarity in perceptions without feelings of actual polarization.

What is noticeable from our data, to state the finding a bit differently, is the "spaciousness" in the Indian imagery, or a cognition of the party system as one in which the parties are "distant" from each other. This can be demonstrated by looking at two measures. If we look at the amount of space comprehended or covered in the spacing of parties, we find that 10 percent used only one or two spaces, while 22 percent used six spaces and 45 percent used seven spaces. Another measure of this is the "range" (the number of spaces between the highest and lowest spaced parties), and 62 percent reveal a range of six or more spaces. Although this is not a direct test of "polarity," it strongly suggests it. And the proportion of this "range" or "polarity" increases with the number of parties spaced, increasing from 52 percent for those spacing two parties to 82 percent for those spacing six parties.

Roughly two-thirds, then, of our respondents were very "spacious" in their location of parties. When one uses a second measure, the number of spaces *between self and the most distant party* located, one arrives at a similar finding, as 58 percent use the maximum or near-maximum number of spaces, and on the other hand for only 9 percent is there no space intervening between self and most distant party. For both of these measures we find that as respondents space more parties, their use of space increases. From 80 to 85 percent of those locating six parties or more appear to cognize the maximum party distance. But even those who space only two parties use much space—up to 50 percent use six or seven spaces and only 20 percent use two spaces. There is strong evidence then that Indians have an image of their party system as including parties ranging over the entire spectrum, not as converging toward a center or to one sector of that spectrum.

Aside from the "spaciousness" and "bipolarity' in Indian images, one also notices a high degree of what might be called "discriminative capacity." Not only do our respondents comprehend a large amount of space, from "very new" to "very old," in their image of the "spread" of parties, but they actually do space parties along the continuum. Approximately 30 percent of the total sample (and 42 percent of those who attempt to space parties) use three or more spaces in locating parties. This varies, of course, by the number of parties located. For those placing three parties, only 40 percent used three spaces, while for those placing five or six parties over 70 percent used three or more spaces. The level of discrimination is high even for those who space only three parties. This suggests a relatively high degree of sophistication and some indication of deliberate "spacing" rather than locating parties in a single space or on two spaces. Perhaps another indication of this is the finding that 56 percent of our respondents locate themselves on a space either not occupied by a party or occupied by only one party, usually the party they identify with. Less than 20 percent actually lump themselves and most of the parties they know together on the same space or two adjacent spaces.

All the nuances and significance of these spacing patterns are not yet entirely clear. They may have a variety of meanings. For instance these latter findings about the use of space and the tendency of a sizable proportion (25 percent) to locate self on a space not occupied by a party may actually be the result of dissonance in images. And their possible implications for lack of affect for the party system also need to be unravelled. It appears, however, that the Indians in our study did not take the easy, quick way out in responding to our request that they place themselves and the parties on our continuum. They attempted generally to locate themselves and the parties along the continuum, utilizing much of the space, conveying the impression at least of deliberative and meaningful behavior.

The Linkages between Party Space and Other Variables

Many questions can be raised concerning the explanation of party space perceptions of the Indian public. These are essentially of two kinds: What factors best explain the differential ability of Indians to space parties, that is, their awareness and sophistication about their party system, and does this awareness of the party system help to explain other kinds of behavior of Indians? In a sense, the utility and meaning of party space behavior hangs on these two questions.

We have already noted that the ability to space *one's own* party is associated with party identification strength. Party identification is also related to the *total number of parties* a person could space (table 10.6). The fact of identifying and the strength of identification clearly enhance the probability that one will space parties. Over 50 percent of strong identifiers can space more than three parties, while this it true of approximately a third of nonidentifiers.

TABLE 10.6 Party Identification and Party Space Capability

Party Identification*	Can Space No Parties (%)	Can Space 3 or More Parties (%)	N
Strong	20	54	1,056
Weak	27	48	351
No party identification	48	32	495

* Major parties only.

If we turn table 10.6 around (asking what percent of those who can or cannot space parties are strong identifiers), we find that only 36 percent of those not able to locate the parties are strong identifiers, in contrast to the 64 percent of those who can space six parties. This suggests again the importance of party identification for the Indian analysis, as well as indicating that the responses we got from our sample were not "guesses." "Awareness" of other parties in the party system is linked as expected to psychological involvement with a party.

When we look at information and political involvement measures we find the same positive relationships. We use the measures here of education and campaign exposure (attendance at campaign meetings, meeting the candidates, receiving party propaganda, exposure to party canvassing) (table 10.7). There are very sharp differences by educational level—only 5

TABLE 10.7 The Relationship of Education and Campaign Exposure
to the Ability to Space Parties*

Party	Education Level (%)					Campaign Exposure (%)				
	College	High School	Pri- mary	Some Lower	Illi- terate	Very High	High	Some	Very Little	None
Congress	5	9	16	30	41	12	14	25	32	50
Jan Sangh	14	32	48	66	67	41	45	56	59	74
Communists	17	26	39	59	71	35	37	54	63	72
Swatantra	18	24	45	59	66	32	45	49	60	72
PSP	21	42	52	70	74	43	50	61	69	78
SSP	21	42	52	74	76	47	50	65	71	78
N	118	82	407	379	453	148	314	475	568	468

* Each percentage is a proportion of the total who were *unable* to locate the party
on our innovation-tradition continuum.

percent of the college-educated being unable to locate Congress party
while the figure is 41 percent for the illiterates. There is a monotonic increase in ability to space parties with educational level. The inability of all
respondents, but particularly for the illiterates, is much greater for the lesser parties—at the 70 percent level for non-Congress parties. The ability of
the college and high school educated remains fairly high for non-Congress
parties. The findings for the campaign exposure index are almost as impressive. Those with no contact with the campaign were much less likely to
be able to locate the parties on our continuum, but there was a 40 percent
increase in spacing capability for all parties for those exposed to the campaign. Campaign informational involvement as well as educational level,
therefore, seem to be relevant to party system awareness.

Further evidence that both education and campaign exposure are relevant factors emerges when we control for one or the other. Thus

	% Not Able to Space Congress	% Not Able to Space the Com- munist Party
High campaign exposure		
College educated	2	6
Illiterates	20	50
Some campaign exposure		
College educated	14	21
Illiterates	38	72
No campaign exposure		
College educated	15	23
Illiterates	57	78

Illiterates with a high campaign exposure are much more aware of party space than illiterates isolated from the campaign; the difference is not as dramatic for the college educated but it is a significantly greater capability. Perhaps the most significant finding attesting to the function of the campaign activity of the parties is the difference for the illiterates between the 57 percent (*not exposed* to the campaign) who cannot locate Congress spatially and the 20 percent (*exposed* to the campaign) who cannot locate Congress. On the other hand the linkage of education to awareness of the party system in India is striking; in the absence of campaign exposure, cognition of the party system is high for the educated.

Age and income level, of the other socioeconomic variables, also seem to be somewhat related to ability to cognize the party system spatially. Those in the younger age cohort, particularly in the twenty-six to thirty age bracket, have the highest capability and awareness. There is a gradual decrease in awareness of the party system with age. As for income, the differences are striking. Whereas only 8 percent of the affluent cannot locate Congress, 39 percent of the very poor cannot. Whereas 30 percent of the wealthy cannot locate the CPI, 66 percent of the lowest income group cannot. There is one interesting deviation in the findings on income—Jan Sangh and Swatantra are parties which are more easily spaced by the high income group than any other non-Congress parties. It is obvious that, aside from Congress, they are the parties most salient to the wealthy.

Three types of variables, therefore, help explain differences in the Indians' knowledge of their party system and their ability to communicate any spatial images about it. These three are strength of party identification, socioeconomic status (education and income), and political informational involvement. Age is another variable revealing some differences in spacing capability.

A second theoretical concern is the explanation of the rationale or basis for the location of specific parties at various points on the continuum. Why do many see Congress as a "very old" party while others see it as "very new"? Why does the public generally locate the Communists at the "new" end of the scale, but a small minority locate it at the "old" end? And the same queries hold for all parties—what are the terms of reference, the dimensions, the orientations to politics or to the society which underlay these spatial perceptions?

The first discovery is that the images of the parties do not vary a great deal for the different age, educational, and income strata of Indian society. It is remarkable in fact how constant the basic distributions are. As discussed earlier, we found Congress to be seen by the majority of our respondents (57 percent) to be at the "old" end of our innovation-tradition scale. In contrast we found our sample (67 percent) picturing the Communists at the "new" end of the scale. The same basic distributions hold

127

for illiterates and college educated, for young and old, for wealthy and poor. Thus, 57 percent of those age twenty-one to twenty-five see the Communists as "new," as do 59 percent of those over age fifty-one. Basically the same findings hold true for the other parties also. It seems clear that each social stratum divides as the general public does and one does not find unique images of any party in particular social sectors. Jan Sangh and Congress are seen by a majority in each social sector as "old," and the rest of the largest parties are seen as "new," with sizable minorities placing the self-same party at the opposite segment of the scale.

Differences in party spatial images seem to be only slightly a matter of the utilization of those personal psychological orientations to politics measured in our study. In the Indian case the "traditionalness" of a person's orientation, and perhaps also his "authoritarianness," might be hypothesized as related to the way he spaces parties. Our findings reveal that this is so only to a very small extent. In table 10.8 we set forth our findings using a "traditionalism-modernism" index as a predictor of the spacing preferences of our respondents.[14] We do find some evidence of association. Those with the most modern orientations are most likely to see Congress, Jan Sangh, and Swatantra as "old" and the Communists (as well as SSP and PSP) as "new." It is interesting that while only 33 percent of our sample see Swatantra as "old," 56 percent of those with modern perspectives see Swatantra as "old." And while 29 percent of our sample see the Communists as "old," only 13 percent of those with modern views see the Communists as "old."

TABLE 10.8 "Traditional" and "Modern" Orientation to Politics as Related to Party Spacing Preferences

Seeing Party as "Old"	"Traditional" on Both Statements (%)	"Traditional" on Strong Leaders Statement (%)	"Traditional" on Parochial Statement (%)	"Modern" on Both Statements (%)
Congress	58	56	51	73
CPI	31	37	25	13
Jan Sangh	47	37	54	63
Swatantra	32	41	39	56
N	1,148	103	330	91

There seems to be, then, some relationship between our respondents' perceptions of the innovation-tradition scale on which we asked them to locate parties and the traditional-modern orientations of the individual. But the relationship is not strong enough to suggest that the two dimensions are

128

the same. In fact, the more analysis we engaged in led us to the feeling that the "innovation-tradition" party space concept is an independent dimension not closely linked to any other. We looked at the responses to campaign issues, for example, and found very little relationship. The three issues were governmental control of the economy, the banning of cow slaughter, and the use of fasting as a political weapon. On none of these issues is there a close overlap with our party space scale. In fact the proportions among "conservatives" and "liberals" who see each party as "new" is virtually identical in most cases. Thus, of the liberals on the economic control issue, 38 percent see Congress as "new" while 35 percent of the conservatives see Congress as "new." Further, 65 percent of the liberals see the Communists as "new," compared to 71 percent of the conservatives. It is, therefore, not the conservatives who see Congress as "new," or vice versa, or the liberals who see the Communists as "new," or vice versa, because the proportions are similar. The images of the Indian parties exist independent of the attitudes Indians have on the political issues of the day. And our party space innovation-tradition dimension is one which exists in Indian minds separate from their issue ideologies. It is a dimension which triggers perceptions which seem to permeate all ideological and social strata, uninfluenced by the linkage of parties in spatial terms to specific issue postions.

A third theoretical concern is the relationship of party space behavior to other behavior. Whether a person locates himself in party space at the same point as his location of his own party, or, conversely, at some distance from his party or other parties, might well be linked to his other behavior. One type of such behavior we are interested in here is his perception of the party closest to him on political issues. If party spacing is relevant and meaningful, it might reveal an association with such party-issue congruence. The relationship need not exist, but one could hypothesize such a relationship. A careful and detailed inspection of a subsample of our data proves that this is indeed the case under certain conditions. We do not find that spatial distance from party of identification is *by itself* the major relevant factor. Persons who see their party as six or seven spaces removed from them still are almost as likely as those located coincident with party of identification to select their own party as issue-congruent. Rather, it seems to be the positioning of self *with reference to the party system itself* which is critical. An extremely high percentage (84 percent) of those who locate themselves and the party of their identification on the same space on our continuum also consider that party as closest on the economic controls issue. (The percentage is 73 percent on the cow slaughter issue.) Of that group, only 5 percent picked a spatially distant party on this issue. On the other hand, almost 50 percent of those locating themselves distant from their own party picked a spatially distant party on this issue. The level of issue-party noncongruence, therefore, increased with spatial noncongruence, suggesting again that use of party space has some meaning for Indians, inducing, or being consistent with, more "rational" behavior. It is also interesting to note that about 70 percent of those locating any parties (and whose behavior was ascertainable on this question) selected a party relatively close to them in space as the party closest to them on the economic controls issue.

A further analysis was made of spatial congruence of self and party system in relation to the "parties least likely to do what you want on this issue." We found a similar, striking difference between those who spaced themselves with their own party and those who did not. On the issue of economic controls, almost 70 percent of those spatially congruent with their own party did what one would hypothesize—they selected parties least favorable on the issue, as one would expect them to in accord with spatial distance expectations. On the other hand, among those not spatially congruent with own party, only 30 percent selected parties in accord with distance expectations.[15] This attests again to the relevance of spatial patterns to other orientations and perceptions about the system.

Spatial perceptions of the party system seem to be somewhat linked to voting behavior. In 1967, when defection from Congress was abnormally high, we find that those who were strong Congress party identifiers *and* who spaced themselves identically with Congress were overwhelmingly inclined to vote for Congress for the Lok Sabha in 1967 as they had in 1962, whereas a smaller proportion of these strong Congress identifiers who did not space themselves coincidentally with Congress were consistent party voters. Weak identifiers also showed less party loyalty if spatially distant from their party. The data are summarized for Congress identifiers in table 10.9. A similar analysis for the party identifiers of all parties reveals a 5 percent greater likelihood of switching from one's own party if a respondent located himself distant from his own party. In a special subsample analysis we found that those who located self and party on the same space were more likely to be spatially consistent if they did switch to another party than those who located themselves one or more spaces removed from party. Thus, 73 percent of those coincident in self-placement either voted for their own party or the next closest party, while only 43 percent of those locating themselves at a distance were consistent in this way.

Those who saw themselves as "removed" or "distant" from the party system reveal less consistent behavior—they were more inclined to desert their party and to select a party which is spatially distant from them. Further, we find that awareness of the party system and the ability to locate parties on a continuum is also linked to consistent and spatially "rational"

130

TABLE 10.9 Voting Consistency by Party Space Perception
(Congress Identifiers Only)

Spatial Patterns	% Supporting Congress in 1962 and 1967 (of Voters in Both Elections)	% of Total Who Voted Congress in Both Elections	N
Strong Congress identifiers			
Self located coincident with party of identification	84	56	229
Self distant from party of identi- fication by one space or more	79	50	237
Weak Congress identifiers			
Self located coincident with party identification	73	41	46
Self distant from party of identification	68	27	86

* Each percentage is a proportion of each spatial pattern subgroup.

behavior. Some evidence exists, therefore, to support the linkage of party spacing perceptions to actual voting. And, in the main, of those Indians who can space parties and are also identifiers (about 50 percent of the total) fully 40 percent exhibit behavior which is "rational" and consistent with party choice. If their party system spatial awareness is high and congruent (for self and party), about three-fourths reveal high behavioral consistency.

Are party space perceptions an index of an individual's involvement with or alienation from the system? This intriguing inquiry constitutes our final theoretical concern in the analysis of our Indian party space data. We could well expect that citizens who have an image of themselves as spatially distant from the political parties might be less likely to support the political system, while those whose self-placement in party space is coincident with the parties would be more system-supportive. This theory is indeed borne out by our data, although the analysis is limited. Congress party identifiers are, of course, consistently more supportive of the government and the system than non-Congress identifiers, independents, or nonidentifiers. But if one controls for party identification, those who are "spatially coincident" with the party(ies) are most system-supportive, those who are "spatially proximate" are almost as supportive, but those who are "spatially distant" reveal the lowest system and government support scores. Thus, while normally 33 percent of our sample of Congress identifiers had relatively high general system support scores, 41 percent of Congress supporters spatially identical with their party had high support scores, but *none* of those "spatially distant" from their party and from the other parties had high system-support scores. It is probably significant that only 6 percent of those perceiving themselves as distant from the parties on our space continuum were broadly supportive of the system. There is some partial evidence here, then, that the party space images of Indians had meaning for them and help explain their political behavior to some extent. Indeed, for some Indians there is evidence that party space perceptions may tap a vital aspect of their political integration or political alienation.[16]

A Suggested Model of Party Space Behavior
In exploring these theoretical concerns, our empirical discoveries suggest some tentative recapitulation of the nature of the relationships operative here. As figure 7 suggests, there are apparently four different types of factors which may be helpful in explaining the capacity of citizens to think in terms of party spatial images and their own place in party space. These are the strength of party identification, socioeconomic status, exposure to political communication, and psychological orientations toward society (such as that tapped by our traditionalism-modernism index). The latter factor may be more helpful in India in explaining the way in which some citizens visualize the parties in space, rather than explaining their ability to space. The party space behavior of Indians may be conceptualized as an intervening variable relevant for explaining certain other aspects of political behavior. We have found a partial behavioral linkage to "issue-party congruence" (the extent to which the individual perceives his party, the party spatially most close to him, as the party closest to his position on an issue), to "government support" (acceptance of, or minimal hostility to,

FIG. 7. Diagram of relationships.

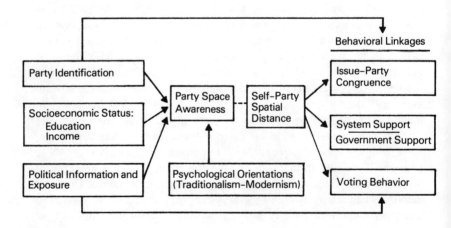

officials, government, and parties). Enough evidence exists in this preliminary analysis for India to indicate that party spatial behavior for many Indians is deliberate and meaningful, and can be useful in helping to explain his political behavior. It is one important indicator of the Indian citizen's "integration" in his rapidly expanding polity.

ELEVEN·

Party Identification, Political Exposure, and Systemic Orientations

T HE RELEVANCE OF PARTY IDENTIFICATION FOR THE INDIAN CITIZEN'S involvement with his political system and, hence, for the functioning of the Indian system, is a complex and many-faceted inquiry. So far we have explored four aspects of that problem: the citizen's belief in the party system, his awareness of the differences between parties, his capacity to relate to parties in issue terms, and his capability for awareness of the party system and himself spatially. One major facet or set of relationships remaining to be analyzed in our model concerns the citizen's attitudes and orientations toward the political system and the extent to which party identification is engaged in such involvement.

In the preceding analysis we have presented data describing the extent of party identification, particularly the relatively high incidence of strong identification in India, its penetration throughout the society, its apparent stability over time, and its linkage with perceptions of the party system. Impressive as these findings are, they only begin to speak to the key functional concerns of "system maintenance" and "system change." Is party identification in India associated with providing stability to the system, or is it associated with the developmental changes in the system, or both, or neither? There are those who would argue that party identification legitimizes and stabilizes, provides equilibrium to a system; others have argued that under certain conditions such "psychological involvement" can lead to change or that the essence of such identification is change. In a developing polity like India we would argue that party identification is linked to both mobilization and stability, and that in fact it may be a major component in a set of attitudes and behaviors in India which on the one hand is evidence that political development has occurred and on the other hand itself feeds the political development process. Party identification is, then, associated with and conducive to stability *and* change, commitment *and* reorientation, political constancy *and* mobility. Rajni Kothari suggests a basic outlook similar to this in his analysis preceding the 1971 election:

> The factor which has provided stability to the Indian political system despite the momentous changes through which it it passing—and the inherently "destabilizing" consequences of these changes—is "party

loyalty" or what, in the literature of social science, has come to be known as "party identification." Increasing politicization, the growth of new values and the permeation of secular symbols and institutions at all levels of society have given rise to new forms of identification which cut across other differentiations and bonds.[1]

D. C. Sheth has also stated this position well in his analysis of partisanship in the 1967 election:

A competitive party system, then, by mobilizing voters into organized politics and creating allegiances among them, produces a kind of stochastic effect, so that those individuals and groups which on the basis of other indicators display a low potential for politicisation, can also develop political orientations necessary for their participation in the processes of decision-making.[2]

Although Kothari places major emphasis on the stability function of party identification, it is clear that he sees party identification as related to political changes taking place and as significant for the political development process. One way of restating this theory is as follows. In the modernization process parties are playing a major role, "a catalytic role," in the restructuring of public attitudes and affect toward the political system and the institutions in that system. Thus, as citizens become "psychologically involved," as they take on *party* identifications and allegiances, as one type of such involvement, allegiances which are critical for party system *stability,* they are also taking on new orientations and attitudes which represent *change,* an integration of the modern with the traditional past. These orientations are functional to system support. "Identification," therefore, is the product of *change;* it leads to or is associated with more *change* (in system-supportive attitudes and behavior), which then leads to *stability* (or, indeed, to more change!). It is this basic theory of the meaning of party identification for India which we wish to empirically pursue here.

Party Identification Linked to Political Exposure and Mobilization
Prior to 1975 we can say that India's party and election system constituted the institutional opportunities and environment for the emergence of a public with strong partisan attachments. Evidence that these institutions have in fact played a mobilist role in the development of partisan loyalty is strong. Even though only a short time has elapsed since the achievement of Independence in 1947, a large proportion of Indian citizens have been "bound into" the system, apparently, if one accepts party identification as a test of such integration. Our data suggest that exposure to the party system and to the politically relevant elite structure have enhanced this

involvement or commitment (table 11.1). We note, for example, that as the extent of exposure to the campaign of 1967 was increased[3] the proportion of strong identifiers, of all identifiers, and of constant party voters increases. There is a striking difference of over 30 percent between those with no exposure and those with very high campaign exposure in strong identification. Consistent voting support for the same party in both the national elections of 1962 and 1967 also was much higher among those highly exposed— 70 percent compared to 49 percent for those isolated from the campaign. To state the finding another way: there are very few nonidentifiers among Indians highly exposed to campaign politics, only 9 percent in our study, while one-third of those not exposed to the campaign were nonidentifiers.

TABLE 11.1 Party Constancy in Relation to Campaign Exposure

	Party Identification 1967				Voting Constancy 1962–67	
	% All Identifiers	% Strong Identifiers	% Non-identifiers	N	% Supporting Same Party among Eligible Voters	N
Exposure level						
None	63	42	33	367	49	195
Low	75	57	23	495	62	290
Moderate	79	59	19	423	63	280
High	80	59	17	292	60	194
Very high	90	75	9	136	70	89

One must be cautious, of course, in the interpretation of these data. We cannot prove that exposure *caused* party identification. One could argue that the relationship is the reverse: party identification caused exposure. Or, more probably, the reasoning might be that only certain types of people are exposed to politics and they happen to be identifiers also. Our position as presented here is that there is such a strong association between exposure and identification, and a consistent one, and the evidence presented here is so cumulatively impressive, that we feel the case is strong for the "exposure→identification" relationship. It seems clear that the party and election systems are functionally relevant for the development of party group attachments, and the extent of exposure to such institutions is associated with the incidence and emergence of strong allegiances. Our data show that identification covaries with party system exposure.

Exposure to political leadership also is associated with party identification, and interestingly this is true with reference to exposure to both party leaders and caste leaders. We secured data from our respondents on their personal acquaintance of party and caste leaders, and candidates for office, as well as whether they had contacted such leaders or received advice from them. Our data show that strong party identification increases from 53 percent for those not exposed to 78 percent for those highly exposed to *both* party and caste leadership. It is very significant for an understanding of the Indian system that *caste* leadership exposure is relevant to developing strong *party* identification. This suggests many interpretations, but above all the importance of traditional social leadership for cues relevant to inducing strong commitments to the parties in the new competitive party system. It is not those exposed to party *or* caste leadership who tend to be the strong party identifiers but rather those *jointly* exposed to both types of leadership, whose attachments to the party system are reinforced by both types of leaders, who are least likely to be independents or nonidentifiers. Party identification seems also to be reinforced and transmitted by the family. In 1967, 14 percent of our sample (17 percent, 1971) grew up in families which were politically interested, but two-thirds of these thus socialized were strong identifiers, compared to slightly more than 50 percent of those not socialized in the family.[4]

Thus, we find that exposure to campaign activities of the parties, to party leadership, caste leadership, and to political socialization influences in the family all conduce to strengthened party identification. In other words, these party and electoral subsystems and institutions, and the leadership behavior associated with these institutions, seem clearly linked to the emergence of a high level of party identification.

From a cross-national perspective, these findings for India seem very similar to those revealed by the American and British studies. Although the measures available to us for comparison are not exactly equivalent, they may be functionally similar and in any event suggest the same basic relationship. Generally, as exposure (or information) increases there is a sharp increase in party voting.[5] India is no different than these "Western" countries, although it may in fact approximate the British case more clearly since even those with no exposure are relatively constant (49 percent compared to the British 57 percent), which is in clear contrast to the much lower percentage in the United States (30 percent) (table 11.2).

Indeed, one of the most interesting aspects of the Indian data, this large percentage of those who are constant in voting and strong in party loyalty even though apparently unexposed to politics through party, leadership, or family socializing stimuli, is the most difficult and challenging phenomenon to explain. We find 42 percent were strong party identifiers even though isolated (so far as our data indicate) from the campaign; 53 percent are strong party identifiers even though not in contact with, or knowledgeable

TABLE 11.2 Comparison of Linkage of Political "Exposure" to Party Constancy:
India, United States, Britain*

	% Voting for Same Party in 2 Successive Elections		
Exposure Level	India	United States	Britain
High	70	73	83
Medium	63	56	75
Low	49	30	57

* American "exposure" really consists of level of information about presidential candidates (see Philip Converse, "Information Flow and the Stability of Partisan Attitudes," in *Elections and the Political Order,* p. 139); the British study used media exposure (see Butler and Stokes, p. 221); the Indian data on exposure are operationalized as campaign exposure to party propaganda, candidates, election meetings, and canvassing. The elections involved are, for India 1962–67, for United States 1956–60, for Britain 1964–66.

of, party or caste leaders. How should we interpret this finding, particularly in the light of the fact that India's present party system is recent in origin and, hence, attachments are conceivably short-lived? In answering this one must keep in mind the different ways in which people were politically exposed—to caste leadership (11 percent), the family (14 percent), party leaders (32 percent), both party and caste leaders (46 percent).

At least four-fifths of the Indian electorate had some contact with political institutions or activity in 1967 or before. When one takes the percent who were strong partisans despite lack of exposure, one is in reality dealing with a very small fragment of the voting population, probably 10 percent or less of the electorate. If one analyzes this fragment one notes that over 70 percent of the "unexposed" but strong identifiers are loyal to Congress, whose loyalty for many is associated with the Independence movement. Thus the basis of their strong party identification is at least partially explicable in terms of historical commitment. Even though they do not now appear to be in contact with the party leadership or its activities, or caste leadership either, these people have a historically based, symbolic attachment to Congress which has deep roots. Current exposure to politics is not necessary to crystallize and maintain their party loyalty.[6] If one accepts this explanation, then the problem of explaining strong party identification of political isolates is eased considerably. There are no more than 3 percent of the electorate who are strong identifiers (with non-Congress parties) despite their apparent nonexposure to politics. These are evenly distributed among the major non-Congress parties. Keeping in mind the possibility of informal social and political influences and stimuli, not all of which we could explore in our study, the problem of explanation is considerably minimized.

The high level of exposure to politics in India thus seems to be linked to party identification incidence and strength. In addition the role of caste leaders in conjunction with party leaders in reenforcing party identification is suggested strongly by the data. Another way to state the position elaborated here is that the party organizations and their leaders, as well as many caste leaders, have been engaging in the mobilization of the electorate in the sense that they have legitimized parties and encouraged citizens into a clear and strong attachment to particular parties in that system.

A striking way to demonstrate this linkage between mobilization and strength of commitment to parties is possible in our 1967 data. If we contrast those "new entrants" in 1967 (that is, those who voted for the first time in 1967 though eligible previously) with those "isolates" (nonvoters in 1967 and previously, though eligible previously), we can see the juxtaposition of mobilization with identification. Of those who were "brought into" the electoral arena for the first time in 1967, 67 percent were identifiers (53 percent strong), whereas for the isolates or nonvoters 54 percent were identifiers (38 percent strong). Those mobilized had a stronger attachment than those not mobilized. Combined with the earlier data we see the suggestion here of a continuous mobilization and socialization process. There seems to be a considerable proportion of the nonvoters who are latent identifiers even though nonparticipant. As they become voters, over 50 percent of them reveal strong party identification, and this can increase to over 70 percent with strong identification as they are exposed to campaigns, party organization influences and activities, caste leaders and party leaders.

The Attitudinal Basis of Party Identification

To understand whether party attachments in India represent or are linked to systemic transformations at the mass level, one must look at citizen orientations and attitudes toward politics, particularly to see whether party attachment converges with citizen attitudinal engagement with the system. Another way to put this is to ask what type of "partisanship" is emerging in India and is loyalty to party symbols an isolated phenomenon or is it associated with the expansion of public involvement in other respects? Almond and Verba have written of the need for "open and moderate partisanship."[7] For India it is necessary also to ask if partisanship is informed, aware, interest-related, system-supportive, and combined with a sense of personal political efficacy. In other countries as well as India, if such linkages with partisan loyalty are present to a marked degree we have the basis for an "effective" and "enduring" participant polity; if such linkages are not formed, partisanship may be irrelevant for mass participation or may have a transitory meaning for political life. The style and basis of partisanship in a society is a central question in understanding its political behavior.

If we look at available evidence on citizen orientations in the United States, Britain, and India we see some interesting variations in the pattern of citizen involvement (table 11.3). India is inclined to be low compared to "Western" countries in level of interest in politics and very low (in 1967) in citizen sense of political efficacy. However, on certain measures (such as awareness of party differences or attitudes about the role of parties and elections in making government responsive), Indian citizens give a greater indication of attitudinal support or optimism. On balance, it is certainly true that on key dimensions Indian citizens are less positively oriented toward participation, but this is not uniformly true on all dimensions and the gap with "Western" citizens is not very great in any case. Yet, probably no more than 10 to 12 percent of Indians appear to see politics as a salient interest for them, with perhaps another 20 percent displaying some feelings of awareness. This may leave 60 to 70 percent rather uninterested, and not engaged with politics.[8]

Keeping these comparative differences and similarities in mind, we return to our basic question, Is party identification linked with greater citizen attitudinal involvement with the system? As table 11.4 reveals, there is some evidence that party identification is associated with greater political interest (particularly interest in the campaign) as well as political awareness (at least one central aspect of political awareness in India, the political preferences of caste leaders and members). The strong identifiers are the most interested citizens, while the nonidentifiers have the least interest and awareness. The "independents," however, or those supporting (identifying with) independent candidates are not the lowest in political interest and awareness, almost matching the strong identifiers on the latter measure. As to knowledge of candidates, the nonidentifiers do quite well at both the national and state assembly level while the "independent" supporters do poorly in their knowledge of national parliamentary candidates. We will return to these findings for nonidentifiers and independents later. Here we note merely that party identification is somewhat inclined to be linked to greater political interest and awareness, but not demonstrably so insofar as information about candidates is concerned.

An interesting comparison is possible between the Indian and American data in the linkage between campaign interest and party identification (table 11.5). The level of interest is higher for all identification categories in the United States, but in both countries strong identification is associated with

TABLE 11.3 Comparative Percentages of Citizen Orientations: India, United States, England, Netherlands

	India	United States	Britain	Netherlands
Interest in the campaign— "very much"	12	30	31	21
General political interest— "great deal"	11		16	10
Differences between the parties—"good deal of difference"	29	21	42	
Sense of political efficacy Politics too complicated (for me)—disagree	9	28		34
People like me don't have any say—disagree	21	66		40
Officials don't care what people like me think— disagree	13	62		34
Parties make government pay attention to the people— "a good deal"	29		19	
Elections make government pay attention to the people—"a good deal"	41		42	

SOURCE: Indian data came from the 1967 study; American data from the 1956 or 1952 studies of the SRC; British data from the 1966 study. For the Dutch data we relied on Robert J. Mokken's "Dutch-American Comparisons of the Sense of Political Efficacy," a paper presented at the Institute for Social Research, University of Michigan, 1969. See also *De Nederlandse Kiezer '71* (Meppel, Netherlands: Boom, 1972) reporting the results of the 1971 national study, for data on the Dutch voter.

greater interest in the campaign. The contrast in the United States is not as sharp, however, because weak identifiers and independents have a relatively high proportion of interested persons—80 percent for strong identifiers and 65 percent for weak identifiers; in India it is 42 percent and 27 percent. Further, those "very much interested" are not likely to be found among weak identifiers and nonidentifiers. Here the contrast is great—only 7 percent of the weak identifiers are "very much interested" in the campaign, which is only one-third of those "very much interested" among the strong identifiers (20 percent). It is significant again, however, to find that the same percentage (20 percent) of the independents in India are "very much interested" in the campaign. While strong party identification, therefore, converges with relatively high political interest, strong support for independent candidates also seems to be associated with the same level of

TABLE 11.4 Supportive Orientations for Party Identification:
Information, Interest, Awareness

	Strong Identifiers (%)	Weak Identifiers (%)	Non-identifiers (%)	Independents (%)
Candidate knowledge*				
Knows 2 or more parliamentary candidates	42	35	41	19
Knows 2 or more state assembly candidates	74	70	70	75
Interest in politics				
Interested in campaign	42	27	20	31
General interest in politics	42	37	21	28
Politically aware of caste				
Very aware	41 ⎱74	30 ⎱64	20 ⎱52	63 ⎱70
Moderately aware	33 ⎰	34 ⎰	32 ⎰	17 ⎰
N	960	328	379	46

* The "don't knows" and "not ascertained" responses, which constitute about 20 percent of the sample, have been eliminated from this table.

TABLE 11.5 Comparative Data on Levels of Political Interest for Party Identifiers: India and the United States*

	India		United States		N	
Political Campaign Interest	% Very Much Interested	Total % Interested	% Very Much Interested	Total % Interested	India	United States
Strong identifiers	20	42	42	80	847	624
Weak identifiers	7	27	23	65	279	651
Nonidentifiers	5	20	...	...	321	...
Independent	20	31	25	68	46	415

SOURCE: United States, 1956 election (*The American Voter*, p. 144); India, 1967 national study.
* Each percentage is to be read as a proportion of an identifier category who has a given level of interest.

campaign interest.

So far, then, we see some limited evidence that Indians identifying with parties are also more "effective citizens." But the nonlinkage of other citizen political orientations with party identification, based on 1967 data, raises questions as to whether partisanship in India is actually rooted in and

142

linked to affirmative orientations to the political system and to political action. Analysis based on the 1971 data, presented in the concluding chapter, reveals a stronger association.

We constructed four indexes for our 1967 data to help code Indians as to their (1) sense of political efficacy; (2) and (3) supportive attitudes toward parties and elections; and (4) "modern" as contrasted to "traditional" political predispositions. Our analysis reveals that in 1967 party identification strength did not necessarily link with these political orientations as one might expect. Thus strong identifiers are no more efficacious in their feelings about political action than weak identifiers or nonidentifiers (about 11 percent in each category have a high sense of efficacy), nor are they more "modern" (the "independents" actually are more modern on our measure—81 percent compared to 70 percent for identifiers), nor are they basically more supportive of the party and election system. One would expect party identifiers to have a high sense of efficacy, or vice versa, but virtually no evidence exists of such a relationship in 1967. In 1971 identifiers had a much greater sense of efficacy than nonidentifiers (see chap. 19).

The picture of the Indian electorate which emerges from this analysis is that in 1967 there still was much nonconvergence of orientations or a weak perspectivist infrastructure as the basis for party identification. Almost 40 percent of our respondents were strong identifiers with a low sense of political efficacy, and only 7 percent were strong identifiers with a high sense of efficacy. This nonconvergence of identification with efficacy is a key element and problem, no doubt, in the development of the Indian system. It is a phenomenon which can be demonstrated by looking at other citizen orientations. These nonconvergent attitude patterns also exist, however, in Western societies, and certainly are to be expected in India. Our concern is more with the nonlinkage of supportive orientations to party identification and perhaps our data are most useful in revealing the marginality on the basis of the 1967 data of the attitudinal support for a meaningful Indian partisanship. There are signs of linkage of partisan loyalty to effective attitudinal involvement with the system, but the signs in 1967 were not yet convincing. In 1971, as indicated in our final chapter, they are more convincing.

It is important to note here that there often are considerable differences by party in the attitudinal orientations of party identifiers (table 11.6). This suggests that it is not identification per se which does or does not associate with other perspectives, but the type of party one identifies with and the political and social context and norms within that party, which appear to be linked to citizen orientations. Thus while 87 percent of Swatantra strong identifiers were low on political efficacy, and 80 percent of Jan Sangh were also, the Communists were more optimistic (only 59 percent were pes-

143

TABLE 11.6 Wide Differences by Parties in the Attitudes of Strong Party Identifiers
(% of Strong Identifiers in Each Group Who Have a Particular Attitude)

Attitude	Con-gress	CPI	JS	SW	Soc	DMK	Norm for Strong Identifiers
High interest in the campaign	19	27	19	10	16	45	20
High political aware-ness of caste	40	29	44	31	56	16	41
"Modern" on political predispositions	71	54	71	77	78	42	70
Low on political efficacy index	66	59	80	87	75	17	67
Critical of the role of parties	24	29	18	40	21	16	25

simists) and the DMK were astoundingly confident of being efficacious in political action (only 17 percent were pessimists). Similarly there was twice as much negativism about the party system among Swatantra strong identifiers (40 percent) as in Jan Sangh or DMK (18 percent and 16 percent). Peculiarly, the Socialists seemed much more politically aware of caste voting (56 percent), as were Jan Sangh (44 percent), not as peculiarly, compared to the low level of such awareness among Communists (29 percent) and the DMK (16 percent). No doubt the differential party clienteles have a great deal to do with the differences on this measure.

Let us attempt a recapitulation of the above findings. One should not be prematurely critical of Indian political development as tested here by an analysis of the linkage between party identification and political orientations. First, because there is virtually no comparative data for other countries suggesting that this level of attitudinal involvement and its linkage to party identification is low in India. Indeed, one might suspect that even in comparison with some Western systems India would rank high in certain respects. Second, except for the measure "sense of political efficacy" these are findings suggesting a significant degree of political development in India. Political interest is rather low but political awareness is moderately strong, acceptance of the party system is actually high, knowledge of candidates is high at the state assembly level and moderate for the Lok Sabha, "modern" psychopolitical predispositions are surprisingly high. True, strong identifiers do not necessarily have these attitudinal orientations more than weak identifiers, although there is a slight tendency in that direction. Perhaps at this stage of the public's involvement with partisanship and political participation in India this is a very acceptable state of affairs. At a later stage, perhaps there will be both strong party identification and identification linked to public interest, more knowledge, personal efficacy, and optimism about the party system. There were already signs in 1971 that this was the case.

The Linkage of Party Identification and Other Political Behaviors

The facts about Indian political *behavior,* as distinguished from political attitudes and orientations, attest more strikingly to the viability and meaning of party identification. The data on leadership contact, first, show that nonidentifiers have limited personal contact with any elites (caste, party, or government) while identifiers (with party or with independent candidates) are much more in elite contact. This is so when respondents are asked specific questions about certain categories of leaders or when they are asked who are important people in their village or locality, and then whether they have "dealings" with them. Less than 10 percent of the nonidentifiers are personally in touch with local leaders, whereas from 15 to 22 percent of the identifiers are in such contact. There is only a slight difference for strong and weak identifiers. It is particularly interesting that the supporters of independent candidates are also closely in touch with the leadership structure, over 20 percent having a "great deal" of personal contact with community influentials.

Participation in campaign activities also reveals that there is a connection between identification with a party (or an independent candidate) and the person's behavior. We asked our respondents detailed questions about their campaign involvement with respect to canvassing, helping voters to the polling stations, raising money, organizing election meetings, joining processions and demonstrations, distributing polling cards or party literature. Slightly over 11 percent engaged in one or more of these activities. The strong party identifiers and those identifying with independents had the best record of participation. Only 2 percent of the nonidentifiers were active at all, contrasted to 17 percent of the strong identifiers. It is also interesting to note that potentially strong identifiers were more inclined to be active in the parties in the future. When asked if they would consider joining a party, 15 percent of the strong identifiers said they would, compared to 7 percent of the weak identifiers, and 5 percent of the nonidentifiers.

Consistency in voting is also linked to party identification, more strongly in fact than our previous behavioral measures. The strong identifiers had a high record of participation—only 6 percent never voting or voting only once—compared to the nonidentifiers, 20 percent of whom never voted or voted only once. In this analysis we find that the supporters of independents participate less than either party identification group (table 11.7).

145

TABLE 11.7 Voting Turnout and Party Identification*

Voting Record	% Strong Identifiers	% Weak Identifiers	% Non- identifiers	% Identify with Independent Candidates
Voted in all 3 elections	75	65	55	61
Voted in 2 of 3 elections	19	28	25	29
Voted in one election	5	6	15	10
Never voted	1	1	5	0
N	490	164	211	21

* This table is computed only for those eligible to vote in the three elections of 1957, 1962, and 1967.

We constructed a "political involvement index" based on party membership, campaign activity, and voting, and looked at the variations in involvement by identification. Although the differences are not striking, they again confirm the observation that strong identification is associated with more, and different types of, political activity. Whereas 19 percent of the strong identifiers not only voted regularly but were active as members or in the campaign, this was true of only 11 percent of the weak identifiers and 2 percent of the nonidentifiers. The supporters of independent candidates were rather involved, 14 percent being regular voters *and* campaign activists.

Compared to the United States, for which we have similar, if not exactly equivalent data reported in connection with the 1952 study, we find results which deviate somewhat, although the direction of the differences are also somewhat confirming[9] (table 11.8). On the one hand the strong identifiers are also those with the best participation record, but the American nonidentifiers or "independents" were not those with the worst record. While 27 percent of the nonidentifiers were highly involved by the American index, only 22 percent of the weak identifiers were highly involved. There is no monotonic decline, therefore, in amount of involvement in the United States as there is in India.[10] However, in both countries strong identification is more strongly associated with high political involvement. The proportion of strong identifiers who are very active is double in the United States—35 percent compared to 17 percent. But the relationship is similar. Above all these data suggest that the political development process in India is one which finds the public including citizens who both identify with the parties and are at the same time more likely to take an active political

TABLE 11.8 United States and India Compared: Party Identification and Political Involvement*

	% Voting & Other Participation		N	
	United States	India	United States	India
Strong identifiers	35	17	586	960
Weak identifiers	22	6	624	327
Nonidentifiers	27	2	365	378

* "Participation" in the U.S. study included campaign contributions, attending meetings or rallies, and work for the parties and candidates, as well as voting in 1952; the Indian measure was virtually identical, including voting in the 1967 election.

participant role. In this respect India and the United States show parallel behavioral patterns.

One can finally pose two basic questions to summarize our observations: (1) To what extent are Indians both *knowledgeable* about politics *and also active participants* in the system? (2) To what extent is this true of party identifiers? If we look at the knowledge our respondents (eligible to vote in the last three elections) had about the candidates for office in 1967 and then look at their participation record we find the following: 18 percent strong identifiers were very knowledgeable and involved in politics; for weak identifiers it is 8 percent; for nonidentifiers 1 percent; for those identifying with independents 14 percent. (An additional 40 percent of the sample had "some" knowledge and "some" involvement; 29 percent for those identifying with independents.)

Clearly, party identification shows some linkage to meaningful participation at election time. The basis for relevant citizen involvement exists for close to 50 percent of the Indian electorate, and particularly for strong identifiers. While one must surely hope for further development for the Indian public of more supportive and efficacious orientations toward politics, the evidence we already have indicates that the public is developing considerable interest, awareness, and information about politics and that this is associated with the developing loyalties of Indians to political parties. In this sense, effective democracy has been emerging in India.

The Independent "Partisan": "Floating Voter" Hypotheses

India is one of the few countries where the number of independent candidates for the national Parliament and state assembly seats is large and where the public's identification with these nonparty candidates, while small proportionately, is durable. The number of independent candidates for the Lok Sabha almost doubled from 1962 to 1967 (from 480 to 829), and the number winning seats more than doubled (from 20 to 43).[11] The number of candidacies at the state assembly level remained over 5,000 in 1967, of which 371 were elected.

Supporters of the independent candidates are an interesting category in India. We isolated those in our sample who identified with these independent candidates and compared them to those who were nonidentifiers, to see what the data reveal about their political involvement and orientations (table 11.9). The evidence is clear that those citizens loyal to independents are consistently distinguishable from nonidentifiers. Supporters of independents are reasonably well involved, interested, and exposed to politics, and they are more likely to have "modern" orientations toward the system than nonidentifiers. Where they differ, quite predictably, is in their support for the party-elections system and in their personal feelings about being effective within that system. Only 14 percent of the "independents" feel parties are necessary *and* help make the government responsive to the needs of the people, while 35 percent of the nonidentifiers hold this belief (and 37 percent of strong identifiers). As to efficacy, "independents" are very pessimistic—82 percent score zero on our sense of efficacy scale (compared to 65 percent of the nonidentifiers). It appears then that supporters of independents in India are relatively highly involved, but unusually skeptical about the efficacy of that involvement.

TABLE 11.9 The Special Character of the Independent Identifiers

Profile Characteristic	Identify with Independent Candidates (%)	Nonidentifiers with Party or Candidates (%)
High campaign exposure	26	16
Knowledge of candidates at state assembly level	91	82
Interested in politics generally	28	23
Interested in 1967 campaign	31	20
"Modern" orientations toward authority and nation	81	63
Consistently supportive of parties	14	35
Consistently supportive of elections	23	52
Scores high on efficacy scale	2	10
N	59	361

Discussions concerning the characteristics and role of the "floating voter" have focused on (1) the extent of his genuine, meaningful involvement with the system, (2) whether the extent of his exposure is linked to his inconstancy in party affiliation behavior, and (3) his role in election outcomes.[12] Interpretation of the meaning of our Indian data for these controversies may be instructive.

The first question is whether "the stronger the individual's sense of attachment to one of the parties, the greater his psychological involvement in political affairs."[13] This observation about American political behavior does not hold consistently in India, as our previous analysis revealed. One must refrain, therefore, from concluding that there is a "syndrome" of the effective partisan who is attached to a party and at the same time more likely to exhibit the characteristics associated with strong partisanship in the United States. The strong partisan in India will probably be more interested, more exposed to parties and political leadership, and more active in campaigns, but he will not necessarily be more knowledgeable, more supportive of the system, more "modern" in psychological involvement, or more optimistic about his chances of influence within the system.

A comparison of those in our survey who were "constant party voters" and those who were "switchers" in the 1962 and 1967 elections reenforces these findings. Here are a few of these comparisons:

	% Constant Party Voters 1962–67 (N=632)	% Switchers 1962–67 (N=277)
High campaign interest	19	12
Care about election outcome	48	42
Scored high on political efficacy index	13	12
Scored high on issue and problem awareness index	9	17
Know two or more parliamentary candidates	44	52
Know two or more state assembly candidates	72	77
Know parliamentary contest winner	94	93

The conclusions for these data are inescapable. We have already seen that the supporters of independent candidates have a relatively high degree of involvement. We see also that "party switchers" are more knowledgeable and only slightly less concerned or interested in politics than constant party voters. Finally, our comparison of strong and weak identifiers reveals important differences in level of political interest, exposure, voting behavior, and campaign activism, while revealing no significant differences on other involvement measures. This evidence strongly points, therefore, to a different pattern of partisanship in India in 1967, one which embraces the existence of independents, switchers, and weak party identifiers who may in many respects be as involved as strong partisans and constant party voters, and in some respects may exceed them in their psychological involvement with politics.

On the other two controversies concerning the "floating voter," the Indian evidence is easily summarized. The classic theory concerning exposure and party constancy is confirmed for India by our previous analysis, both for data on party identification and voting consistency 1962–67. The relationship is not a perfect one since at the middle exposure levels there is very little variation in either strength of party identification or constant party voting. Yet the differences at the extremes are striking—33 percent difference in strong party identification between those not exposed and those highly exposed, and 21 percent difference in constant party voting 1962–67. Apparently a slight exposure to party produces a sizable increment in strong identification (from 42 to 57 percent), but then it takes a multiplication of many stimuli and influences to increase this to the 75 percent level. Constancy in party commitment and support is enhanced by much exposure to politics, and not by low exposure, at least at this stage of political development in India.

The role of the body of voters who do not identify with parties can be calculated in various ways. First, the supporters of independents constitute about 3 percent of our sample, which seems negligible, but these supporters in 1967 sent forty-three members to the national Parliament (over 8 percent of that body). The "nonidentifiers" constitute approximately 24 percent of the sample (of those in our study who were ascertainable on identification) (table 11.10). The weak identifiers make up 18 percent of the sample. The voting participation record of those not committed to parties was high—over 70 percent (according to the recall of our respondents). Thus, the Indian electorate consists of a sizable proportion of mobilizable nonparty participants. As table 11.10 reveals, only 53 percent are strong identifiers who vote regularly, 17 percent are weak identifiers who vote regularly, and 21 percent are nonparty, noncommitted, or independent supporters who vote regularly.[14] Thus there is room for great movement and change within the electorate. Of our total 1967 sample, 12 percent were defectors from Congress (they had supported Congress in 1962) and 3 percent were defectors from non-Congress parties, for a total of 15 percent. Seven percent were dropouts (nonvoters in 1967). The proportion of the Indian electorate which is inconstant in party support from one election to the next approaches one-fourth, almost half of the proportion of those who do not identify strongly with a party. The "defec-

150

TABLE 11.10 Distribution of Indian Electorate: Party Identification, Voting Record, and Activism*

	Strong Identifiers (%)	Weak Identifiers (%)	Non-identifiers (%)	Identify with Independents (%)	Total (%)
Active and vote regularly	11	2	†	†	14
Vote regularly	42	15	19	2	77
Vote irregularly	3	1	4	†	7
Do not vote	†	†	1	0	2
					100

* This is based on a sample of 878 respondents who were eligible to vote in the elections of 1957, 1962, and 1967.
† Too few cases for even 1 percent.

tion'' in 1967 of party supporters who split their vote between one party for the Lok Sabha and another party for the state assembly was at a similar level—27 percent. While the potential for a ''floating vote,'' therefore, is high in terms of strong or weak party identification (over 40 percent), the actual movement of voters from party to party is closer to 25 percent.

In 1967, the party preferences of respondents who did not identify with a party were distributed over the party spectrum. Approximately a third voted for Congress, 36 percent voted for opposition parties, close to 20 percent did not vote, and about 10 percent backed independent candidates. The vote for these opposition parties by the uncommitted was rather dispersed—4 percent Swatantra, 8 percent Jan Sangh, 7 percent Communists, 6 percent Socialists. Thus, although Congress received only three out of ten votes from the ''floaters,'' probably a decline from Congress support in the past, no particular opposition party benefited primarily in 1967. The Right and the Left as well as independent candidates profited fairly equally from this uncommitted vote.

One cannot ignore the ''floating vote'' in India, or rather the theoretical and practical possibility that those uncommitted to the party system, or weakly committed, are yet considerably interested in elections, rather well informed, and participant in predisposition, and that they can decide elections for or against Congress. But the problem of mobilization and concentration of this body of ''floaters'' is difficult. In 1967 the effort was considerable, but because of the dispersion of the opposition and the basic loyalty of Congress identifiers, Congress's losses, while serious, were not catastrophic. And in 1971 Congress again scored an overwhelming success. The role of the floaters seemed to have been inconsequential, though only subsequent analysis can confirm this. Nevertheless, as Kothari warns in 1971, the threat is always there:

> Actually, despite a firm base of the Congress in the electorate in terms of party commitment as well as the existence of a sizeable proportion of voters committed to opposition parties, there is still a large section of "floating vote" in the Indian electoral system ... the point that the opposition vote is based on less positive commitment to the parties voted for, than is the case with Congress voters, has also an obverse to it which the Congress organisers need to grasp: the opposition is better able to mobilise the floaters than is the Congress party.... Here is a large mass of potential supporters whose actual vote in the next election will depend on (1) the image that the rival parties project, (2) the ability of their electoral organisation to mobilise these voters, and (3) the degree of voter turnout.... In an election which is likely to be pitched to the demand for a clear mandate for the Prime Minister and her party on the one hand and an all-out offensive of the alliance parties against her, the behaviour of the "floaters" will perhaps turn out to be the chief deciding factor.[15]

A Few Summary Observations

The theoretical argument advanced here has emphasized the incremental reenforcement and "recycling" aspects of political development in a society like India. As Indian citizens become exposed to political parties, political leadership, and the campaign and election processes they are gradually "bound into" an interlocking system of new identifications (such as party loyalty), new images of the political system, new information about and interest in that system, supportive attitudes toward that system, feelings of efficacy about involvement in that system (although this doesn't really appear until 1971), and patterns of activism and behavior in that system (which in turn have feedback consequences for politicizing and mobilizing instruments such as political parties as well as for political elite behavior). In India it has been argued here that parties play a major role in these new political acculturation and mobilization sequences and that party identification and commitment thus become focal aspects of the development process (see fig. 8). Party identification is associated positively with the "learning" of a whole new set of systemic images and orientations. One cannot say that party identification is a causal agent but rather that it is part of a new political configuration in the cognitions of citizens of a developing polity. The political change that takes place then is a complex pattern of interrelated and associated small changes in loyalties, values, attitudes, beliefs, and behaviors. And while this is "change," it also

152

FIG. 8. Configuration diagram of linkages of party identification to Indian political development.

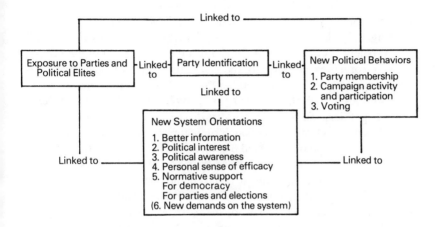

produces "stability" over time for the system. This at least has been the theory we have been working with in the analysis presented here.

To a certain extent our data support this set of theoretical propositions. We have found a gratifyingly large proportion of the Indian public exposed to parties and the leadership in the political system—50 percent have some exposure and 25 percent have a great deal of such exposure. Further, such exposure seems clearly linked to the emergence of party identifications, strong and weak, by the Indian citizens. Seventy percent are identifiers, 51 percent strong identifiers; above all, at least 75 percent of those highly exposed to parties and political elites are strong identifiers, one of the most significant findings in our study. Further, we find a strong linkage of party identification to participation in the political system—party membership (both present membership and willingness to join in the future), campaign participation, and voting consistency. It seems clear that party identification, together with exposure to parties, is relevant in India to mass behavioral involvement with the system.

Our findings in 1967 are less conclusive, however, as to the linkage of party identification to attitudes and orientations, cognitive and normative, to the political system. We can observe three different types of relationships. First, there does appear to be some linkage between party identification and extent of political interest. Strong identifiers are twice as interested in the campaign and in politics generally as nonidentifiers. There also seems to be a relationship between strong identification and political awareness. The linkage of identification with "modern" orientations to authority and on the question of loyalty to central government versus the locality is much weaker, however. And the same weak association is found for other attitudes in 1967. This prompts a second observation—that party identification is unrelated to knowledge of candidates because there was an amazingly high level of information which pervaded all levels and sections of the society. For example, we found that over 70 percent of our sample knew two or more candidates for the state assembly. Party identification as a phenomenon may be less important for the high informational level.

This brings us to the lack of linkage of party identification to the citizen's sense of political efficacy. Strong identifiers scored no higher than weak identifiers or nonidentifiers (although supporters of independent candidates scored lowest). In 1967 we found that the overwhelming majority (close to 70 percent) of the Indian public was pessimistic about the possibility that they might have influence over, or be taken into consideration by, decision makers. The interesting finding is that party identification is apparently unrelated, is virtually irrelevant to, the existence of personal feelings of efficacy. In 1971 much more relevance can be demonstrated. Above all, party identification is linked to increased voting participation and campaign involvement. Thus, strong identifiers, and identifiers in general, are more behaviorally involved but have no greater sense of the personal efficacy of this involvement than nonidentifiers.

One can become quite disturbed about this or view it with equanimity, as part of the evolution of mature and effective citizen activity in a democracy. A negative interpretation would join with Edward Shils' view of the consequences of a traditional, hierarchically structured culture for a society like India when it moves toward participant democracy:

> The chief effect of the hierarchical structure of authority, in both the traditional and the modern sectors of society, is to generate either excessive submissiveness among the ordinary people, or an extremist egalitarianism by way of reaction against it. Insofar as the people are used to living in a hierarchical traditional society, they have little conception of their rights as citizens. *Although they can be brought to vote in elections, they do not feel that their preferences will be considered in the decisions of their rulers;* and above all they are little inclined, unless there has been a great break in tradition, to speak out their own views and preferences on the largest questions of policy.[16] (italics supplied)

There can be no doubt that Indian voters are identifiers who participate but are pessimists about their role in the system. Perhaps this is the natural result of their lack of prior socialization to politics and their newness to the system, as well as the congruence of having a one-party dominant system in India and their previous "learned pessimism" in dealing with that system. It by no means vitiates the meaningfulness of their involvement with that system, as our data dramatically demonstrate has been occurring. Indeed, in the face of such personal pessimism and frustration about politics, the Indian citizen's emerging partisan loyalties, interest in politics, knowledge about candidates, and willingness to participate is gratifying. Perhaps it is the real evidence that development is occurring, a tribute to the capacity of the Indian democracy to massively change a political culture and to socialize its public to the acceptance of that new culture.

To interpret these data in the light of the 1975 developments is difficult. One may argue that the weak association between party identification and certain attitudes and predispositions will now, with an "interruption" in democracy, become even weaker. Or one may argue that the development of strong identification which showed considerable stability and penetration and behavioral consequences, despite pessimism about one's role in the system, attests to the probable durability of citizen partisan loyalties. When democracy resumes in India, the impact of the crisis on the depth of commitment to parties will in a sense be a key test of the democratic politicization of the Indians from 1947 to 1975.

Part Four

POLITICAL INVOLVEMENT IN INDIA
IN COMPARATIVE PERSPECTIVE

TWELVE

Theoretical and Conceptual Approaches:
The Functions of "Involvement"

T HE INVOLVEMENT OF THE INDIAN MASSES IN POLITICS IS A RECENT, dramatic, and sustained phenomenon of great significance for modern democracies. It has much more than political relevance, narrowly conceived. It has supported and undergirded the new political institutions of this large nation. It has occurred during a period of remarkable social and economic change. It is an involvement which embraces and transforms the total society. At the same time it reflects and conserves the uniqueness of Indian culture. It is an involvement by "traditionals" who are "moderns" while they remain "traditional."

The Indian citizen for over twenty-five years has been the object of a massive political socialization and mobilization effort seeking to persuade him to become an actor in the political system. Since 1947 he has been instructed in politics, exhorted to participate in politics, and importuned for his support. And this effort has been nothing short of remarkable. Over 150 million Indians have come to the polling places. Over 20 million have taken on party campaign work. More than twice that number appear at political rallies, meet candidates, and contact governmental leaders on personal and political matters. This image of mass mobilization to politics in such a short span is almost incomprehensible, but it is reality. It is unique Indian reality and must be understood in the context of Indian society, culture, and politics. What has this massive political involvement of Indians done for the system? What is its meaning for the Indian citizen as newly involved, politicized citizen? What is its relevance for elite performance? These are the critical questions which take priority over all others in the analysis and interpretation of mass involvement of Indian citizens in their political society.

Among students of Indian politics there is no more important and recurrent concern than the extent and meaning of public participation in politics. For certain scholars, indeed, this is a critical test of the success of Indian political development. Gopal Krishna has stated this very clearly: "The contemporary democratic political system in India has at its centre the system of free elections based on adult franchise."[1] He argued that at least three basic assumptions or interests motivated the founders of the Indian Republic and those in power after Independence: "legitimate authority

159

rests on popular consent,'' competition is the best means of ensuring the "beneficial exercise of power,'' and "democracy represented ... an aspiration for a more open egalitarian society."[2] For all of these, widespread citizen participation was focal in his opinion. This feeling (that the electoral system, electoral politics, and the public's involvement with politics constituted the heart of the democratic order) has been echoed by many writers both in India and abroad.

As recently as 1968 Edward Shils concluded that India was not yet a "political society'' because most of the preconditions for such a society had not been met. Among these was the following precondition: "A degree of interest in public affairs sufficient to impel most adults to participate in elections and to follow in a very general way what is going on in the country as a whole, with a reasonable and temperate judgment of the quality of the candidates and the issues."[3] Applying this to India he observed, "It is only the personal qualities of the Indian elite which compensate for the fact that India is not yet a political society."[4] Although other scholars are not as negative in their assessment of the success of participant democracy, certainly there is general agreement that meaningful political involvement by Indian citizens is central to an evaluation of the Indian system and its progress since Independence.

System-Theoretical Concerns

If we sort out the specific theoretical interests and arguments of those writers emphasizing various aspects of political participation, the reasons for the concern become more apparent. One recurring theme is the integrative-functional role of political involvement. Rajni Kothari has been particularly preoccupied in his writing with the problem of building consensus and the achievement of political integration. "Elections,'' he theorizes, "not only determine the nature of the party system under which the deliberative, competitive and representational elements of the polity function and change. They also give rise to a convergence of values, styles, and behaviours of different levels of the political structure, lead to integrative or divergent outcomes, and determine the strength and content of political consensus."[5] Along with this theme is his emphasis on political mobilization and the "penetration-response'' image of the development process, with the party system as "the operative core of a framework of consensus,'' establishing links with the social infrastructure, mobilizing support, and "aggregating interests and cleavages."[6]

A second major theme in this writing is the importance of participation for the functioning of political institutions, particularly the special "competitive dominant'' Indian party system and the parliamentary representative system. The public's involvement with politics has been crucial for making this party system truly competitive, both within Congress party and in its relationship with opposition parties. The emergence of a meaningful mass-elite reciprocal interaction system, slow in arriving, is dependent on public participation in the periodic selection of leaders, the use of electoral reprisal against elites, and the development of leadership accountability to the public.

Along with this concern is a third basic interest—the ideological and pragmatic objective of achieving a more egalitarian society. Gopal Krishna writes that the electoral system was conceived of as a way of "loosening the rigid hierarchical structure of status and power in the traditional social order." Further, he asserts that "the struggle for power through elections has proved to be a force for bringing about major social changes and re-alignments of social groups and . . . a redistribution of power in society, giving the once oppressed communities for the first time a measure of effective influence in public affairs."[7] Kothari also writes of the relevance of parties and elections, and the participation of people through these channels, for the rise of new social groups to power and the "social displacement" of others. He notes that social strains and tensions have occurred in India during the political development process. The social base of the polity has been expanded as a result of participation through political mobilization and socialization, and new groups have begun to be involved. But this has also brought alienation and sometimes deliberate exclusion of formerly participant groups and individuals under the logic of a changeover "from movement to party" or "from elite politics to mass politics." The earlier "homogeneous urbanised and 'westernised' elite" has been broken up, modified, displaced, and reformed into a different type of coalition based on a new network of social relationships.[8] On the impact of this concerning caste he argues that this penetration "downwards" of electoral and developmental politics "has led to momentous changes in the hierarchy of influence and status in Indian society." Particularly he feels that it is leading to the drastic modification of "the closed system of loyalties," that it has broken down caste solidarity in political action and altered the manner in which caste is related to party politics.[9]

In systemic-functional terms, then, scholarly reflections on the meaning of electoral participation and the public's involvement in politics in India has emphasized at least three major theoretical areas of interest. It is argued that public involvement is (1) central to the achievement of political integration, legitimizing authority and building national consensus; (2) central to the articulation of a democratic mass-elite relationship, to developing a more responsible leadership, and the effective functioning of the "competitive dominant" party system; and, (3) central to the redistribution of the political power of social groups, to altering the hierarchy of influence, to achieving more social equality, and presumably therefore to more "beneficial policy" related to social change.

161

If we operationalize these highly generalized concerns, we can specify particular theoretical objectives in the study of mass involvement. One can look at such activity as relevant for four levels of analysis—the individual citizen (how does participation fulfill his needs), the group (how does participation enhance its status), the political process (how does participation affect the working of the legislature), and the system (how is the goal of legitimacy or integration achieved). We are interested in all these levels and questions, but the focus of our investigation is (1) on what mass involvement behavior tells us about the Indian citizen's engagement with the political system and its institutions, and (2) what is the meaning and relevance of this for understanding the development of the Indian system. In the process of probing these questions we hope to shed some light on other matters, such as who among the public is most involved and has influence, what factors or conditions are conducive to political participation, and what are the probable consequences of political activity for elite behavior.

Studies of political participation are usually concerned with similar initial inquiries—who is involved, types and styles of participation, "determinants' and "conditions" for involvement, and the association of participation with basic political attitudes and orientations. But studies differ sharply in their theoretical goals, in the basic dependent phenomena to which they wish to relate these data. These theoretical concerns can be diverse, as seen below:

Mass Political Participation Studies

Common Descriptive- Analytic Concerns	Different Theoretical Levels of Concern
1. Who is active?	A. For the individual "Self-interest" "Influence" "Politicization," etc.
2. In what ways?	
3. Because of what social and economic factors?	B. For the group "Cohesion" "Status" "Equality," etc.
4. Conditioned or stimula- ted by what types of political environment?	C. For the processes of politics "Representation" "Interest articulation" "Elite responsive- ness," etc.
5. Linked to what norms, values, perceptions, and attitudes?	D. For the system "Legitimacy" "Integration" "Democracy" "Social transformation" "Development," etc.

There are indeed many significant uses to which participation analysis can be put, ranging from politicization of the individual and his influence to group interest, elite behavior, and system performance.

The thrust of our inquiry comprehends all four levels of analysis, but it is primarily concerned with the nature of individual political behavior and its relevance to system functions. We start with a desire to discover as much as we can about the ways in which the individual Indian citizen is "engaged with" or "involved in" his political system. We want to explore these types of involvement carefully, looking at the forces, factors, and environments which seem to lead him to this involvement. Above all, we are interested in the meaning of political participation for him, what it seems to mean for his cognitions and perceptions of the political order. At the other extreme we wish to generalize about the meaning of this mass political involvement of Indians for their society. At the system level we are interested in the levels of "effective citizenship" and the integrative consequences of this for the society. Yet, the great crisis in India is over social and economic policy, the difficulties in the achievement of an egalitarian society. We are therefore concerned with interpreting our data (rather inferentially, no doubt) with that theoretical interest in mind. In between the extremes of focusing on "the individual" and "the system" we advert from time to time to observations concerning the relevance of our data for the *social group* and for the *policy process,* particularly the possible consequences of mass participation in India for public policy, social conflict, and for the competitve party system. In the larger sense one cannot meaningfully study political participation without seeing its relationship to a variety of system processes and functions.

The Indian Cultural-Historical Context

The study of political participation in India presents special problems. One senses, if he or she has had any serious exposure to the Indian scene, that there may be great differences in the nature and role of political activity there, in contrast to Western societies. At the same time one is certain that there are basic uniformities. Particularly one senses that the societal context, and the historical and cultural environment, within which participation takes place must be incorporated carefully in any attempt to understand political involvement in India. This may well affect the definition of the phenomenon of participation itself. It will certainly affect the meaning of participation for citizen, elite, and system.

Thus while India and the United States may both have 10 percent or 12 percent who are politically active, the meaning of this in the context of the society's culture and development probably differs widely. As the Rudolphs, Edward Shils, and others have pointed out, one must remember that Indian culture originally emphasized "self-restraint," "nonviolence," respect for legitimate authority, avoidance of conflict and "groupism," a minimal or nonexistent role for the individual in political life, and overwhelming apathy.[10] With the Independence movement before and after 1947, India's new political elite, primarily within the Congress party, initiated the great democratic experiment, which Kothari has called the ongoing "structural crisis": the adult franchise, the "competitive-dominant" party system, "democratic decentralization," and the mobilization of public involvement. They were interested in the expansion of the polity to the illiterates, the deprived, the untouchables, the periphery, and in the process sought to mobilize public support for the programs for economic development and social change. The early period was a mobilist one; elite initiatives were communicated to the public, and support was generated for developmental goals, but within a "consensus system." The leadership style was not initially populist, and the public response was support-, not reprisal-, oriented. But this period produced internal strains and tensions throughout the society and system. Certain groups gained influence, other groups lost. The party system was in the flux of great change. Internal organizational tensions within the Congress party finally produced a schism in 1969. The role and strength of opposition parties increased considerably in certain areas. So within the party system and among the groups at its social base, great change has been occurring. The question is whether in this twenty-five years or more since Independence the role of the public and its participation in the political system has changed. How does it participate, for what reasons, and with what consequences for the system?

The essence of the matter is that the Indian public—uneducated and unread about politics, loyal to local groups and symbols, unsocialized to participate in the larger political system, indeed having no sense of personal efficacy in that system—was called on to be involved in the politics of the large society virtually overnight. This is the heart of the theoretical issue of political participation in India. As Gopal Krishna has put it, "Paradoxically, the process of modernization ... has ... accentuated certain forces of parochialism by requiring mass participation in the political process when the attitudes of most of the population have not been modernized. The elections in these circumstances have come to play a major educative and mediating role between the modern, modernising and traditional aspects of Indian society."[11]

It is in the light of the cultural norms, social conditions, historical experience, and the ongoing development of the Indian political system that one must try to understand the meaning of political involvement by Indian citizens today. It is not an easy task.[12]

Purposes of Our Study

We have several aims in the analysis of political involvement in India. They are connected to certain key theoretical questions about which there is some controversy among scholars and which we wish to explore with our data, keeping the Indian political and cultural context constantly in mind.

1. What is the extent of political involvement—has the norm of participation penetrated into all social groups, at the periphery as well as at the "center," or is political activity still remote for most Indians? How does the pattern of involvement in India compare with other nations, especially those in "the West"? Further, what is the potential for political involvement of the adult population; to what extent are the apathetic able to be mobilized? What seems to be the meaning of political involvement for social groups—particularly caste groups, educational sectors, and income or occupational categories?

2. Are the "newer" social groups on the periphery, who have been mobilized and who now participate, different in their demands, identifications, and expectations than the "older" social groups at the center? Does this (as Kothari observes) suggest a basic tension for the system? Has there been a concomitant withdrawal or displacement of "older groups" frustrated by these trends? Above all, is political participation in India a social group phenomenon?

3. How have Indian citizens been stimulated to participate, as the result of what pressures, forces, circumstances? Has the family begun to assume a socializing role? Are the political parties important as socializing agents and, above all, is the caste assuming a politicizing function?

4. What is the probable relevance of the patterns of participation in India to the political process, particularly for the (*a*) adoption of certain types of policies, (*b*) nature and quality of competitive relationships among the parties, and (*c*) support for governmental economic and social goals?

5. What is the probable relevance of the pattern of political participation in India to such large system characteristics as the achievement of system stability, political integration, system adaptability, and redistribution of social power and a more egalitarian society?

6. What has political participation done for the Indian as an individual? Has it changed perspectives toward society, replacing the old cultural norms of apathy, inefficacy, distrust of politics, with greater interest, knowledge, and a more optimistic view of the political world, and the citizen's role in it? Or does there seem to be very little difference in perspective and do the earlier basic orientations persist? Has participation played the role of educating and enlightening while mobilizing and involving Indians?

These six sets of questions constitute the context of our inquiry. Most of

165

these are too big for any single investigation to resolve, but on the other hand for most of them our data have some relevance and it is our hope to demonstrate what our data say which may shed some light on these central queries about the Indian system. Wherever possible we shall present the Indian findings comparatively so that some view of the performance of the Indian system in cross-national perspective can be obtained.

System comparisons are always difficult and utilizing survey data to generalize across nations about the incidence, style, and ways in which political involvement occurs is no exception. Comparative data must not be taken in an absolute sense because of the possibility of measurement error. Nevertheless we are presumably studying the same phenomenon in two or more societies, one of which is India—the phenomenon of the adult citizen's "engagement" with the political system. Although this phenomenon may not be operationalized and measured in exactly the same way, due to the special systemic restraints which require conceptual modifications, we are still generalizing about the same phenomenon for several countries. This has some value in the search for knowledge, even if one is primarily interested in "understanding" India. For comparative data leading to comparative generalization may indeed tell us how unique India is (or how nonunique), what patterns of political involvement in relation to social groups set India apart from "the West" (if any), and, if India's development thus far appears special, what India's pattern of mass behavior in politics may become in the future, based on our knowledge of the factors associated with mass involvement in politics in other countries. Finally, comparative analysis may reveal the relevance (or irrelevance) of certain political environmental factors—systemic or subsystemic—for explaining political behavior.

Our primary focus here is not to identify the characteristics of the "ideal" participant citizen. Obviously from our analysis one can secure ample information concerning the background of those Indinas involved with politics, their attitudes and their assumptions, and their orientations toward the polity. Our interest is, however, not to derive a "syndrome" of the Indian activist, but to investigate the variety of ways Indians are involved, the conditions under which this has occurred, and the probable consequences of this for the citizen and the system.

Previous studies have begun to deal with some of these questions. Gopal Krishna's article in 1967, which used aggregate analysis to deal with the integration of peripheral groups and regions classified by developmental status, caste or tribal reserved constituencies, and minority religion (Muslims) raised some significant questions.[13] Bashirrudin Ahmed's analysis of the 1967 data in his 1971 article examines the different types of political activity in India, their interrelationships, and the pattern of political stratification of the Indian society which these data suggest.[14] Subsequently, using data from four Indian states, Verba et al. did a comparative analysis with the United States, Nigeria, Austria, and Japan to demonstrate the noncumulative patterns of participation and to test in a very preliminary way a social mobilization model for the explanation of activism.[15] We have now made a beginning, through these pioneer efforts, at understanding the extent to which the public votes and engages in other types of participant behaviors. It remains for us to move beyond this description of the *extent* of participation to the crucial queries concerning the *meaning* of participation for the Indian system.

The Conceptualization of "Involvement" or "Participation"

Political participation studies are inclined to use a narrow definition of the phenomenon. Thus Lester Milbrath emphasizes behavior "which affects or is intended to affect the decisional outcomes of government."[16] And Verba and Nie, in their studies of participation, are preoccupied with the conception as including only "activities by private citizens that are more or less directly aimed at influencing the selection of governmental personnel and/or the actions they take."[17] This emphasis on purposive, instrumental behavior relevant to public policy making or decisions as being at the heart of the meaning of political participation or involvement may be satisfactory for the United States or "the West," but as Verba and Nie themselves suggest it may not be adequate for all societies.[18] There is much "participation" and "involvement" which is not explicitly instrumental, as Milbrath has pointed out.[19] In India particularly, but in other countries as well, the public's participation may be "passive" as well as "expressive," demonstrating general support or opposition, or merely demonstrating interest and attention to politics without seeking to, or expecting to, influence decisions, at least not specific decisional outcomes.[20] Sometimes individuals are involved for information-gathering purposes, or for sharing experiences with others in a political context, or for communicating a need for help or for advice, and sometimes it may be a ritualistic, though meaningful, type of involvement. Further, although certain types of activities may appear on the surface from a "Western" perspective, as designed to influence the personnel of government and/or their decisions, it is quite conceivable that the activity, such as getting out the vote on election day or distributing campaign literature, may be not purposeful in that sense at all. It would seem that for India the public's involvement can be quite varied and probably very meaningful for determining the nature and function of the system, even though not purposefully linked to decisional outcomes. Looked at from only one of several possible perspectives, at least eight levels and contexts of involvement can be comprehended:

1. Acts or expressions of allegiance or nonallegiance for the system or the regime and its political institutions.

2. Voting, in the Schumpeterian sense of participating in the selection of political leaders.

3. Information-seeking and knowledge-acquiring behavior, exposure to politics, and "paying attention" to politics.

4. Leadership contacts for a variety of purposes—help on a personal problem, maintenance of a personal social relationship, or a desire to influence a governmental action.

5. Mass protests and demonstrations aimed at opposing or supporting governmental leadership or decisions.

6. Acts of associating with others in a social-political context which may or may not be designed to influence governmental personnel or policy.

7. Campaign participation which may result from many types of motivations. This participation may be concerned with decisional outcomes, or relevant to procuring immediate support for party and/or candidate(s).

8. Potential participation, or an indication of a willingness or readiness to be involved under certain conditions in the future.

In the study of political involvement of the public in a developing democracy like India, one cannot ignore any of these forms of "participation." They are all very relevant to understanding the role of the public, actual and potential, in the political order. And they all may have significant consequences for the functioning of that order.

The Plan for Analysis

Our major focus in the presentation here is the meaning of the public's political involvement for Indian society. What are the implications of the various types of activities and ways of participating politically for the development and functioning of Indian democracy? Is the Indian society not a "political society" as Edward Shils contended in 1968, or has it become one in certain respects but not in others? In what respects is there progress and in what respects not? In addressing ourselves to these fundamental theoretical concerns, we shall follow a very straightforward sequence for presenting our data. First, we shall discuss the various types of political involvement in India, as other scholars have done, comparing the evidence for India with that for other countries. This will provide us in aggregate and gross terms with a general picture of the extent of political activity in India. Next, since the pattern of participation for different social groups and sectors seems critical for "theories" of the meaning of Indian participation, we shall ask the questions "Who is participating in what ways?" and "Who is not involved politically?" The social character and base of the participant polity should then become apparent to us, as well as the extent to which certain social groups have been "displaced" or have withdrawn or are persistently apathetic. In the next two chapters we examine the linkage between political involvement and the political attitude structure of Indian society, on the one hand, and the conditions of political exposure and socialization—the political environmental role—on the other hand. In chapters 15 and 16 we address ourselves to such questions as (1) Have the older cultural norms, militating against personal involvement in politics, persisted or disappeared? (2) Has exposure to the "modern" electoral and party institutions and processes become important in explaining increased political involvement? We then turn to an assessment of the probable consequences of participation. In chapters 17 and 18, we present data relevant to four questions: the meaning of participation for the individual citizen, for the role of social groups in the system, for the functioning of the party and leadership system, and the probable consequence of participation for the achievement of system goals. The scheme of this presentation is shown in figure 9.

FIG. 9. A design for analysis of political participation.

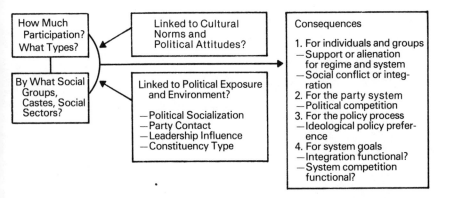

We will then attempt to emphasize the conditions under which Indians become participants, the social group context of their participation, the environmental conditions linked to their participation, and the probable relevance and impact of participation on their own lives, that of their social groups, and political life in their society. We are less interested in demonstrating the impact of participation on specific policy outcomes than other studies and more concerned with discussing the meaning of participation for the development of Indian democracy. This, it will be noticed, affects

169

the way we conceptualize the phenomenon "participation," the type of analysis we engage in, particularly our emphasis on the social group context of participation, and the use of our data to explore the basic functional theoretical problems we have posed as the essence of our inquiry.

THIRTEEN·

The Extent of the Indian Citizen's Engagement with the Political Process

E XCEPT AT ELECTIONS," WRITES EDWARD SHILS ABOUT THE NEW states, ". . . the countryside leads a slumbering political exis-tence." "Citizenship is not among the virtues" which traditional societies "prize."[1] This corresponds closely to the view of David Butler and Donald Stokes about the state of the British public's involvement. They comment on "the remote and marginal nature of politics for the British voter . . . " except "in rare moments of social and political upheaval."[2] And in *The American Voter,* Angus Campbell and his colleagues have a similar con-clusion: "For most Americans, voting is the sole act of participation in politics."[3] The summaries by Lester Milbrath and Sidney Verba and his associates are phrased similarly: "Few, if any, types of political activity beyond the act of voting are performed by more than a third of the Ameri-can citizenry."[4]

Despite such low estimates of the extent of public involvement in poli-tics in both "modern" and "developing" states, paradoxically there is considerable preoccupation with the study of this subject. It is widely felt that the extent and manner of the public's involvement is a key test of the democratic character of the system, and is central to democratic theory. Put another way, we are interested in the performance of the political system and feel that the extent and pattern of the public's participation can be related to the system's performance, both in the narrow sense of the deci-sional outcomes from that system, and in the much broader sense of the nature of the political process and the achievement of certain functional goals for the system, such as "integration," "stability," and "democ-racy."

The Operationalization of Involvement Behavior

If we are to concentrate our attention on this question of the public's involvement, and do so in a useful cross-national context, it is necessary to develop a broad approach to the phenomenon. Two important considera-tions must be kept in mind. There are a variety of *ways* in which citizens can manifest a meaningful "engagement" with a political system, many of them not overt acts of "influence." And there are a great variety of *motivational orientations* which underlie a citizen's "engagement" with

171

the political system. As many scholars have demonstrated, the frequency of types of participatory activities can range from 70 or 80 percent who vote, to 30 percent who discuss politics with others, to 1 percent who hold political office. Yet one must be careful not to presume that one type of activity is more meaningful "engagement" in the political process than another. This depends on the individual and the culture he or she resides in. Thus, distributing party literature or attending a political meeting may be no more, or less, meaningful as a measure of a citizen's involvement than voting, or keeping informed on politics via the media, or joining a political procession. It is deceiving, on the one hand, to accept voting as the true test of involvement or, on the other hand, to limit oneself to actions related to directly "influencing governmental decisions."[5] There are many other ways in which citizens are "engaged with" or "involved with" their political system, and such narrow approaches limit the study of the role of the public in that system.

The second consideration concerns motivations for public involvement. It is a very dubious procedure to assume that a particular type of activity in the political sphere is necessarily related to a specific purpose attributed to it by the investigator. Attending a political meeting may in no way be motivated by a desire to "influence governmental decisions," nor objectively need it be instrumental to that end. And if there is anything that our research on the motivations of political activists has revealed it is that one can by no means generalize that the activist is motivated by a desire to influence governmental decisions. Indeed, most activists are involved for quite other reasons, whether for personal careerist ambitions or social gratification or from a general philosophical sense of civic obligation.[6] To isolate, therefore, one set of public activities in politics and argue that these are the most essential because they are linked to, and motivated by, desires to influence political decisions is both empirically unsound and leaves out much of the important meaning of the public's "engagement" with the political order. Indeed, in a country like India, if one would operationalize participation in "decisional influence" terms, subjectively, most citizens and most participatory acts would not qualify. As Shils observes, in such societies, "insofar as the people are used to living in a hierarchical traditional society . . . they do not feel that their preferences will be considered in the decisions of their rulers."[7] Decision-making impact is not their involvement referent.

In essence, one must recognize that citizens engage in a great variety of activities and for a great variety of purposes. If one is interested in discovering and analyzing the extent and manner of the public's relationship with that political system, one should not limit oneself to specific acts or attribute particular motivations or probable outcomes to such citizen acts.

One may leave out, by concentrating on a narrow group of activists (say, 10 percent or even one-third of the public), large numbers of citizens who are "engaged with" the system, but not as operationalized "activists." Or, the relationship of individuals to the polity may be only narrowly conceptualized, as "decisional influentials," while leaving out other, equally important, aspects of their involvement. In the study of Indian participation a broad perspective is necessary if we are to assess the extent and meaning of the public's role in their system.

If we look at the variety of ways in which Indians manifest their engagement with the political system, we could order them, or list them, in many different ways making many different distinctions: electoral and nonelectoral; in a local context, or state or national context; in a social group interactional setting or individually initiated; passive or active; expressive versus instrumental; and so on.[8] In our analysis we find these distinctions suggestive but not precisely applicable. Rather, we see *eight* basic ways in which the ordinary citizen relates to the political system and then we identify *three* basic objects toward which this behavior is relevant. We ask whether the individual's involvement is focused on or oriented to the *general political system as system,* or the *sociopolitical group structures* within the system, or *the system's political leadership subsystem.* Figure 10 explains the relationships we would emphasize. In addition we are concerned with *potential* involvement as well as *actual* involvement, focusing on the possibility that citizens could be mobilized in the future for political activity.

We do not assume that these types of activities or involvements are "cumulative" or have a "hierarchy." Obviously most of those involved through voting will have manifested some affiliation or identification with the system, such as party identification, but not necessarily and not always clearly. And those who campaign for leadership at election time are usually voters. This is not the key "pattern" concern we have, however. Rather than assume that these activities are probably interrelated, we take a different posture toward the problem. We see the citizen acting within the system and relating to it (or not) and seeking to comprehend the meaning of his or her behavior in systemic or subsystemic terms. This behavior has consequences for the system as well as for the individual. Citizens engage in varieties of discrete types of behaviors focused in different ways and toward different parts of that system. We feel it is extremely important for us in our study of Indian political behavior to discover the "pattern" and "meaning" of the citizen's involvement in the sense of determining to what extent and in what ways citizens are "engaged" with the (political) system (knowledgeable about it, psychologically identifying with it, supporting it or protesting against it), with the political group infrastructure of

Fig. 10. A model of political involvement types relevant to India.

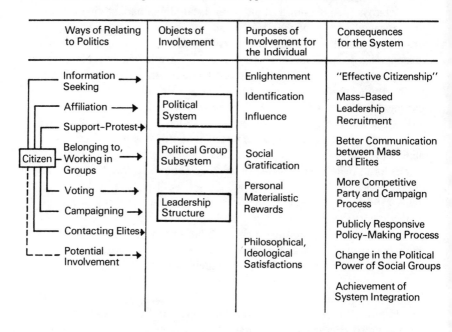

Ways of Relating to Politics	Objects of Involvement	Purposes of Involvement for the Individual	Consequences for the System
Information Seeking		Enlightenment	"Effective Citizenship"
Affiliation	Political System	Identification	Mass-Based Leadership Recruitment
Support-Protest		Influence	
Belonging to, Working in Groups	Political Group Subsystem	Social Gratification	Better Communication between Mass and Elites
Voting		Personal Materialistic Rewards	More Competitive Party and Campaign Process
Campaigning	Leadership Structure		
Contacting Elites			Publicly Responsive Policy-Making Process
Potential Involvement		Philosophical, Ideological Satisfactions	Change in the Political Power of Social Groups
			Achievement of System Integration

(Citizen)

that system (joining political parties or other groups, associating actively with others in a political group context), or with the leadership sector of the society (selecting leaders, mobilizing support for leaders, contacting leaders).

This approach, then, is designed to tell us how general systemic, or group subsystemic, or leadership subsystemic the citizen's activity orientation is. Obviously, one can interpret political involvement behavior differently—for example, affiliation behavior may be interpreted as either affiliation with the system, the party (or other group), or specific leadership or leadership cliques or aggregations. Mass demonstrations are interpretable as opposing the system, certain groups within it, or certain leadership. These alternative interpretations require careful analysis. The basic question we pose, however, is clear, How involved is the Indian citizen with his political system and the political groups and leadership structures within it?

A Comparison of Involvement Types for India and the West

The general comparison between India and other countries is afforded by table 13.1, where we take eight types of involvement with the system and present our 1967 data for India, in some cases supplemented by the data from the Verba study even though this was not a national study. (In our conclusion to this book we present the same data for India for 1971.) It becomes readily apparent that Indian involvement is relatively high when compared to that in the United States and England. The one striking difference is in following politics in the mass media. In 1967 only 34 percent of our Indian sample were media followers (that is, exposed at all via radio or newspaper), while U.S. and British citizens were allegedly exposed at over the 90 percent level.[9] Indians also were significantly lower in levels of political interest, generally and in the campaign specifically. Slightly more than one-tenth had high campaign interest compared to about one-third in the "Western" countries. On the other hand it is interesting to see that the Indian elector is more likely to engage in mass participative behavior, such as going to election rallies and political meetings, and is slightly more likely to meet candidates. Further, 43 percent of our Indian sample indicated to us they had "dealings" or associations with persons influential in their villages and local communities. This seems comparatively high, though no equivalent data are available for other countries. It suggests that, despite limited exposure to newspapers and radio, many Indian citizens pay attention to politics, are informed about politics, and are exposed to politics through other channels and media, in some cases exceeding citizens in the "West." Despite attending more meetings, and being in contact with local leaders to a greater extent, however, there can be no doubt that 50 percent or more of the Indian public is not involved with politics regularly through communication media and other channels.

Indians rank comparatively high on certain types of involvement. They identify with political parties to the same extent as in the United States and almost as much as Britain. In 1967 they had a strikingly high proportion of strong identifiers. This tendency has been analyzed in detail in another section of this study. Further, the level of political knowledge or information of Indians is equal to that in the "West," despite less exposure to the mass media. We used a simple test of information level, the ability to identify the representatives from the local area in the national legislature or Parliament. The British proportion is highest, but the Indian percentage of 50 percent exceeds that for the United States. (It increases to 60 percent for identification of state assembly representative.)

Belonging to political parties and engaging in other social interactional behavior in politics is at relatively the same level as elsewhere: 25 percent of our Indian sample had worked for a political party, and 8 percent belonged to a party—rather significant evidence of involvement. Indian voting turnout may be slightly lower, although in comparison with the U.S. national election turnout of 54 percent in 1972 India comes off well.

TABLE 13.1 A Comparison of the Frequency of Political Involvement in India, the United States, and the United Kingdom

Types of Involvement	India Men (%) 1967	United States		Britain	
		Total Sample (%)	Men (%)	Total Sample (%)	Men (%)
Allegiant					
Party identification	70	76	(72)	90	(89)
Strong party identification	51	37	(36)	32	(36)
Attentitive					
Follow politics in mass media	34	91	(94)	92	
Met political candidates	26	16	(22)	35	
Interested in politics considerably	11	32	(39)	16	(24)
Interested in campaign considerably	12	30	(34)	34	
Knowledgeable about politics	50	40		51	
Mass participative					
Attend political rallies, meetings	25	7	(8.5)	8	(11)
Join protests, demonstrations	5	...		...	

Social group associative					
Belong to political parties, clubs	8	3	(3.6)	12	(16)
Ever worked for a party	25	26		17	
Work with community groups	18	32		...	
Voting					
In national election	78	72		77	
In local elections	42	47		43	
Electoral campaign					
Active in specific campaign	12	3–5		3	(4)
Gave money in a campaign	21	10	(11)	...	
Elite contact					
Party leaders	9	21		6	
Government leaders	20	17		...	
Potential involvement					
Would join a party	10			...	
Would contact party leaders	25			...	
Would contact government leaders	32			...	

SOURCE: See note 10 for the sources for table 13.1.

In various forms of campaign activity Indian citizens are involved at levels probably greater than the "West." Almost 12 percent were active in the 1967 campaign, with 9 percent reporting some campaign canvassing effort, 6 percent involved in organizing meetings and rallies, 7 percent involved in the campaign through associations and groups, and 7 percent distributing literature.[11] These percentages are higher than those found in studies of political activity in the United States or Britain. The parties and candidates obviously have been able to mobilize large numbers of citizens as workers at election campaign time. Campaigns are exciting, with workers participating enthusiastically in a wide variety of vote-mobilizing efforts, and in certain areas observers of campaign activity have noted the thoroughness and efficiency of Indian campaign organization and strategies as implemented by local leaders and workers.

One form of involvement that many Indians spend time on is contacting governmental and political leaders. Verba distinguishes here between those contacts which are to get help for personal needs from those which are motivated by a "social referent." He suggests that three-fourths of the Indian contacts are personalized, while only one-third of the U.S. contacts are. Whether this distinction is valid in these terms is open to argument. There is no question, however, as to the relative magnitude of elite contact efforts in India. According to our national study, up to a fifth of Indian citizens have contacted officials or party leaders, and another 25 to 30 percent indicate that they would make such efforts to contact elites if the occasion arose, if they needed help, or if a problem existed which required elite attention. It is this "potential" involvement which is as interesting as the actual involvement, and indicates the "mobilizability" of Indian citizens for political purposes, or in political contexts.

Parenthetically one might comment here that the proportions of political involvement used here should not be conceived of in absolutist terms. These proportions are derived from a sample survey where the margin of error must be kept in mind. Further, not all studies produce the same results. This is partly due to the particular time of the study but not altogether explicable in this way. Sometimes questions of phrasing occur as, for example, whether the British question of being "active in parties" is the same as "ever worked for a party." One should keep these conceptual and technical problems of equivalence in mind in using the data presented here. These are, frankly, only rough comparisons.

We use data for men in India throughout this analysis because our female sample was very small (some 300 cases) in 1967. The differences between men and women were indeed striking and suggest that on many of our measures few women are effectively involved.

	Men (%)	Women (%)
Party identifiers	74	64
Followed election in the newspaper	34	15
Met the candidates	26	10
Had an interest in the campaign	33	12
Knew a candidate for the Lok Sabha	59	31
Knew a candidate for state assembly	82	50
Attended election meeting (some or many)	26	6
Was a party member	7	1
Worked on the campaign	12	2

In some respects this looks like a "male political society." Women seem particularly underrepresented in party membership, campaign work, and attentive behavior (meeting candidates, attending meetings, and so on). Nevertheless 50 percent demonstrated the beginnings of knowledge about politics and 64 percent were identifiers. Given the status of women in the Indian system, this reveals considerable involvement with the democratic party process.

The Differential Magnitudes of Involvement Activities

Gradations in the extent of the Indian public's involvement in the political system are suggested by figure 11. Protest behavior is at the bottom of our list, with 5 percent of the public involved in 1967. Then follows a variety of party and campaign activities, with no more than 25 percent indicating involvement through parties. Attentive behavior is at the 26 to 34 percent level. Voting and party identification is found among much larger proportions of the population, reaching 70 percent. Although the location in such a graph of particular activities varies for the United States or Britain, the basic picture is very similar.[12]

Can we distinguish basic types of participation? Lester Milbrath long ago distinguished between the "spectators" and the "gladiators."[13] Others have used different language for distinguishing the patterns of involvement. Verba and his colleagues suggest four categories for those members of the public who do more than vote: "parochial" participants (who only contact leaders for personalized reasons), "communalists" (who work with others on local problems), "campaigners," and "com-

FIG. 11. Frequency of forms of public involvement in politics in India in 1967.

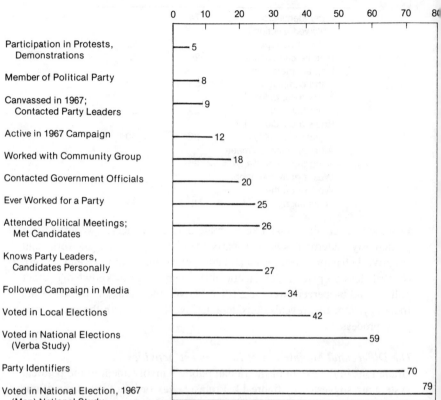

The following types of involvement were taken from the Verba et al. study based on four states only:Worked with community groups, Ever worked for a party, Voted in local elections, and the 59 percent national voting participation figure (Sidney Verba, Norman Nie, and Jae-On Kim, *The Modes of Democratic Participation* [Beverly Hills, Calif.: Sage Publications, 1971], p. 36). The other data are from our 1967 national study.

plete activists'' (who engage in a wide range of activities beyona voting). Ahmed, in stratifying the Indian electorate, sees two categories beyond those who only vote: ''auxiliaries'' (activists beyond voting who have a medium level of interest in politics and political knowledge), and ''politists'' (who are engaged in two or more types of political activity and have a high level of political interest and information). Depending on the focus of one's investigation, these are useful approaches. Ahmed's concern

180

is with activity level *and* political interest and information level. Verba's concern is with the direction and/or object of one's activity.

It is interesting to note that both approaches seek to identify at the extreme end of the continuum the participants who are the most involved. And it is striking that in their studies of political involvement in the United States and India how close they are in the magnitude of involvement. Ahmed found 47 percent in India participating in some activity beyond voting; Verba found 50 percent for the United States. Ahmed found a most activist group at 11.8 percent of the Indian population; Verba found 11.0 percent for the United States. If a summary comparison of the degree of political involvement is necessary, perhaps for the time being this would be most useful.[14]

An Image of Political Involvement for the Total Indian Community

A basic image of the Indian public's political involvement emerges from our data. Using all the types of involvement referred to so far (except party identification, which is analyzed separately), we can generate the distribution of table 13.2. We have first sorted out our population on the basis of an index of involvement emphasizing three types of activity: voting, party membership, and campaign activity. We then look at the distributions for each of these activity categories of other types of involvement. We note that those who seem to have no party or campaign involvement are often, nevertheless, attentive to politics in a variety of ways (24 percent follow politics in newspapers, 17 percent have met a candidate, 15 percent have a general interest in politics). About a fourth of those who might be considered "campaign apathetics" do have an involvement with the system. On the other hand, not all of those who vote regularly are attentive to politics. In fact only one-fourth of the regular voters are attentive, although another one-third seem to be fairly knowledgeable about the candidates. Even the most active persons in our sample, the 12.5 percent who participated in campaigns and/or were party members, were not all attentive to politics. One can derive a great variety of perceptions of the Indian public's engagement with the political order from table 13.2. There are "potential activists" among the apathetics, as well as quite a few "apathetics" who are fairly knowledgeable about the candidates and to a limited extent interested in politics. Above all, one does not get the impression that the great majority of Indian citizens are completely isolated from the system. In fact, quite the contrary.

We can represent this reality better by calculating proportions of the total population who are characterizable as at different levels of engagement with politics in India (table 13.3). This overall picture based on our 1967 data clearly reveals the different involvement sectors of the public. Several

TABLE 13.2 Patterns of Indian Political Involvement: Convergence of Campaign Activism, Political Attention, Political Knowledge, and Noncampaign Involvement*

	Index of Party, Campaign, and Voting Involvement (%)		
	No Activity, Nonvoting, or Irregular Voting	Nonactives, Vote Regularly	Actives Who Vote Regularly
Politically attentive			
Follow campaigns in newspapers	24	26	56
Met candidates	17	23	54
Personally knew party leaders, candidates	18	24	65
Aware of local groups, active in campaigns	16	19	35
Some or much interest in politics	15	27	64
Political knowledge			
Knew candidate for Parliament	30	42	64
Knew candidate for state assembly	39	60	82
Noncampaign involvement			
Received advice on voting from religious or caste leader	6	9	13
Received help from party leader	9	9	22
Belonged to religious caste groups	8	5	15
Would be willing to join a political party	4	7	13
N	105	787	127
% of national sample	10.3	77.3	12.5

* Voting in the 1957, 1962, and 1967 elections was used in constructing the index, and "actives" were those voting in two elections, active in some way in the campaign, and/or party members. Based on 1,019 respondents eligible to vote since 1957.

TABLE 13.3 An Aggregate Image of the Indian Public's Engagement with Politics*

	Nonactive in Party and Campaign Work, Nonvoters Usually (%)	Nonactive in Party and Campaign Work, Vote Regularly (%)	Party and Campaign Actives, Vote Regularly (%)	Total (%)
Not attentive to politics, no knowledge	6.3	30.9	2.3	39.5
Not attentive to politics, some knowledge	1.6	26.3	3.2	31.1
Attentive, no further exposure outside of party and campaign work, knowledgeable	1.6	13.1	5.1	19.8
Attentive, other exposure outside of party and campaign work, knowledgeable	.8	7.0	1.9	9.7
Total	10.3	77.3	12.5	100.1

* These data, one must be reminded again, are based only on the male sample. The overreporting of the vote turnout is high. As reported earlier, the "attention" measure used is *general* interest in politics and public affairs. The knowledgeable measure is based only on ability to name candidates for Parliament for the constituency respondent lives in.

observations stand out. Only 7 percent of the public are both active in campaigns and/or parties and are attentive to politics. Another 8 percent are not campaign actives but are involved in politics in other ways. Only 6 to 8 percent of the population are completely withdrawn from politics, inactive, and totally disinterested and uninformed. Over 30 percent of the population seem to be regular voters who are otherwise inactive *and* inattentive as well as ignorant of politics—the uninformed but participant sector. Almost 40 percent of the population seem to have a minimal knowledge of candidates. In sum, while our basic index of party and campaign activity suggests that only 12.5 percent were "actives," this is in fact a misleading characterization of the Indian public's involvement with the polity. The percentage is much larger, depending on the criteria used—27 percent are attentive voters, and to this might be added other voters who seem quite knowledgeable about politics. True, 33 percent are voting without being very knowledgeable about politics and over 5 percent are active in campaigns or parties without giving much evidence of being otherwise very attentive to politics. But the dimensions of involvement in all the various ways we have explored it are impressive. While one can be concerned about the low level of political attention (70 percent are not very attentive), and the fact that 33 percent of the population are apparently voting without much knowledge, one must be encouraged by both the high proportion who *are* knowledgeable about candidates (60 percent) and by the rather small proportion who are completely isolated from the system.

Political Involvement Typologies

If one is interested in typologies of involvement, our theoretical interests suggest that there are certain key groups one should focus on in the study of the public's behavior in the Indian system: (1) "The campaign and party actives," those who are highly involved and seek to work through party and electoral institutions. They are, however, not always well informed (12.5 percent). (2) The informed, politically interested, and attentive regular voters (20 percent). (3) The moderately informed but rather uninterested and unattentive voters (26 percent). (4) The ignorant and uninterested voters, a large group which somehow has been mobilized to vote despite no other evidence of genuine interest (31 percent). (5) The "inactives" or completely uninvolved, a small percent of whom, however, are reasonably informed (10 percent).

Then there are several special subgroups which cut across these basic types and which are interesting to study: (1) The "mass participative" citizens—especially those involved in protests, demonstrations, and so on (5 percent). (2) Those who belong to political parties and other political groups (8 percent). (3) Those who contacted party or governmental leaders directly for help or advice (9 percent party contacters, 20 percent government contacters). (4) Potential participants, who say they may join a party or contact leaders for help (from 10 percent potential party members to 30 percent who may ask elites for assistance).

Some of these groups parallel or cut across those identified by other students. Thus, Verba and his associates speak of the "communalists" who in the United States at least are "high in overall level of political activity" but who are preoccupied with "general communal goals" rather than with campaigns. These are individuals who presumably have a high level of attention to politics and information, as well as voting consistency, and they would then be found in several of our categories. The "parochial participants" which the Verba study identifies, who in the United States at least are limited in their involvement except for contacting leadership for personal interests, and who are low in "psychological involvement" with politics, would fall into our categories of minimally attentive "inactives." In an earlier study Bashiruddin Ahmed used categories parallel to the types used here. He also used level of information and interest by which to distinguish participant types. He referred to the "apathetics" as inactives who may vote but who have low interest and knowledge. Within this group (21 percent in his estimate then) are obviously individuals whom we have screened out on the basis of voting regularity and attention to politics. He used the terminology "auxiliaries" and "politists" for those at the highest levels of involvement, the "auxiliaries" being those actives with less interest and information. These are not the same but are obviously similar to the most active category of participants used here.

We are not addicted to labels. Our major concern is in the identification of key groups or types of citizen involvement in India as they are broadly conceived. We do not want to concentrate exclusively on those who are "most active," or most involved theoretically in influencing policy decisions, or most "psychologically involved" in politics. The characteristics, orientations, motivations, and roles of a variety of types of involved citizens concern us in this comparative analysis.

India and the United States: A Comparative Evaluation of Political Involvement, Interest, and Information

How does one evaluate this evidence of the *extent* of the Indian citizen's engagement with the political system? One approach is to look at these data in system-functional terms, which we do later in our analysis. Another approach is comparative, and the key question there is, What does this image of the Indian public look like when compared to that of other countries? No perfectly comparable aggregate distributional images are available, but certain approximations are possible in U.S. data. We attempt this in figure 12.

There are several ways to look at such comparative data. We have used Indian and U.S. data on voting participation and level of interest and information. We have then compared interest and information for the population, divided into voters and nonvoters.

Indian *nonvoters* are twice as likely to be uninterested in politics as in the United States, but are basically not less informed (figure 12). The difference is between 88 percent and 46 percent on interest level (or a difference of 42 percent), and only 6 percent difference on information level. Indian voters, however, are three times as likely to be uninterested, but again their information level is respectably close to that of the American voter. For voters the differential in interest level is 44 percent, but only 18 percent in informational level. Actually, if one asks the question differently—what percentage of Indian and American voters are highly

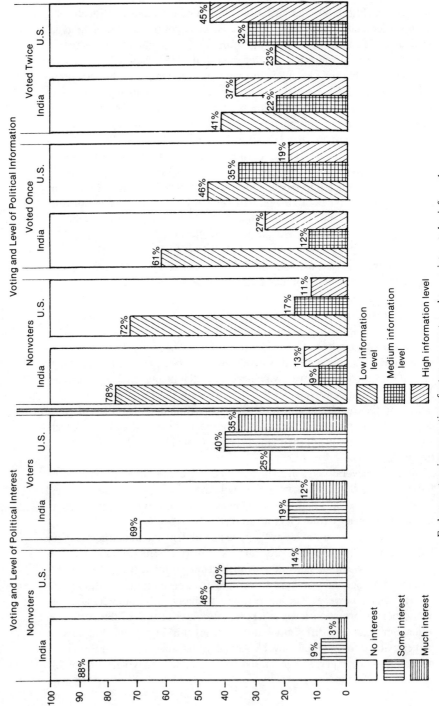

Fig. 12. Comparative public involvement images: two approximations for India and the United States.

Each percentage is a proportion of voters or nonvoters who were interested or informed.

informed—there is only an 8 percent difference for regular voters, 37 percent for India are highly informed and 45 percent for the United States. Thus, the low level of interested and informed involvement of nonvoters is the strikingly different picture for the two countries. But, among regular voters, while the Indians are much less interested in politics they are almost as well informed as American voters. This is the most significant comparison which probably can be made at this point.

On most tests of involvement the Indian public is remarkably similar to the United States and probably to other Western countries if comparable data were available. In two respects Indians are much lower in involvement—exposure to politics through the mass media and extent of expressed interest in politics.

Is it true that the Indian public is "slumbering," is overwhelmingly apathetic, is excluded from the "political dialogue" between elite and activist, is uninfluential in the political process? This is the argument that is generally advanced and the one quoted at the beginning of this chapter. The 1967 election study data support this observation only in part.

Over 50 percent of the Indian public consists of persons who not only vote but are fairly knowledgeable. True, only half of this 50 percent (or 28 percent of the population) are interested, by their own admission, in political affairs. But if one sticks to the requirement of voting accompanied by a basic minimal knowledge, the 50 percent plus in India stands up very well to the American percentage (53 percent). Actually, a larger proportion of the American sample consists of ignorant nonvoters than does that of India. Yet the level of political interest among nonvoters in the United States is higher (14 percent with much interest in United States, compared to 3 percent in India). If one applies other tests as to whether the Indian public is "slumbering," such as the proportion who are behaviorally engaged in some purposive way beyond voting, one of course finds usually less than one-third so involved: campaign work (12 percent), ever worked for a party (25 percent), contacted government leaders (20 percent).[15] But if this criterion is also applied to the United States, one finds most of *that* public "slumbering" also.

In aggregate, summary terms the Indian public's level of involvement is impressive. What is necessary now is to look at the level of involvement of the various social segments and groups in Indian society to see to what extent the peripheral, depressed, remote social sectors are engaged with politics and what the meaning of political participation and attention is for them.

FOURTEEN

The Social Basis and Relevance of Political Involvement in India

T HE POLITICAL BEHAVIOR OF SOCIAL GROUPS AND SECTORS IN INDIA IS central to the analysis of Indian development. In a society as diverse demographically and as structured socially as India is, the analysis of the political participation of social groups is important. It will tell us which groups or levels of the society, if any, are most active, and whether there is a hierarchy of political involvement. It will suggest what the role of such groups might be in political development. Above all, it will tell us whether social origin and status are at all important in explaining political activism as well as the nature of political conflict at the mass level.

One of the theoretical controversies to which such data are relevant is the "integration-diversity" issue in intellectual perspectives about Indian development. Do the data reveal that the system since 1947 has mobilized more and more social groups into participation, even those at the remote periphery of the society, integrating and assimilating them into the new political order? Or do the data reveal that social diversity and cleavage have continued and that the differential participation patterns reveal more conflict and segmentation than homogenity and aggregation—either because certain groups still have limited access and/or desire for involvement, or because the demands generated by the social penetration of the system have exacerbated the conflict among or within social groups? Perhaps this is the most basic and relevant query, comprehending other subordinate questions, which we must keep in mind in looking at the political involvement of social groups. As one scholar has remarked, the extreme social cleavages in the Indian subcontinent should have resulted in breakup of the Indian nation-state.[1] It is remarkable that, despite predictions to the contrary, India seems to be as politically integrated a nation as before (some would say more integrated), despite continuing if not deepening social and cultural-geographical diversity. Perhaps it is a special genius of the Indian system to accomplish political aggregation in the context of social segmentation, to bring peripheral groups into political life without undue conflict and to mobilize traditional groups for the new polity by involving them side by side with the urban, educated, "modernizing" social groups without such traditional groups losing their identities. At least this is one of the basic tenets of the theory of developmental strategy in India. As Rajni

Kothari contends, this "assimilative capacity" is the product of a "long history of incorporating all newcomers in the framework of Hindu civilization."[2] It is the *actuality* and *effect* of this assimilation, this political mobilization of social groups, which we seek to explore with these data.

The Extent of Involvement for Social Groups

The first fact we can establish from our data is that there were sharp disparities in political involvement in 1967 by social status. The contrast is particularly noticed when one looks at level of education (table 14.1). The illiterates are particularly isolated in comparison to all other education groups—in extent of political interest, knowledge about politics, and campaign activity. One must note, however, that the highest education levels are not necessarily the most politically involved on all measures. Those with middle or even primary schooling do better on campaign and party activity than those with a high school or college education (22 percent compared to 17 percent). It is the acquisition of *"any education,"* not *"much education,"* that makes a difference in India. The differences by caste status follow the same pattern, but not as dramatically, and the differences between political involvement for higher and lower castes and Harijans do not reveal a monotonic pattern. Thus a large proportion (13 to 14 percent) of middle castes and Harijans/Tribals demonstrate campaign and party activity while only 11 percent of the upper castes do. Thus, there are social status differences but not on all types of involvement, and not consistently in the expected direction. This is in contrast to the findings for the United States, where Verba and Nie found consistent and sharp differences by education level.[3] (See also the summary of the findings from *The Civic Culture* on the role of education,[4] and the conclusions by Milbrath.[5])

One must note here the relatively high involvement in the campaign and party process of lower castes and those with little education—this is the second fact of importance. Thus 8 percent of the Harijans and Tribals in our sample were party members and 11 percent of those with no more than primary school education had joined the party. This plus the evidence of the extent of "knowledgeable voting" for these groups—true for 30 to 44 percent of them—suggests that periphery groups are being mobilized and involved with the electoral process.

The differences for other social sectors also reveal the penetration of the involvement "ethic" widely in Indian society. The contrasts for income groups are again considerable, indeed the greatest for all categories when one looks at the proportions involved in campaign activities. There are three times as many activists among those with the highest incomes (24 percent compared to 8 percent). Yet 8 to 10 percent at the lowest economic

TABLE 14.1 Caste and Education Groups: Extent of Political Involvement*

	% Interested in Politics Generally	% Regular Voters and Knowledge-able about Politics	% Active beyond Voting	% Party Members	N
Education group					
High school completed and those who attended college	44	61	17	8	75
Middle schooling	43	54	22	12	158
Primary only	36	44	18	11	195
Illiterates	23	34	7	4	570
Caste groups					
Upper castes	36	54	11	6	298
Middle castes	28	43	14	7	168
Low castes	31	35	11	8	205
Harijans/Tribals	28	30	13	8	178

* This and the following two tables are based on those in our sample who were eligible to vote in the elections of 1957, 1962, and 1967. Involvement items were operationalized as follows: "interest" includes those "somewhat" or "very much" interested; "regular voters" includes those voting in all national elections; "knowledge about politics" was based on the ability to name two or more candidates standing in the constituency for Parliament (Lok Sabha); "active beyond voting" includes any kind of campaign activity or party membership.

levels are active, as are 13 percent of the nonfarm workers. The activists are not exclusively the urban, educated sectors of the population. Also, 18 percent of the Muslims are active, compared to 12 percent of the Hindus. It is interesting to note that the most residentially mobile persons—those moving from village to town or city— are both the most uninvolved (25 percent) and are relatively active (16 percent). While there are indeed differences in political participation by social status, what is outstanding in these data is the mobilization for political involvement of those we might consider least likely, and the latest in point of time, to become active—the very poor, the illiterate, the untouchable, the Muslim.

Contrasting Patterns of Involvement for High and Low Status Citizens
Although this mobilization has occurred, there remain extreme contrasts between upper and lower status groups, as shown in table 14.2. On one hand, there is very little difference in one form of "allegiant" involve-

TABLE 14.2 Special Types of Political Involvement for Contrasting Social Status Groups*

Attentive and Allegiant Behavior			
	% Identifying Strongly with Party	% Exposed to the Campaign	% Knowing the Candidates
Highest education	55	40	62
Illiterates	52	14	13
Upper castes	51	29	38
Harijans, Tribals	52	17	16
"White-collar" occupations	49	39	62
"Blue-collar" nonfarm workers	52	17	24
Farmers	53	19	20

Elite Contact Behavior		
	% Knowing Party, Religious, or Caste Leader(s) Personally	% Received Political Advice from Religious/ Caste Leader
Highest education	55	6
Illiterates	22	10
Upper castes	42	8
Harijans, Tribals	24	12
"White-collar" occupations	53	4
"Blue-collar" nonfarm workers	21	6
Farmers	31	11

* See notes to table 14.1. "Exposed to the campaign" refers to those in the highest two categories of our exposure index (based on campaign meetings, party canvassing, meeting candidates, receiving handbills).

ment, namely strong party identification, for these social groups. They are all fairly close to the 50 percent level. But data on campaign exposure show clearly that the highest educated, upper caste, white-collar respondents are more involved. They also are the most knowledgeable about candidates and are much more likely to know party, caste, and religious leaders personally. For example, over 50 percent of those with "white-collar" occupations and at the highest educational levels know political and caste/ religious leaders personally, but only 21 percent and 22 percent of the "blue-collar" workers and illiterates do. This is a sizable 32 percent gap, and attests to the great difference that still exists despite the mobilization of "the periphery." On one type of involvement, lower status groups are more active—they clearly are more frequent contacters of elites for help and advice.

The Overrepresentation and Underrepresentation of Social Groups
To summarize the overrepresentation or underrepresentation of these social sectors in political activity compared to their population proportions, we have used the same measure used by Verba and Nie.[6] The calculations used in table 14.3 are simple and clearly express the imbalances in the social composition of the activist population. On all measures the illiterates, who constituted 57 percent of the special sample we used for this analysis (those men whose activity was ascertained 1957 to 1967), were grossly underrepresented. For example they only constituted 25 percent of

TABLE 14.3 Overrepresentation and Underrepresentation of Social Groups in Types of Political Involvement*

		Index of Representation (%)				
Social Group	% of Our Sample	Campaign Exposure	Elite Contacts	Knowledge of Candidates	Campaign Activists	Party Members
Caste						
Upper castes	32	+34	+34	+37.5	−12.5	−19
Middle castes	18	− 6	−38	+27	+ 6	− 6
Low castes	22	−23	− 9	−32	−14	+ 9
Harijans, Tribals	19	−21	−26	−42	+ 5	+11
Muslims	9	0	+22	−11	+56	+33
Education						
High school/ college	23	+83	+70	+126	+61	+61
Middle-low	20	+ 5	+15	0	+40	+60
Illiterates	57	−37	−33	−53	−56	−46
Occupation						
White-collar— business	17	+76	+65	+129	+41	+41
Farmers and farm workers	64	−13	− 6	−30	−13	− 5
Nonfarm workers	19	−26	−37	−16	+ 5	−21

* See notes to tables 14.1 and 14.2 for operationalization of involvement variables, and note 6, chapter 14, for the formula for the computation of overrepresentation and underrepresentation.

the campaign activists in our study, netting a −56 score on our representation index. Similarly, the lower castes and those with farm occupations were inclined to be underrepresented, although not as seriously as the illiterates.

Lower status persons are not consistently underrepresented in all political involvement types, however. In this respect the Indian data may be unique. Among party members, for example, lower castes, Muslims, and middle education groups are actually overrepresented, and to a considerable extent. The same is so if one looks at the composition of campaign activists—Harijans, Tribals, and "blue-collar" workers exceed the proportions one would expect in terms of their proportions in the sample population. Again, therefore, the Indian case is not one of consistent, single-directional representation of upper status groups on all political involvement measures. There is strong evidence here that while illiterates are consistently underrepresented, lower castes and low status workers have been participating in certain ways beyond normal expectations.

Comparative Findings on Social Status and Political Involvement: India, the United States, and Norway

How do these findings for India compare with data for other countries? Verba and Nie assert without reservation what their U.S. data demonstrate: "Citizens of higher social and economic status participate more in politics."[7] While true that this has been confirmed "many times in many nations," one must recognize, as they implicitly do, alternative paths to participation in different systems. A 1960 study in Norway found that those with upper educational and occupational status did not necessarily reveal the highest levels of political activity and that instead social status differences in participation were linked to the type of party to which the individual affiliated. The basic proposition advanced was that educational level and occupational position "make less of a difference in the level of political activity in a class-distinct party system such as the Norwegian and more of a difference in a system of two socially and economically highly heterogeneous parties such as the American."[8]

A presentation of comparative data for the three countries—the United States, India, and Norway—is found in table 14.4. The United States is clearly distinct in the linkage of educational level to political activity. As educational level increases, the proportion of activists increases significantly from 10 to 25 percent. This is not so for either India or Norway, but these two societies also differ. The presence of a large body of illiterates with low political participation (7 percent) makes the Indian situation unique. But one notes also that those with a high school or college education are not the most active politically. In Norway, this is also true, those at

193

TABLE 14.4 Three-Nation Comparison of Educational Level and
Political Involvement*

	U.S. % Active	India % Active	Norway % Active
Educational level			
Highest	25	22	26
Middle-secondary	16	26	32
Primary-grade school	10	17	30
Illiterates	. . .	7	. . .
Occupational position			
"White-collar"	21	19	24
Manual worker-nonfarmer	11	17	22
Farmer	8	12	27

* Norwegian national sample of 1,406 in October 1957; U.S. sample of 1,772 in November 1956. Based on men only for all three countries. The political activity measure includes basically the same types of activities in all countries. The educational and occupational categories are as comparable as possible. Each percentage is a proportion of the educational and occupational group who were active.

lower educational levels being more active than the upper educational elite. Although use of these figures in absolute terms is unwarranted, it is striking to note that while only 10 percent of those with lower ''primary'' school education are active in the United States, 17 percent are in India and 30 percent are in Norway.

The Indian data on political activity by occupation are also basically different than the American. The gaps by occupational level are not great. This same pattern suggests that the relationship between SES and political involvement differs interestingly among countries, depending on other systemic conditions. In India the gaps by social stratification in political activity are not as great as in some Western societies.

The differences by age reveal that it was the generation who came to adulthood from 1947 to 1957, our age category ''thirty-one to forty,'' who sustained the greatest interest in political activity. That group was slightly more active than those who came to maturity just before 1967. The one exception to this pattern seems to be the Muslims, for the oldest category among them consists of rather involved citizens—24 percent active compared to 12 percent for other older adults. It is particularly in the middle and lower castes where one finds the immediate post-Independence adults revealing this involvement with politics—20 to 21 percent in these groups are active beyond voting. Among the middle caste youth who had just become eligible for voting in 1967, one also finds a high incidence of political involvement. But in all of these groups except the upper castes, it is the immediate post-Independence exposure to politics which seems linked to participation, suggesting that that period was one in which politics was most salient and the mobilization of the public most effective.

Proportionate Contributions of Low and High Status Persons to the Politically Active Cadre

Social profile data for different political involvement types in India dramatically demonstrate that it is not high status persons who constitute the bulk of the politically active. In table 14.5 we turn the analysis around and ask what proportions of the politically attentive "public" and the "campaign active" cadres come from upper and lower castes and from the different educational groups. Those with low or no education comprise a relatively high percent of the "attentives" (47 percent) and a majority of the actives (63 percent). And lower castes, while not as likely to be "attentive" as higher castes, have a respectable proportion among the campaign actives (39 percent). Perhaps this tells the more significant story for India—the heavy proportionate involvement of low status people in politics.

TABLE 14.5 Social Profiles of Campaign "Actives" and "Attentives"*

	% Campaign Actives	% Politically Attentive
Castes		
Upper	28	44
Middle	19	23
Low	19	15
Harijans/Tribals	20	11
Muslims	14	7
Education		
High school/college	10	21
Middle	27	32
Primary	28	20
Illiterates	35	27

* Based on those in the eligible electorate 1957–67, "actives" were those who were party members and/or took part in campaign work. "Attentives" here refers to those who knew two or more candidates for the Lok Sabha in their constituency.

The same basic finding emerges when we look at the social composition of other politically involved types (tables 14.6 and 14.7). Much of the mass demonstrating is obviously engaged in by those with little education, although the proportion of illiterates is low (9 percent). On the other hand, those involved in personal contacts with elites come overwhelmingly from the illiterate and lower educated sectors. And the parties can look to these

TABLE 14.6 Social Profiles of Politically Active Types in India: I*

	% Mass Protesters (N=94)	% Elite Contacters (N=387)	% Potential Activists (N=200)
Caste groups			
Upper castes	28	33	35
Middle castes	25	10	16
Low castes	16	22	20
Harijans/Tribals	11	17	15
Muslims	15	11	9
Others	6	7	6
Education groups			
College educated	7	8	5
High school completed	7	5	4
Middle	51	25	33
Primary	26	22	23
Illiterate	9	41	36

* "Mass protesters" refers to those who said that they did "join in any procession or demonstration." "Elite contacters" were those who went to or personally received political advice from party, governmental, or caste leaders; "potential activists" are those who said they would be willing to join a political party.

same sectors for future members. While political involvement by caste status seems more closely linked, low castes do constitute sizable proportions of mass-protesters (27 percent), elite contacters (39 percent), and potential activists (35 percent).

Perhaps what is most impressive is the realization that the peasant who has never left his village dominates the political activist cadres in India. This is impressive even though it is well known that India still is close to 80 percent rural (table 14.7). From two-thirds to four-fifths of these active participants are nonmobile villagers, attesting to the penetration of the participant "ethic" into the countryside. The occupational distributions underscore this also—48 to 68 percent of these activists are farmers and farm workers. The urban, white-collar, educated sectors of Indian society constitute a relatively small minority of the political activists, even though they participate proportionately more than their relative strength in the population.

A final comparison of the Indian with the American data is suggested by the analysis of Verba and Nie. They found that among those at the lowest participation levels, only 10 percent come from the highest third of the population on SES, while among those at the highest participation levels,

TABLE 14.7 Social Profiles of Politically Active Types in India: II*

	% Mass Protesters (N=94)	% Elite Contacters (N=387)	% Potential Activists (N=200)	% of Sample
Occupations				
White-collar, business, profes-sional, clerical	19	19	13	17
Farmers and farm workers	48	62	68	60
Nonfarm workers				
Skilled and semi-skilled	21.5	10	14	11
Unskilled	7.5	5	3	7
Unemployed	3	3	2	3
Age				
21–25	17	11	25	17
26–30	15	12	24	16
31–40	37	34	23	27
41–50	16	19	14	18
50+	15	25	14	21
Residential mobility				
Always in village	66	73	80	76
Always in town or city	26	19	14	15
Moved from village to town	6	6	6	7
Moved from town to village	3	1	1	1

* Since these are social profile data, each percentage is a proportion of the activist group.

57 percent came from the highest third of the population on SES. A rough comparison with India is provided if we use educational level as the mark of SES. The comparable Indian figures would be approximately 27 percent and 65 percent. Thus, the differences are in the same direction but not of the same magnitude. If we use caste as the indicator of social status, however, the findings are strikingly different (fig. 13).

The lowest caste groups (Harijans/Tribals) constitute an increasingly large proportion of the political participants as one moves along the scale from least to most involved. While 17 percent of Harijans and Tribals are completely inactive, 24 percent are party members. On the other hand, there is a decrease in the proportion of high castes as one moves along the involvement scale. Such data as these attest again to the ambivalent and

Fɪɢ. 13. Caste distributions by level of political involvement.

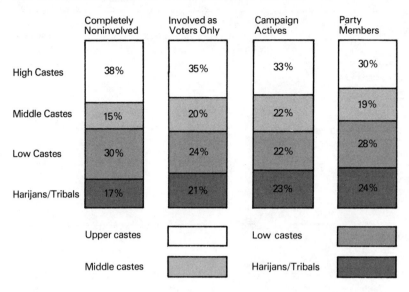

inconclusive relationship in India between social status and political involvement.

Social Status and Political Activity Linked Differently by Political Party
The failure of SES to be consistently linked to political involvement in India is partially attributable to differences among parties (table 14.8). In the left-wing "class-distinct" Communist party social status is not at all linked to political activity—42 percent of the manual workers who are Communist identifiers are active while only 21 percent of the white-collar Communist identifiers are active. This is true also for the Socialists (31 percent vs. 14 percent). And the Jan Sangh, which has a high proportion of low social status supporters, also reveals more political activity among those with only primary and middle education than those having high school or college education. This is the same type of finding discovered in Norway by Rokkan and Campbell. Their 1957 findings for Norwegian men were that 36 percent of those in the Socialist party with primary education were active, while only 21 percent of those with such education in non-Socialist parties were active. India and Norway, in part because of the characteristics of their party systems, thus differ significantly from the United States in the linkage of SES to political activity.

What is outstanding in these data about India is that there is not the sharp

TABLE 14.8 Socioeconomic Status and Political Involvement among Party Identifiers*

Party Identification	Illiterate (%)	Primary School (%)	Middle Schooling (%)	High School/ College (%)	Manual Worker (%)	White-Collar Occupations (%)
Congress	11	21	24	25	16	19
Swatantra	2	14	29	†	†	†
Jan Sangh	4	27	27	15	16	26
Communists	8	46	43	29	42	21
Socialists	6	28	33	†	31	14
DMK	27	33	79	†	57	†

* Each percentage is a proportion of those in each party of a certain educational level who were active beyond voting.
  † Too few cases for analysis.

social stratification in political involvement that one finds in other countries, especially the United States. True, the illiterates in India are inclined to be much less active generally, yet, they are the most active in contacting elites, and are proportionately high in receiving advice from party and caste leaders. They also are high in party identification (52 percent are strong identifiers). Above all, we should not forget that illiterates make up the largest proportion of campaign actives, understandable because of the sheer bulk of their numbers. They are underrepresented, but still are numerically strong among the politically involved. If this can be said for the illiterates, it is doubly true for the lower caste groups. They manifest as much political interest, campaign activity, party membership, and party identification as middle and high caste groups. They, too, are underrepresented among the activist group but not by as much as the illiterates.

John Kautsky has said that a democratic system is "a political system in which all or most significant groups in the population participate in the political process or, to say the same thing somewhat differently, in which all or most significant interests have access to effective representation in the process of making government decisions, i.e., of allocating scarce resources."[9] One certainly cannot equate participation with influence or with democracy, and this is only one test of a system. Nevertheless, despite disparities, there is evidence here that groups previously excluded were, prior to 1975, gradually securing some access to the representative process.

If one reflects on these data for social status and political involvement, one sees considerable evidence that the message and stimulus of political involvement has penetrated to the social extremities of Indian society. The lower caste, illiterate peasant who lives in the village of his birth demonstrates a remarkable level and diversity of political participation. While the wealthy, "white-collar," well-educated are overrepresented, they are not dominant numerically. There appear to be quite a few different types of social and economic environments within which such political socialization and mobilization has occurred. There is more "homogenization" than sharp cleavage in these data, and there is considerable evidence that India's leaders since Independence have indeed attracted those in the lower reaches of Indian society to involvement in the new polity. In Western theory, we have assumed that those with the highest social status participated to a greater extent because they had greater stakes in politics, more knowledge about politics, and thus greater motivation for political activity. In a society like the Indian, this is, in fact, not the case. Those at the lower status levels of Indian society are aware that politics is very meaningful to them and therefore they are involved more than one would have predicted on the basis of Western politics. Otherwise, it would be difficult to explain why 20 percent of the campaign actives are Harijans or "Tribals" and another 20 percent are from low castes. They obviously must see politics as very relevant to their lives; they must sense high stakes in political involvement for them; they must sense a feeling of confidence in their capacity to participate effectively in the Indian polity.

FIFTEEN·
The Normative and Attitudinal Basis for Political Involvement

T HE POLITICALLY ACTIVE SEGMENT OF A SOCIETY HAS A SET OF ORIEN-
tations, perceptions, beliefs, and attitudes distinguishing it from the
nonactive segment. at least this is the conclusion from a variety of studies
in the West, although not all studies arrive at the same findings.[1] What the
exact *direction* of this linkage is has not been closely established—whether
the attitudes predetermine political involvement, or the political activity
results in attitudinal change. Two different models of political life can be
employed.[2]

We start with the position of so many scholars that the traditional cultural environment, the attitudes about politics and the social system on
which most Indians for generations had been reared, predisposed Indian
citizens against political activity. As Edward Shils has put it: "Insofar as
the people are used to living in a hierarchical traditional society, they have
little conception of their rights as citizens. . . . the prevalent beliefs of most
traditional societies are almost exclusively characterized by the absence of
elements of civil politics."[3] Thus, put this way, the key empirical question
is whether Indian citizens with attitudes and beliefs which are the heritage
of their traditional system are less active politically than those whose
attitudes and beliefs have been changed, who have become less "traditional," if you will. We are interested then in the linkage between traditional
orientations, contrasted to nontraditional, and political involvement, in
looking at attitudes as a basis, as "leading to" involvement.

We also wish to look at our data using political activity as the "independent variable." We will do this in a later chapter, asking, What are the
attitudinal consequences of political involvement in India? Are the actives
inclined as a result of their involvement to become more interested in
politics, less alienated, less "traditional?" Both types of questions can be,
and must be, put to our data. In the absence of any clear indication of the
causal process involved here, we must investigate the evidence that Indian
citizens become attitudinally socialized as a result of their political involvement, as well as vice versa. In the analysis in this chapter we will
work with the assumption that attitudes are theoretically antecedent to
activity. In a later analysis we reverse this theoretical relationship.

"Traditional Norms" and Political Involvement

A basic question to begin with is whether Indians who espouse traditional norms and attitudes, presumably inhibiting their involvement with new political institutions and processes such as parties and elections, do indeed reveal an aversion to such "modern" types of political activity. Our data suggest that this is not the case (table 15.1). It depends, of course, on how "traditional" attitudes are defined. As examples of the problems faced in operationalizing "traditional" orientations, we can use two short-answer statements which might have been considered to be tests of this phenomenon. These two items on which our respondents were asked to express agreement or disagreement were (1) "We should be loyal to our own region first, and then to India." (2) "What this country needs more than all the laws and talk is a few determined and strong leaders." We soon found that we could not be sure that responses to these items could be construed as relevant to "traditionalism." Loyalty to a region, although initially appearing "parochial" in orientation, need not be an exclusively traditional view; neither need a desire for strong leaders be interpreted as traditional in the Indian context. Our findings here were very interesting (table 15.1). Those with the most parochial view (agreeing to statement 1) had one of the highest records of political involvement, if they also took a "nonauthoritarian" position (disagreement with statement 2). Twenty percent engaged in political activity beyond voting, the same proportion as the nonauthoritarian "centralists" (who disagreed with both statements 1 and 2). Though suggestive, as a test of traditionalism we could not rely heavily on these responses.

In a more convincing test we asked our respondents to place themselves on a seven-point "tradition-innovation" scale.[4] Almost 50 percent of our sample placed themselves at the "tradition" end of this scale, and they were fully as participative in politics as those who saw themselves as at the "new" or "innovative" end of the scale. Other indications generally support this basic finding. An exception, perhaps, are those most strongly opposed to cow slaughter, but the difference there is not extreme. One of the most interesting tests we used was with reference to the type of family in which the respondent was brought up—whether "authoritarian" or more "democratic" in its style of decision making. One of the highest levels of political involvement is found in the most "traditional" family decisional environments where the decisions are made by the head of the family or by family elders. Over 20 percent of these respondents engaged in some type of activity besides voting while only 9 to 10 percent of those coming from more "democratic" family decisional environments were active. These data strongly suggest that traditional orientations and environments do not

TABLE 15.1 "Traditional" Attitudes and Their Linkage to Political Involvement

Integrative System Attitudes	% Active beyond Voting	% Very Active in Campaign and Party Work	N
Localist, nonauthoritarian	20	11	54
Centralist, nonauthoritarian	20	11	47
Centralist, authoritarian	8	2	160
Localist, authoritarian	14	4	603
Self-location on "tradition-innovation scale"			
Very traditional	13	4	265
All traditional	14	5	387
Very innovative	14	5	171
All innovative	14	4	313
Ideological or issue traditionalism			
Favor banning cow slaughter (traditional)	11	3	721
Oppose banning cow slaughter (nontraditional)	14	7	291
Type of family decision-making pattern			
By head of family or elders	22	9	248
By collective discussion	10	3	219
By each individual for himself	9	2	501

inhibit, but rather may even facilitate involvement with parties and election processes.

Caste Orientations and Political Involvement

A special set of traditional attitudes concerns caste, the question here being whether those who demonstrate a high level of "caste consciousness" and who value the political role of caste associations are less or more inclined to participate politically. We have attempted again to use a variety of tests to see what the relationship is (table 15.2). Again, there is no clear evidence that those "traditional" in caste perceptions and values are less participative. Those who are most aware of caste in politics on our index (that is, know how their caste votes and know the caste of the candidates) are relatively very active beyond voting (20 percent, compared to only 1

TABLE 15.2 Caste Perceptions and Orientations as Linked to Political Involvement

	% Active beyond Voting	% Very Active in Campaign and Party Work	N
Caste awareness index			
Highest (Score 3)	20	7	324
(Score 2)	12	3	314
(Score 1)	8	3	257
Lowest (Score 0)	1	1	124
Attitude toward role of MP			
Very important to work for caste	12	1	248
Somewhat important	12	3	189
Not important	17	8	365
Voting preference of R and of his caste leader			
Respondent agreed with leader's party choice	16	4	360
Respondent did not agree with leader	23	10	40
Respondent not aware of leader's preference	9	4	620
Perception of caste voting (among voters)			
Saw own caste as voting for one party	17	3	235
Saw own caste as voting for more than one party	18	7	448
Considered it important that his caste voted a certain way (among regular voters)	14	4	202

percent of those low in caste awareness). Since this is as much a measure of awareness generally as of knowledge about the political aspects of caste, we used other tests. Those who are "traditional" in the sense of agreeing with the party preference of the caste leader who advised them are high in political activity (16 percent, but not as high as those who did not agree [23 percent]). Those whose caste was identical to that of the candidate they voted for, possibly evidence of "traditional" behavior, were virtually as involved in politics as those for whom this was not so. On one normative test—whether the MP or state assembly representative should work in the legislative body for his caste—the theoretically more "modern" types who said this was not important were more active, and particularly had a higher proportion of very active persons (at the 8 percent level). But the evidence is by no means indicative of great differences. Above all, our data support the proposition that Indians who were very aware of, and approved of, the political aspects of caste—perceptually, normatively, behaviorally—had a high percentage of people considerably involved in party politics and the election process.

We can particularize these findings by partitioning our respondents by their caste status and then discover whether the highest, middle, or lowest castes, *if they are oriented to "caste,"* are most active in politics (table 15.3). The basic trends noted earlier are by and large confirmed for caste categories: caste awareness (which is probably a measure of knowledge and not of "traditionalism") is associated with higher levels of political activity for all caste groups. Our "modern" orientations generally seem to be linked to higher activity for most caste groupings. The exceptions, however, are notable. The major new discovery here is that *for lower caste groups, particularly the Harijans and Tribals,* those who "value" caste and appear to identify normatively with "caste" and "tradition" have extremely high levels of participation. Thus, 19 percent of those among the Harijans who feel representatives should work for their caste are politically involved, as are 22 percent of those who see themselves as "traditional." Similarly 32 percent of the "caste-aware" Harijans are active in parties and elections. These are among the highest proportions of political involvement found in any of our groups. And it appears to be a consistent finding. (There is some limited evidence from our scale of innovation-tradition self-perceptions that "traditional" upper castes are also highly involved, but the evidence is not supported by all our tests.) This is then a significant finding, indeed—in the lowest social strata of Indian society, where traditional orientations predominate, high levels of involvement with "modern" political institutions are revealed.

The total distribution of the Indian activist population by caste and caste awareness is represented in table 15.4. It is clear that the overwhelming majority of Indian activists are politically conscious of caste. They know how their caste votes, the caste of candidates, and how the caste leader voted. Among upper castes the ratio is 6 to 1 that activists are aware of caste, in the middle castes it is better than 8 to 1, and for the lower castes and Harijans it is 3 to 1 that activists are caste conscious. This does not necessarily mean that activity is functionally linked to caste perceptions, nor that "traditionals" are more active than "moderns." These would be improper and incautious conclusions from these data. These data merely

TABLE 15.3 Caste, Tradition Orientations, and Political Involvement (by Caste Status)*

	% Upper Castes	% Middle Castes	% Lower Castes	% Harijans and Tribals
Caste awareness index				
Highest (Score 3)	19	21	16	32
(Score 2)	8	21	11	10
(Score 1)	7	7	13	6
Lowest (Score 0)	0	0	0	0
Importance that MLA's represent their caste				
Important	6	10	6	19
Not important	16	21	19	14
Self-perception on tradition-innovation scale				
Very "new"—innovative	9	21	10	15
All "new"—innovative	10	23	8	12
All "old"—traditional	11	15	8	22
Very "old"—traditional	14	10	7	22

* Each percentage is a proportion of those in a caste category with a particular orientation who were active politically beyond voting.

TABLE 15.4 Distribution of All Political Activists (N=119) by Caste Level and Caste Awareness

	% Upper Castes	% Middle Castes	% Lower Castes	% Harijans, Tribals	% Muslims	% Totals
Aware of caste	24	17	12	17	12	82
Not very aware of caste	4	2	7	2	2	17
						99

document that India's political activists are inclined to have a fairly accurate set of cognitions, or mental image, of the linkage between caste, caste leader, and voting behavior in India.

Attitudes toward the Regime and Political System as Linked to Involvement

We looked for the linkage between other basic attitudes and political involvement (table 15.5). There is no consistent set of findings which would suggest that those alienated or dissatisfied with the regime or the system are less active. In fact, we find those who were most critical of national and local officials were most likely to be active, but on the other hand, those who felt Congress had provided inadequate leadership were least active.[5] When we analyzed the political activity of Indians who supported parties and elections as contrasted to those who were critical of the party and election system, we found those accepting the system to be more active. On the other hand, those who disapprove of party conflict, parodoxically, were more active in the campaign (15 percent) than those who approved of party conflict (9 percent). These findings create an interpretive problem for us. One cannot conclude that system alienation or system support is, or is not, consistently linked to political involvement. One interpretation consistent with these data is that those who accept today's party and electoral institutions are more likely to be active, even though (or perhaps, despite the fact that) they disapprove of party conflict. Over 80 percent of our sample, in fact, disapprove of party conflict, but despite this commitment to consensus, given the *fact* of party competition, over 60 percent are supportive of the parties. And, these system supporters tend to be more politically active than those who reject the system.

Psychological Orientations and Involvement in Politics

A third type of attitudinal linkage concerns what has been called "psychological involvement" in politics. The measures used to determine the individual's psychological orientation vary by study, including attention to politics, political interest, as well as attempts to determine the individual's basic sense of personal political competence.[6] Here we use three separate measures and they yield somewhat different results, although suggesting strongly that personal expressions of political interest and, to some extent, competence are linked to political involvement (table 15.6). Our two measures of political interest show a striking relationship, the most striking of any of our attitudinal findings in percentage terms. Thus only 5 percent of those who say they had no interest in the campaign were active, while 43 percent of those who were very much interested were active in the campaign. Whether this is a significant finding depends on

TABLE 15.5 Attitudes toward the System and Regime as Linked to Political Involvement

Attitude	% Active beyond Voting	N
Index of support for government officials		
High support	11	353
Medium support	19	93
Low support	15	391
Attitude toward Congress leadership		
Congress failed in providing leadership	12	663
Congress did not fail in providing leadership	21	184
Feels parties made government pay attention to ordinary citizens		
A good deal	18	294
Somewhat	14	346
Not at all	11	208
Don't know	2	169
Attitude toward party conflict		
Not desirable	15	754
Is desirable	9	155
Feels elections help make government pay attention to ordinary citizens		
A good deal	16	417
Somewhat	15	310
Not at all	10	157
Don't know	3	131
Type of party system favored		
One-party system	10	443
Two or more parties	18	481

one's view. In one sense, all it tells us is that politically interested people are politically active, at least much more so than politically disinterested people. And we might have expected that in India, as well as in the United States, or any other country. Whether "interest" means "psychological involvement" is unclear, and even if it is a type of "psychological involvement," whether this tells us much about the psychological basis of political activity could be argued. In any event, the facts are clear for

TABLE 15.6 Measures of "Psychological Involvement" as Linked to Political Activity

	% Active beyond Voting	% Very Active in Party and Campaign Work	N
General political interest			
None	6	1	708
Some	23	9	200
Great	31	13	111
Campaign interest			
None	5	1	721
Some	21	6	180
Great	43	22	118

India—approximately 70 percent of the public said they were not interested in politics, yet 5 to 6 percent of these did participate, while from 21 to 43 percent of those who were interested were active.

The measure of political efficacy is more useful and no doubt taps more underlying orientations of a person toward parties, elections, governmental officials, and "politics." Its emphasis is on subjective feelings of competence in the context of the political process as the individual perceives that process. The specific items used to determine one's sense of political efficacy have remained fairly constant since the early study of the 1952 election by the Survey Research Center at the University of Michigan.[7] The items used in the Indian study and their relationship to political involvement are found in table 15.7. On two of the measures there seems to be some evidence that feelings of personal inefficacy or incompetence are associated with low levels of political involvement (items 1 and 3). On two other items this relationship is much less clear (items 2 and 4). The differences, however, are by no means all-or-none differences. We find that over 10 percent of those who revealed low faith in their role in the system nevertheless were active. This is high involvement for people whose subjective competence is low.

As noted in another context, large proportions (up to almost 80 percent) of the Indians in our 1967 sample respond with the "pessimistic" or "inefficacy" response to these items. The 1971 responses were less pessimistic. In the United States efficacy is usually higher, though in recent years it has declined. Although for the total sample political efficacy in the United States is much higher than in India, there are extreme variations by social groups and geographical regions in the United States. The 1952 study disclosed that 72 percent of southern men with only a grade school

TABLE 15.7 Political Efficacy Measures and Their Linkage to Political Involvement

Measures	% Active beyond Voting	% Very Active in Party and Campaign Work	N
"People like me don't have any say about what the government does"			
Agree	11	3	724
Disagree	20	9	206
Don't know	5	0	78
"Voting is the only way that people like me can have any say about how the government runs things"			
Agree	13	5	785
Disagree	12	4	146
Don't know	5	0	88
"Sometimes politics and government seem so complicated that a person like me can't really understand what is going on"			
Agree	13	4	828
Disagree	17	8	92
Don't know	4	0	98
"Government officials do not care much what people like me think"			
Agree	13	5	813
Disagree	14	1	134
Don't know	6	0	72

education, for example, had a low sense of political efficacy and that 67 percent of northern women with a grade school education also were low in this respect. These are percentages of low subjective competence very similar to those in 1967 in India, although the cross-national levels of subjective competence for *total* populations are very different.[8]

Comparatively, the key question for us is whether and to what extent political efficacy is linked to political involvement in the two countries. These data, using similar indexes of political efficacy and participation for the United States and India, are presented in table 15.8. One notices at once that political participation declines in both countries as sense of

TABLE 15.8 Relation of Political Efficacy to Participation: United States and India*

Efficacy Scores	United States	N	India	N
	% Engaging in Voting and Other Political Activity			
High 4	42	106	24	80
3	43	326	20	82
2	27	629	23	259
1	20	202	13	1,133
Low 0	12	331	9	235
	% Nonvoting and Nonparticipant			
High 4	13		10	
3	15		10	
2	23		8	
1	26		12	
Low 0	47		15	

* Using the 1952 U.S. data as a model (found in *The Voter Decides,* especially pp. 31, 187–91), we constructed an efficacy scale for India using the same four items as in the United States, and a participation index using the same type of items in both countries.

efficacy declines, but the contrast is much sharper in the United States than in India. The difference in participation in the United States between high and low efficacy is 30 percent while in India it is 15 percent. It is only at the lowest efficacy levels in India that political involvement really decreases, and actually those highest in efficacy are not much more participant than those ranking at the middle levels in efficacy. Another contrast to note in the two countries is that while high efficacy in the United States is linked to much higher participation (42 percent compared to 24 percent), low efficacy in the United States also means much more nonparticipation (47 percent compared to 15 percent). Thus in India, where much larger proportions of the population have very little sense of political efficacy, this does not necessarily mean withdrawal from political involvement. If the same relationships prevailed in India as in the United States, close to 40 percent *of the electorate* would have very little sense of efficacy *and* be completely nonparticipant. This is not the case—the proportion is actually closer to 10 percent.

A final major comparison between India and the United States for educational subgroups, using these same data for political efficacy and political

211

activity, demonstrates the similarities and differences for the two countries (table 15.9). Generally, for all educational groups in the two countries, participation declines as efficacy declines, although this is much more consistently so for the United States than for India. But the two countries differ directly when one seeks to pinpoint where among the educational groups one finds the greatest participation. As expected in the United States, the college educated with a high sense of political efficacy are the activists (+43) and those with a grade school education with a low sense of efficacy are the most inactive (−48). But in India the picture is much more mixed, and actually it is those with a primary school education with a high sense of political efficacy who are the most active (+24) and those with a higher education and low sense of efficacy who are least active (−18). So while degree of political self-confidence is generally linked to political participation in India within each educational level (except for those in the middle education categories), the linkage between political efficacy and activity is most pronounced among those with a small amount of education. Those Indian citizens with a limited education, and with perhaps a new sense of political competence, a sense of being able to have some impact on the system, are the most active with parties and in campaigns. This again underscores the socially penetrative character of political development in India.

Personal Financial Perspectives and Involvement in Politics

In a society of high economic deprivation one might well expect a close relationship between perceived economic condition and political behavior. But what the exact nature of that relationship is likely to be is conjectural—whether the deprived are "activist" or "alienated" and withdrawn. We asked three questions in 1967 probing attitudes toward personal financial status. On two of these the sense of dissatisfaction was a majority opinion: 63 percent were not satisfied with "your (you and your family's) present financial situation" (11 percent were well satisfied), 53 percent felt that during the last few years their "financial situation had been getting worse" (17 percent getting better). Somewhat more optimism was revealed in "looking ahead and thinking about the next few years." The distribution of personal financial expectations was as follows: 32 percent, getting worse; 14 percent, the same; 36 percent, getting better; and 16 percent, don't know. Generally we found that those Indians who felt the most deprived on these measures were less inclined to be active politically than the others. But the differences were not large. And the distinctions by social status (such as educational level) were considerable (table 15.10).

The deprived illiterates are consistently low on political involvement,

TABLE 15.9 Relation of Sense of Political Efficacy to Political Participation for Educational Groups: India and the United States*

Education Groups	Degree of Political Efficacy (%)		
	High	Medium	Low
India			
Illiterates	0	−5	−11
Primary school only	+24	+5	−3
Primary and middle	+14	+17	+6
High school and			
college	+14	+10	−18
United States			
Grade school	+17	−16	−48
High school	+26	+8	−8
College	+43	+31	†

* This table is based, as is table 15.8, on a direct comparison of 1967 India and 1952 U.S. total sample data. See *The Voter Decides,* p. 193. A plus score means that those in a particular educational category at a particular efficacy level were more participant than nonparticipant (that is, the percentage with low participation was subtracted from the percentage with high participation). A minus sign means the reverse—the percentage not participating was higher than the percentage participating.

† Too few cases for analysis.

while those illiterates who are more financially optimistic are consistently somewhat higher in activity. But the proportions who are politically involved among the economically well-satisfied and optimistic middle education groups is striking—29 percent to 33 percent are politically involved. Yet, the differences *within* the middle education groups are not large or consistent. Among the respondents with middle schooling, even those who feel very deprived economically and who see things getting worse are active—23 to 27 percent. And the other education groups show no evidence of a clear linkage between degree of financial optimism and political participation. Indeed, although the deprived illiterates are particularly low in involvement, the evidence of political activism, present and potential, among those who are depressed about economic conditions is strong. Up to a third of the high-school-educated cadre, a fourth of those with middle schooling, and even more than 10 percent of those with a primary school education who are pessimistic about economic conditions are active in politics. The possible implications of these data for agitation for political relief and policy change are unambiguous.

213

TABLE 15.10 The Relation Between Financial Perceptions and Political Participation by Educational Level*

	Educational Level (%)					
	Illit-erate	Pri-mary	Mid-dle	High School	Col-lege	All Res-pondents
Perception of financial situation for self and family						
1. Well satisfied with present financial situation	9	9	33	17	15	15
2. Moderately satisfied	8	25	18	27	17	16
3. Not satisfied at all	6	14	27	21	12	13
Opinion as to whether personal financial condition has changed in the past few years						
1. Getting better	7	16.7	29	26	25	17
2. Staying the same	6.5	21	29	19	22	16
3. Getting worse	6.5	14	22	22	12	12
Expectation as to how personal financial situation will change in the next few years						
1. Get better	9	17	30	19	18	16.5
2. Stay the same	6	24	24	21	19	15
3. Get worse	6	13.5	23.5	30	18.5	12

* Each percentage is the proportion at a given educational level and with a particular attitude on personal financial situation who were active beyond voting. Based on the voting eligibles from 1957 on.

Involvement Despite "Alienation"

In the analysis presented in this chapter we have seen that India is a polity whose masses remain considerably "traditional" and highly aware of caste and its role in politics. Yet, many of these people are politically involved, often participating in acts beyond that of voting. The level of involvement is comparatively high and it is linked to attitudes which in the West would be considered contradictory or dysfunctional. Lower castes and illiterates with attitudes suggesting high criticism and rejection of the system, the regime, and its leadership, as well as high cynicism about the ordinary citizen's possible role in that context, and in addition, opposition to party conflict and the competitive style of political life—many of these people are the regular voters and the highly active. Perhaps this is the most revealing discovery in the exploration of this aspect of India's political behavior. There is "alienation" (in the sense of low efficacy, rejection of conflictual aspects of the system, and so on) *and* involvement at the same time for the same citizens, in the lowest and most socially deprived sectors of the society. This does not mean that support for the system has not also brought more involvement. And, there is strong evidence that the citizen's engagement with "modern" parties and elections is producing supportive attitudes, a point we will develop later. But, the large mass of the Indian electorate by Western standards holds "alienative" orientations toward politics—distrust of party conflict (83 percent), cynicism about officials (58 percent), loyalty to the locality rather than the central government (76 percent), very low feelings of personal competence in the political arena (71 percent), and low interest in government generally (70 percent). Yet, these citizens contributed the bulk of the voters and the activists. As the distributions in table 15.11 reveal, the Indian electorate is both alienated and involved. Only a small proportion of the total electorate can be characterized as rejecting the system and withdrawing from political involvement incidental to that rejection. It is almost as if these data are suggesting that many Indian citizens find themselves as part of a new post-Independence polity which they question or even distrust (a distrust which is the product of a long legacy of unhappy exposure to governmental authority) but which they, for a variety of reasons, have decided to participate in. Party and election politics is salient and important to many of them, too important to allow their traditional and cynical orientation toward "government" to interfere. And, significantly, as we shall demonstrate in a later chapter, as they do participate in this system there is

TABLE 15.11 Distribution of Alienation and Political Involvement for the Total
Electorate (N=937)*

	% Inactive	% Some Activity as Voters	% Political Activity beyond Voting	% Total
Greatly alienated	8	55	8	71
Somewhat alienated	2	15	3	20
Supportive	1	7	2	10

* This is based on those men in our sample who were eligible to vote in the elections of 1957, 1962, and 1967, and for whom political activity and sense of efficacy were ascertainable. "Alienation" is operationalized here on the basis of our efficacy index.

evidence that some of their negative feelings about the system and their involvement in it are being modified. Perhaps that is the basic finding: political involvement despite alienation eventually leads to commitment and support. This will become apparent as we proceed with the analysis. This finding makes the antidemocratic hiatus of 1975 more tragic, for it may lead to more cynicism, less exposure to democratic party processes, and thus less trust and support.

SIXTEEN·
Political Environment: The Context and Stimulus for Involvement

Two Approaches to the Problem

T HEORIES OF POLITICAL DEVELOPMENT EMPHASIZE THE RELATIONSHIP between the political institutional environment and political participation. There is a strong tendency to argue that the types of institutions matter a great deal, because they provide the context, stimuli, and opportunity for citizen participation. There are two different ways of looking at this relationship, however. For some scholars the problem is operationalized in participation *pressure* terms, for other scholars it is conceived of in participation *response* terms. Thus, Huntington sees the stability of developing societies as the product of the emergence of "modern" institutions, such as a coherent party system, which can cope with and contain the pressure for participation by economically and socially frustrated citizens.[1] The presence of effective and adaptive political institutions as channels for participation are, in his view, crucial for the establishment of a legitimate political order.

There are those, however, who see institutional development as preceding and providing the stimulus and context within which participation is encouraged and promoted. Thus, Kothari argues that "the achievement of independence did provide a moment of choice to the Indian leadership with regard to the institutional strategy it would like to adopt for the new republic." The political elites developed a set of institutions which were partially a continuation of the pre-Independence period and partially innovative attempts to deal with the crises and problems confronting the society at Independence. Kothari concludes: "The institutional structure that emerged was essentially modernist in character but with important departures from the Western model designed to facilitate national integration and social assimilation."[2] The argument implies that the new institutional environment created by the elites provided the opportunity and facilitated citizen participation. If this is true, the 1975 "interruption" would constitute an inhibiting environment.

There appear, then, to be two different emphases on the relationship between institution building and citizen involvement—one theory concerning institutions as being created to deal with the needs and demands of citizens, and the other theory emphasizing the development of institutions which then generate citizen involvement, which in turn is functional to elite developmental goals of mobilization, support, and integration. It is this latter theoretical position concerning the nexus of institutions and participation which is generally apropos of the analysis presented in this chapter. We wish to explore whether the political stimuli to which citizens were exposed under the post-Independence institutional conditions seemed to be relevant for political involvement.

Many scholars have discussed, outside of the theoretical context of "development," the probable importance of political environmental conditions for political behavior. The type of party system—whether integrated or pluralized, ideologically polarized or nonideological, or whether reflecting social class differences or not, to mention only a few differences—has long been considered such an environmental or systemic condition relevant to political behavior. Certain party systems may contribute to strong identification with parties, or political participation, and others may not.[3] Further, there has been much discussion of the legal environment, particularly whether certain types of suffrage and election laws facilitate involvement or discourage it.[4] Then, also, the type of constituency environment, or political subculture, within which a person lives—particularly whether it is competitive or not—has been advanced by many as significant in explaining a variety of political phenomena.[5] Finally there are some studies which sought to characterize the party *organizational* environment at the local level and to determine its role in mobilizing the vote.[6] There are, then, a considerable variety of studies preoccupied with theorizing about, or analysis of, the political environment's relevance for political involvement. Our analysis builds on these previous efforts.

Early Political Socialization and Involvement

Before looking explicitly at the relevance of the post-Independence party environment, we should note that socialization to politics in the family is a belated phenomenon for most Indians. Actually only 18 percent of our respondents said their fathers, or other members of the family, were politically interested; only 11 percent could recall the party identification of their father; and only 41 percent indicated that the age they became aware of politics was before twenty (only 15 percent before age sixteen). Yet it is interesting to observe that earlier exposure to politics was related to political activity in subsequent adult life (table 16.1). An extremely high proportion, 33 percent, who were politically aware before age sixteen engaged in politics beyond voting, and 20 percent were active among those aware by age twenty-five, but only 6 percent were active of those becoming aware later in life. Similarly over a fifth were active if they had politically interested fathers.

TABLE 16.1 Political Socialization as Influential in Political Involvement

	% Active beyond Voting	N
Age first politically aware of politics, parties, etc.		
<16	33	58
16–20	17	170
21–25	20	182
26–30	8	133
31–40	9	142
40+	6	76
Never	4	168
Family's political interest		
High	22	50
Moderate	14	73
Not at all	12	826

Exposure to Political Leadership

Since late adolescence and the early adult periods seem to be the times of developing political awareness, an important question is, What types of "adult exposure" to what types of environment, and particularly whether exposure to political leadership and party institutions, seem to be most relevant? We asked a variety of questions concerning citizen's contacts with political leadership: whether they had dealings with influential persons in their village or town; whether they knew party, caste, or religious leaders and had contact with them; whether they had gone to a party or governmental official for help; whether they had received a caste leader's advice on voting. The importance of such exposure for political involvement is obvious (table 16.2). Respondents who were isolated from caste and party leadership were relatively nonparticipant—only 5 percent were involved at all beyond voting. Those who knew leaders personally were the most involved (21 percent), and if in addition they reported contact with one or more leaders their political involvement escalated to the 30 or 40 percent level. There is a monotonic increase in participation with increased leadership exposure.

This finding in itself, of course, tells us very little about the factors determining political involvement. All it does tell us is that those who are "active" in contacting, or knowing, leaders are also "active" in parties and campaigns. It suggests but does not demonstrate that leadership exposure preceded political participation, and indeed the relationship might very well be reversed. However, at least we know that large numbers of Indians are in contact with political and caste leaders, and as closeness or

219

TABLE 16.2 Leadership Exposure as Linked to Political Involvement

Leadership Exposure (with Candidate, Party, or Caste Leader)	% Active as Party Member *or* in Campaign	% Active as Party Member *and* in Campaign	Total % Active beyond Voting	N
No contact, knows no leader	4	1	5	531
Knows none personally, but contact with 1 leader	8	2	10	125
Knows none personally, but contact with 2	8	8	16	26
Knows 1 leader, but no contact	12	9	21	160
Knows 1 leader, *and* contact with 1 leader	19	11	30	121
Knows 2 or 3 leaders, has had contact with 1 or 2	20	11	31	55
Knows leaders personally, and received help from them	26	22	48	46

frequency of association with leaders increases one also finds increased political activity. One should not discount the possibility, however, that this exposure is a function of involvement.

Exposure to the 1967 Political Campaign
Political involvement is also, in the same covariant sense, linked to campaign exposure (see table 16.3). Those respondents who were subjected to the party and candidate stimuli were more likely to be active participants (19 to 44 percent) than those who were more isolated from the campaign (1 to 8 percent). On individual types of exposure items, the contrast is striking. Thus, those who had not followed politics in the newspapers (a large proportion in India—close to 70 percent) were less likely to be politically involved, as were those who had not met the candidates or who had not been canvassed by the parties. Again one can discount this relationship by arguing that either the parties are selective in their campaign techniques (which would not account for certain types of exposure, such as reading about politics in newspapers or meeting candidates) or that naturally those who were politically involved were subsequently exposed to campaign and party activities. Nevertheless, there is a juxtaposition again of political

TABLE 16.3 The Linkage between Campaign Exposure and Political Involvement

Type of Campaign Exposure	% Active as Party Members *or* in Campaign	% Active as Party Members *and* in Campaign	Total % Active beyond Voting	N
Followed politics in newspapers?				
Yes	15	9	24	300
No	6	2	8	714
Met the candidates?				
Yes	15	11	26	268
No	6	2	8	749
Canvassed by the parties?				
Yes	12	7	19	353
No	6	2	8	659
Index of campaign exposure				
High Score 4	21	23	44	73
Score 3	13	6	19	154
Score 2	12	7	19	242
Score 1	6	0	6	301
Low Score 0	1	0	1	249

involvement with exposure to the party system and although the direction of the relationship is not demonstrable from these data, the relevance of the findings is clear. Those Indians who are exposed to "modern" party processes and leadership are the most likely to be the activists who are most involved politically with the vote mobilization and leadership support tasks at the base of the polity.

One comparative piece of evidence is interesting in this connection. Lester Milbrath, using the Survey Research Center's 1956 election data, presents the relationship between party contact and what he has called "gladiatorial" activity (engaging in at least one type of activity beyond voting). His data permit the following comparison:[7] in both the United States and India 20 to 25 percent contacted or canvassed by the party organization are campaign actives, while 10 percent or less of those not thus contacted are active. This is not tautological although it suggests a close linkage. In both countries personal contact by the party seems similarly efficacious, or vice versa. The two patterns of political involvement go together, but not perfectly.

*The Causal Linkage between Party Effort and Voting or Nonvoting: India
and the United States*

The relationship between party campaign exposure and one type of political involvement—voting—can more clearly be expressed in "causal"
terms. Our Indian data clearly establish the relevance of party exposure for
voting turnout (see tables 16.4 and 16.5). If we look first at those in our
sample who were nonvoters previously (in 1957 and 1962) and classify
them by the *extent* of their exposure in 1967, the "impact" of the party
appears strikingly. The contrast at the extremes is between the 91 percent
who voted among those highly exposed and the 38 percent among those not
exposed—a 53 percent differential. Clearly the party's role seems to be
significant.

TABLE 16.4 Vote Mobilization by Degree of Total Campaign Exposure

Among Non-voters of 1957 and 1962*	Campaign Exposure Index				
	Low 0	1	2	3	High 4
% voting in 1967	38	54	66	77	91
% not voting in 1967	62	46	34	23	9
N	100	91	61	52	23

* These were eligible to vote in previous elections.

The reduction of nonvoting and of party defection, whatever the *type*
(party origin) of campaign exposure, is clearly apparent in table 16.5. Here
we control by party predisposition and then look at the extent of nonvoting
for those exposed to Congress, to non-Congress parties, and not exposed at
all. Among those not exposed the extent of nonvoting among previous
party supporters rises to 15 percent, and to 26 percent for previous nonvoters. What is also striking in the table is the role of exposure in reduction of
party defection. Only 13 percent of Congress supporters defected if they
were exposed to Congress campaign stimuli, but 48 percent defected if
exposed to the opposition parties. The proportions of defection are 10
percent and 45 percent, respectively, for non-Congress supporters.

The exposure of voters to rival campaign efforts of the parties was
considerable in 1967, and these efforts appear to have been relatively
competitive. The voters were subjected to non-Congress stimuli almost as
much as to Congress stimuli. For example, of the electorate canvassed 41
percent were approached by non-Congress parties. And the parties were
approaching each other's partisans. Thus, 18 percent of the 1962 non-

TABLE 16.5 The Role of the Partisan Origin of Exposure in Reducing Nonvoting and Party Defection*

Category of Respondents	Party Exposure (1967)	% Not Voting in 1967	% Defecting in 1967 from Party of Support in 1962	N
Congress supporters in 1962	Exposed to Congress (18%)	9	13	816
	Exposed to non-Congress (6%)	8	48	
	Not exposed (76%)	15	29	
Non-Congress supporters in 1962	Exposed to Congress (18%)	5	45	217
	Exposed to non-Congress (24%)	6	10	
	Not exposed (58%)	15	22	
Nonvoters in 1962 (but eligible to vote in 1962)	Exposed to Congress (11%)	10	. . .	781
	Exposed to non-Congress (10%)	15	. . .	
	Not exposed (79%)	26	. . .	

* This table is based on one type of campaign exposure: attendance at election meetings held by the parties during the campaign.

Congress supporters were canvassed by Congress and 14 percent of the 1962 Congress supporters were canvassed by non-Congress workers. Party organizational effort seemed to be relatively high. The evidence that this work had an impact, both in keeping predisposed regulars in the fold as well as reducing nonvoting, is clear. It is interesting to note that of all the "dropouts" in 1967 (partisan supporters of 1962 who did not vote in 1967) 63 percent had no, or little, campaign exposure and only 6 percent were highly exposed to the campaign.

How do these findings for India on the relevance of party and campaign exposure compare with other societies? Unfortunately only limited efforts have been made to study this phenomenon in the West. A simple comparison of Indian and American data is presented in table 16.6. The role of canvassing in the two countries is remarkably similar, although the proportion of Indians in our study who reported being canvassed was considerably higher (36 percent) than in the United States (17 percent). The Indian parties, if active, apparently can be effective agents, in conjunction with other forces, in bringing citizens to the polls, much as in the United States.

TABLE 16.6 The "Impact" of Party Canvassing in India and the United States

	Canvassed by One or More Parties	Not Canvassed by any Party
	(% Not Voting in the Election)	
India (1967)	11	21
United States (1956)	12	28
N (India)	647	1,169
N (United States)	301	1,448

SOURCE: The U.S. figures come from Lester Milbrath, *Political Participation* (Chicago: Rand McNally, 1965), p. 100. An almost identical set of percentages is found for the 1952 presidential election in Morris Janowitz and Dwaine Marvick, *Competitive Pressure and Democratic Consent* (Ann Arbor: Bureau of Government, Institute of Public Administration, University of Michigan, 1956), p. 80.

The *degree* of exposure to the parties as organizations in relation to voting turnout is a more difficult proposition to demonstrate comparatively. The availability of evidence on this point is limited. Verba reports that "multiple active membership" in organizations, accompanied by evidence of involvement in these groups, enhances the probabilities of political participation, but the role of party organizational activity in Verba and Nie's study is not isolated.[8] Several studies have demonstrated that the *existence* of strong local party organization and leadership in the United States may account for an increment of 5 to 10 percent in the party vote.[9] On the other hand a study of this in Norway in 1956 revealed that the strength of the local party organization was not related to its capacity to mobilize the vote beyond normal expectations. Social class variables were powerful predictors of the vote in Norway.[10]

In India exposure to the party effort in campaigns is clearly productive in mobilizing previous nonvoters (table 16.4). It is also linked to political activity, and to the reduction in party defections. Those isolated from the campaign and the party effort were clearly more chronic nonvoters, less likely to vote in the 1967 election, and less likely to be at all personally active. The evidence is inconclusive as to whether party organizational effort and campaign activity is more productive in India or in the United States. In both countries there is a strong suggestion that such effort has a "payoff" for the party as well as for increasing public involvement in the system generally.

The Effect of Campaign Exposure in Reducing Status Group Differences in Participation

One of the interesting questions is whether party campaign exposure reduces the discrepancy between high and low status groups in political involvement. Do illiterates and lower castes, as they become politically exposed, approximate the political participation levels of higher status persons? (One should recall, however, that our previous analysis revealed that in India it was those with middle level education who had the highest involvement levels, and among caste groups the differences were minimal.) Verba and Nie have argued that "organizational activity" has given blacks in the United States a "particularly large boost upward in political participation."[11] Similarly Morris Janowitz and Dwaine Marvick demonstrated that in the 1952 presidential election in the United States the lower social classes and the ethnic-religious minorities narrowed the gap considerably in voting participation, in comparison to the middle classes and white Protestants, as a "result" of party canvassing.[12] A summary of their findings can be presented as follows:

	United States: % Nonvoting in 1952	
	Canvassed	Not canvassed
Upper middle-class	0	12
Lower lower-class	19	47
Class difference	−19	−35
Protestant whites	13	25
Ethnic-religious minorities	10	32
Group difference	+3	−7

Status group differences in political activity are a different type of phenomenon in India. In comparison to the United States there seem to be two differences: at the lowest party exposure levels there is practically no difference in involvement for castes and education groups, but as exposure increases it is "middle" status groups who move considerably ahead in involvement (table 16.7). Thus, campaign exposure means that the lower castes become active (jumping from 3 to 24 percent), and become in fact as active as the upper castes, but by no means as active as the middle castes who are activated by high exposure to the 37 percent level. Similarly illiterates are activated as they are exposed to the campaign (rising in participation from 1 to 15 percent), but again those with middle schooling increase phenomenally in political involvement—to 43 percent. All three measures we use in table 16.7 demonstrate these tendencies. Socialization to politics in the family also has its impact on political involvement for all caste and educational groups, but, again, particularly for the middle castes.

225

TABLE 16.7 Political Exposure as Linked to Political Involvement, by Social Sectors*

Political Exposure Variable	Educational Groups (%)			Caste Groups (%)		
	Highest Educated	Middle Schooling	Illiter- ates	Upper Castes	Middle Castes	Lowest Castes Plus Harijans/ Tribals
Campaign exposure index						
High	31	43	15	23	37	24
Medium	19	26	16	13	21	22
Low	12	4	5	4	8	7
None	0	4	1	2	0	3
Exposure to party or caste leader						
Yes	31	34	16	21	42	29
No	7	8	5	5	7	6
Socialization: whether fam- ily was inter- ested in politics						
Yes	27	29	14	14	36	17
No	18	16	7	10	10	11

* Each percentage is the proportion of each social status category and exposure group who were active beyond voting.

A summary measure using educational status and party canvassing, simi- lar to the American measure, tells this story simply:

	India (1967) % Active beyond Voting	
	Canvassed	Not Canvassed
Highest education	20	14
Middle education	32	15
Illiterates	12	6
Group differences		
Higher and illiterates	8	8
Middle and illiterates	20	9

Whereas social status differences in political participation are diminished by party activity in the United States, the disparity between lower status and middle status groups (but not with upper status groups) is widened in India.

TABLE 16.8 Exposure to Campaign Politics for Caste and Education Subgroups

	Campaign Exposure Index		Specific Types of Exposure	
	% in 2 Highest Categories	% Not Exposed at All	% Who Met the Candidates	% Canvassed by the Parties
Caste groups				
Upper	30	16	35	42
Middle	21	33	21	31
Lower	17	27	24	28
Harijans	18	31	17	37
Muslims	21	16	25	31
Education groups				
Highest	51	5	57	61
Middle	35	13	39	39
Primary	24	24	25	36
Illiterates	14	30	19	29

The relevant query then is, What percent of upper, middle, and lower status groups are indeed exposed to politics in India? The difference between caste and educational subgroups is consistent: upper status groups are more exposed, the lower castes and illiterates are the least exposed (table 16.8). But the differences are much more striking by educational level than by caste. Indeed the Harijans were almost as likely to be canvassed by the parties as the Brahmans (37 percent compared to 42 percent). But it was the illiterates who were most disadvantaged—six times as many, compared to the upper castes, were not exposed at all. Only 19 percent of the illiterates met the candidates and only 29 percent were canvassed, while over 50 percent of the upper castes met candidates and were approached by party canvassers. Thus, although campaign exposure did have a considerable effect on lower status people, larger proportions of them were not exposed. This suggests the potential for political mobilization and involvement in the Indian system, as in all systems. In the United States the extent of the public's exposure to the party's campaign efforts is not great—in the Detroit study in 1956 it was discovered that 44 percent of the eligible electorate was completely unexposed, and another

16 percent had practically no contact with the parties.[13] In 1952, only 12.3 percent of the U.S. national sample was canvassed by the parties.[14] The Indian campaign effort is therefore impressive by comparison—25 percent were exposed to the campaign, 12 percent participated in it. The lower status groups in India were less exposed but by no means excluded from the campaign process. And as they were exposed they narrowed the "participation gap" with upper status persons while middle status Indian society assumed relative dominance among political participants.

Constituency Environmental Characteristics as Linked to Involvement

A fascinating inquiry concerns the role of constituency environment in political behavior. Does the type of party-competitive situation in a community or election district influence the citizen's readiness to be involved in politics? And which constituency situation maximizes participation? We have attempted here to find answers to these questions by looking first at differences in participation for types of parliamentary constituencies. Our data suggest that there may be a relationship between the type of party contest in a constituency and political involvement. The number of parties or candidates in a constituency by itself did not have a relationship to participation beyond voting, but the presence or absence of Right parties (Swatantra and Jan Sangh) and Left parties (Socialists or Communists) seems to be relevant. It was the *pattern of ideological conflict* in the constituency which seemed to matter most. Where Congress was opposed in 1967 by a Left party, political involvement was highest; where it was only Congress versus Jan Sangh, involvement was lowest. The difference was 19 percent between these extremes.

We looked at the party and candidate contest in 1967 as compared to 1962 and noted that where there was an increase in Left parties there was higher participation than where more Right parties appeared on the scene in 1967. In those constituencies where a Right party competed in 1962 but *not* in 1967 there was a 20 percent political involvement beyond voting, but when Right parties were present in *both* elections there was only a 10 percent participation beyond voting. Thus, in terms of the ideological conflict pattern in 1967 and in terms of the historical pattern of party appearance and disappearance from 1962 to 1967 there is very suggestive evidence that a Left-oriented constituency political conflict pattern was most conducive to political involvement beyond voting.

As for the incidence in nonvoting, we discovered striking differences by type of conflict. These differences can be illustrated as follows:

Type of Constituency Conflict	% of Sample Not Voting in 1967
Congress vs. DMK	8
Congress vs. one Left party	13
Congress vs. local party or Independent	15
Congress vs. two Left parties	17
Congress vs. one Right party	19
Congress vs. a mixture of Right and Left parties	19
Congress vs. two Right parties	30

It appears that both a multiplicity of Left and Right parties or the absence of a Left party is related to low voting turnout.

There were other candidate conflict situations which produced high voting participation, particularly in those constituencies where Congress fought it out with the DMK. But in addition to this situation, and specific contests with local parties and independents, nonvoting seemed to be lowest where Congress competed in "straight fights" and where the opposition included a party on the Left.

In this chapter we sought to look at political environment in India as facilitative of political involvement. We have limited ourselves to certain types of environmental conditions for which we could get measures of citizen exposure. In essence we asked whether the Indian citizen's exposure to the "new" political elites, the "new" party structure, the "new" campaign process, and the "new" competitive party system seemed to lead to more voting participation and political activity. Our data are dramatic evidence that this is the case. Exposure by Indian citizens to the new party and campaign institutions and processes is associated positively and strikingly with political involvement. The differences in involvement between those not exposed and those highly exposed are great. Those in contact with no leaders are inactive; those in contact with several leaders are more likely to be active. Those exposed to the campaign stimuli of candidates and parties are very active; those not exposed are politically inert. Among those previous nonvoters greatly exposed to campaign efforts in 1967, 91 percent voted; only 38 percent of those not exposed voted in 1967.

Obviously the actions and efforts of leaders and parties were very relevant to citizen involvement, as important in India as in the United States. And in India lower caste groups keep pace with upper caste groups in participation as exposure to political leaders and parties increases. It is

229

the middle caste and middle education groups who exhibit the greatest increase in participation in India and who therefore have become a much more prominent force among the participant political elite. Yet the differential proportions of status groups who are exposed at all to politics remain large—up to 30 percent of lower castes, middle castes, and illiterates are not exposed at all, compared to only 16 percent of upper castes and 5 percent of the most educated. Here then lies a future for political mobilization, either by the government or by the opposition. With the dissolution of free and competitive party democracy in 1975 these findings take on added significance. If exposure to the "new" party and electoral institutions now is minimal, one can indeed wonder what the long-range consequences for the Indian citizen's involvement will be. Without a reenforcing democratic elite and party environment, the habit and desire for participation, if the Emergency is long in duration, could certainly decline for many citizens.

S E V E N T E E N·
Alternative Models for Explaining Political Involvement and for Assessing its Impact

FROM OUR ANALYSIS THUS FAR, IT IS OBVIOUS THAT A GREAT VARIETY OF factors may be linked to, and may possibly explain, why Indians become involved in politics, whether as voters, party members, campaign activists, or elite contacters. Conversely, our data also suggest strongly that political activity and involvement have considerable impact on political attitudes and behavior in India. To determine which of all the factors apparently related are most useful, and in what pattern, is a difficult task. Are the basic orientations of Indians toward the political system, its policies, symbols, and leaders most important in their politicization; and, if so, which orientations are most relevant? What is the utility of social status for explaining involvement—particularly educational level and caste status? Is it their sense of identification with political parties, and particularly the strength of that identification, which is important in explaining why, and how, they become active participants? Is it their exposure to the political environment—to the parties, to other groups, to caste and political leaders, to the mass media, or even to politics in a particular type of family? Or is it some more general personal philosophy or value commitment or psychological orientation which seems to have the most explanatory relevance? In this brief summary chapter we shall attempt to identify the factors or conditions which seem most powerful as explanatory variables, for India first, and then for India in comparison to other countries. And, in the process, we hope to suggest alternative approaches or models by which we might look at the relationships between these different factors.

The Path Model Explaining Political Activity
There are several different models or ways of presenting data to demonstrate the linkage between political involvement and the host of social status, attitudinal, and environmental variables which we have been working with in this analysis. If one wishes to "explain" political involvement, the most common model, perhaps, is the following: Social status→Attitudes→Political involvement. This model assumes that the social and economic environment in which a person was brought up and in which he now lives provides or limits the opportunities, skills, resources, impulses, and social reenforcements for political participation. The basic assumption

is that social status leads to certain basic political attitudes which in turn encourage or discourage political activity. Various scholars have employed this model, most recently Verba et al. in their study of political participation in the United States and abroad. They present simple "path models" of the correlations between SES (combined into an index based on occupation, education, and income, or, earlier, using education alone) and a set of so-called civic attitudes. These attitudes are of four types in the U.S. study ("psychological involvement in politics," political efficacy, political information, and a sense of contribution to the community), while in the comparative study "partisan affiliation" is used.[1] There is some difficulty in attempting to present our data comparatively with these studies due to problems of operationalization, separation of attitudinal components, and availability of equivalent data. The variable "psychological involvement" is rather loosely conceived, for example. Nevertheless, sufficiently comparative analyses are possible to permit us to present our Indian data, as it fits into this path model, so as to see the differences between India and other countries for which data are available.

An illustration of the correlational linkages for India in this type of model, based on our data, is provided in figure 14.[2] As can be seen, we have relied here on education as the indicator of social status and have utilized six different "intervening" measures of personal attitudinal or psychological involvement[3] in order to explain campaign activism. These partially replicate the measures Verba and his associates used (political interest, media exposure, efficacy, knowledge of leaders, and party identification) and use an additional measure for India—caste awareness (based on items concerning knowledge of how the castes voted, the caste of the candidates, and whom caste leaders supported.)[4]

Fig. 14. Path model of variables related to campaign activity.

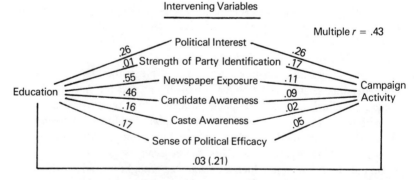

The correlation in parentheses is the direct original relationship before the effects of the other orientations are removed.

Educational level correlates poorly in India in 1967 with party identification, and rather poorly with caste awareness and sense of political efficacy. Previously, we demonstrated that strong party identification declines at the higher education levels in India—only 37 percent of college educated are strong identifiers and 46 percent of those with a high school education, while 54 percent of the illiterates are strong identifiers. Education is not a good predictor of campaign activity either when the effects of other attitudes are considered. Education perhaps has a more important linkage to knowledge about candidates (.46), newspaper exposure (.55), and political interest (.26). And as the model suggests, education seems to work with these latter two variables to induce people to become campaign actives.

Party identification and political interest, and to a lesser extent newspaper exposure, are important factors associated with campaign activity. Party identification has no relationship to educational level, so that the connection of party identification to other antecedent variables is not demonstrable from this model. It is significant that there is virtually no linkage between candidate knowledge, caste awareness, or political efficacy as contributors to campaign activity when we use this type of path model.[5] Thus, education, mediated through political interest and newspaper exposure, and party identification strength unrelated to education are the factors which, in terms of this model, seem to best explicate campaign activity in India.

A Comparison of Path Models for India and the United States: Campaign Activity

We can attempt an explicit comparison of our findings using basically the same path models as Verba and his associates used for five countries, including the same basic variables they used.[6] In figure 15, the path models for campaign activity are presented for India and the United States. There are slight modifications in the "psychological involvement" variable as operationalized in the two studies.[7] And the Verba study includes an attitudinal variable—"contribution to community"—which we did not use in the Indian study. This, however, does not modify the set of relationships drastically.

In both India and the United States, the linkage between education—"psychological involvement"—campaign activism is consistent, and seems to be the most important configuration of variables. Partisan intensity is linked to activism also, but not necessarily associated with education. This is the major distinction between our findings and those of Verba and his associates. Verba found in India a simple correlation of .23 between education and party identification strength in India, while we found virtually no relationship (.01). This is surprising, and difficult to explain.

233

Fig. 15. Comparison of path models for India and the United States: correlations for campaign activity.

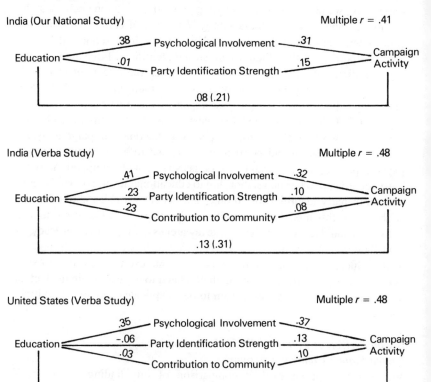

India (Our National Study)   Multiple *r* = .41

Education — .38 — Psychological Involvement — .31 — Campaign Activity
Education — .01 — Party Identification Strength — .15 — Campaign Activity
.08 (.21)

India (Verba Study)   Multiple *r* = .48

Education — .41 — Psychological Involvement — .32 — Campaign Activity
Education — .23 — Party Identification Strength — .10
Education — .23 — Contribution to Community — .08
.13 (.31)

United States (Verba Study)   Multiple *r* = .48

Education — .35 — Psychological Involvement — .37 — Campaign Activity
Education — -.06 — Party Identification Strength — .13
Education — .03 — Contribution to Community — .10
.13 (.25)

One notes that in no other country, including the United States, does the Verba study demonstrate a significant relationship between education and partisan intensity. And in other respects our findings are similar for India to those of the Verba group. Thus, the fact that their Indian study was done in only four states (West Bengal, Andhra Pradesh, Gujarat, and Uttar Pradesh) and not in the same year as ours may not be relevant explanations. The fact remains that in our 1967 national election study in India we found no meaningful relationship between educational level and the strength of party identification.[8]

Path Coefficient Correlations, Four Nations: Campaign Activity
Placing the Indian findings side by side with these data from the United States and all the other countries reveals interesting similarities and differences (table 17.1). In no country is there a strong correlation between

234

TABLE 17.1 Some Path Coefficient Correlations "Explaining" Campaign Activity Comparatively: Four Nations*

	Correlation between Education and Party Identification	Correlation between Education and "Psychological Involvement"	Correlation between Party Identification and Campaign Activity	Correlation between Education and Campaign Activity	Multiple r for Education, Attitudes, and Campaign Activity	Correlation between "Psychological Involvement" and Campaign Activity
	(Simple r)	(Simple r)	(Residual r)	(Simple r)		(Residual r)
India (our study)	.01	.38	.15	.21	.41	.31
India (Verba study)	.23	.41	.10	.31	.48	.32
United States	−.06	.35	.13	.25	.48	.37
Austria	−.11	.32	.15	.12	.55	.52
Japan	.05	.28	.18	.04	.45	.36

SOURCE: Data other than Indian is from Sidney Verba, Norman Nie, and Jae-on Kim, *The Modes of Democratic Participation* (Beverly Hills Calif.: Sage Publications, Inc., 1971), appendix, pp. 75–79. The Indian data are from our 1967 national election study.
* The correlations in the first two columns and column 4 are strictly comparable; for the remaining columns the correlations are comparable for the last three countries, but since slightly different attitudes or orientations were used in our Indian study, the correlations for India are not strictly and perfectly comparable to the other countries. We feel the differences are not great enough, however, to discredit the comparisons.

education and party identification. Only in the United States is there a strong independent relationship between education and campaign activity. This reinforces our earlier argument that the United States may be relatively unique in the relationship between education and this type of political participation. In all countries here analyzed there is a relatively high correlation between party identification and campaign activity. This may be a little surprising to those who have studied the Austrian and Japanese systems, and indeed American scholars might have expected a higher correlation for the United States. The comparatively high correlation for India, however, is not unexpected, given our earlier findings. There is also a high correlation in all countries between "psychological involvement," however measured, and campaign activity. The relevant model, therefore, might be reconceptualized as shown in figure 16, based on the analysis thus far. For India in addition we found a linkage between educa-

FIG. 16. A summary comparative path model for campaign activity.

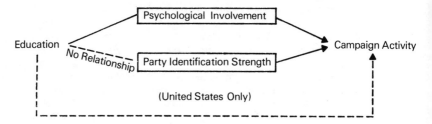

tion and candidate awareness, caste awareness and sense of political efficacy, but no linkage between these last three factors and campaign activity.

Path Models, Five Nations: Voting and Elite Contact Behavior

If we now turn from campaign activity and use the path model to explicate the variables linked to other types of political involvement, we see similar types of findings. Figures 17 and 18 are concerned with voting and elite contact in India. Educational level is even less relevant for explaining voting in India. Again, party identification strength is relatively important (.14). But the variables "explaining" campaign activity do not hold equally here. Level of general political interest and newspaper exposure are not important as factors linked to voting (.07 and −.03). But candidate awareness and caste awareness are important, two variables which were not useful in "explaining" campaign activity. Thus, sophistication about the identity of candidates and awareness about the relationship of caste to politics, plus party identification strength, among these variables seem most important. But overall these variables "explain" much less about voting than they do about campaign activism (multiple r of .31).

FIG. 17. Path model of variables related to voting in India.

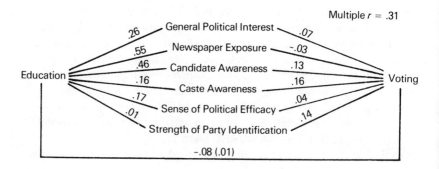

FIG. 18. Path model of variables related to elite contact in India.

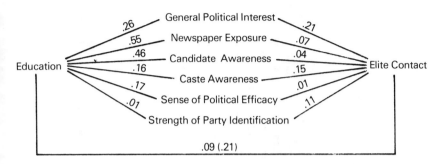

Multiple *r* = .40

The path model for "explaining" the participation of Indians by contacting elites is again somewhat different than the preceding models.[9] Again, political efficacy is of no help in predicting such contacts, nor is candidate awareness or newspaper exposure. General political interest and, significantly, caste awareness plus party identification are the most relevant variables here in explaining elite contacts.

To summarize, the one "psychological" or "attitudinal" variable, then, which seems to be linked to all three forms of political participation in India is strength of party identification. Of equal importance, except for explaining voting behavior, is general political interest. Caste awareness is next in significance, being linked to voting participation and elite contacts. Of partial utility is newspaper exposure and candidate awareness. Sense of political efficacy is of no relevance, a corroboration of our previous findings on the role of efficacy in explaining Indian political behavior.

To again put India in comparative perspective we can look at the Verba analysis for other countries, using the more limited and explicitly comparable models (as in fig. 15, tables 17.1 and 17.2). The first major conclusion concerns the relevance of party loyalty. India is apparently the only country where party identification is a consistently relevant variable in "explaining" different types of political involvement. It is important for the United States in relation to campaign activity and voting, but not in elite contacts by the public. It is also important in Japan for all except elite contacts. A second observation is that India and Japan are the only two countries in this comparative set for whom psychological orientations are consistently important factors in "explaining" all three types of political involvement measured here. In the United States (and Nigeria) mass contacts with elites are not explicated at all by the political-psychological variables used here; in Austria these variables seem irrelevant to voting participation. Third,

TABLE 17.2 The Path Coefficient Correlations "Explaining" Voting and Elite Contacts: Five Countries*

	Voting				Elite Contacts			
	Multiple r for Education, Attitudes, and Voting	Correlation between Education and Voting	Correlation between Party Identification and Voting	Correlation between Psychological Involvement and Voting	Multiple r for Education, Attitudes, and Elite Contacts	Correlation between Education and Elite Contacts	Correlation between Party Identification and Elite Contacts	Correlation between Psychological Involvement and Elite Contacts
India (our study)	.26	–.03	.23	.085	.39	.19	.10	.24
India (Verba study)	.26	–.13	.23	.09	.34	.17	.02	.20
United States (Verba)	.38	.13	.16	.23	.11	.03	–.02	.09
Australia	.24	–.09	.08	.08	.13	–.02	–.02	.13
Japan	.26	–.05	.13	.17	.17	.02	.08	.13
Nigeria	.32	–.09	.17	.21	.17	.10	.08	.05

SOURCE: The same as for table 17.1.
* As the note for table 17.1 explains, the variables operationalized for India are not perfectly comparable. These are all residuals after the effects of other variables are removed.

only in the United States does educational level seem to be a useful factor linked to voting, but even in the United States this factor shows virtually no relationship to elite contacts by the public. Paradoxically, in India education seems clearly related to elite contacts. And fourth, as the "multiple *rs*" indicate, India is again the only country where this type of model (excluding educational level, of course) seems consistently useful. In fact, while the multiple *r* for the other countries declines considerably in exploring elite contacts (to .17 or lower), it is at a high level for India (.39). There is strong evidence here then that party identification strength and psychological-attitudinal orientations toward politics may be key variables in helping to explain the Indian citizen's voting, and political involvement beyond voting. The model using such variables (again excluding the educational variable) is much more questionable for other countries for understanding public contacts with elites. It has more utility in explaining voting. It is relatively most useful for all countries in understanding the factors which compel persons to engage in campaign activity.

Extensions and Refinements of the Path Models for India: Using Caste and Party Exposure Variables

We have discovered for India, then, a possible path model which identifies at least suggestively certain variables and their possible linkages to different types of political involvement. This can be diagrammed as shown in figure 19. Certain factors seem clearly linked to political involvement, although we don't know the direction of the linkage. Where one finds high political interest one is also more likely to find considerable campaign activity than among those with low political interest, but campaign activism may "cause" interest or interest may cause activity, or the two may work so jointly or reciprocally that it is impossible to unravel the causal direction. Similarly educational level seems linked to certain other vari-

FIG. 19. The differential relevance of variables linked to participation types.

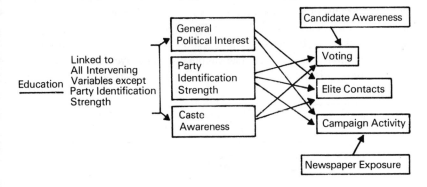

239

ables, as sense of political efficacy, which in itself is not linked to political activity, but which may be related to other attitudes or orientations, such as political interest, which itself is linked to political activity. The only antecedent factor chronologically which we can be sure of is education. Its direct impact on political involvement is negligible but it is strongly linked to other attitudinal variables which are linked to political activism.

In trying to improve on this empirical model we explored the relevance of caste status in India, using it in place of education. As our previous cross-tabulations suggested, the correlations were negligible in two cases and relatively small in the third instance:

	Product Movement Correlations Caste Status
Campaign activity	.05
Voting	.01
Elite contacts	.13

Caste seems only directly linked to some extent with elite contact behavior by the Indian public. It seems largely irrelevant to other types of political participation.

To expand the range of our analysis we next decided to add some political exposure variables to these models. Up to this point we had primarily used attitudinal or "psychological involvement" variables as mediating between educational status and political activity. We now add a "campaign exposure" variable reflecting four kinds of contact with parties or candidates during the 1967 campaign (receiving handbills, attending election meetings, meeting candidates, and being contacted by party canvassers). Second, we used a "leadership exposure" variable based on the number of *local* influential persons whom the respondent knows and with whom he has had associations or "dealings."[10] Our primary interest here was to see whether such exposure variables, if incorporated into these models, were useful for "explaining" political involvement. We had seen in our previous analysis that those highly exposed in the campaign were also very likely to be active. The question is whether this relationship would hold up in a path model. The simple product movement correlations for these two variables already suggested the limits of possible relevance:

	Campaign Activity	Voting	Elite Contacts
Campaign exposure	.376	.215	.285
Leadership exposure	.084	.090	

Exposure to local (primarily village) leadership is not related to other types of political involvement. Campaign exposure, however, seems to be highly relevant.

The path models certainly bear out this importance of campaign exposure. Using the more abbreviated form of the path model used previously in comparison of our Indian data with other countries, we added these exposure variables in figures 20 through 22. If we concentrate first on understanding which variables help "explain" campaign activity, we note that by adding "campaign exposure" to the model we introduce a variable which is now even more important than psychological involvement—its correlation is .25 and that of "psychological involvement" is .24. Further, there is a slight decline in the importance of party identification strength. And the amount of variance "explained" increases slightly—the multiple *r* is .47 rather than .41 as previously.

FIG. 20. Path model of campaign activity with campaign and leadership exposure variables added.

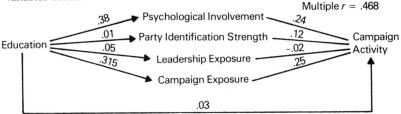

FIG. 21. Path model of voting with campaign and leadership exposure variables added.

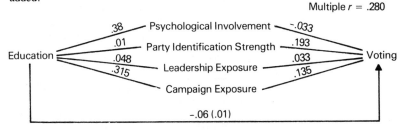

FIG. 22. Path model of elite contacts with campaign exposure variable added.

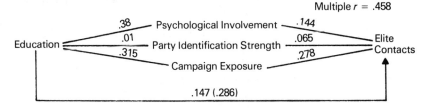

This decline in the relevance of "psychological involvement" is apparent also when we use campaign exposure in the path models for voting and elite contacts (figs. 21 and 22). Psychological involvement becomes completely unimportant in explaining the vote, and campaign exposure becomes the next most important variable (.135) after party identification (.193). The party identification correlation declined (from .229). One notes, however, that this combination of variables is less successful in "explaining" the vote than in our earlier path model when we used such variables as candidate awareness and caste awareness (fig. 17).

Campaign exposure apparently is extremely relevant in its linkage with elite contact behavior among the Indian public. As figure 22 demonstrates, the citizen's contact with parties and candidates during the campaign is more important than any other variable. "Psychological involvement," which in the earlier model had .24 correlation, declines now to .14. And party identification strength becomes even less relevant.

Perhaps the most striking discovery here is that education is now linked to campaign exposure, as well as to "psychological involvement" and it is the constellation of these variables, plus party identification (which is not linked to education), which is most helpful for understanding the forces at work in inducing political involvement. The diagram which most fits what we now know if we use only the highest correlations that have emerged may look like that shown in figure 23.

FIG. 23. An empirical model of Indian participation.

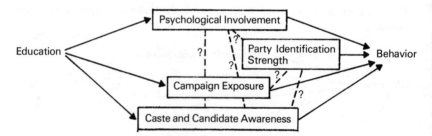

The Model of Attitudes as Derived from Political Involvement
One of the most intriguing questions in political analysis is whether political behavior results in or contributes to attitudinal change. Normally, we see behavior as a derivative of orientations, beliefs, and attitudes, and this approach has been utilized in the data presented here thus far for India. We now wish to turn this analysis around and ask whether being politically involved in India seems to "result in" or "be relevant for" different perceptions of and attitudes toward the political system, a basic query if we are to understand political development in India.

242

It is quite clear that presenting our data this way reveals that the "be-havior→attitude" relationship is indeed suggested by the data from our study. First, if we look at the differential levels of knowledge and interest by involvement status, we see striking differences (table 17.3). Those who are very active are much more informed than the uninvolved or those who only vote—a 49 percent difference. Campaign interest is high for 61 per-cent of the very involved, while none of those who are not involved were interested. Caste awareness, general political interest, and awareness of party differences similarly is high for the involved but not for those who are less active. It is interesting to note that it is not just voting participation which seems to "produce" high levels of knowledge and awareness. Rather it is extra involvement as a party member and in some form of campaign activity which is closely linked to such attitudes.

TABLE 17.3 The Relevance of Political Involvement for Knowledge, Interest, and Awareness about Politics*

	% Uninvolved	% Irregular Voters	% Regular Voters	% Campaign or Party Actives	% Active in Campaign and Party Member
	(N=24)	(N=81)	(N=787)	(N=85)	(N=42)
Knowledge of candidate Names 2 or more (Parliament)	13	23	25	41	62
General political interest high	0	6	9	23	36
Election campaign interest high	0	4	8	29	61
Caste awareness high	8	20	29	51	55
Sees differences in party programs	9	21	27	44	59

* Each percentage is a proportion of the involvement category.

Basic attitudes toward the party system may be greatly "influenced" if one is politically involved (table 17.4). And being a regular voter is appar-ently an additional type of behavior which by itself relates to, or induces,

TABLE 17.4 The "Consequences" of Political Involvement for Basic Attitudes*

	% Uninvolved	% Irregular Voters	% Regular Voters	% Party or Campaign Actives	% Active in Party and Campaign
Strong party identification	16	27	54	76	90
Parties help make government pay attention to people					
"A good deal"	17⎱ 30	23⎱ 49	28⎱ 63	40⎱ 79	43⎱ 79
"Somewhat"	13⎰	26⎰	35⎰	39⎰	36⎰
Elections help make government pay attention to people					
"A good deal"	25⎱ 54	32⎱ 57	41⎱ 71	45⎱ 82	55⎱ 88
"Somewhat"	29⎰	25⎰	30⎰	37⎰	33⎰
Favors more than one-party system	37	43	46	63	76
Party conflict not desirable	67	68	74	88	86
Political efficacy					
People like me have no say (agrees)	79	73	73	68	57
Voting has an effect (agrees)	42	69	78	81	86
Government officials don't care what people like me think (agrees)	74	75	80	75	95
Approves of same or greater government controls over the economy	29	37	40	51	57
Satisfied with government officials					
At local level	33	36	44	41	36
At district and central levels	33	44	41	34	46

* Each percentage is the proportion of the involvement category who hold a particular attitude.

more positive attitudes toward the party and election system. Only 16 percent of the uninvolved are strong party identifiers, but 54 percent of the regular voters are, and 90 percent of the very active are. The uninvolved have a rather negative view of the role of parties and favor a one-party system, but approximately 80 percent of the very active are supportive of the party system. Few approved of party conflict, however, and being politically active actually leads to an increase in disapproval of such conflict. This is obviously an inherent paradox in public attitudes toward the Indian system. People would strongly prefer a consensus party system, yet they can support and identify and be active in a party system even though it is a conflict system.

Another paradox which emerges here is that on certain measures of personal political efficacy high proportions of active as well as uninvolved persons feel "inefficacious," and yet they continue to support the system. For example, 74 to 95 percent of the actives feel that "government officials don't care what people like me think." A third interesting finding, if not a paradox, is that there is high dissatisfaction with government officials at both the local and central government level, and yet this seemingly does not affect political involvement. In terms of basic attitudes, then, political involvement is high despite criticism of the regime, lack of a feeling of efficacy, and a strong opposition to party conflict, but such activity seems to "lead to" or be "linked to" strong loyalties to parties and increasing support for the multiple party system within a context of free elections. One should note also that the actives are "liberals" on the issue of governmental controls—over 50 percent favor controls over the economy compared to less than 30 percent of the uninvolved.

Political involvement seems to "result in" somewhat less traditional attitudes, although the evidence is by no means conclusive (table 17.5). Many of the actives still hold "traditional" positions. The very active cadre, however, perceive themselves as more "innovative" on our "traditionalism-innovation" scale than those who were uninvolved; they are less supportive of a ban on cow slaughter and are less likely to feel a legislator should work for caste interests. These are by no means such convincing findings as those on other basic attitudes, however. And in fact we find our political actives in India giving evidence of *both* strong support for the post-Independence institutions of parties and elections *and* yet revealing a great deal of traditionalism in their responses. It seems clear that traditional attitudes persist and are meshed with, and not considered contradictory to, activity within the "modern" political arena.

When we partition our sample by educational level, we can see the striking differences in the proportions who hold "supportive" attitudes (table 17.6). On the first three types of orientation in that table the illiter-

TABLE 17.5 The Possible Consequences of Political Involvement for a Change from "Traditional" to "Modernizing" Attitudes

	% Uninvolved	% Irregular Voters	% Regular Voters	% Party or Campaign Actives	% Active in Party and Campaign
Sees self as "very new" (innovative) on party space scale	0	17	21	21	22
Favors banning cow slaughter	71	75	73	69	55
Feels legislator should work for caste interests	21	24	26	33	7

TABLE 17.6 The Relevance of Political Involvement for Basic Attitudes and Levels of Political Knowledge and Interest: By Contrasting Education Groups

	% Upper Educated*			% Illiterates		
	Inactive	Voters	Actives	Inactive	Voters	Active
Knowledge of candidates (Lok Sabha)						
Can name 2 or more	67	76	92	10	13	23
Can name 1 or more	71	85	94	18	41	53
General political interest						
"Some" or "great"	33	34	100	8	23	44
Supports parties: feels they make government "pay attention"	67	88	100	29	56	73
Feels national government officials are doing a good job	50	38	7	42	41	40
Government officials don't care what people like me think (disagrees)	25	22	15	8	12	18
Opposes party conflict	67	82	69	65	70	87

* Includes those with upper secondary, high school, or some college education.

ates are far below those with a higher education, in political knowledge, interest, and support for parties. But there is a sharp increase in these orientations as political participation increases. In some cases, these are dramatic increases, for both the well-educated and the illiterates. Just being a voter seems to mean a sizable jump in knowledge of who was a candidate for office—from 18 to 41 percent among the illiterates. And support for the party system increases from 29 to 56 percent among the illiterates. In addition, being a campaign or party active means an extra increment in knowledge, interest, and support for parties, particularly, but not exclusively, among illiterates. Illiterate "actives" have very respectable levels of political knowledge and acceptance of the system. However, in the latter three types of items in the table, one finds that political involvement may not be as relevant, or, in fact, may be somewhat associated with less "modern" or less "system-support" types of attitudes. For example, cynicism about government officials does not decline with involvement (among the upper-educated it actually increases).

One senses from these data, then, that despite social status differences, political involvement does not necessarily soften antisystem orientations, or feelings of cynicism and inefficacy, but it does heighten knowledge about politics, interest in politics, and support for parties, particularly among the large mass of illiterates—all very salutary consequences if one is concerned about political development.

When we look at caste differences (table 17.7) we note the same pattern of findings. The lower castes, ordinarily low in political sophistication in terms of their knowledge about caste elite and mass political behavior, become highly "caste aware" if involved in politics—a striking increase from 17 to 88 percent if the uninvolved lower castes are compared to the involved lower castes. Simple knowledge of the caste of the winning candidate also increases dramatically (although the difference between the inactives and actives among the upper castes is also great). Further, the lower castes show a significant contrast in support for the party system—22 percent of the inactive lower castes are supportive while 83 percent of the active lower castes are. Again, we find very little evidence that political involvement reduces traditional attitudes. Lower caste actives are actually more likely to think that a legislator should work for caste interests (71 percent) and are only slightly less pessimistic about their political efficacy (62 percent). On balance then one can be gratified to see lower castes and Harijans reveal, coincidental with political activity, or as a result of it, knowledgeable, aware, and supportive behavior and attitudinal patterns, but one must realize that basically traditional orientations toward the system and their role in that system persist, among upper castes as well as lower castes.

TABLE 17.7 Differences by Castes in the "Consequences" of Political Involvement for Basic Political Attitudes

	Upper Castes (%)			Lower Castes and Harijans and Tribes (%)		
	Inactives	Voters	Actives	Inactives	Voters	Actives
Has high caste political awareness	65	67	85	17	54	88
Feels it is important for legislator to work for caste interests	38	47	32	50	50	71
Knows caste of winner in constituency in parliamentary election	27	38	71	11	15	33
Favors banning cow slaughter	78	81	81	78	82	68
"People like me have no say"	76	78	71	69	70	62
Supports party system	62	69	80	22	52	83

We can now return to our path analysis used previously and attempt to illustrate this suggested relationship (behavior→attitude) (figure 24). Using

FIG. 24. Path model of the "impact" of campaign activity on psychological involvement.

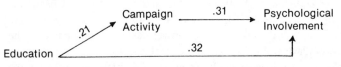

Multiple r = .49

education as the social status variable and "psychological involvement" as previously defined (political interest and media exposure) as the "dependent" variable, we can compute a correlation for the possible influence of campaign activity on such attitudes as are comprehended in "psychological involvement." The product moment correlations are as follows:

	Campaign Activity	Psychological Involvement
Education	.21	.38
Psychological involvement	.37	

In the path model, campaign activity has a considerable "impact" on psychological attitudes toward politics (path coefficient of .31) which is almost as great as the reverse relationship in the same type of path model (a path coefficient of .35 for the "impact" of psychological involvement on campaign activity). Yet, the path model in figure 24 has more explanatory power it appears (multiple *r* of .49) than if one looks at activity as "dependent" (multiple *r* of .38). In a sense nothing has been definitely established by this as to the actual "flow" of relationships, in reality, although this is a very suggestive finding. There seems, in fact, to be a reciprocal relationship obtaining which can be most properly diagrammed as shown in figure 25.

FIG. 25. The interaction of variables linked to involvement.

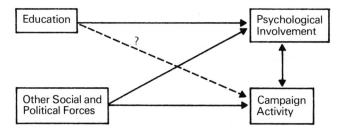

For the time being our analysis does not permit a more complete unravelling of these relationships. Certainly our data strongly suggest that these variables may in reality be linked as suggested. But such models, including path models, are too simplistic. With other variables such as "campaign exposure" and "party identification strength" added to this model, a more complex configuration of variables emerges, which is probably less a simple "path flow" model than a complex set of mutually linked and re-enforced variables incrementally producing more meaningful involvement, behaviorally *and* attitudinally, over time.

The controversy over the utility of particular path models is difficult to resolve. It may be that the "behavior→attitude" model is more useful in certain circumstances in certain societies, and with certain social groups than is the "attitude→behavior" model. In our Indian data the linkage between party support attitudes and political participation for educated people is rather poor. For illiterates there is inclined to be a better "attitude→behavior" relationship. Similarly if we look at the relationship between political efficacy attitudes and political activity for caste groups we see the same type of difference. Lower caste respondents, Harijans and Tribals particularly, who are active in campaigns and parties seem to develop a sense of political efficacy, but at the upper caste levels there is no such relationship. Similarly if we use an orientation like "political interest" we find that at the upper educational and caste levels it is strongly linked to political activity (a 40 percent difference in activity proportions between those high and low in interest). But for the lower educational and caste groups the differences are marginal (less than a 10 percent difference). On the other hand, if we turn the analysis around, and use the "attitude→behavior" model we find that consistently for lower status groups, but not for all middle and higher status groups, activity seems to produce more support for parties and a heightened sense of political efficacy. For illiterates and lower castes the differentials by political involvement in attitudes toward the party system are large. It seems to make a great deal of difference for these lower status people if they are politically involved; it seems to result in much more affirmative attitudes toward the political system and toward their role in that system.

Concluding Observations: A Suggested "Joint Pressures" Model
In this chapter we have explored the possible linkage patterns for a variety of variables as they interact with political involvement. We have envisaged behavior as both the "effect" and "cause" in constructing these models. It is clear that a configuration of variables operate together, such as party identification strength, political interest, campaign exposure, and political participation. But what their mutual relationships are with each other—how they "explain" political activity or how they are affected by such activity—remains to be more perfectly analyzed. Yet that these variables are relevant for explaining political behavior is indisputable.

The role of social and economic environmental factors is much less clear. We found neither caste status nor educational status by itself as very important in its direct relationship to political activity. Education seems to influence political interest, as well as other attitudes (but not partisan intensity), even though it has no direct relationship to political activity. Thus social status as reflected in education appears to be important as an indirect influence on political activity.

Path models are interesting but they rest on the assumption of "linear" causal relationships. Thus, in such a model education presumably determines psychological involvement to a great extent, which in turn has an impact on political behavior. But as we have seen, this "linear" type of model may be spurious and other models may be equally as powerful, or even more useful. In the case of a society such as the Indian, one model which may be more useful is a "cross-pressures" or, perhaps better labeled, a "joint pressures" model. Indeed many of our findings suggest that many Indian citizens are caught in a cross-pressure or combined pres-

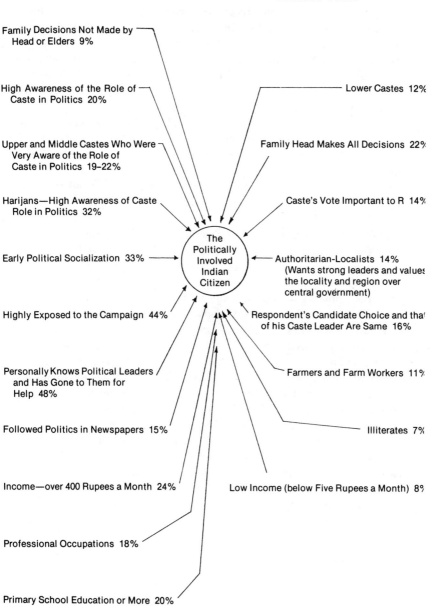

FIG. 26. A "joint pressure" model suggesting "traditional" and "modern" influences as related to political involvement in India.

"Modern" Forces   "Traditional" Forces

Family Decisions Not Made by Head or Elders 9%

High Awareness of the Role of Caste in Politics 20%

Lower Castes 12%

Upper and Middle Castes Who Were Very Aware of the Role of Caste in Politics 19–22%

Family Head Makes All Decisions 22%

Harijans—High Awareness of Caste Role in Politics 32%

Caste's Vote Important to R 14%

The Politically Involved Indian Citizen

Early Political Socialization 33%

Authoritarian-Localists 14% (Wants strong leaders and values the locality and region over central government)

Highly Exposed to the Campaign 44%

Respondent's Candidate Choice and that of his Caste Leader Are Same 16%

Personally Knows Political Leaders and Has Gone to Them for Help 48%

Farmers and Farm Workers 11%

Followed Politics in Newspapers 15%

Illiterates 7%

Income—over 400 Rupees a Month 24%

Low Income (below Five Rupees a Month) 8%

Professional Occupations 18%

Primary School Education or More 20%

The percentages are proportions of each subgroup who were active in the campaign or as party members in 1967.

sure situation, being subjected to stimuli facilitating and inhibiting political participation. Particularly one is inclined to see the Indian citizen as conditioned by "traditional" forces and by more "modern" influences, al- though this a great oversimplification of reality. There is no question that a variety of pressures from different sources impinge on the Indian citizen. The unanswered question is which of these types of forces conduce to political involvement. In figure 26 we suggest a model of the influence of "traditional" and "modern" forces as only one way of visualizing the differential pressures as they may be shaping the political participation of the Indian citizen.

What stands out in this model is the variety of factors which may be associated with political involvement. And many individuals who exhibit "traditional" characteristics are nevertheless active politically. Thus, those who are brought up in the most "traditional" homes, where the head of the household and/or elders made the decisions for all members of the household, are very active in politics. Even the "authoritarian-parochials" are relatively active.

On the other hand, the evidence that modernization pressures and conditions are linked to political involvement are indisputable. Family socialization to politics is clearly relevant, as is campaign exposure, and personal acquaintance of and contact with political leadership. Those with some education, holding professional and managerial occupations, and in the higher income brackets are also relatively involved in politics.

What this indicates, therefore, is that there are a variety of conditions under which Indians may be led to political involvement. And it is not only those who have been exposed to "modernizing" stimuli who are active. Under certain circumstances those coming from traditional environments are involved with India's modern politics. Indeed one is inclined to conclude that "traditional" and "modern" influences are merged in the backgrounds and attitudes of many Indians in such a way that it is difficult to determine which is of the greatest importance. "Tradition" has by no means given way to "modernity" but is in fact commingled with it. The two, "modernity" and "tradition," both are dominant perspectives in the Indian polity and together give great reason for political involvement while at the same time giving greater meaning for the system to a large number of Indian citizens.

EIGHTEEN

The Functions and Consequences of Political Involvement: For the Party System, Social Conflict, Policy Decisions, and Effective Citizen Action

T HE RECURRENT CONCERN OF SCHOLARS OF POLITICAL DEVELOPMENT IS in the system relevance and consequences of political activity, particularly for a society like India during the period from 1947 to the present. The meaning and effect of voting and other types of political activity for such a society has been closely questioned by some writers. Generally participation through parties and elections is viewed as probably having a considerable impact on the polity. Kothari argues that "party politics became the great vehicle of national integration," "that a country as vast and pluralistic as India can be effectively united only through a participant and accommodative model of politics."[1] Similarly Shils, though at times pessimistic about the importance of political participation, states at one point:

> The granting of universal suffrage without property or literacy
> qualifications is perhaps the greatest single factor leading to the
> function of a political society ... The drawing of the whole adult
> population periodically into contact with the symbols of the
> center of national political life must in the course of time have
> immeasurable consequences for stirring people up, giving them a
> sense of their own potential significance and for attaching their senti-
> ments to symbols which comprehend the entire nation.[2]

Although one may well question the validity of the models of political development advanced by such scholars as S. N. Eisenstadt, Gabriel Almond, Karl Deutsch, and Samuel Huntington, they all generally view political participation as part of a "systemic process" of social-political change in developing societies.[3] There are, of course, considerable differences in the ways in which they conceptualize the development process and in the way in which, in their theories, political involvement is phased into and interacts with societal transformations in social status and social organization, economic behavior, the revolution of technology and cultural development. The virtues of alternative theories or models will not be argued here. Our basic position advanced earlier is that in India political participation and activity occurred after Independence, *after* elite initiatives had established the new constitution, party structure, Parliament, and bureaucracy.

Now, however, in this chapter we wish to argue empirically the reciprocal of that basic theoretical position—that political involvement can have an impact on the political and social order. As indicated in the introduction, we feel that political involvement is functional to the achievement of political integration, to the development of elite-mass relationships critical if democratic institutions are to perform well, and to the achievement of a more egalitarian system in the redistribution of social power. Without political involvement the Indian society would be decidedly different. In the absence of political involvement the inputs, the process, the outputs, and the very character of the political system would be, and would have been, quite different. And whether genuine democratic political development could have occurred is open to serious question.

The Theoretical Roles of the Political Activists
Up to now we have concentrated on an analysis of political involvement which demonstrated the diversity of participant activities and the relatively high proportion of Indians who engage in such activities. We found a high level of voting turnout and over 12 percent of the population engaged in political activities beyond voting. We then analyzed the social and demographic characteristics and correlates of political involvement as well as the extent to which psychological and attitudinal variables help explain activity. We found political involvement by no means concentrated in the higher social strata of Indian society, and that those with "traditional" as well as "modern" orientations toward the political system are politically active. Finally we discovered that exposure to the environment of competitive parties and campaigns was linked to high political involvement. Implicit in this analysis already, then, is the functional relevance of political participation for the Indian system: it has penetrated the society, it is tied to critical systemic attitude patterns, it is occurring within the environment of the new party politics.

Going beyond such analysis of the extent and sources for participation, we can now ask the question, What are the potential consequences of having such political activists? These activists, 12 percent of the adult population, engage in a variety of political acts, some nominal or sporadic, others more purposive and sustained in nature. What is the meaning for the society of having such a new functional subelite? What are the consequences for the activists themselves as well as for their society? Perhaps the central question is, Has a new stratum of active citizens assumed participant roles in India since Independence in 1947, a group which reflects attitudes, perceptions, values, and orientations toward the political system which potentially or actually already have had (or can have) an impact on a wide range of public activities in India, local as well as national? In

Eisenstadt's phrase, Is there an activist stratum which could manifest a "transformative capacity" for the Indian polity? In reflecting on this question we can suggest a variety of possible system impacts. First, do these involved people play an important role in the mobilization of support or opposition for regime goals? Related is the question of whether they are in fact, or may be, generating pressure on the top elites for new policies based on the policy preferences of these lower level activists. This is a "consequence" explored very specifically by Verba and Nie in their study of participation in the United States, to which we will refer later in our Indian analysis.[4] Second, what is the communication role of these activists, as opinion and action leaders, in their relations with the public? Not only may their role be important in interpreting elite policy goals but also in contributing to public consensus, or dissensus, concerning system performance and practice. Third, one must view the individuals in this activist cadre as coming from different social groups and political structures, and thus potentially contributing to the tension and conflict within the system, as activists compete with each other in the parties and campaign context. In this connection one might ask, What is the potential for exacerbation of group conflict or for revolution among those within the activist cadre and in their relationships to the masses? In all of this one must inquire whether political involvement is a legitimizing force or a force of disequilibrium, an integrating force or a conflict/competition maximizing force? Are these activists contributing to system maintenance and acceptance or to its rejection? There are thus many vantage points from which to view the possible functional relevance of political involvement in India. And in the analysis which follows we will seek to explore the possible meaning of our data for these large theoretical concerns, by looking at specific answers to specific operational questions.

The Political Sophistication of the Activists

It is important to recognize at the outset that the profile of these Indian activists reveals that they probably are, or can be, "effective" and "sophisticated" citizens. This states in a different way our earlier presentation of evidence that political participation had "consequences" for political perceptions and orientations. A few summary characteristics are presented in table 18.1. In contrast to the nonactive public they are very knowledgeable about politics, well-informed on who the candidates were, who was successful in the election, and who had a high level of caste awareness (that is, know how castes voted, what the caste of candidates was, and how caste leaders voted). The differences between activists and the nonactive public are extreme—13 percent compared to 83 percent, for example, know who the candidates were. Further, the activists have much

TABLE 18.1 Profile of Indian Activists as "Effective Citizens," Contrasted to Less Active Groups in the Population

	% Completely Nonactive	% Very Active in Party or Campaign
Political knowledge		
Can name 2 or more candidates for state assembly	13	83
Can name 2 or more candidates for Parliament	13	62
Political interest and exposure		
Level of general political interest		
Great	0	36
Some	8	43
Learned about politics from newspapers	21	64
Party perceptions		
Strong party identification	16	90
Sees party programs as different	9	59
Contact with political leaders and groups		
Personally knows 1 or more political leaders	12	81
Met the candidates in the campaign	0	70
Active in groups (other than parties) in the constituency during the campaign	0	17

more interest in political affairs—79 percent of the very active have an interest in politics while only 8 percent of the nonactive public are interested. Activists are much more exposed to the newspapers as well as to the parties, of course. Almost two-thirds learned about the election campaign from newspapers, compared to a fifth of the nonactives. Actives are a bit more likely to be members of social groups (other than caste or religious associations), although the level of such membership is uniformly low in India. They are also more likely to be active in groups other than parties, although the proportions are small—less than 20 percent.

Actives are strong party identifiers—over 90 percent compared to 16 percent or less for those not involved. They were consistent party voters from 1957 to 1967—67 percent compared to 47 percent of the regular electorate. About 15 percent were "switchers" and 14 percent were newly mobilized in 1967, having been nonvoters previously.

Actives were more inclined to feel there were differences in party programs, while nonactives were less likely to see such differences. Their exposure to political leadership and the party process was considerable. Up to 80 percent of the actives knew political leaders personally, up to 70 percent had met the candidates, and from 42 to 61 percent had been exposed to the campaign. It seems clear then that this 12 percent of the Indian electorate consisting of individuals who have exhibited some activism are a relatively well-informed, interested, aware, and politically exposed group, highly committed to support for the parties. They could be conceived of as not only a "campaign activist cadre" but also as an "opinion leadership cadre," having potential influence with the public generally while performing essential tasks in elite support.

If we divide our activist group by social status characteristics, we can see that there are different levels of political awareness and exposure. Examples of some of the differences are as follows:

	Upper Caste Actives	Lower Caste and Harijan Actives
% personally knowing political leaders	79	64
% active in campaign groups	18	13
% meeting candidates	70	38
% able to name 2 or more candidates for Parliament	62	43

The same differences exist for educational groups among the activists. Higher status activists are clearly more likely to be informed and in contact with political leaders and influentials. But the proportion of lower caste activists who are in touch with leaders and who are knowledgeable is nonetheless surprisingly high.

Differences among the Activist Cadres by Party

Having established the high level of political sophistication of these activists, our second concern is their distribution by political party. As table 18.2 reveals, there is a preponderance of Congress identifiers among the activist sample, with 55 percent belonging to that party. No other single party has over 10 percent of this activist stratum. And there is a fairly

257

TABLE 18.2 Party Identification of Political Activists

	% of all Party and Campaign Actives (N=253)
Congress	55
Swatantra	5
Jan Sangh	8
Communist	8
Socialist	7
DMK	10
Independents, and nonidentifiers	7

balanced distribution to the "right" and "left" of Congress. Interestingly, the DMK had 10 percent of the activists, and this compared to 8 percent for the Communists and 8 percent for Jan Sangh. Also interesting is the fact that 7 percent of all activists said they supported Independents or would not identify with a party.

The opposition to Congress, then, is somewhat underrepresented in terms of their strength in the population, but all major parties have sizable cadres of active supporters. According to our calculations, approximately 20 million adults in India in 1967 engaged in some type of party work. Over ten million of these were Congress workers, but over one and a half million worked for the Communists, the same number for Jan Sangh, two million for DMK, one million for Swatantra, and over a million and a quarter for the Socialists.[5]

Congress activists tended to be somewhat stronger in party loyalty when compared to non-Congress activists—88 percent compared to 68 percent. This tendency was also found in comparing Congress voters with non-Congress voters—77 percent having strong party identification among Congress voters and 65 percent for non-Congress voters. There were great variations by individual party, however, with the DMK marked particularly by strong party identification among activists and voters.

All parties rely heavily on those with low social status for the work that has to be done in campaigns. This was particularly true for Congress activists, over 50 percent of whom had no education or very little education (table 18.3). But all parties recruit close to 40 percent of their activists from these low status groups. The opposition Right and Left parties have more activists with a college education than does Congress, but the total proportion of such high status persons is below one-fifth. The net result of having 55 percent of all activists supporting Congress and a heavy concentration of lower status people among these Congress activists is that, if we reverse the

TABLE 18.3 Social Status of Activists of the Different Parties

Activist Group	Educational Categories (%)					
	Illiterates	Primary	Middle	High School	College	N
Congress	31	24	31	6	7	139
Swatantra and Jan Sangh	9	30	38	6	18	34
Socialists and Communists	16	27	35	5	16	37
DMK	15	23	58	4	0	26
Independents and nonidentifiers	29	12	47	6	6	17

analysis, we discover that of all our lower status activists, 80 percent are found as working for Congress. This is the proportion for both activists who were illiterates and lower caste. There is considerable evidence here then that the educationally and socially deprived or unprivileged sectors of Indian society contribute the bulk of the personnel from the general population who engage in campaign and party activity. Congress profits particularly from this tendency. Yet, this is not an exclusively "Western," educated, upper-class, Congress-controlled activist cadre. It is more properly characterized as a lower social status cadre including many very loyal Congress followers but also including sizable cadres of supporters in the opposition parties.

Views of the Political Process Held by Party Activists
If we look at these different sets of activists for Congress and the opposition parties, one basis for assessing their present and potential impact on the system is their level of system criticism, rejection, and alienation. And for opposition parties particularly it would be instructive to determine the depth of their antagonism to Congress and its policies. We have already noted the contrasts in attitudes toward the political system and process for all activists and nonactives. A brief summary may be useful here (table 18.4). The activists' view of parties and elections is generally supportive, much more so than that of irregular voters and nonactives. However, there is a traditional fear of dissensus as a result of party conflict which activists even more than ordinary voters are concerned and articulate about. Activists also feel that voting can be efficacious, even though they are heavily pessimistic on other efficacy items. Finally, activists are on balance dissatisfied with local and higher government officials, their negative support scores matching those of the inactives on these measures. Thus actives

TABLE 18.4 Differences in System Support for Actives, Voters, and Nonactives*

	Index of Support			
	Actives	Regular Voters	Irregular Voters	Non-actives
View of parties: feel they make government responsive	+60	+43	+23	−7
View of elections: feel they make government responsive	+71	+56	+31	+37
Preference for competitive party system to one-party system	+35	−1	−4	−5
Satisfied with local officials	−17	−1	−15	−17
Satisfied with state and central government officials	−16	−1	+6	−17
Satisfied with the results of the election here (in the constituency) for Parliament	+25	+35	+32	+5
Efficacy: "People like me have no say about what the government does"	−33	−52	−57	−66
Efficacy: "Government doesn't care what people like me think"	−67	−67	−61	−65
Efficacy: "Voting has an effect on what the government does"	+69	+64	+57	+9
Views party conflict as desirable	−76	−58	−53	−51

* These support scores were arrived at by subtracting the proportions who were not supportive from the proportions who were supportive. The "don't knows" were eliminated from the calculation of the support scores. A plus score indicates more support, or less criticism.

seem clearly distinguishable from nonactives in that they do strongly support the party and election system within which they are active, they accept the results of elections, but they are critical of governmental officials and appear cynical about the effectiveness of their own personal role in the system. They are by no means a complacent, completely supportive subelite. They could well be motivated to work for change in the system, but most of them apparently do not hold antisystem orientations.

A clue to the views of activists about the legislative process is afforded by their responses to our question as to whether MPs should work for the interests of their caste. Many, including activists, still take the position that this is important. But only 21 percent of our most active cadre do (5 percent are undecided), while 38 to 53 percent of the less active do (and up to 25 percent are undecided).

Added to the evidence of activist skepticism about the system cited above is the evaluation of the Congress record. On evaluations of Congress leadership and policy (on controlling prices, food distribution, rooting out corruption), from 60 to 80 percent of the activists were critical. This suggests that the level of unrest and dissatisfaction was high, and the potential for these citizens for mobilization to change the regime was considerable.

These observations concerning the existence of conditions among activist citizens which could be exploited against the regime, if not against the system, make much more sense if we divide our activists by party allegiance. As stated earlier, 70 percent of Indian activists (88 percent of Congress activists, 68 percent of opposition activists) were *strong* party identifiers. There is a high level of psychological commitment to party, with Congress activists particularly strong in their loyalty. Keeping this in mind, the distribution of political sophistication and system, or regime, support by party activists cadre is enlightening (table 18.5). Activists in all parties are very supportive of the party and election system generally. From 80 to 90 percent, irrespective of party, feel parties and elections make the system responsive, and they are generally not interested in a one-party system. On the other hand they are uniformly pessimistic or cynical about the political efficacy of the ordinary citizen. In all parties the activists feel that "government doesn't care," "politics is too complicated" for the ordinary citizen, and "people like me have no say." The proportion of activists who have a sense of efficacy is extremely low, particularly for Swatantra and Jan Sangh participants on the Right.

In addition to cynicism about subjective political competence, most opposition activists are dissatisfied with the job local, state, and central government officials are doing. Congress and DMK activists are much more supportive but party activists on the Right and Left as well as those activists working for independents are largely critical—from 20 to 40 percent. And their criticism of the policies and leadership of Congress is overwhelming. Only Congress activists are inclined to defend Congress in its handling of price control, food distribution, law and order, agricultural problems, and similar problems. And Congress activists are more likely to defend Congress than Congress identifiers who were not active—on the average a 5 percent differential.

In all other parties the activists are more critical of Congress than those who were inactive. The difference, for example, on "providing strong leadership" is 10 percent more criticism of Congress by activists in the parties on the Right, 19 percent difference by activists for parties on the Left, and 36 percent difference for DMK.

Although actives in opposition parties are generally inclined to be more critical of Congress than those not active, we do not find this to be true for all social status groups. In fact it is interesting to note that illiterate activists

261

TABLE 18.5 Differences in Political Orientations for Political Actives by Party

	% Congress	% Swatantra and Jan Sangh	% Socialists and Communists	% DMK	% Independents
View of parties					
Feel they make government responsive	84	85	87	84	81
Prefer a competitive party system to one-party system	64	71	76	70	69
View of elections					
Feel they make government responsive	89	85	97	97	95
Satisfaction with officials					
With local officials	48	41	25	62	35
With state and central government officials	54	19	27	60	38

Knowledge of politics

Knows 2 or more candidates					
For Parliament	53	68	74	72	71
For state assembly	87	94	92	96	71
Efficacy					
High on 4 items of efficacy index	15	3	19	11	12
Criticism of Congress (% strongly agree)					
"Failed to provide strong leadership"	33	66	77	69	38
"Failed to keep prices down"	37	86	89	96	65
"Failed to distribute food properly"	36	69	78	96	59
"Failed to handle the problem of agricultural production"	22	56	58	67	60

and lower caste activists generally are less critical than the inactives in these social groups. There was a 10 to 20 percent difference, respectively. It was the middle and upper social status activists, particularly in opposition parties, who exhibited the greatest rejection of Congress leadership.

This high anti-Congress criticism, combined with dissatisfaction of the job officials at all levels were doing, plus cynicism about the efficacy of political action, suggests a high potential for disaffection as well as political involvement focusing on change. In effect we have here a set of activists who are rather knowledgeable about politics, believing in the competitive party system, who differ basically in their evaluation of the job the Congress party and the Congress administration was performing. Congress activists, while having a minority of dissidents and critics among their number, were basically supportive and satisfied. But the other half of the activist cadre had rejected the type of leadership Congress was providing.

One final distinction of interest in this connection. When we asked our respondents to place themselves on our seven-point "innovation-tradition" scale, the differences for party activists were striking. Only 38 percent of our Congress activists place themselves at the "new" or "innovation" end of the scale (that is, see themselves as "standing for new ideas"), while for the activists of Swatantra and Jan Sangh it is 58 percent, for the Socialists and Communists 73 percent, for DMK activists it is 92 percent, and for activists who worked for independents it is 62 percent. In terms of self-perceptions, then, opposition activists do see themselves as more innovative, working for "new programs" and for social and political changes.

Policy Preferences of Activists
The role that these activists conceivably might have over policy is suggested if we look at the distinctions between activists and others in the population in attitudes on policy questions. We utilize here basically the same procedures employed by Verba and Nie in the study of political participation in the United States.[6] Verba presents data suggesting that the most activist cadre in the United States is the most conservative on social and economic issues. Thus, while 48 percent of the 5 percent most active segment of American society reject the need for governmental responsibility in social and economic welfare, only 21 percent of the 5 percent least active segment of U.S. society reject governmental action.[7] Thus activists are much more conservative than those who were inactive, a product no doubt of the high social status background of American party activists. In India the relationship is reversed. The most active stratum is also the most "liberal" on the question of governmental intervention in the economy. As figure 27 reveals, 57 percent of the most active are liberal while only 29

FIG. 27. Differential levels of "liberalism" for involvement categories (percentage desiring the same or greater governmental controls over the economy).

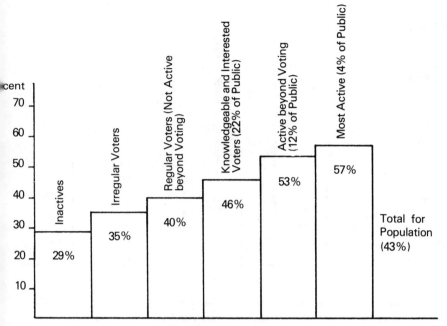

In sum, while in the United States those with higher social status predominate among activists and contribute to conservatism among activists, this is not so in India. There those with higher social status do not predominate among activists and they are not consistently conservative. As a result Indian activists are liberal in their policy outlooks.

percent of those completely uninvolved are liberal. Similarly, although the opinion of most Indians for religious reasons opposes cow slaughter, the activists are least traditional in this respect—43 percent opposing a ban on cow slaughter, compared to 16 percent for those who are inactive (fig. 28).

In the United States Verba found that those activists with upper social status were most conservative on economic and social issues. Again, in India one usually does find this tendency also, although not consistently. Upper- and middle-caste activists are more conservative (but upper castes less conservative than middle castes) while Harijans, low castes, and Muslim activists are more liberal. The differences are striking—a difference of as much as 35 percent. As for educational level, activists with a high education have a very "liberal" view (54 percent favoring greater government control), although those with a primary school education are slightly higher in liberalism. In sum, while in the United States those with higher social status predominate among activists and contribute to conservatism among activists, this is not so in India. There those with higher social status do not predominate among activists and they are not consistently conservative. As a result Indian activists are liberal in their policy outlooks.

265

Fɪɢ. 28. Differential levels of "liberalism" for involvement categories (percentage opposing a ban on cow slaughter).

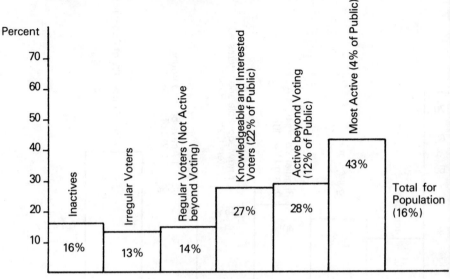

Activity Level

The issue of cow slaughter reveals a somewhat different picture of policy preferences for activists by social status. The least "traditional" are found among those with the highest education. Activists are, however, consistently less traditional on this issue than those who are not active. The differences range from 19 percent at the highest educational level to 3 percent for illiterates.

Party differences in policy preferences among activists are considerable (table 18.6). On the issue of governmental controls it is clear that Congress, Socialist, and Communist activists are committed to the liberal position, or the position of maintaining or increasing governmental controls, while Swatantra and Jan Sangh activists are overwhelmingly opposed to controls, and the DMK and independents are in between. The preponderance of activists are supporters, then, of governmental controls of some sort, including 62 percent of the activists of the ruling party. It is also interesting to note that in some parties the activists are less "liberal" on this question than those not active, notably the Socialists, Communists, and independents.

Party activists differ also in their attitudes on the cow slaughter issue. The most "traditional," favoring the ban, are the Right activists of Swatantra and Jan Sangh (91 percent favoring the ban); Congress follows next (77 percent), and then the Socialists and Communists (65 percent), DMK (60

TABLE 18.6 Party Differences among Activists in Support of Governmental Activity

	% Favoring Greater Controls		% Favoring the Same or Greater Controls	
	Actives	Nonactives	Actives	Nonactives
Socialists and Communists	49	56	61	67
Congress	39	34	62	56
DMK	31	15	46	34
Independents	24	33	41	51
Swatantra and Jan Sangh	12	17	21	34

percent), and the independents (43 percent). The nonactive identifiers in these parties, however, are heavily "traditional" and their activist leaders are apparently unrepresentative of rank and file opinion. Thus 84 percent of Socialist and Communist inactive identifiers support the cow slaughter ban, almost 20 percent more than among their activists. The same is true for DMK inactives (79 percent favoring the ban) and independents (83 percent supporting the ban). Activists, therefore, are a relatively liberal group in India on this issue which finds the overwhelming majority of the Indian population very "traditional."

If we look at the position of activists on policy questions, therefore, we find the same basic pattern as in the United States—the activists differ from the inactive sector of the population significantly. But the two systems are strikingly contrasted. In the United States activists are much more conservative on economic and social issues than those not active. In India activists are much more liberal than those not active. The probable relevance of this for policy action in the two societies is clearly suggested by these data.

Evidences of Social Group Conflict and Congruence in Involvement
One interesting way of interpreting our data is to assess the meaning of differences among activists in social groups in their orientations toward the system. We have already noted the differences in policy preferences by social groups. The contrast between the "liberalism" of the Muslims and lower castes and the "conservatism" of the middle and upper castes on the issue of governmental economic controls is considerable. This suggests a basic policy preference conflict. And on the cow slaughter issue also there is a tension, particularly between the less traditional upper educated group and those with lower education, who are more traditional on this issue.

On other orientations toward the political system one finds social group differences, and, perhaps, "conflict" also. The actives within the caste categories, for example, differ greatly in their sense of political efficacy. Interestingly both the low and high caste actives are most cynical, while the Harijans and middle castes are most optimistic—as much as a 26 percent spread. The contrast among actives by education level is equally large— only 20 percent of the illiterates feel that "people like me have a say," while 46 percent of those with the highest education are optimistic. On the other hand those actives with a college or high school education are most critical of the job the national officials are doing, while those less well educated are much more supportive—a 37 percent spread.

There is, however, much congruence also in perceptions and evaluations of the political system by these activists from different social groups. Thus, from 74 to 83 percent are very supportive of parties despite caste status. From 77 to 93 percent support the election system despite educational status. The level of general political interest is relatively high for activists, although it does vary by social status. The Harijans and Muslims are low in interest (50 to 53 percent) while the upper castes are high in interest (73 percent). The illiterate activists are low (44 percent), while those with primary and middle schooling are higher in interest (66 to 71 percent) and those with a high school or college education are very high—100 percent expressing an interest in politics. There is therefore basic interest in the system and support for it among actives, but those actives coming from different social groups manifest different degrees of cynicism or optimism about their capacity to work in the system.

Final Observations on the Functions of Political Participation
What obviously stands out, first, in this analysis is the consistent set of differences between those Indian citizens who are involved with the party and campaign processes and those who are not involved. The former are much more knowledgeable about politics, interested in politics, and politically exposed. They are also more supportive of the party and election system on most measures, while also being very critical of government officials and Congress leadership, and cynical about personal political efficacy. The activists are significantly more "liberal" ("interventionist") on economic and social questions than those not involved, although there are great variations by educational status. Indian activists differ strikingly from American activists on this dimension.

A second major finding here is that in certain important respects the political activists differ considerably by party. They are by no means a homogeneous group, although all parties "recruit" activists from lower and middle social status categories. They also tend to be strong party identifiers and to view the party and elections systems favorably. They differ in the extent to which they appear to be alienated from the present regime. Congress and DMK activists are relatively supportive of state and central government officials, while the activists of other parties are much more negative. And there is strong criticism of Congress leadership and policies by activists in all opposition parties. Finally, the activists differ greatly by party in their attitudes on the extent of governmental control over the economy. This ranges from 21 percent "liberalism" among Swatantra and Jan Sangh activists to 62 percent "liberalism" among Congress, Socialists, and Communist activists.

In reflecting on the meaning of these data in functional terms, several interpretations are possible. One is obviously that political activism in India is conducive to the maintenance, if not the accentuation, of political competition. But this is not necessarily a "Congress vs. all others" type of competition. Within Congress there is considerable disaffection as well as internal factionalism. Perhaps a third of Congress activists are highly critical of Congress leadership, while approximately 40 percent are relatively conservative on the issue of governmental intervention in the economy. Further, a majority of Congress activists on certain ideological divisions seem to join with the Left parties against the Right. So the pattern of competition in terms of activist orientations and attitudes is a complex one, but it is obviously a competitive-functional one. The evidence suggests the presence of considerable protest, criticism, and pressure on elites and a clear momentum toward "liberal" and "innovative" initiatives. By 1975 this pressure seemed to be particularly manifest.

On the other hand the evidence also suggests that the beliefs and orientations and behavior of these activists are integration-functional. The actives, after all, do support the system of competitive parties and elections much more than those not involved. The differences in support scores in this regard are striking (table 18.4). These are certainly "legitimizing" types of orientations. And they are reenforced by the fact that the activists are informed and their views are based on considerable exposure to the parties and their leadership. Indian activists are also strong party identifiers, engaging in work in support of the party system. Finally, the integration potential for political involvement is strongly suggested by the fact that lower social status groups as well as upper social status groups are apparently engaging in political activity. "Peripheral" groups are noticeably involved: 18 percent of the Muslims, 13 percent of the Harijans and Tribals, 12 percent of nonmobile villagers, 8 percent with a monthly family income of under fifty rupees, 6 percent of the Christians. True there are considerable differences between illiterates and those with a higher education (7 percent compared to 22 percent) and similarly for occupational

269

groups, in political knowledge and exposure. But there is a remarkable social inclusiveness about Indian political involvement which may moderate social conflict and may help translate social needs into political action.

While noting these integrative implications one must also recognize that social and political dissensus emerges from our data on political involvement. This appears in the differences among the parties in their criticism of Congress policies—Congress activists tend to defend Congress, other party activists are overwhelmingly critical. But more importantly, dissensus appears when we look at the attitudes of social sectors toward governmental policy. One striking evidence of possible conflict is in the attitudes of the activists by caste groups toward governmental controls over the economy. Here there is a 35 percent difference between lower caste and Harijan activists combined (61 percent taking a "liberal" stance and desiring strong controls) as opposed to middle and upper castes (only 26 percent and 38 percent of whom want strong controls). Activists from lower castes are both more liberal and more likely to defend Congress than are upper and middle caste activists. We do not find these differences for education. We do find, however, a sharp difference among upper and lower educated activists on the cow slaughter issue. On that issue those activists with the highest education are most "modern," the illiterates most 'traditional''— a significant 42 percent difference. Pronounced differences do exist, then, among activists on these critical issues dependent in part at least on differences in social status and origin. In addition, we noted sizable differences between activists in caste and education groups in their sense of political efficacy. Illiterates who are activists seem particularly cynical as to whether people like themselves can have "a say" in what the government does.

The new participant activist, subelite in India is clearly not a ritualist, immobilist, consensual cadre engaging in only symbolic types of political activity. It seems basically committed to the values of the new political system while also critical of governmental performance. Considerable disagreement exists among activists in their perceptions of and support for governmental officials and programs. It is a competitive subelite with intense loyalties to the dominant party as well as to opposition parties on the Right and Left. It is an activist subelite coming from a highly diversified set of social backgrounds and these social differences seem relevant to their issue preferences. It has the potential, therefore, of putting great pressure on governmental leaders as well as acting as opinion leaders in influencing the public toward both protest and support for the system and the regime.

David Apter's view of the role of parties is perhaps helpful here. He says:

> In modernizing systems.... parties play an active entrepreneurial role in the formation of new ideas, in the establishment of a network of communication for those ideas, and in the linking of the public and the leadership in such a way that power is generated, mobilized and directed. [8]

On balance this Indian activist elite looks like a potentially "transformative" set of activists, innovative, "liberal," knowledgeable, committed. As yet, however, the data do not suggest that this subelite is interested in working outside the system, or in completely changing the system, nor indeed in making such intensive demands on the system that their activism imposes impossible strains on the system and leads to instability. Rather, these data suggest that this is a subelite functioning within the viable Indian political order, a stimulus for policy and leadership change, and constituting the hard-core cadres of parties, competing for power and arguing for change, but in all this is a subelite whose values are basically democratic, whose beliefs are legitimizing, and whose collective patterns of activities contribute a dynamism to Indian political, social, and economic development.

A final postscript: Obviously Mrs. Gandhi saw this activist subelite as a threat in 1975, rather than a salutary force; yet our data reveal it as a basically democratic and effective force in modern India.

NINETEEN·
Trends and Prospects in Indian
Political Development

The Two Images

PEOPLE HAVE TWO CONTRASTING VIEWS OF INDIA SINCE INDEPENDENCE. One is that very little has changed and that India is still very much a traditional, illiterate, village society with citizens perfunctorily and ritualistically participating in elections and campaigns but with little real change occurring in political sophistication and meaningful political behavior. The other is that India is an Asian democracy in which political "modernization" has occurred at a rapid pace in the face of great social and economic crises, with citizens becoming genuinely involved with new democratic institutions and processes—parties, elections, legislatures—and developing a sophisticated knowledge of, and belief in, such institutions, while retaining many practices and orientations of traditional society. As our presentation in this book has indicated, we are very much inclined to the latter interpretation and image, and continue in that conviction despite the "happenings" of 1975.

Our initial analysis of mass political behavior was based on the interviews conducted with a random adult national sample in 1967. These were valuable for establishing the first empirical generalizations of citizen political involvement, party identification, and cultural orientations toward the political system. The crucial question, lingering throughout that analysis, is whether those findings based on 1967 conditions are "short-term" or "long-term," reflective of idiosyncratic stimuli of that election year or "normal" patterns of citizen behavior. The 1971 election, and our national cross-sectional study of that year, designed and carried out with essentially the same approach as four years previously, provided us with the opportunity to see if the patterns observed in 1967 were enduring or not, even for this short developmental span of modern India.

General Trends: 1967 and 1971

If we look at the trends in general responses to the questions we put to Indian citizens in these two election years, it is clear that the public's engagement with the political system remains relatively high and constant, and there are some signs that the public is more meaningfully involved. Let us look at some of these "signs" and attempt to assess their importance. Table 19.1 provides a quick summary comparison of responses for 1967

272

TABLE 19.1 Trends in Political Orientations and Behavior, 1967 and 1971

	1967 (%)	1971 (%)
Interest		
Political interest generally	35	38
Personally care about election outcome	40	52
Knowledge		
Accurate information about the candidate winning in R's constituency	50	67
Efficacy		
Feels "government officials care much about what people like me think"	21	40
Feels "people like me have a say about what the government does"	30	63
Thinks "politics and government are not so complicated that a person like me can't really understand what is going on"	20	43
Behavior		
Voted consistently in 2 national elections	34	45
Helped in campaign on election day	6	10
Has contacted a government official	20	26

and 1971. It appears that at the time of the latter election political interest was up, concern about the election was also up, people were more informed about the candidates, they also felt more efficacious about politics, and their behavior revealed increased, and possibly more consistent, involvement with politics. Perhaps most impressive in 1971 was the increase in sense of political efficacy and knowledge about politics. There were many fewer resigned defeatists in 1971, that is, individuals who perceived themselves as helpless in the great political system, in "traditional" terms. Only 37 percent were saying they had "no say" in politics. Combined with great concern about the outcome of elections, greater knowledge, and greater consistency in voting behavior this suggests that there is, indeed, political development in India.

So far as general trends in party identification are concerned, the evidence is more mixed. Those who do identify with political parties behave similarly in 1967 and 1971. Thus, 73 percent of the identifiers in both years voted consistent with their identification, a striking finding in any system. Further, identifiers continue to exhibit consistency in their issue politics— 53 percent and 51 percent of the identifiers in these two years, respectively, select their own party as the one they prefer on the issue of governmental

273

control of the economy. For strong identifiers the proportion was 67 percent in 1971 and 60 percent in 1967.

We found, as indicated earlier, that party identification was down in 1971. The proportions fell from 70 to 47 percent (all identifiers) and 51 to 35 percent (strong identifiers). If people identify with a party in India they are still inclined to be "strong," but the proportion who do indicate affiliation was much lower in 1971. This may be due to a change in the sequence of the questions which actually may have made the identification measure a better one in 1971. We first asked respondents in 1971 to name the parties (which was not done in 1967), and then we asked them which party they were "closest to." As a result, some respondents in 1971 may have been "screened out" and were less willing to indicate a party affiliation.

One must consider the possibility that party identification did in fact decline in India (as it has in the United States). Other questions revealing attitudes to parties and elections indicated that there was less affect for these institutions in 1971. Thus, on the basic question of whether parties (and elections) "help to make the government pay attention to the people" the proportions were 66 percent in 1967 and 42 percent in 1971. Support for elections as institutions declined from 73 to 51 percent. This suggests some particular (1971) or developing cynicism toward the party-electoral subsystem. The antagonism was particularly noticeable among strong identifiers. For strong Congress supporters the pro-party sentiment declined from 94 to 55 percent. This was higher than for any other party group, contrasting, for example, with the Communist strong identifiers, 66 percent of whom were still pro-party in 1971 (compared to 75 percent in 1967).

Although some decline in party identification occurred as well as some lessening in support for the parties, the level of loyalty to parties is still considerable and probably close to the level of many Western societies. This is, in a genuine sense, remarkable since the extent of family socialization to the new system is still very low in 1971. Only 17 percent reported that their fathers had an interest in politics (compared to 14 percent in 1967) and only 15 percent (11 percent in 1967) could recall their father's party affiliation. For the vast majority of Indians, their socialization to politics occurred as adults—43 percent (1971) were never exposed to party politics in their youth and subsequently have become party identifiers. Three-fourths of these are voting consistent with that identification.

The Linkage of Party Affiliation to Other Attitudes and Behavior
A more important type of evidence indicating that Indian citizens are meaningfully engaged with their system is the linkage between an orientation like party identification and other types of attitudes and behaviors. Are

identifiers more knowledgeable about political candidates, for example, than nonidentifiers? As table 19.2 reveals, while the level of interest and knowledge in 1971 was up generally for the sample, the major leaps in these orientations were among strong identifiers. Indeed, in 1967 there was very little difference by party identification in knowledge; by 1971 there was a sizable, 24 percent, spread between strong identifiers and nonidentifiers. This was not as pronounced when the degree of interest is analyzed, but the trend in 1971 is still observable.

TABLE 19.2 Trends in Political Orientations among Party Identifiers, 1967 and 1971

	Strong Identifiers (%)		Nonidentifiers (%)	
	1967	1971	1967	1971
Knowledge of candidates	42	74	41	50
General interest in politics	42	54	21	23
Campaign interest	42	53	20	24
Parties make government pay attention	81	67	79	48

One should also note that support for parties seems much more closely linked to party identification in 1971 than in 1967. On the item we used to probe whether the respondent felt that parties made government responsive, in 1967 there was virtually no difference by party identification (81 percent compared to 79 percent) but in 1967 there was a sharp difference (67 percent of the strong identifiers feeling parties were responsive, compared to 48 percent for nonidentifiers). This again points to the evolution of a more internally consistent and structured set of orientations among Indian citizens.

A similar point can be made concerning political efficacy. There were only slight differences by party identification strength in 1967; on such items almost all identifiers (70 to 90 percent) revealed a very low sense of political efficacy. In 1971, however, whereas few of those with no party identification felt efficacious, identifiers were much more confident. From 45 to 55 percent of the strong identifiers gave efficacious responses, and weak identifiers were on the average about 8 percent lower in self-confidence.

Strong identifiers attached to either Congress or opposition parties were markedly involved in the campaign in 1971, much more so than noniden-

275

tifiers. Thus, 28 percent of strong Congress supporters attended election meetings, and 36 percent of strong opposition supporters did, while only 11 percent of the nonidentifiers were thus involved. The strong party supporters did house-to-house canvassing (15 to 20 percent, compared to only 3 percent of nonidentifiers), took voters to the polling station (21 percent compared to 4 percent), contacted officials (39 percent strong Congress, 32 percent strong opposition, but only 17 percent nonidentifiers). These findings attest to the continued and increased meaningfulness and relevance of party identification for the Indian citizen's engagement with politics.

We found striking consistency among the identifiers of the particular parties in their attitudes on issues. One question which was identical in both studies dealt with governmental control in society, "Do you think that for the progress of the country the government should exercise greater controls over industry, trade, and agriculture than at present, or less controls, or keep them as they are?" This was followed by the question, "Which party is closest to what you want on this issue?" The responses to this question indicate no basic change from 1967 to 1971 by party. The parties' identifiers are arrayed as follows for the two years:

% of Identifiers Favoring Greater Controls

```
              JS  SWA  DMK  Cong  SSP              CP
1967   0 ─────────────────────────────────────────────────── 100
              15   19   27   35   41                70


              JS  DMK  SWA  Cong  SSP   CP
1971   0 ─────────────────────────────────────────────────── 100
              25   29   33    40   42   60
```

The stability of attitudes for party identifiers thus emerges clearly. Although there seems to be a clear movement "to the Left" for all parties, except oddly enough the Communists, the relative status of the parties on this dimension remains the same. The attitudes of identifiers are stable between 1967 and 1971, with no dramatic shifts.

A variety of evidence suggests, therefore, that party identification is a political orientation that persists in India and appears to be consistently linked to other types of political engagement. Those who are committed to parties in 1971 revealed an even greater tendency to be knowledgeable about politics than in 1967, to express a greater political interest, to reveal much more political self-confidence or a sense of efficacy, and to participate more in politics. There is evidence of decline in support for the party system, possibly associated with the schism in Congress in 1969. This is certainly not a "collapse" in support. It is a phenomenon similar to that in other lands, such as the United States. Above all, there appears to be great

276

consistency in the meaning of party identification over time and its persistent linkage to the kinds of behavior one would be inclined to say one should find in a democratic society.

The Trends in Political Participation

We noted earlier the relatively high levels of political activity in the 1967 and 1971 elections (although voting turnout seems to have declined slightly in 1971). In some respects the magnitude of political participation in India exceeds that of Western democracies. What we are concerned with here is whether this political participation in 1971 was linked to critical orientations and behavior which are functional to a democratic and effective polity. The key question is whether the system continues to attract activists from many sectors of the society, activists who are informed, concerned, and supportive of the system, whether critical of the regime or not.

It is interesting to note at the outset that again in 1971 the politically activist cadre consisted of people with diverse social backgrounds. Indeed, the social penetration is a little "deeper" in some respects in 1971 than in 1967[1] (table 19.3). More of the illiterates were active (but only 9 percent compared to 7 percent in 1967), as were those near the bottom of the income ladder. Political participation increased generally throughout the society; this "ethic" or predisposition appears to have been contagious. The greatest increases in such activity were among the following groups: high school and college educated (12 percent increase over 1967), upper castes (12 percent increase), Muslims (7 percent increase). While the lowest income groups and castes are maintaining or only slightly increasing their political involvement, upper status groups seem to be more active. Yet one should not ignore the significance of the behavior of lower socioeconomic status groups. Thus "nonmobile villagers" (those who have not left the village in their lifetime) report a 15 percent level of political involvement in 1971 (12 percent in 1967). And the participation of Muslims is particularly noticeable. The political activist cadre in India thus appears to be numerically and socially more inclusive. These data document a high level of public engagement with politics. These findings may be particularly significant in the light of increasing radicalization of certain sectors of the Indian public, a subject on which D. L. Sheth has written recently.[2]

The functional relationship between political participation and attitudes toward politics is even more striking in 1971 than in 1967. Table 19.4 illustrates some of these findings. On every orientation except attitude to parties the politically active cadre is consistently more committed and engaged with their political system. On some items they are much more sophisticated. Take, for example, the level of political knowledge. The

TABLE 19.3 Social Backgrounds of Politically Involved Citizens, 1967 through 1971*

	1967	1971
Educational level		
Illiterates	7	9
Some primary	18	17
Primary and middle	22	28
Higher—high school,		
and above	17	29
College	22	35
Age†		
31–40	14	20
41–50	11	17
50+	12	13
Occupation		
"White-collar"	18	23
"Blue-collar"—nonfarm	13	17
Farmers and farm workers	11	15
Religion		
Hindu	12	16
Muslim	18	25
Income level		
Lowest	9	9
Upper-lower	11	16
Middle	17	23
Upper-middle	24	27
Caste		
Harijans/Tribals	13	13
Low castes	11	14
Middle castes	14	17
Upper castes	11	23

* Table gives percentage of each social category who were in the top two categories of our involvement index.

† Since the involvement index covered voting in the past three elections, the younger age categories in each year's study had to be eliminated.

salience of politics to the ordinary Indian citizen emerges strongly from these 1971 data. Even nonvoters do well in identifying candidates—a fourth can identify two parliamentary candidates! Among regular voters it is close to three-fifths, and for the actives it is 80 percent or more. In 1967 we had noticed this level of knowledge of state assembly candidates, but

TABLE 19.4 The Association of Political Involvement with Attitudes toward the
Political System, 1967 and 1971*

Attitudes	% Inactives	% Irregular Voters	% Regular Voters	% Actives	% Very Active
General political interest					
1967	8	17	27	56	79
1971	13	24	30	67	83
Knowledge of parliamentary candidates (can mention 2 or more candidates)					
1967	13	23	25	41	62
1971	27	44	58	79	89
Parties help make government pay attention to the people ("somewhat" plus "a good deal")					
1967	30	49	63	79	79
1971	14	25	39	58	74
Efficacy Politics and government too complicated (agree)					
1967	75	73	82	86	81
1971	58	65	60	43	23
People like me have no say (agree)					
1967	79	73	73	68	57
1971	33	37	37	34	28

* Each percentage is a proportion of persons in each activist category who hold a given attitude.

not at the national parliamentary level. The change in four years is dramatic and impressive.

Equally dramatic is the change in feelings of political efficacy. The extent of the increase in self-confidence is so great it is scarcely credible. Consider the standard efficacy item such as: "Sometimes politics and government seem so complicated that a person like me can't really understand what is going on."[3] Responses to this item were much more efficacious in 1971 for all (male) respondents, 58 percent agreeing with it in 1971 but 80 percent agreeing in 1967. The significant difference between the two years, however, is not the 22 percent greater sense of efficacy in the total sample but rather the linkage of efficacy to political participation. Whereas in 1967 there was actually greater "cynicism" among the actives than the inactives, in 1971 the actives were clearly more self-confident about the public's role in the system—a 35 percent spread in efficacy. So those most active in the system now are much more optimistic about the meaningfulness of political activism than before. The fantastic difference in feeling among the very active group between 1967 and 1971—almost a 50 percent difference—suggests that political involvement is seen more than ever as functional. Other efficacy items indicate a similar change in 1971 (see the "people have no say" item in table 19.4). Clearly this is a change in public orientations of great significance![4]

We noted in our earlier analysis that the most active Indians were also the most "liberal" ideologically, contrary to the finding in some other societies, such as the United States. The 1971 data again document this observation. On the question of governmental controls over industry, trade, and agriculture, the differences for the total male samples were as follows:

	1967 %	1971 %
Favor no controls	6	2
Favor less controls	32	27
Favor some controls	4	3
Favor same controls as now	11	11
Favor greater controls	26	34
Don't know	18	22

There was greater endorsement of governmental controls in 1971, although the movement in that direction was not striking. Among activists there was a similar slight tendency in the same direction. So we find that the 50 percent among the activists who favored "the same or greater controls" in 1967 increased in 1971 to 54 percent. Although this is so, a sizable percentage of 31 percent of the activists take a conservative stance, and, thus, the activists are ideologically divided roughly 55 percent to 30 percent on this key issue. What is perhaps even more interesting is the increase in liberalism among the inactives from 25 to 37 percent. (There was also, however, a 15 percent increase in "don't knows" among the inactives.) Other influences and forces, besides political activity, are at work by which the apathetic Indian public has been moved more toward acceptance of governmental interventionism. In 1971 only 23 percent of the inactives favored less governmental controls, which is also true of only 28 percent of the regular voters. While a sizable stratum of conservatism still remains, as well as much ambivalence and uncertainty, the trend is definitely toward more liberal positions on this type of issue, led by the activist minority.

Indian activists, while "liberal" ideologically, are often "traditional" in their views about politics. In an earlier chapter we explored this tendency at length with the 1967 data. Repeatedly, using different measures, we found that "traditionals" were as likely to be politically active as the "moderns," and, turned around, politically active people included relatively high proportions of those expressing "nonmodern" views. This is illustrated again in 1971. We asked a variety of questions concerned with the role of caste and caste leaders in politics, and followed with specific questions, such as, "Do you think it is important or not important for you to vote the same way your caste/religious group votes?" For the total sample, 52 percent responded "important," 35 percent "not important," and 13 percent "don't know."[5] This indicates considerable evidence of commitment to caste as a relevant reference group for self in the political decision-making process.

Where do activists stand on this question? As table 19.5 indicates, they remain considerably "traditional," if the "caste support" has that connotation. The actives are much less ambivalent on this matter and a majority clearly feel that conformity to caste voting is important for them. In fact, the regular voters are not as caste-conformity oriented as are the activists! In some respects this finding corresponds with our 1967 observations. On our "traditionalism index" of 1967, almost 75 percent of the actives scored high, that is, were very traditional, while 60 percent or less of the inactives and irregulars were. They also scored highest on "caste awareness," and were almost as inclined to place themselves at the "traditional" end of the continuum of "innovation-conservatism" as were those who were less involved. Thus 45 percent of those who were not active beyond voting favored following the "old ways" of doing things, while 50 percent of the "very active" placed themselves at this end of the continuum.

A direct comparison for the two years is possible if we look at the extent of awareness of and conformity between the perceived candidate choice of

TABLE 19.5 Importance of Caste for Political Involvement (1971)
("Do you think it is important or not important for you to vote the same way your caste/religious group votes?")

	% Inactives	% Irregular Voters	% Regular Voters	% Actives	% Very Actives
Important	37	44	49	63	57
Not important	27	44	37	30	36
Don't know	37	12	13	7	4

281

the caste (or religious) leader and that of the respondent. There appears to be only slight diminution in caste consciousness and, indeed, some evidence that the politically active sector of the Indian population is inclined in 1971, as before, to value conformity to the political choice of caste and religious leaders. The data are summarized in table 19.6. One must keep in mind here that usually less than half of the respondents *knew* what the candidate preference of their caste or religious leader was. This awareness increases with political involvement, however, so that among the actives close to 50 percent asserted that they did know that preference. And there was overwhelming agreement with that preference—at the 80 percent and 90 percent level—with no diminution in that agreement level for the activists, and no decline in this tendency in 1971. Thus the activists are (1) more knowledgeable and aware of where the caste or religious leader stands politically, and (2) as likely to agree with him as are the inactives. One cannot impute causality or interpersonal influence from these data. Individuals obviously may vote for the same candidate as the caste leader as a result of a variety of other stimuli and pressures. These data are suggestive, however, of the saliency of caste and religion for the most

TABLE 19.6 Caste Awareness and Conformity Patterns by Political Involvement

	Inactives and Irregulars		Regular Voters		Active beyond Voting		Very Active	
	1967	1971	1967	1971	1967	1971	1967	1971
% aware of the candidate choice of caste/religious leader	30	21	38	24	60	47	43	45
% of those aware who agreed with the candidate choice of the caste/religious leader	75	82	92	88	90	92	78	83
% of all respondents in the group who were *both* aware and agreed with caste/religious leader	23	17	35	22	54	43	33	38

active citizen, as well as the fusion of traditional forces such as caste and religion with Indian party politics.

An additional word of caution is necessary concerning the interpretation of the meaning of caste for political perspectives, particularly for the actives. One should not infer from the above data that Indians feel caste is the only factor or even an important factor in elite decision making. We note, for example, that when we asked in 1967 whether it is the duty of the legislator to work for caste interests we got the following responses from actives and inactives:

	% Seeing the Caste Role of Legislators as "Important"	% DK
Very active	21	5
Voters	45	14
Inactives	38	24

Thus, though actives are aware of caste and indeed feel a caste leader's candidate preference is important to know, it does not follow that the majority of actives (or of all citizens, for that matter) feel that governmental leaders should base their decisions on caste interests.

In summary, the 1971 data strongly reinforce many of our earlier observations about the magnitude and relevance of political participation in India. Activists have, more than ever, a broadly inclusive social base, with individuals at all class and status levels involved to a greater extent than before. Political activity is linked functionally to attitudes and orientations, clearly suggesting that there is a configuration consisting of activity, greater political knowledge, greater political interest, and a greater sense of political efficacy. The change in this direction, associating efficacy and involvement, is dramatic in 1971. On the other hand we also note a decline in support for the party system in 1971, not in an alarming sense, but clearly apparent, although those most active remain most supportive of parties. Finally, while Indians are becoming active and remaining active, and taking on attitudes functional to the democratic party-electoral subsystem, they also continue to reveal their strong engagement with traditional institutions and leadership. Caste is still salient and normatively important for those most active in the Indian polity.

Correlations Demonstrating the Trends in These Associations
in Political Orientations
To document further the reality of change from 1967 to 1971 in as concise a way as possible, we present here the correlations of a variety of factors with three critical measures: (1) party identification strength, (2) political

efficacy, and (3) "psychological involvement" with politics. The magnitude of the correlations of these three measures with a variety of sociodemographic, attitudinal, and behavioral variables will suggest what seems to be the direction of change.

To begin with, a look at the correlations for party identification show a remarkable consistency in that this phenomenon was more strongly associated with *every one* of our attitudinal and behavioral variables in 1971 than it was in 1967 (table 19.7). And some of these correlations became respectably high in 1971—such as "political interest" (.333), "care about outcome" (.449), some of the efficacy items (.280), and the campaign activity measures (for example, canvassing, .232). Whereas efficacy was virtually unrelated in 1967 (.013), it is now more positively associated. This is true also, one notes, of the "caste saliency" items, such as the agreement with caste leader's candidate preference—in 1967 the correlation was .039, but in 1971 it was .259! There is considerable confirmation

TABLE 19.7 Correlations of Selected Variables with Party Identification

Variables	1967	1971
Social background		
Education	.007	.218
Caste status	−.028	.112
Income	.037	.153
Urban-rural residence	−.007	.089
Age	−.051	−.024
Attitudinal		
General political interest	.208	.333
Campaign interest	.238	.316
Care about election outcome	.246	.449
Political efficacy		
"Politics too complicated . . ."	.013	.280
Voting has an effect	−.052	.266
Voter has no say	−.055	.204
Knowledge of candidates	.103	.232
Caste vote important	.100	.125
Agree with caste leader's decision	.039	.259
Behavioral		
Index of campaign exposure	.225	.292
Meetings attended	.176	.229
Vote in election	.088	.134
Took voters to polling station	.179	.263
Member of political party	.166	.223
Canvassed in campaign	.197	.232

here, then, for the observation that party identification is now more closely associated than ever before with "positive" system orientations. As noted earlier, our party identification measure in 1971 may have been more rigorous but this is, if at all, only a partial explanation of these trends.[6]

Social status differences may be more significant in Indian mass political behavior than previously. This is not so for age differences, or urban-rural differences, where the correlations remain close to zero. But for education (for which we found virtually no relationship in 1967) and income, and to a lesser extent caste status, the 1971 data indicate that higher social status now seems to be linked to greater party identification, a greater sense of efficacy, and more psychological involvement. Although these are not generally urban-rural residential or life-style phenomena, they suggest a current engagement in politics of those higher social status groups that previous research indicated were rather inactive or alienated from the political scene.

The correlations with political efficacy are remarkably similar to those just presented for party identification. Among the many correlations, perhaps the most interesting are as follows:

	Correlations of Political Efficacy	
	1967	1971
Political interest—general	.170	.388
Care about election outcome	.193	.458
Knowledge of candidates	.193	.256
Attended election meetings	.189	.314
Member of political party	.114	.210

Those who have a sense of political efficacy are, in 1971, clearly more concerned about politics, more interested, more knowledgeable, and more likely to be active in politics. This orientation—self-confidence about the capacity of the citizen to be involved and to have some say about politics—is linked to other involvement orientations for the first time in 1971. One notices also that the correlation between campaign exposure and political efficacy has increased markedly—from .200 in 1967 to .354 in 1971. Though one might argue that this is a "circular" set of relationships, the correlation is still notable. Those who are exposed to campaigns feel that their own role in politics can be more efficacious.[7]

The relationship between psychological involvement in politics and behavioral involvement are strong in both 1967 and 1971. The following correlations are illustrative:

	Correlations with Psychological[8] Involvement	
	1967	1971
Knowledge of candidates	.277	.309
Attend election meetings	.504	.459
Canvas	.393	.423
Take voters to polling station	.359	.414
Political party member	.271	.297
Vote in election	.120	.174

Those who care about politics and are interested also tend to be involved with the parties behaviorally and in campaigns. The correlations are quite strong for these measures, and they usually reveal an increase in association in 1971 over 1967.

These are often fairly high correlations, equally significant in 1971 as in 1967 or even more so. They suggest the direction of Indian political development. There is more "constraint" in political attitudes and orientations than before. Those who are identifiers tend also to be more interested, more knowledgeable, and more behaviorally involved. Those who have a sense of relevance and optimism about being active in the system are also those who are knowledgeable, care about politics, and are engaged in political activity. This is what one might predict as a system develops in a free competitive party and electoral climate. More than ever this is precisely the direction in which the Indian system is moving. This does not, however, mean that it is "modern" and not "traditional." This is a meaningless way to characterize the Indian development. It is greatly "traditional," while at the same time traditional forces adapt to, are mobilized by, and enrich, the new institutions and processes of the post-Independence polity.

Reflections on Political Development in India
If one were interested in evaluating the accomplishments of Indian political development and assessing where India stood prior to 1975, there are certain aspects of the system one would focus on. These phenomena are knowledge about politics, level of political interest, psychological involvement with the outcomes of political actions, extent of political socialization, extent of political activity, belief in and acceptance of the competitive party system and elections, support for the ideological goals of the regime, strength of identification with the system (and parties as a

subsystem), sense of political efficacy, and actuality of penetration of the involvement ethic to the social periphery of the system.

As the trend data presented in the tables and graphs of this chapter demonstrate, on virtually all of these measures the Indian system is clearly a developed polity, and one which in 1971 showed clear signs of continued growth in citizen political awareness, sophistication about politics, and involvement. Figure 29 documents the consistent rise in general trends from 1967 to 1971 on a variety of measures. The sharpest increases were in political knowledge and sense of political efficacy. As figure 30 reveals, the measures concerning regime support also are consistently increasing in 1971. Support for the Congress party among identifiers is at the 67 percent level (61 percent in 1967) and support for the same or greater controls is now 45 percent (up from 37 percent). The decline in support for Indira Gandhi's government, which may have occurred more recently certainly, was not apparent in these 1971 data. As indicated earlier, the only critical measures which indicate a decline in commitment to the system in 1971 are party identification itself and the public's attitudes toward parties. There is no doubt that in 1971 Indian citizens were less supportive of parties and elections. Nevertheless, there was not a clear and consistent rejection of the system in 1971. For most measures, system support was high among strong identifiers and the most activist cadre. As our data presented earlier indicate, and as figure 31 particularly shows, those most involved were most knowledgeable, interested, supportive, and efficacious.

The level of political socialization in the family is still low in India, lower than for any other democratic system for which we have data. Less than 20 percent of Indian citizens report that they became aware of politics through parental influence.[9] Nevertheless, the evidence is strong that their postadult exposure to politics has been pronounced and lasting. Indian citizens match most Western societies in level of political sophistication and involvement.

What can we say, then, in evaluating this developing Indian system? In final analysis, based on the empirical observations from our studies of Indian mass behavior, a model of the Indian polity emerges. The new Indian elite in 1947, and since, established a set of institutions (a party system, a Parliament, a bureaucracy, and so on), adopted an ideology and a set of developmental goals, and a strategy for involving the Indian public with the new system. Gradually the Indian public, as a result of exposure to these institutions and leaders and adult socialization influences, has moved away from its original apathy and ignorance of politics and its unfamiliarity with democratic norms and values to an early participation in the voting process, the beginnings of interest in political matters, and some elementary information about political issues, candidates, and processes. This

287

FIG. 29. General trends in political orientations and involvement.

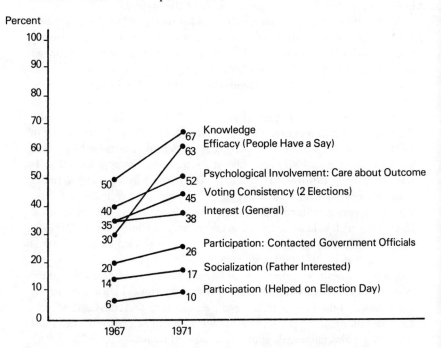

early involvement stage was probably completed by the 1957 election. Over time, after 1957, this engagement with politics penetrated into the villages, the lower castes, the lowest socioeconomic sectors and the rural hinterland of the society. Along with this arousal of interest came a sense of identification with parties, an acceptance of system goals, and increased political activity of several different types. As the years passed this exposure to party and electoral politics was intensified, and became very salient to the majority of Indian citizens. By 1971 we note more activity, a greater psychological involvement with politics, and, for a strikingly large number, a sense of political efficacy—a feeling that they can become effective through the system.

Thus by 1971 we find that Indian citizens demonstrated considerable political sophistication. They know the parties—over 50 percent can identify two or more parties (and 31 percent three or more parties). A large minority (39 percent) discuss politics in the home fairly frequently. They are contacted by the parties at election (45 percent reported being canvassed in the 1971 campaign). They are more likely to attend election meetings and rallies than is usually true in Western democracies (20 to 24 percent), and they are more likely to listen to the speakers of two or three

FIG. 30. Trends in regime support.

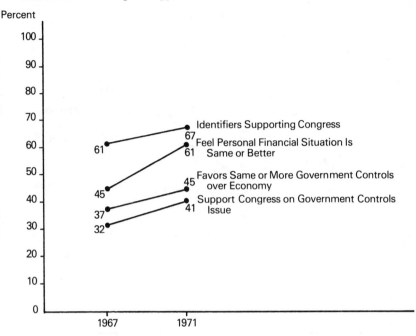

Percent

parties than to be confined to their own party exclusively. And 60 percent or more feel that the citizen can have an influence in the system.

The consequences of these developments in political behavior in India have been tremendous, both for the individual and for the system. The individual has seen new opportunities for realizing himself politically and for influencing the actions of the elites in a democratic society. A new political culture has emerged which is a fusion of "traditional" orientations and values and more recent "modernizing" orientations and values. Caste is still an important influence on, and a part of, the Indian citizen's life, but it has been integrated with new associations and beliefs. The Indian system prior to 1975 achieved political legitimacy through the combination of belief in the democratic political processes, by both elites and citizens, active participation in those processes, and confidence in the elite's capability to govern effectively. Pressures from below in this politicized, traditional society may well auger more protest, agitation, and radicalization for the future. Perhaps that is the most natural consequence in a society which in the first twenty-five years after Independence manifested the most striking accomplishments in democratic development of any modern polity.

289

FIG. 31. Political orientations of identifiers and activists compared to the public in 1971.

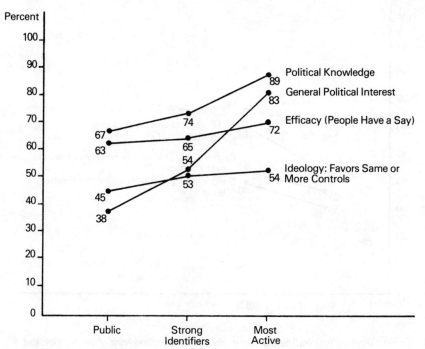

TWENTY

Epilogue: 1975 and Beyond

T HE CESSATION OF DEMOCRACY IN ANY SYSTEM INVARIABLY LEADS TO speculation as to causes or factors explaining such a phenomenon, as well as to arguments over the conditions which will obtain if and when rejuvenation of the democratic system occurs. The "interruption" of democracy in India in 1975 certainly invites such discussions. We have argued consistently in this analysis, backed up, we think, by an over-whelming body of evidence, that significant segments of the Indian public had been drawn into democratic political life by 1971 and that a sizable activist minority, growing in size and sophistication over time, had re-sponded to elite overtures and were indeed participating responsibly and intelligently. While this conclusion is essentially correct and empirically demonstrable, in our opinion, the question naturally is raised as to whether there were counterdevelopments in the period before 1975 which could raise doubts about the genuineness of mass democracy and provide reasons for the abrogation of democracy, while also providing clues as to the direction of Indian political behavior in the future.

If one has read our analysis carefully, caveats will have been noted throughout. While basically optimistic about the expansion and deepening of the Indian democratic polity from 1947 to 1971, we have called attention frequently to findings which might provoke concern. One of the most obvious is the apparent decline in support for the party system revealed in our 1971 data, as reflected in both attitudes toward parties and psychologi-cal identification with them. Strong party identification declined from 51 to 35 percent. Although part of this may be an artifact of question phrasing, other responses seem to bear out this trend. One must note also that accord-ing to official statistics there was a slight (4 to 5 percent) decline in voting turnout in the 1971 election, although we found an increase in the propor-tions of the public who were engaged in political activity. Another major problem uncovered in the 1967 study was the low level of personal efficacy which the ordinary Indian has felt about political participation. This cyni-cism decreased somewhat in 1971, but from 40 to 60 percent of the sample still was inclined to be doubtful about their capacity to have a say or about the responsiveness of officials, or both. Thus one notes, as we indicated in the text, much "political participation despite alienation" and persistent pessimism. The 1971 study also revealed more evidence that a sizable minority of the Indian public was thinking more radically about politics, approving of strikes and demonstrations (32 percent) and the seizure of property (48 percent)—in a sense supporting the confrontation (or "bandh-gherao") tactics which many elites have recently deplored.

It would be a gross injustice to these data, however, to suggest that the participation of Indians had by the 1970s become overwhelmingly based on personal cynicism, radical perspectives, and antisystem orientations. There was clearly a deeper interest in politics, much more knowledge about candidates, and a commitment to parties which was linked to positive orientations toward the system. At least two-thirds knew the winner in their constituency, and over 70 percent could identify two or more candidates for state assembly. Over two-thirds could spatially locate Congress plus one other party (and 47 percent could locate Congress plus two or more other parties). Over 50 percent were exposed to party organization efforts and revealed stronger identifications, possibly as a result of such contacts. And at least 50 percent showed some minimal consistency between party preference and own-issue positions.

The actives were predominantly ideologically "liberal," supporting governmental action to deal with economic and social problems. There were indeed conservatives among them on the Right, but they were not in the majority. Further, actives were drawn from all social sectors, particularly from the lower status groups who previously had been noninvolved. A very high proportion (approximately one-fifth) of lower caste citizens who were "traditional" in their caste perceptions and preferences were active beyond voting.

By the 1970s the Indian public was becoming more socialized to democratic politics, both as adolescents and adults. They were as attentive, interested, concerned, knowledgeable, and supportive of their system as people in any Western society whose comparable data on mass behavior we could examine. Above all, although we have data at only two points in time, there clearly seemed to be a movement over time in the development of an Indian citizenry which, while remaining very traditional socially, was accepting the participant norms of a modern polity.

If this is the empirical reality about the state of the Indian public's commitment to political involvement, obviously there are "big questions" to raise and to speculatively seek to answer. The Emergency decrees and the way in which power has been exercised under them finds the Indian system today then in a state of elite-mass dysfunction. Freedom of the press has been abolished, elections postponed, popular participation in politics suspended, and most parties placed virtually in a limbo with the large-scale arrests of their leaders and cadres. The ruling elites have repudiated the democratic development preceding 1975 while large segments of the public, probably a majority, have now been socialized to believe in that system and to participate in it. What is the meaning of this for India today and tomorrow?

The first point that probably should be made in dealing with this question is that we should not expect Indians to necessarily behave otherwise, or to do more, than we have noted has occurred elsewhere in the history of mankind when interruptions in democratic systems have occurred—whether in France, or Germany, or Italy, or Greece, or other Third World countries. No doubt much of the public is now relatively apathetic, observing developments and evaluating their relevance for their own private lives. No doubt also thousands of the activists who were mobilized by the process of democratic developments over the years, and for whom politics was an important, and even profitable, career line, while chafing and restless, are for the time being adapting to the Emergency. True, there are some signs of tension, sullen acceptance of the Emergency, as well as periodic challenges.[1] But, one should not expect a public rebellion, in India any more than elsewhere, even though there surely is a politically involved and socialized sector unhappy with developments in the past two years. This sector, ironically, was also overwhelmingly oriented to support the progressive policy initiatives of Mrs. Gandhi. The absence of a public revolt should not be interpreted as the absence of commitment to democracy. India, the land of political contradictions, is today a system where many of its people socialized to acceptance of free and open politics must now live, perhaps for some time, under an antidemocratic regime.

A second major reflection concerns the question of whether the Emergency of 1975, the events leading to it and the actions following from it, permit one to conclude that the Indian democracy established by the leadership of Nehru and his followers after 1947 was unsuitable for India or was a failure. Much criticism has been leveled at the Indian constitution, the bureaucracy, the Parliament, the role of the states, the party system, and particularly the irresponsible behavior of India's pragmatic politicians. Richard Park concludes: "In the widest sense . . . . the task ahead for India is to construct a political order that is more suited to its own genius—the experiment, in general, has been the most successful in Asia.—But it is not adequate for India."[2] There are those who would say that a system of free and open participation in a competitive party system produces too much conflict, a lack of discipline, and irresponsible behavior, and leads to the disintegration of the system. There are, of course, others who will argue that until one has economic and social development—literacy, urbanization, an adequate GNP—one cannot have the necessary preconditions for democratic development. It seems to us that these arguments miss the mark. They play into the hands of the critics of democracy. They ignore the great progress in economic and social change in India, the establishment of a unified integrated society, and the accomplishment of a remarkable fusion of traditional and modern values in a spirit of justice and freedom. True, democracy in India had its excesses, but the system was fundamentally sound. It was only through the "open society" political pluralism and through competitive party politics that integration, legitimacy, and social progress were achieved. Those who would argue otherwise should only look at Pakistan. In emphasizing India's failure in economic policies in recent years one ignores the tremendous progress made earlier under the democratic constitution.

Rajni Kothari, it seems to us, expressed well the proper evaluation one should place on India's condition today. While recognizing that distortions in the system occurred, and agreeing that reforms certainly are necessary, he reaffirmed the essential soundness of the pre-Emergency Indian system:

> Here it is necessary to grasp the logic of the Indian model of politics that emerged in the first twenty years of independence out of the twin facts of a highly diverse social structure and its territorial spread, on the one hand, and the need to provide a framework of consensus and integration to carry out the major tasks facing the country. The model had two interrelated aspects: a structure of governance which allowed for an authoritative exercise of power ... and a wide and diffuse sharing of power at various levels which legitimized such a structure of authority and made it responsive to the diverse needs and demands of the population.... The "system" that emerged out of such a structure of participation ... continued to enjoy widespread acceptance.... it worked and worked rather well for almost two decades.... And central to its success was one key factor: the ability of the operators of the system to understand its logic and their willingness to play it out.[3]

This is an insightful and courageous evaluation.

The empirical analysis presented in this book attests to the emergence of such a system at the mass level. At all levels of the society by 1975 Indians were involved with an active political process. One sees in our data the development of meaningful perceptions of and commitments to democratic political values and practice. This being so, one can only hope that the "operators of the system," as Kothari refers to them, steeped as they have also been, in their personal and political lives, in democratic orientations, will again return India to the pursuit of the democratic goals of individual freedom, self-government, and the "open society" on which the India of 1947 was founded. Politically the Indian citizen has learned much about democracy. His civilization can now only prosper properly through the democratic spirit of the masses, nurtured again by opportunities for expression and involvement, and finally realized in political decisions made by leaders who cherish that spirit, decisions which lead to economic and social justice for the Indian masses.

TWENTY-ONE.

A 1977 Postscript: Democracy in India Has Roots

I N THE THIRD WEEK OF MARCH 1977 A TOWERING EVENT OCCURRED IN India—nearly 200 million Indians voted for freedom. This was a momentous act, a veritable revolution, one which changed the course of history. With unprecedented decisiveness and clarity the voters defeated Indira Gandhi's government, removed the operators of the Emergency from office, and brought their incipient authoritarianism to an end. From 26 June 1975 on, for over twenty months, the Indian people had been subjected to arbitrary and capricious rule, following the abrogation of their freedoms, the destruction of their party system, and the arrogant violation of a wide range of democratic norms. When given the chance to express their opinions they reacted with great courage, overwhelmingly rejecting the authoritarian regime. In its simplicity and grandeur this was a magnificent electoral event. As Acting President B. D. Jatti said in his formal opening address to a joint session of Parliament:

> The people have given a clear verdict in favor of individual freedom, democracy and the rule of law, and against executive arbitrariness, the emergence of a personality cult and extraconstitutional centers of power.[1]

With the election of March 1977, the restoration of democracy in India began. India was again an open society.

This great episode in mass political behavior occurred after we had completed the analysis for our study presented in this book. It also occurred without the opportunity for a careful national survey comparable to our studies in 1967 and 1971. No sample data are, therefore, available with which to interpret the results of the election and to assess the factors responsible for the momentous electoral outcome of March 1977.[2] Nevertheless, the basic results can be presented, interpreted in a preliminary way, and some of the major questions emerging from the election can be specified. Above all, the election can be viewed in the light of the basic theoretical model which is at the heart of our investigation.[3]

The specific results of the election are by now fairly well known. Not only was Mrs. Gandhi defeated in her own constituency, but her son Sanjay was also rejected, as were others in her government closely associated with the rule under the Emergency—Defense Minister Bansi Lal, the Law Minister H. R. Gokhale, and Information Minister V. C. Shukla. In certain northern states Congress was almost shut out. In Delhi and in the states of Punjab, Haryana, Himachal Pradesh, Uttar Pradesh, and Bihar, Congress failed to get even a single seat. In Madhya Pradesh and Rajasthan, Congress got only one seat, and in West Bengal and Orissa it was victorious in only three and four constituencies, respectively. Out of a total of 302 seats in those states, Congress's share was only 9.

The nationwide election results as summarized in table 21.1 reveal the magnitude of the vote and the nature of the defeat of Congress. The turnout was relatively high, 60.54 percent of the 320 million eligible voters, compared to 55.3 percent in 1971. Almost 50 million more people voted in 1977 than six years previously. There were a large number of candidates in the field—2,439—second only to the 2,790 in 1971.

The Congress vote did not decline absolutely, remaining at about 65 million, but its percentage share of the vote did decline dramatically, from 43.6 to 34.5 percent. The combined opposition party movement of Janata-CFD mobilized *and* concentrated a tremendous vote against Congress—over 81 million votes, compared to less than 40 million for these same parties in 1971. Indeed this is the crux of the Congress defeat. The ability of these opposition parties to combine for the election, to prevent the fragmentation of their vote through multiple candidacies, and above all to make democracy versus authoritarianism the main issue in the election—this was the strategy and the genius leading to the Congress defeat. Unlike past elections, the electoral battle was essentially between the Congress and a singularly well-knit formation of non-Communist opposition parties (the Jan Sangh, the SSP-Socialist Party, the BLD-Indian Peoples Party, the Congress-O, and the Congress for Democracy) formed on the eve of the election by several leaders, among them Jagjivam Ram, who left Mrs. Gandhi's cabinet after the elections were announced. Of the two Communist parties, both of which are recognized as multistate parties by the Election Commission, the CPI (Marxists) had an electoral alliance with the Janata/CFD in most states, and the CPI with the Congress in some areas. Likewise, the important regional parties, like the Akali Dal in Punjab and the DMK in Tamil Nadu, fought the elections in alliance with the Janata/CFD, while a new party in Tamil Nadu, the All-India Anna DMK, established a few years previously by rebels from the old DMK, had an electoral understanding with the Congress in that state.

This time a smaller proportion of the vote went to the two Communist parties, the other small parties, and independents, all of whom together received 22 percent of the vote compared to 32 percent in 1971. In contrast to these parties and independents there was a surge of support for the

Chapter Twenty-one

TABLE 21.1 The 1977 Election Results Compared to 1971

Party	% of the Total Vote		No. of Seats Won		% of Seats in in Lok Sabha		Total Votes Received	
	1971	1977	1971	1977	1971	1977	1971	1977
Congress	43.6	34.5	352	153	68	28	64,040	65,100
Combined Janata-CFD	24.5	43.2	51	299	10	55	35,645	81,400
Two communist parties								
CPI	4.7	2.8	23	7	4	1	6,935	5,300
CPM	5.1	4.3	25	22	3	4	7,510	8,100
Other parties	13.6	9.15	53	51	10	9	20,200	17,200
Independents	8.6	6.0	14	7	2.7	1.5	12,270	11,333
Totals			518	539			146,600	188,433

* The 1977 data are drawn from provisional figures released by the Election Commission immediately after the election. Elections for two seats, one in Himachal Pradesh and another in Jammu and Kashmir, were not included in these returns in 1977. The 1971 data actually have to be understood as utilizing a special calculation: they combine the results for the parties which eventually became part of the 1977 Janata/Congress for Democracy coalition. The data for the 1971 election come from the Election Commission of India, *Report on the Fifth General Election to the House of the People of India-1971*, 1973, vol. 2.

Janata-CFD opposition, which apparently attracted most of the "new voters" and probably a substantial number of Congress defectors as well. The exact nature of the vote exchanges 1971–77 between parties will not be known because of the absence of national survey data. One can note, however, that the difference in the Janata-CFD vote in 1977 and the equivalent vote in 1971 (46 million) matches closely the aggregate influx of new voters. The addition of almost 50 million voters was linked to the tremendous election totals amassed by the Janata-CFD coalition, and thus was linked to the Congress defeat.

The defeat in terms of seats was equally dramatic. Congress lost over 200 seats, the final total being 153. On the other hand, the Janata-CFD coalition won 299 seats, compared to 39 at the time of dissolution. This was indeed a catastrophic reversal for Congress. In one fell stroke the election terminated thirty years of the party's rule at the national level, and reduced it to a party with barely more than one-fourth of the seats in the lower house of Parliament. Further, it deprived it of most of its support in the north. The 153 seats of Congress came primarily from the South: Andhra (41), Karnataka (26), Madras/Tamil Nadu (14), Kerala (11). The other sizable victories for Congress were Assam (10), Gujarat (10), and Maharashtra (20), even though losing heavily in Maharashtra in 1977. Congress lost in almost every state in the country, but its losses were extreme and severe in the north.

The surge of votes, the phenomenon of a mobilized citizenry, is undeniably one of the fascinating aspects of the election to analyze. If one disaggregates this by states one can begin to locate the areas of greatest surge as well as observe the extent to which this was a nationwide development. In table 21.2 one can compare the state voting turnout for 1977 with that of the previous elections of 1971. In only one state was there a decline in turnout—Tamil Nadu—while in two others there was no change or a small one—West Bengal and Maharshtra. The turnout increase was manifest throughout the country, with certain states producing a truly remarkable surge—Gujarat (16 percent increase over 1971), Kerala (15 percent), Punjab (14 percent), Bihar (13 percent), Uttar Pradesh (12 per-

TABLE 21.2 Comparison of State Voting Turnout 1971–77, and Seats Won and Lost by Congress*

| State | State Voting Turnout | | | No. of Seats Won or Lost by Congress 1977 | Congress Seats Won 1971 |
	1971 (% in Rank Order)	1977 %	Rank		
Tamil Nadu/					
Madras	69	67	5	+5	9
Kerala	64	79	1	+5	6
Haryana	63	73	3	−7	7
West Bengal	59	59	11	−10	13
Punjab	59	73	2	−10	10
Andhra Pradesh	58	62	7	+3	38
Maharashtra	58	60	10	−22	42
Jammu and					
Kashmir	58	58	12	−3	5
Karnataka/					
Mysore	55	63	6	−1	27
Gujarat	53	69	4	−1	11
Rajasthan	52	57	13	−13	14
Assam	50	50	16	−3	13
Bihar	48	61	8	−39	39
Madhya Pradesh	45	55	15	−20	21
Uttar Pradesh	45	57	14	−73	73
Himachal					
Pradesh	41	61	8	−7	7
Orissa	41	44	17	−11	15

* Comparable data for small states and territories are not included here because they were not available at the time these results were assembled.

cent), Haryana (10 percent), Madhya Pradesh (10 percent). Perhaps most outstanding were certain states where Congress lost heavily and states where voting participation had been low previously—Uttar Pradesh, Bihar, and Madhya Pradesh. In these states Congress lost 132 seats, while voting turnout, which had averaged 46 percent in these three states in 1971, jumped to an average 58 percent in 1977.

To establish a pattern of Congress losses and gains in relation to turnout is, however, not simple. States like Kerala and Gujarat, where Congress gained or lost only minimally, were high turnout states. And in other states like Orissa and West Bengal it did not take a tremendous surge in votes to win seats from Congress. This suggests that in those states it was the defection of Congress supporters, as well as the concentration of the opposition voters, which produced the Congress defeat. Perhaps the only appropriate summary on this matter at this point is the following:

	Average Increase in State Turnout in 1977 (%)	Average State Turnout in 1977 (%)
States where Congress won seats	5.7	69.3
States where Congress lost seats	8.5	61.0
Six northern states where Congress lost 162 seats	10.7	62.7

Despite some irregularities in the data, there appears to be a strong covariation between the surge in votes and the reprisal against Congress.

There will be much written about the major factors explaining the social, political, and motivational forces behind the vote. Particularly, why was there a difference in voting preferences between the north and the south? Is it because the southerners are people with levels of sensitivity different from those of northern citizens, so that while the latter were outraged by the policies of the government under the Emergency, the former did not react so sensitively? Or is it because there was inadequate information about, and exposure to, governmental policies in the south? There may be some support for both theories. But it is important to note that there seems to be a strong and positive relationship between the degree of suffering experienced by the people of an area and the extent of retribution visited on the Congress government at the polls. It was in the north that the government's "revolutionary" sterilization program was enforced in an allegedly arbitrary and high-handed fashion, and it was in these areas where Congress losses were greatest. An explanation which takes these facts into account, which links voting behavior to the actual life experiences of the people, which indeed varied considerably from state to state under the Emergency, is necessary in order to comprehend the meaning of the election. The social, economic, and political conditions in Kerala, for example, at the time of the 1977 election were much different than in Uttar Pradesh or Bihar and other northern states. In Kerala the voters were acting in a context of the impressive six-year record of stability and progress under the United Front Government in which Congress participated. The result—an increase in Congress seats in Kerala. And in Tamil Nadu a complex set of partisan developments following the dismissal of the DMK government some eight months after the Emergency, while viewed initially as a capricious act of Mrs. Gandhi's government which would hurt it in 1977, did not induce voters to reject Congress, apparently because of the long record of corruption in the state. But in northern states different conditions prevailed. The harshness of Congress rule was either directly experienced or was a proximate reality for most people. Under the circumstances Janata-CFD appeared to the northerners as a major and in fact the only real instrument for overthrowing a government whose actions had become intolerable.

The electoral response was of course produced by a variety of stimuli, experiences, pressures, interests, and attitudes, the relevance of which must be subsequently assessed. But certainly the election must be seen as a mass democratic action against a political leadership which had stripped the people of their liberties, imposed an authoritarian regime based on fear, and inflicted great suffering on a helpless public. It is a great tribute to the Indian voters that they acted so massively against the government even though economic conditions had to a certain extent improved, the Emergency had not been lifted, and therefore the possibility of severe reprisals remained.

This was, then, a decisive election, and the consequences could be far-reaching. The Congress party's status has been drastically altered, converted as it is to a minority opposition status with, for the time being at least, primarily regional public support. New leaders have been brought into office in Delhi and new policy positions are being articulated. With the dissolution of the state assemblies on 30 April new leaders may well emerge also at the state level after the next round of state elections scheduled for June. Further, the vast cadre of party activists who were displaced, silenced, or imprisoned under the Emergency can now return, and many already have, to compete for candidacies and to participate in organizational activist and leadership positions. And a public socialized to the acceptance of, and participation in, parties and competitive elections, a participation proscribed for twenty months, will now be free to engage in partisan behavior. In short, the election results returned India to a competitive, pluralistic, democratic polity. As such it was a "critical election" indeed.

The interruption of democracy may well have consequences, now as well as in the future when the system returns to "normal." This is a matter on which we as yet have very little knowledge, for any country experiencing a hiatus in democracy. One can only engage in speculation. What will be the long-range effect on party loyalty, particularly on the public's identification with Congress? Will partisan commitment to such specific parties as Jan Sangh or the Socialists be superseded by a new commitment to Janata? Will a new sense of political efficacy develop in public orientations toward the political system and its institutions, replacing the highly negative, cynical, and pessimistic beliefs of the past? And how radicalized will the activist segment of the public be now that it has displaced Indira Gandhi and Congress from power? What instruments for political action will they prefer, particularly how important will Indians view political parties as the preferred structures for action? Above all, will the tempo of commitment to political involvement and to democracy itself be maintained now that the threat of authoritarianism has been removed? These and other similar queries will concern us in this period of the 1977 election aftermath.

Throughout this study we have emphasized certain basic theoretical positions. We have argued that from the time of Independence in 1947 India has demonstrated remarkable political development. There emerged a democratic political culture at the mass level. The public came to accept the new political institutions, particularly the party system and the election system. Indians developed a sense of belonging to parties and a capacity to think knowledgeably and perceptively about the party system and the place of their party in it. They engaged in a variety of political activities, at a level of involvement and sophistication equal to that of the West. Yet, they retained their own unique system and ways of thinking about politics, a fusion of "traditional" and "modern" orientations. And this developmental process was pervasive, continuous, and widespread. Indians believed in their system and manifested these beliefs in a variety of ways. Finally, these behavioral and attitudinal phenomena penetrated deep into the countryside. Democratic activism became part of the thoughtways of village, as well as urban, political and social life. Now, in 1977, we see the harvest, the validation of this developmental process. The Indian public has acted democratically and massively against authoritarian abuse of governmental power. This was possible because for thirty years, from 1947 to 1977, despite poverty and illiteracy, that public learned about the meaning of mass participatory democracy, came to believe in it, and practiced it. This, indeed, is the great lesson of modern India.

Part Five

APPENDIXES

APPENDIX 1

Description of the 1967 Study[1]

The sample for the 1967 study was drawn in a multistage probability design and ultimately included 2,632 citizens as potential respondents.[2] Given our primary concern with the impact of different party systems on the politics of India, we began by developing a typology of party competition into which each of the 471 accessible parliamentary constituencies was placed.[3] A sample of 10 percent was drawn from each of the eleven divisions of that typology, giving a full array of competitive milieus within which to mount the survey. In each of the sampled parliamentary constituencies, a probability selection was made of two state assembly constituencies, with the chance of inclusion being in rough proportion to size, and then a random selection of two polling stations was made within each assembly constituency. Evidence of the representativeness of the sampled parliamentary and assembly districts vis-à-vis the whole of India in terms of voting turnout and partisan distribution is presented in table A1.

TABLE A1   The 1967 Election Results for the Set of Sampled Constituencies Compared with the Results for All Constituencies

Parliamentary Election			State Assembly Elections	
All Constituencies (%)	Sampled Constituencies (%)	Points of Comparison	All Constituencies (%)	Sampled Constituencies (%)
61	62	Voter turnout	61	63
41	38	Congress vote	40	40
18	22	Vote for "rightist" parties	16	17
17	18	Vote for "leftist" parties	17	21
22	21	Vote for other parties and independents	27	22
(520)	(47)		(3,467)	(94)

SOURCE: Election Commission of India, *Report on the Fourth General Election to the House of the People of India,* 1969, vol. 1.

On the whole, the evidence in this table is quite satisfying. The relatively small deviations from the actual results—no more than five points for any entry—permit some confidence that the first stages of the sampling procedure did not lead the final data to be badly skewed on these important political dimensions. Of course, because the opposition to Congress is grouped in the table, there is a somewhat smaller sampling error for each group than would occur with party-by-party tallies, given the fact that so many of them contest a rather small number of seats. For example, an estimate of the proper proportion of the total of fifty-seven constituencies in which the Marxist Communist party ran could easily go wrong, or the six seats (in West Bengal) contested by the Forward Bloc could be missed altogether. Nevertheless, the evidence presented in table A1 serves to make the point intended: in the overall distributions of turnout and partisanship, the sampled constituencies at both the state assembly and parliamentary levels do not seem unlike their pooled counterparts for India as a whole.

The final step in the sampling process was to choose respondents from lists of eligible citizens which are maintained by polling station officials and which had just been brought up to date for the election. Only men were allowed into the pool of eligibles. This decision was based on assumptions concerning the accessibility of women as well as the cost and difficulty of sending female interviewers into each polling station. (In the 1971 study the sample included men and women proportionate to their presence in the adult population.) The individual sampling was done on a random basis, with the sampling fraction allowed to vary with the size of the unit so as to produce no more than nineteen interviews in the largest and no fewer than twelve in the smallest. Because past experience indicated that the rate of response would be somewhat lower in urban areas, an upward adjustment in the list-sampling rate was made in these areas. Finally, for purposes of validating the all-male sampling strategy, interviews were taken with women in a randomly chosen subsample of twenty-eight polling stations.

Of the 2,632 potential respondents, interviews were taken with 2,287 of them, a completion rate of 87 percent. This completion rate is, in comparison with surveys elsewhere, very high and reflects the currency of the polling station lists, the geographic stability of the Indian population, and the quality of the field work. Interviews began immediately after the late February elections and by the end of March well over half of them had been completed. In the first two weeks of April an additional 24 percent were added, and 12 percent more by the end of that month. The final 6 percent were interviewed in May. On the average, just over one hour was needed for each interview, although the range was from thirty minutes to almost four hours. Most of the interviews (59 percent) were taken in the respondents' homes. Eleven percent were completed in the workplace, 17 percent in a public place, and the balance in various other locations. For about one out of seven interviews, permission was needed from another person for the respondent to be contacted.

In the important matter of privacy, the results were not ideal. Only 36 percent of the interviews were conducted without others being present. For an additional 56 percent, others were present but did not enter into the question-and-answer exchange. However, for the final 8 percent, there was intervention by onlookers. This potential contamination of the interview by others, which field interviewers found it impossible to avoid, called for subsequent special checks of the relationships within the data. Happily, with statistical controls for this factor applied, no significant differences in those relationships could be found.

The initial external test of the data involved a comparison of the survey percentages with figures taken from the then most recent census of India, that of 1961. Evaluation of the adequacy of the survey can be made on the basis of residence, occupation, literacy, and scheduled caste and tribe distributions. The comparisons are presented in table A2. On the whole, these results are quite pleasing. The 5 percent difference in the proportion from rural settings reflects the higher sampling fraction used for urban polling stations and affects the distribution of agricultural occupations. Although on the literacy figure there is an 11 percent differential, the survey being high, this appears to be a result of the fact that the census figure is six years older. If the difference between the 1951 literacy figure for men (25 percent) and the 1961 figure is taken as an expected growth rate, the projected 1967 figure would be 50 percent. This is very close to what was actually obtained in the survey data.

TABLE A2 Comparison of Census Data and Sample Data on Selected Demographic Factors

Point of Comparison	Census %	Sample %
Rural population	82	77
Farm owners and cultivators*	49	45
Farm workers*	13	11
Literate population*	41	52
Scheduled castes and tribes	21	20

SOURCE: *Census of India, 1961,* pt. 2 and 5.
* Men only.

A second external test of these data was made with official election returns, and the results are to be found in table A3. Here the two sets of figures are somewhat discrepant. The reported vote for Congress in the state elections is 9 percent higher than the actual one, and more seriously, the turnout figure is 25 percent above the national figure. However, there is an obvious adjustment to be made inasmuch as the survey figures are for men only. In making such an adjustment, we first examined the subsample where women were included and found that nonvoting for women was about twice that for men. Had women been included in the sample, then, the turnout figure for the survey would have been about 79 percent, closer to the actual one but still 18 percent higher. India is not unique in this respect. Inflation of reported vote turnout is also found in American studies, where it approximates 15 percent.

If we assume the discrepancy between the survey and census figures to be the result of false reporting by respondents rather than the result of sampling problems, we can predict that this false reporting would also affect the Congress vote figure. American election studies suggest that with respect to politics, nonvoters are less interested, less informed, and less involved than are the citizens who cast ballots on

TABLE A3 Comparison of Official Returns and Sample Data on Voting Turnout and Distribution in State Assembly Contests

Point of Comparison	Official Returns (%)	Sample Results (%)
Voting turnout	61	86
Congress vote	40	49
"Rightist" vote	16	14
"Leftist" vote	17	15
Vote for other parties and independents	27	22

SOURCE: Official Returns from Election Commission of India, *Report on the Fourth General Election to the House of the People of India,* vol. 1.

election day. As a consequence, only very intrusive political stimuli will reach them. Moreover, awareness is confined to only the most visible of political organizations. In the Indian case, this would probably be the Congress party. Hence, any claimed voting by nonvoters would seem more likely to be attached to Congress than to any other party and, for that matter, more likely to be so attached than the reported voting of actual electors. Examination of the party preferences of respondents in the Indian sample who reported they had not voted lends credence to this argument. Of the nonvoters who had a preference, 60 percent opted for Congress, a much higher percentage than that given by actual voters. Moreover, claimed Congress support did actually go up among those respondents who expressed small interest in the elections and who were little exposed to the campaign. If the point is granted and the 60 percent figure is used to estimate how many of the "false voters" claimed to have voted for Congress, the increment to the Congress vote would be 11 percent, giving it a total percentage of 51. This, of course, is very close to the survey results.

A final external test was made by examining the extent to which the survey data and the actual voting percentages had the same pattern across the ninety-four state assembly constituencies included in the sample. Here for each unit a score based on about twenty-one respondents is compared with the real voting behavior of the 150,000 citizens who reside within the average assembly district. The product moment correlation measured the closeness of the covariation. Once again the results encourage confidence in the data. The correlations for voting turnout and for Congress voting are moderately strong, both just over .40. More impressive than these, however, are the relationships for the rightist parties, the leftist parties, and the residual category, other parties and independents. For those three matches the correlations were .73, .81, and .77, respectively. All of the five relationships were significant. These figures strongly suggest that the survey data capture a very substantial part of the true variation in electoral fortunes across India in 1967.

All of these external tests are designed to permit a judgment of how well the survey data match the population from which the sample was drawn. For the variables checked here, the match was remarkably good. However, it must be noted that these tests were confined to the relatively "hard" survey data for which comparison figures in the census or electoral records could be obtained. No such tests are possible on the attitudinal items. Hence, although it appears that the sample is nicely representative, our confidence that it is representative on all counts cannot be total.

The first internal check of the survey data involved examination of the noncommittal response figures. When a large proportion of the respondents answer "don't know" to a set of questions, it may mean that a problem exists with the translation, or that the field work was inadequate, or both. Of course, other explanations are possible as well. Nevertheless, this "nonresponse" level and pattern is one indicator of the quality of the data. Here tests were run across the states and across the legislative districts with simultaneous controls for education and interest in politics, both of which could account for noncommittal responses to many questions.

The initial finding was that very little evidence exists of this type of answer being a form of noncooperation. A subset of items asking exclusively about routine personal behavior was used in this test. Any items which required information or which asked about political attitudes were not included. The proportion not answering the questions in this subset never exceeded 1 percent and typically was very much smaller.

A second finding, this time based on the entire set of questions, was that the proportion answering "don't know" averaged about 10 percent. As was expected, education greatly affected this figure. Illiterate respondents averaged 14 percent, a figure which dropped off quickly as education increased up to middle school and then leveled off. For the group at the upper end of the education distribution, the average was 4 percent. Overall, this noncommittal response rate is quite acceptable and compares very favorably with experience in other nations.

The final test here involved the search for areas where noncommittal responses were particularly frequent. With the aforementioned controls in effect, one state, Andhra Pradesh, stood out as having an excessive level of "don't knows" within the interviews. However, the variance of that score was also substantially higher than it was for any other state, indicating that whatever it was that caused this high level, the effects were far from uniformly felt across the entire sample from Andhra Pradesh. Further examination at the level of parliamentary constituencies revealed that only two of the four constituencies sampled within that state showed the high levels of nonresponse, and for each of them, the variance also was very high. All of this suggests that factors other than the translation of the questionnaire were involved. Unfortunately, it is impossible to investigate the possibility that particular interviewers produced these results.

Further examination of noncommittal response levels within the parliamentary constituencies revealed that two others, one in Tamil Nadu and the other in Rajasthan, also had high levels and with much smaller variance, suggesting a more general effect. When the assembly constituencies were run through the same tests, little more could be uncovered, partly due to the small number of cases available with the controls in effect. Overall, what differences could be found were clear at the parliamentary level.

Altogether, 170 respondents were clustered in the four parliamentary constituencies where the nonresponse level was high. Clear education effects were found in these districts, just as in the others sampled. In sum, it appears that about one-third to one-half of the interviews in these settings, mostly with illiterates, had high numbers of noncommittal responses.

The "don't know" results are quite satisfactory as a whole. The problems which led to the high levels of nonresponse in the four parliamentary districts remain somewhat mysterious. It may be that with higher numbers of interviews in each polling station it would have been possible to uncover a local milieu effect which is presently obscured. Be that as it may, these results do not discourage the belief that the data are sound.

The next internal check involved examination of responses to find patterns which might indicate that in some instances those answers had little meaning. One examination dealt with cue taking, a situation in which the respondent repeatedly answers with the first—or the last—alternative posed within a question. No evidence of any such pattern was found. A second examination checked for another type of response set, sometimes called a "courtesy bias," where the respondent repeatedly chooses the answer which he feels will please the interviewer, usually the affirmative one. This test was somewhat ambiguous because of the failure to include appropriately reversed items in the questionnaire. However, a dichotomous measure was constructed from those instances where the respondent was offered questions under either an agree-disagree or a strong-agree through strongly-disagree format and always chose an affirmative reply. There were 385 such respondents. This was then cross-tabulated with other questions which under a different format asked for affirmative or negative replies. The results indicate that, at most, the consistent yea-sayers are no more than 120 in number or about 6 percent of the total. While this very rough test leaves much to be desired, it does suggest that any acquiescence problem in the data is not an unmanageable one.

The final test of the internal structure of the data was in effect a validity check at the assembly constituency level. Just as for the entire sample examination of expected attitude relationships is made to assess the validity of measurement, so here an examination was conducted for each of the assembly districts. There is, of course, the problem of small numbers, the average per district after elimination of missing data being only nineteen cases and in some instances dropping to nine or ten. Moreover, there certainly are many differences in the socioeconomic and political characteristics of the subsamples. Nonetheless, by looking at the patterns of expected relationships across a set of intercorrelated variables, a number of points could be seen. First, only a single district, one in Haryana, deviates significantly from the expected relationships, and this is not a district where nonresponse was also a problem. An additional fifteen districts, spread across ten states, exhibited moderate deviation, only two of them among those with higher numbers of "don't know" responses. All of these deviations lie well within a normal distribution of such scores. In fact, the district from Haryana is located only two standard deviations above the overall mean. Particularly given the small number of cases for each district, this suggests that no single set of constituency interviews has gone terribly awry.

Altogether, these external and internal tests of the survey data represent a comparatively elaborate evaluation of their adequacy. The results indicate that, as far as

312

can be measured, these data are very good indeed. Again, however, it is useful to point out that the evaluation is necessarily limited and that error is no doubt present. What is reassuring, however, is that the error is not unmanageable, nor is it systematically concentrated in one geographic area. This certainly lends credence to the belief that both the questionnaire design and translation and the field work were well handled. And the external checks also suggest that the sample is quite representative.

APPENDIX 2
The Major Indexes Used in the Study

A variety of compound measures were used and presented at various points in this study. They are listed below with the items included in their composition. The particular answer option used is included in parentheses at the end of the item.

A. *Political Efficacy Index*
Items
1. People like me don't have any say about what the government does. (Agree-Disagree)
2. Sometimes politics and government seem so complicated that a person like me can't really understand what is going on. (Agree-Disagree)
3. Government officials do not care much what people like me think. (Agree-Disagree)

Procedure
Variables were recorded such that a nonefficacious response is scored 1. The three variables are summed, with a score of 3 indicating high efficacy and a score of 0 indicating low efficacy.

B. *Campaign Exposure Index*
The index is simply a summation of dichotomized responses to the following: received handbills, attended election meetings, met candidate(s), was contacted by party canvasser(s). This resulted in a scoring ranging from all four positive (score of 4) to none positive (score of 0).

C. *Caste Awareness Index*
This index is a simple summing operation based on binary coding of questions pertaining to knowledge of candidates' caste, how own caste voted, and which candidate the caste leader preferred. The range is from 3 for high caste awareness to 0 for low awareness.

D. *Political Involvement Index*
This index includes the voting frequency of the respondent in the three most recent national elections and whether he was active in the campaign and/or a party member. The index is assumed to be cumulative such that for those few respondents who say they have never voted but have been active or have been party members, the information is simply coded as "missing data." The index thus

314

varies from ''0'' (never voted, no campaign activity, not a party member) to ''4'' (voted two or more times, was active in the campaign, and was a party member). The index is constructed only for those age cohorts who would have been eligible to vote over the three elections.

The 1967 Questionnaire[1]

(Interviewer's Introduction)

I come from Delhi—from the Centre for the Study of Developing Societies. The Centre is a non-governmental body sponsored by the Indian Adult Education Association. This study is about the general elections and we are interviewing adult citizens and leaders. We need your co-operation to ensure the success of our study. I hope you will be kind enough to spare some time to answer some questions.

1. I would like to ask you first about this (village/town) you live in. How long have you lived here?

   IF NOT ALL LIFE:

   1a. From which village/town do you come? (CHECK WHETHER IT IS A VILLAGE OR TOWN.)

   1b. Where have you lived most of your life—in towns or villages?

2. What are the most import problems the people in this (village/town) face?

3. What are the main castes here?

   3a. To what caste do you belong?

4. In many places, we have found that castes and religious groups set up organizations for social, educational, and other purposes. What are such castes or religious organizations here?

   IF ORGANIZATIONS MENTIONED:

   4a. Are you a member of any of these organizations?

   4b. Which ones?

5. Apart from caste organizations, what other public organizations have been set up in this (village/town)?

   5a. Are there any others?

   5b. To which of these organizations do you belong?

6. Who is the most influential person in this (village/town)?

   Who else?

   (RECORD FIRST THREE.)

   (ASK FOR EACH OF THE PERSONS RECORDED.)

   6a. What does he do as an influential person?

   6b. So far have you had any dealing with him?

7. What have been the most important changes that have taken place here in recent years?

   (RECORD IN ORDER MENTIONED.)

8. Now I would like to talk to you about the election in February. Who were the candidates from this constituency?

   8a. Was anyone else a candidate?

   (ASK FOR EACH CANDIDATE MENTIONED.)

316

8b. Do you happen to know the caste of these candidates?

8c. Was he a candidate for the Lok Sabha or the State Assembly?

9. Generally speaking, would you say that you personally cared very much who won in this constituency, or didn't you care very much?

10. In this constituency, which party or candidate won the election for the legislative assembly?

   10a. How satisfied are you with these results—very satisfied, somewhat satisfied, or not satisfied?

   10b. And which party or candidate won election for the Lok Sabha?

   10c. How satisfied are you with these results—very satisfied, somewhat satisfied, or not satisfied?

11. Talking of (NAME OF STATE) as a whole, how successful was the Congress Party in this election compared with the last general election—more successful, same as before, or less successful than before?

12. Among the other parties, which party has emerged as the most successful in this election here in (NAME THE STATE)?

   12a. How satisfied are you with these results in the State—very satisfied, somewhat satisfied, not satisfied?

13. Leaving the period of election aside, how much interest do you take in politics and public affairs? Do you take a great deal of interest, some interest, or no interest at all?

14. How interested were you in the election campaign this year? Were you interested a great deal, somewhat interested, or not interested at all?

   14a. How many of the election meetings held by the parties or candidates in this area did you attend? Many, some, or none?

   14b. Which were the different parties or candidates whose election meetings you attended?

   14c. What about newspapers—did you learn about the election from the newspapers?

   14d. From which parties or candidates did you receive handbills?

15. Did any of the candidates meet you personally during the campaign?

   15a. Who were these candidates?

16. Did any party canvassers come to your house and meet you personally?

   16a. For which parties or candidates?

   16b. Was anyone in your family personally contacted by a candidate or canvasser?

   16c. For which parties or candidates?

17. Did any religious or caste leader advise you or anyone in your family as to how you should vote in this election?

   17a. Who was that? (FORMAL POSITION)

   17b. Do you know him personally?

   17c. Do you think this kind of advice helps people in deciding how to vote?

18. Did you vote this time?

   18a. For whom did you vote for the State Assembly?

   18b. For whom did you vote for the Lok Sabha election?

19. If you could vote *again,* would you still vote for the same party/candidate?

317

20. Did the candidates you voted for discuss any issues during the election campaign?

    20a. What were the issues?

    20b. Which candidate was this—the Lok Sabha candidate or the assembly candidate or both?

  (IF "NO" IN Q. 18):

    21a. What was the main reason you did not vote in this election?

    21b. Did the candidates in this constituency discuss any issues during the election campaign?

    21c. What were the issues?

    21d. Which candidate was this—the Lok Sabha candidate or the assembly candidate or both?

22. Five years ago, did you vote in the general elections of 1962?

    22a. For whom did you vote in the State Assembly election?

    22b. For whom did you vote in the Lok Sabha election?

    22c. What was the main reason you did not vote in that election?

23. How about the election ten years ago—did you vote in the general elections in 1957?

    23a. For whom did you vote in the State Assembly?

    23b. For whom did you vote in the Lok Sabha election?

    23c. What was the main reason you did not vote in that election?

24. Have you ever voted for an Independent candidate?

25. Are there any parties for which you would *never* vote?

    25a. Which parties?

26. Did you work in the campaign in any way?

    26a. Did you engage in house-to-house canvassing for any party or candidate?

    26b. Did you help to get voters to the polling stations?

    26c. Did you help to raise any money for a candidate or a party for the election campaign?

    26d. Did you help to organize any election meeting in your area?

    26e. Did you join in any procession or demonstration?

    26f. Did you distribute any polling cards or literature for a party or candidate?

    26g. What else did you do?

    26h. Would you say you did these things for the candidate or for the party?

    26i. Which (party/candidate)?

27. Did anyone in your household work in the election campaign?

    27a. Who was that? (GET RELATIONSHIP TO "R.")

    27b. What were the things he did?

28. Do you personally know any party leaders or any of the candidates in this constituency?

29. Which were the most active groups in the election here? (WHERE UNCLEAR GET SOME DESCRIPTION OF THE GROUP.)

  (IF MENTIONS GROUPS):

29a. Were you active in any of these groups in this campaign? Which ones?
30. Generally speaking, which party do you feel closest to?
    30a. Is your preference for this party very strong or not very strong?
    30b. Was there ever a time when you felt close to another party, rather than (NAME PARTY MENTIONED) party?
    30c. Which party was that?
    30d. What was the main thing that made you change parties?
31. Was there ever a time when you felt close to any party?
    31a. Which party was that?
    31b. What was the main thing that made you change your mind about this party?
32. What are the main difficulties for the Congress Party in finding support *in this constituency?*
    32a. What are the main advantages for the Congress Party in finding support *in this constituency?*
33. Over the years, has the Congress Party been finding it easier or harder to get support *in this constituency?*
34. In general, what gives the Congress Party its *main* strength?
    34a. In general, what are its *main* weaknesses?
35. In general, what gives to the parties other than the Congress their *main* strength?
    35a. In general, what are their *main* weaknesses?
36. Do you think there are important differences in the policies and programmes of various parties?
    36a. In what ways is the party you voted for (or would have voted for) different from other parties?
37. Do you think that for the progress of the country the government should exercise *greater* controls over industry, trade, and agriculture than at present, exercise less control, or keep things as they are?
    37a. Which party would be most likely to do what you want on this issue?
    37b. Which parties are against what you want on this issue?
38. Recently there was a lot of discussion on whether the central government should pass a law to ban cow slaughter. Should the central government pass such a law, or do you think this is not a proper subject for central government action?
    38a. Why do you think so?
    38b. Which party would be most likely to do what you want on this issue?
    38c. Which parties are against what you want on this issue?
39. Some people recently have tried fasting in order to influence the government; others have disapproved of this. How about you—do you approve or disapprove of fasts for influencing the government?
40. Here are some charges that were made against the Congress leadership in the last campaign. I will read them one at a time and you tell me how strongly you agree or disagree.
    40a. The Congress failed to keep prices down.
    40b. The Congress failed to provide strong leadership.

40c. The Congress failed to keep law and order.

40d. The Congress failed to distribute food properly.

40e. The Congress failed to provide help for farmers.

40f. The Congress failed to root out corruption.

41. What do you think of the government officials here in this block/town—are you generally satisfied with the job they are doing or not?

    41a. And what about the government officials at district and *higher* levels—are you satisfied with the job they are doing or not?

42. One way to look at parties is to determine how different they are. Some parties want to preserve old traditions, while some stand for new ideas. (HAND CARD.) On this card the space to the left of the line represents all those parties which stand for new ideas. The space to the right of the line is for those parties which are for old traditions. On which side of the line would you put (GIVE NAME OF EACH PARTY AND SHOW PARTY SYMBOL)? Party list: Congress, C.P.I., Jan Sangh, S.S.P., Swatantra, P.S.P.

    42a. Are there any other parties you would like to put anywhere on this card? Which ones and where?

    42b. (FOR EACH PARTY PUT ON THE RIGHT SIDE OF THE CARD) To what extent does (PARTY) stand for old traditions, very much or not so much?

    42c. (FOR EACH PARTY PUT ON THE LEFT SIDE OF THE CARD) To what extent does (PARTY) stand for new ideas, very much or not so much?

    42d. Where would you put yourself on this card? (PROBE FOR THE EXTENT OF HIS LEANING EITHER ON LEFT OR RIGHT.)

43. Are you a member of any political party?

    (YES)

    43a. Which party is that?

    43b. Do you hold any position in the party, or in a group associated with the party?

    43c. What position is that?

    (NO)

    43d. Would you consider joining a political party?

    43e. What party?

44. Are there any problems on which you would go to a party leader for help?

    44a. What kind of problems?

45. Have you ever gone to a party leader for help?

    45a. Did this leader help you?

46. Are there any problems on which you would go to a government official for help?

    46a. What kind of problems?

47. Have you ever gone to an official in the government for help?

    47a. Did he help you?

48. How much do political parties help to make government pay attention to the people—a good deal, somewhat, or not at all?

49. How much does having elections from time to time make the government pay attention to the people—a good deal, somewhat, or not at all?

50. Recently we talked with some MLA's and MP's from different parties.* Here are some statements they made about their duties as legislators. How important do you consider each of these—very important, somewhat important, or not important?

    50a. To work for the policies and programme of his party.

    50b. To work for the wishes of his electorate.

    50c. To work for the interests of his caste.

    50d. To work for what he believes to be right.

    50e. All in all, which one is *most* important for a legislator to represent: his party, his electorate, his caste, or his own views?

51. Do you think elections are necessary or not necessary in this country?

52. And how about political parties—do you think political parties are necessary or not in India?

53. There have been many discussions about the best way to determine what the people want in India. Some people feel that it is necessary to have *only one* party to determine what all the people want. Others feel that it is necessary to have *more than one* party to find out what the people want. Which do you think is necessary—only one party or more than one party?

54. We are interested in how people are getting along financially these days. As far as you and your family are concerned, would you say that you are well satisfied with your present financial situation, moderately satisfied, or not satisfied at all?

    54a. During the last few years, has your financial situation been getting better, getting worse, or has it stayed the same?

    54b. Now looking ahead and thinking about the next few years, do you expect your financial situation will stay about the way it is now, get better, or get worse?

55. Was your father very much interested in politics, somewhat interested, or not interested at all?

    55a. Which party or movement did he support?

56. Were there any other members of your family who were interested in politics?

    56a. Who were they?

    56b. What party or movement did they support?

57. At what age did you first become aware of politics, parties, and such activities?

58. What was it that first made you aware of such activities?

59. What are the political events during your life which you remember most clearly? (NOTE THE YEAR OF EACH EVENT.)

60. We are interested in how families reach decisions about voting. Some people say that the head of the family or someone else takes decision for the whole family. Others say that decisions are taken by each person on his own. Still others say that decisions are arrived at after discussions among the family members. Would you tell me how voting decisions are reached in your family?

* MLA's=Members of Legislative Assembly; MP's=Members of Parliament.

60a. Is this how your family decides other important matters or not?

61. Which party did the leaders of your caste/religious group support in this election?

(IF KNOWS PARTY):

61a. Did you agree with that position?

62. Who is the *one* person here in this (village/town) whose advice on voting you respect the most?

62a. What does he do? (POSITION/STATUS)

62b. His relationship with "R."

63. Generally speaking, did most members of your caste vote for one party or for different parties?

63a. Which party (or parties)?

(IF ONE PARTY):

63b. Is the fact that your caste votes that way important to you or not?

64. What parties or candidates did the other castes in this village/town vote for?

65. Which party or candidate best protects the interest of your caste?

66. In general, do MLA's and MP's in fact protect the interests of their caste or not?

67. I would like to read some statements we often hear. Would you tell me whether you agree or disagree with each one.

67a. People like me don't have any say about what the government does.

67b. Voting by people like me does have an effect on how the government runs things.

67c. Sometimes politics and government seem so complicated that a person like me can't really understand what is going on.

67d. Government officials do not care much what people like me think.

67e. What this country needs more than all the laws and talk is a few determined and strong leaders.

67f. We should be loyal to our own region first, and then to India.

67g. It is not desirable to have political parties struggling with each other for power.

BACKGROUND DATA

68. Age (years)

69. Religion

70. Who else lives here? (ONLY RELATIVES LIVING IN HOUSE)

71. Who is the head of household?

(IF "R" NOT HEAD):

71a. What is the occupation of the head?

71b. (IF HEAD RETIRED) What was his occupation most of his life?

71c. What was the highest level of education he reached?

71d. What is (was) his monthly income?

(IF FATHER NOT MENTIONED AS HEAD IN Q. 71):

72a. What is your father's occupation.

72b. (IF FATHER RETIRED OR DEAD) What was your father's occupation most of his life?

72c. What was the highest level of education he reached?

72d. What is (was) his monthly income?

73. What is your occupation?

73a. (IF RETIRED) What was your occupation most of your life?

74. What was your very first occupation?

75. What is the total monthly expenditure of your household?

76. What is the highest level of education you reached?

77. What is your monthly income?

78. What is the monthly income of the whole household, including your income?

79. Hou much land is *owned* by you and your household?

80. Have you or members of your household taken any land on tenancy?

    80a. How much?

  (IF YES ON Q. 79 AND/OR Q. 80):

    80b. How much land are you and your household cultivating?

TO BE ENTERED BY INTERVIEWER IMMEDIATELY AFTER INTERVIEW

A1. Date, time, and place of interview.

A2. Was anyone else present?

A3. Was permission needed from anyone other than "R" to conduct the interview?

A4. Was the respondent cooperative?

A5. Describe briefly the style and condition of respondent's dress.

A6. What is the material used in the respondent's house roof (if interview is in house)?

A7. Record name of caste/castes living in the neighbourhood.

A8. Describe the neighbourhood in terms of occupations of the residents. Use broad categories.

A9. Is there anything that would be useful to the research team in understanding the interview question—anything about the respondent, the setting, or anything else?

Notes

1. See Rajni Kothari, *Politics in India* (Boston: Little, Brown & Co., 1970), pp. 38–42, 148–50.
2. Robert L. Hardgrove, Jr., *India: Government and Politics in a Developing Nation* (New York: Harcourt Brace, 1970), pp. 38–39.
3. Ibid., p. 186.
4. W. H. Morris-Jones, *The Government and Politics of India* (London: Hutchinson University Library, 1964), p. 52. See also Myron Weiner, "India: Two Political Cultures," in Lucian Pye and Sidney Verba, eds., *Political Culture and Political Development* (Princeton, N.J.: Princeton University Press, 1965), p. 199.
5. Charles Taylor and Michael Hudson, *World Handbook of Political and Social Indicators* (New Haven, Conn.: Yale University Press, 1972), pp. 94–95. See also Rudolph J. Rummell, *Dimensions of Nations* (Beverly Hills, Calif.: Sage Publishers, 1972), table 11.13, which ranks India fifth in number of persons killed in domestic conflict, 1955.
6. For a good discussion of this thesis and an empirical examination of Indian elites in which it is explored, see W. Ross Brewer, "Game Players and Ideologues: An Examination of Leadership Types in India" (Ph.D. diss., University of Michigan, 1974), particularly pp. 25–26.
7. Samuel Huntington, *Political Order in Changing Societies* (New Haven, Conn.: Yale University Press, 1968), pp. 84–85.
8. As one example, see the articles by Lloyd Rudolph and Myron Weiner in the *Asian Survey,* vol. 11, December 1971, as well as the writings of Rajni Kothari (such as his *Politics in India*) and Edward Shils (*Political Development in the New States* [The Hague: Mouton, 1962]).
9. Among other scholars who have studied these developments, one particularly useful work was by John O. Field, "Politicization and System Support in India: The Role of Partisanship," a paper presented at the 1974 American Political Science Association meeting, Center for International Studies, M.I.T., 1974. Field concludes, "Politicization, especially party politicization," is widespread in India; and among its effects is the "cultural institutionalization of democratic politics in Indian society" (pp. 93–94).
10. See Max Ralis et al., "Applicability of Survey Techniques in Northern India," *Public Opinion Quarterly* 23 (1958): 245–50; Lloyd and Susanne Rudolph, "Surveys in India: Field Experience in Madras State," *Public Opinion Quarterly* 22 (1958): 235–44.

11. Angus Campbell, Philip Converse, Warren Miller, and Donald Stokes, *The American Voter* (New York: John Wiley & Sons, Inc., 1960), p. 484.
12. Ibid., p. 489.
13. Angus Campbell, Philip Converse, Warren Miller, and Donald Stokes, *Elections and the Political Order* (New York: John Wiley & Sons, Inc., 1966), p. 254.
14. Angus Campbell, Gerald Gurin, and Warren Miller, *The Voter Decides* (Evanston, Ill.: Row, Peterson & Co., 1954), p. 197.
15. Ibid., p. 191.
16. Frederick Frey, "Cross-Cultural Survey Research in Political Science," in R. T. Holt and J. E. Turner, eds., *The Methodology of Comparative Research* (New York: Free Press, 1970), pp. 173–294.

Chapter Two

1. Rajni Kothari, "Continuity and Change in India's Party System," *Asian Survey* 10 (1970): 947.
2. See Stanley A. Kochanek, *The Congress Party of India* (Princeton, N.J.: Princeton University Press, 1968), p. 408. Kochanek's interpretations (pp. 410–47) of the meaning of the 1967 "defeat" for Congress are extremely useful.
3. Rajni Kothari, "The Political Change of 1967," *Economic and Political Weekly* 6 (1971): 231.
4. See W. H. Morris-Jones, "India Elects for Change—and Stability," *Asian Survey* 11 (1971): 719–41, for a careful discussion of the observations and predictions. His notes are used for the summary presented here.
5. Ibid., p. 719.
6. Myron Weiner, "The 1971 Elections and the Indian Party System," *Asian Survey* 11 (1971): 1157. See also other articles by Lloyd Rudolph and Stanley J. Heginbotham, interpreting the 1971 election, which appear in this issue of the *Asian Survey*.
7. Ibid., p. 1153.
8. On this point for 1967 see particularly Dwaine Marvick, "Party Cadres and Receptive Partisan Voters in the 1967 Indian National Elections," *Asian Survey* 10 (1970): 963–64. Also relevant is the article by Bashiruddin Ahmed, "Political Stratification of the Indian Electorate," *Economic and Political Weekly* 6 (1971): 252–53.
9. In 1967 only 34 percent reported following the campaign through the newspapers; in 1971 it was less, 29 percent. In 1971, 36.5 percent reported being exposed to the campaign via the radio.
10. S.J. Eldersveld, "Party Identification in India in Comparative Perspective," *Comparative Political Studies* 6 (1973): 276–78.
11. Ibid.
12. Philip E. Converse, "Continuity and Change in American Politics: Parties and Issues in the 1968 Election," *American Political Science Review* 63 (1969): 1084.

13. An earlier discussion of these vote exchanges in 1967 is found in S. J. Eldersveld, "Elections and the Party System: Patterns of Party Regularity and Defection in 1967," *Asian Survey* 10 (1970): 1016–20.

14. See Eldersveld, "Party Identification in India in Comparative Perspective," *Comparative Political Studies* 6 (1973): 227, for the sources for these comparative figures. Of course these may now be inflated proportions for these countries also. After the 1972 election the SRC report revealed that Nixon had received the votes of 42 percent of the Democratic identifiers. See Arthur H. Miller et al., "A Majority Party in Disarray: Policy Polarization in the 1972 Election," *American Political Science Review* 70 (1976): 753–78.

Chapter Three

1. See a most provocative piece by Ashis Nandy, "The Making and Unmaking of Political Cultures in India," *Daedalus* 102 (Winter 1973): 115–37. Kothari's discussion in chapter 7, "Political Culture and Socialization," in his *Politics in India* is also very useful. Many others can be cited also, particularly the work of Lloyd and Susanne Rudolph, *The Modernity of Tradition: Political Development in India* (Chicago: University of Chicago Press, 1967).

2. Myron Weiner, "India's Two Political Cultures," in his *Political Change in South Asia* (Calcutta: K. L. Mukhopadhyay, 1963), pp. 114–51; W. H. Morris-Jones, "India's Political Idiom," in C. H. Philips, ed., *Politics and Society in India* (London: Allen & Unwin, Ltd., 1963), pp. 133–54. See also a criticism of these theories in the light of some empirical data by Peter B. Mayer, "Support for the Principles of Democracy by the Indian Electorate," *South Asia* 2 (1972): 24–32.

3. Gabriel Almond, "Comparative Political Systems," *Journal of Politics* 18 (1956): 391–409.

4. Sidney Verba, "Comparative Political Culture," in *Political Culture and Political Development,* p. 518.

5. We accept here the basic position of Clifford Geertz, who saw the "hermetical approach" to culture as running "the danger . . . of locking cultural analysis away from its proper object, the informed logic of actual life . . . . Behavior must be attended to, and with some exactness, because it is through the flow of behavior—or, more precisely, social action—that cultural forms find articulation" (*The Interpretation of Cultures* [New York: Basic Books, 1973], p. 17).

6. See Kothari, *Politics in India,* for the rationale for this theoretical position.

7. Lucien Pye has argued that in empirical discussions of "political culture" one should start with assumptions concerning those cultural orientations most functional for a particular political system, and then examine the reality—that is, the incidence of such orientations. In a sense, in the ensuing analysis, we move in a similar fashion between macrolevel assumptions and microlevel data. See Lucien Pye, "Culture and Political Science: Problems in the Evaluation of the Concept of Political Culture," in Louis Schneider and Charles M. Bonjean, eds., *The Idea of Culture in the Social Sciences* (Cambridge: Cambridge University Press, 1973), pp. 65–77.

8. Mayer, "Support for the Principles of Democracy by the Indian Electorate," p. 31.
9. One should remember that this analysis in both years is based on data for men only. Our 1967 sample included too few women for proper comparison. In comparing Indian data with other countries we have presented the data for men wherever possible or indicated the extent of the differences between men and women, in the U.S. and British studies particularly. Although we did not in either of these studies systematically set out to study political culture, we did ask questions for other purposes which are useful for assessing system orientations.
10. The U.S. data come from Sidney Verba and Norman Nie, *Participation in America* (New York: Harper & Row, 1972), p. 369; the British figure is from David Butler and Donald Stokes, *Political Change in Britain* (New York: St. Martin, 1971), appendix. The test was in a sense less rigorous for the Indian respondents, since identification by party, symbol, or person's name was acceptable. If two or all three of these identifications were advanced, however, they had to be accurate.
11. Campbell et al., *Elections and the Political Order,* p. 204.
12. The proportion found *after* the 1964 election was much higher—82 percent for women, 88 percent for men. It was 67 percent for men in India in 1971 (but based again on knowledge of party or candidate's name, or both).
13. Our reanalysis of the data in Butler and Stokes, *Political Change in Britain,* appendix. The differences for men and women were extremely small, no more than 1 percent.
14. See *Institute for Social Research Newsletter,* Winter 1974, p. 5. Minimal differences of 2 percent were found for men and women on this item.
15. Dhiru Sheth of the Centre for the Study of Developing Societies, Delhi, is making an intensive study of the extent and implications of these orientations toward direct political action.
16. See Campbell et al., *The Voter Decides,* p. 191, for a comparison of male-female responses on political efficacy.
17. B. Ahmed, "Caste and Electoral Politics," *Asian Survey* 10 (1970): 979–92. See particularly pp. 984 ff.

Chapter Four
1. One finding, possibly provoking more concern, was that in the villages only 42 percent positively assert support for the competitive party system, compared to 64 percent in the cities.

Chapter Five
1. Kothari, *Politics in India,* p. 251.
2. The data on the basis of which the 1962 and 1967 calculations in the accompanying table were made are found in R. Chandidas, Ward Morehouse, Leon Clark, Richard Fontera, eds., *India Votes* (Bombay: Popular Prakashan, 1968; New York: Humanities Press, 1968), pp. 533–643, 362–525. The Haryana 1962 data are for those Punjab constituencies which were included in the new

state by 1967.
3. We completed a state-by-state analysis of the correlations for individual respondents between all these cultural components. It was impossible to include all these findings here, however, and only some of the major observations can be summarized.

Chapter Seven
1. Rajni Kothari, *The Context of Electoral Change in India* (New Delhi: Academic Books, 1969), pp. vii, ix, 25.
2. Ibid., p. 137.
3. Rajni Kothari, "The Political Change of 1967," *Economic and Political Weekly* 6 (1971): 229.
4. Gopal Krishna, "Electoral Participation and Political Integration," in *Context of Electoral Change in India,* p. 27.
5. Dhiru Sheth, "Partisanship and Political Developments," *Economic and Political Weekly* 6 (1971): 259–74.
6. Samuel J. Eldersveld, "Elections and the Party System: Patterns of Party Regularity and Defection in 1967," *Asian Survey* 10 (1970): 1016–20.
7. The article by Sheth referred to in note 5 above employs both components.

Chapter Eight
1. Much of this chapter was published earlier in Samuel J. Eldersveld, "Party Identification in India in Comparative Perspective" (*Comparative Political Studies* 6 [1973]: 271–95) and is used by permission of the publisher, Sage Publications, Inc. Since our Indian data are based on a male sample, we have tried to use male data in comparative studies for other countries also, where these were readily available.
2. The basic distribution of party identification in our total male sample (N of 1973) in 1967 was as follows (1971 in parentheses):

Party	Strong Identifiers (%)	Weak Identifiers (%)	Total Identifiers (%)	
Congress	32	10	42	(29)
Swatantra	3.5	1.5	5	(0.7)
Jan Sangh	5	2	7	(2.0)
Communists	3	1	4	(2.5)
Socialists	3.5	1	4.5	(0.6)
DMK	3	0.4	3.4	(2.6)
Smaller parties	2	1	3 }	(5.2)
Independents			3 }	
Nonidentifiers			18.3	(52)
No answer, don't know, refusals			10	(5)

(Note: in 1971 the Congress identifiers were divided as follows: Congress (N) 29 percent, Congress (0) 2.9 percent, Congress unidentified 3.2 percent.) The dominance of Congress and the fragmentation of the identification with opposition parties is striking. The difference in the proportion of identifiers in 1971, due possibly to the different way in which the series of questions was asked, is discussed both in the introductory and concluding chapters.

3. Another interesting finding to note in India is that there is relatively little "overlap" in generational transmission of loyalties. Thus only 7 percent of those now identifying with a non-Congress party were brought up in Congress homes. And less than 1 percent of Congress supporters were brought up in non-Congress homes. In Kerala we found that 6 percent of Communist identifiers came from Congress identifiers and 2 percent of Congress identifiers came from Communist family backgrounds.

4. These data for "the West" are taken from Jack Dennis and Donald J. McCrone, "Pre-adult Development of Political Party Identification in Western Democracies," *Comparative Political Studies* 3 (1970): 252. These data differ from the Indian data in two important respects: 1. They are proportions of youth or students at these age levels who give political socialization responses and are not based on adult recall of the age of socialization, as is the case for India. 2. These studies were more precisely concerned with identification than with more general political awareness, which may in fact make the contrast with the Indian findings more striking. Thus, while not directly comparable, they are presented here as suggestive and possibly relevant.

5. The U.S. data come from Campbell et al., *The American Voter,* p. 147. The U.S. percent increases to 74 percent if only those respondents whose parents were both Republican or Democrat are used. The British data are from Butler and Stokes, *Political Change in Britain,* p. 49. This figure increases to 69 percent if either father or mother's preference is used. The percentage in England would be over 75 percent if only respondents whose parents were both Conservative or Labour were used. These are proportions of those who recall parent's party choice who are congruent with parent's politics.

6. See the article by Jack Dennis and Donald J. McCrone, "Pre-adult Development of Political Party Identification in Western Democracies," for data on familial agreement by age groups in Western countries.

7. See Eldersveld, "Elections and the Party System: Patterns of Party Regularity and Defection in 1967," *Asian Survey* 10 (1970): 1016–20. Also Kothari, *Politics in India,* and his "The Political Change in 1967."

8. As expected, Indian identifiers who have had ties with other parties are somewhat less strong in their party affiliation, but not to a great extent—76 percent of those with no previous ties are "strong" compared to 70 percent of those with such ties.

9. Philip E. Converse and Georges Dupeux, "Politicization of the Electorate in France and the United States," in Campbell et al., *Elections and the Political Order,* p. 291.

10. The only finding at this level in the United States is for the very lowest income level, which in 1952 was reported as having 50 percent with strong party

identification. See Angus Campbell and Homer C. Cooper, *Group Differences in Attitudes and Votes: A Study of the 1954 Congressional Election* (Ann Arbor: Institute for Social Research, University of Michigan, 1956), p. 56.

11. Lloyd I. Rudolph and Susanne H. Rudolph, *The Modernity of Tradition: Political Development in India* (Chicago: University of Chicago Press, 1967), p. 12.

12. Kothari, *Politics in India,* pp. 85, 225.

13. On this point, see also D. L. Sheth, *Citizens and Parties* (New Delhi: Allied Publishers, 1975), particularly pp. 135–64.

Chapter Nine

1. An exception is Jack Dennis, "Support for the Party System by the Mass Public," *American Political Science Review* 60 (1966): 600–615.

2. Ibid., p. 606. These data came from a study of a Wisconsin cross section in 1964.

3. Jack Dennis, Leon Lindberg, Donald McCrone, and Rodney Stiefbold, "Political Socialization to Democratic Orientations in Four Western Systems," *Comparative Political Studies* 1 (1968): 89, based on responses to a questionnaire administered to schoolchildren in Colchester, Essex, England.

4. S. J. Eldersveld, *Political Parties: A Behavioral Analysis* (Chicago: Rand McNally & Co., 1964), pp. 19–20, 440–41.

5. S. J. Eldersveld, *Political Affiliation in Metropolitan Detroit* (Ann Arbor: Institute of Public Administration, University of Michigan, 1957), p. 129.

6. Dennis, "Support for the Party System by the Mass Public," p. 604.

7. See Butler and Stokes, *Political Change in Britain,* p. 500. See also p. 32.

8. Jack Dennis et al., "Political Socialization to Democratic Orientations in Four Western Systems," pp. 88–92.

9. Henry Valen and Daniel Katz, *Political Parties in Norway,* chapter 8. See also Angus Campbell and Henry Valen, "Party Identification in Norway and the United States," *Public Opinion Quarterly* 25 (Winter 1961): 505–25.

10. See Donald R. Matthews and James W. Prothro, "The Concept of Party Image and its Importance to the Southern Electorate," in M. K. Jennings and L. H. Zeigler, eds., *The Electoral Process* (Englewood Cliffs, N.J.: Prentice-Hall, 1966), for a discussion of the relationship between party identification and "party image" for whites and blacks in the south. At one point (p. 167) in the analysis they conclude, "A man's party identification does not tell you in the South today how he perceives his party and how he evaluates it." It is also interesting to note their view that the "saving grace" which keeps the southern whites and blacks in the Democratic party is, first, 40 percent have no image of that party and "large numbers of others have only the most rudimentary picture," and, second, the "amorphous nature of American parties permits the two races to perceive the same party somewhat differently" (p. 172).

11. Campbell et al., *The American Voter,* chapter 10.

12. Campbell and Valen, "Party Identification in Norway and the United States."

13. Studies in other countries have not addressed themselves precisely to the

question posed here. The American studies have strongly suggested the absence of issue-party congruence as did the recent study of British politics by David Butler and Donald Stokes. One fragment of evidence in that study, again not precisely measuring the phenomenon as done here but nevertheless enlightening, is found in a table on page 194 of that study. For those who had an opinion on the nationalization issue among Labour and Conservative supporters, 52 percent felt the "other party" would do more on the problem and 48 percent felt their "own party" would do more, a level of issue-party ambivalence far exceeding that found in India! See Butler and Stokes, *Political Change in Britain,* p. 194.

14. Samuel Barnes' analysis of Italian data does demonstrate a strong relationship between party identification and a Left-Right location on a policy index. This is not the same as linking party identification to one's perception of which party will do what the respondent wants done on an issue, but Barnes' analysis suggests that this linkage would probably be close in Italy (Samuel H. Barnes, "Left, Right and the Italian Voter," *Comparative Political Studies* 4 [1971]: 170).

15. Of course empirically, on the controls issue, a larger percentage of Swatantra than Jan Sangh strong identifiers desired less controls, as noted above.

16. Campbell et al., *The American Voter,* p. 180. See chapter 8 for the discussion of the problem and the data used here.

Chapter Ten

1. Philip Converse, "The Problem of Party Distance in Models of Voting Change," in Jennings and Zeigler, *The Electoral Process,* pp. 175–207.

2. Butler and Stokes, *Political Change in Britain,* pp. 206–7. Other studies presenting French data are J. Laponce, "Note on the Use of the Left-Right Dimension," *Comparative Political Studies* 2 (1970): 481–502; Philip Converse and Roy Pierce, "Basic Cleavages in French Politics and the Disorders of May and June, 1968," a paper presented at the Seventh World Congress of Sociology, Varnia, Bulgaria, 1969.

3. Barnes, "Left, Right, and the Italian Voter," pp. 157–75. See also, Samuel Barnes and Roy Pierce, "Public Opinion and Political Preferences in France and Italy," *Midwest Journal of Political Science* 15 (1971): 643–60.

4. Hans Klingemann, "Testing the Left-Right Continuum on a Sample of German Voters," *Comparative Political Studies* 5 (1972): 93–106.

5. It is interesting to note that of all the efforts to use party space analysis which we have discovered (Italy, Germany, France, Netherlands, Finland, India, Britain), those studies which use a structured, given scale or continuum and which also give the names of the parties to be spaced report uniformly high ability to locate parties and self. The proportions who are able to locate self are India (78 percent), Italy (76 percent), France (90 percent), Netherlands (93 percent), Germany-Hesse (81 percent). When the structure is not supplied, as is the case of Finland and France (1958), the proportion seems to fall, although there are too few cases to validate this observation positively.

6. See the Converse, Barnes, and Butler-Stokes references cited in notes 1 through 3 above for the actual analysis. In the English study the authors conclude that only 39 percent "correctly" placed the Labour party, and only 16 percent had "fully" or "partially elaborated interpretation" of the "Left-Right concepts" (p. 211). A recent report of a national study in the Netherlands in April 1971, asking respondents to place themselves and thirteen Dutch parties on a seven-point party space continuum characterized as an innovation-tradition ("change everything"–"return to yesterday's life") continuum, reveals 58 to 77 percent spacing the parties and 93 percent locating themselves. See *De Nederlandse Kiezer '71* (Meppel, Netherlands: Boom, 1972), pp. 141–42.

7. Barnes, "Left, Right, and the Italian Voter," p. 165.

8. Ibid., p. 164.

9. Converse, "The Problem of Party Distance in Models of Voting Change," pp. 186–88. Our observations were based on a detailed inspection of a 10 percent random subsample.

10. Based on our subsample analysis.

11. Converse, "The Problem of Party Distance in Models of Voting Change," p. 188.

12. See Klingemann, "Testing the Left-Right Continuum on a Sample of German Voters," p. 97.

13. Based on our subsample analysis.

14. Two items were used in this index: (1) "What this country needs more than all the laws and talk is a few strong leaders." and (2) "We should be loyal to our own region first, and then to India." Agreement with both was the most "traditional" response; disagreement the most "modern."

15. The spatial distance expectations were based on respondent's own spatial locations of parties.

16. We also attempted to see whether party spacing behavior was related to the tendency to support extremist parties on the Right or Left. The findings were inconclusive. Although 30 percent of those locating themselves distant from the parties supported extreme parties, the proportion was only slightly larger than the percentage in 1967 supporting extreme parties among those who spaced themselves with their own or other parties.

Chapter Eleven

1. Rajni Kothari, "The Political Change of 1967," *Economic and Political Weekly* 6 (1971): 248.

2. Sheth, "Partisanship and Political Development," p. 273.

3. This index was based on the following information about each respondent: whether he attended election meeting(s), received party propaganda in the mail, met the candidate(s), and was canvassed by party workers at his home.

4. See chapter 8 for a much more detailed examination of political socialization influences.

5. True, Converse also found that there was a high correlation between party

identification and the vote at the low media exposure level. Converse, "Information Flow and the Stability of Partisan Attitudes," in Campbell et al., *Elections and the Political Order*, p. 146. On party voting, however, the comparison presented here is defensible.

6. This accords, of course, with the theory that under certain conditions the absence of new information and stimuli leads to stability in partisan behavior. See Converse, "Information Flow and the Stability of Partisan Attitudes," pp. 136–57.

7. Gabriel Almond and Sidney Verba, *The Civic Culture* (Princeton, N.J.: Princeton University Press, 1963), particularly chapter 4, "Patterns of Partisanship."

8. Actually, at the state politics level in India we find much greater knowledge. Over 60 percent, for example, could name one or more candidates for the state assembly seats in their districts in 1967, while only 47 percent could do so for the Parliament.

9. See Campbell et al., *The Voter Decides*, p. 108.

10. We find in India that those persons who "identify" with independent candidates are also quite active—15 percent both voted in 1967 and were active in the campaign.

11. For these statistics see Chandidas et al., *India Votes*, pp. 362–643.

12. See Campbell et al., *The American Voter*, p. 143; Converse, "Information Flow and the Stability of Partisan Attitudes," in Campbell et al., *Elections and the Political Order*, pp. 136–41; Hans Daudt, "Floating Voters and the Floating Vote: A Critical Analysis of American and English Election Studies" (Ph.D. diss., Leiden University, 1961); Butler and Stokes, *Political Change in Britain*, pp. 221–28; Kothari, "The Political Change of 1967," p. 249.

13. Campbell et al., *The American Voter*, p. 143.

14. These figures are very rough and by no means absolute. The reported vote is inflated considerably when compared to an actual voting turnout of under 60 percent. Our analysis is based on a male sample only, but the figures here as in all national election studies are still much higher than they actually should be.

15. Kothari, "The Political Change of 1967," pp. 247–48.

16. Shils, *Political Development in the New States*, p. 29.

Chapter Twelve

1. Krishna, "Electoral Participation and Political Integration," p. 27.

2. Ibid.

3. Shils, *Political Development in the New States*, pp. 58, 59.

4. Ibid., p. 59.

5. Kothari, "Party Politics and Political Development," in *Context of Electoral Change in India*, p. 3.

6. Ibid., p. ix.

7. Ibid., p. 27.

8. Ibid., pp. 2, 3, 15, 18.

9. Ibid., pp. 16–18. In a sense his basic hypothesis, presented on p. 18, is: "The politicisation of the majority population living in hitherto unpenetrated areas,

and the resulting shifts in the locus of political power, has led the much earlier politicised and for long privileged minority population represented by the urban middle class to feel deprived and alienated and has led to their withdrawal from the participation and decision-making channels of the democratic polity."

10. See the Rudolphs' essay, for example, on "The Private Origins of Public Obligation," in their book *The Modernity of Tradition,* pp. 240–46. See also Shils, *Political Development in the New States,* p. 29.

11. Krishna, "Electoral Participation and Political Integration," p. 28.

12. Maurice Duverger long ago pointed out the difficulties in the study of participation from a contextual standpoint. See his *Political Parties* (New York: John Wiley & Sons, 1963), pp. 79, 116.

13. See Gopal Krishna, "Electoral Participation and Political Integration," *Economic and Political Weekly,* annual number, February 1967, pp. 179–90.

14. Bashiruddin Ahmed, "Political Stratification of the Indian Electorate," *Economic and Political Weekly,* vol. 6, 1971.

15. Sidney Verba, Norman H. Nie, Jae-on Kim, *The Modes of Democratic Participation: A Cross-National Comparison* (Beverly Hills, Calif.: Sage Publishers, 1971).

16. Lester Milbrath, *Political Participation* (Chicago: Rand McNally, 1975), p. 1.

17. Verba and Nie, *Participation in America,* p. 2.

18. Ibid., pp. 2–3.

19. Milbrath's discussion of "Conceptual Problems of Participation," in *Political Participation,* chapter 1.

20. For an interesting typology of involvement emphasizing this dimension, see Ashis Nandy, "Insiders and Outsiders: Aspects of Political Alienation," in Sheth, *Citizens and Parties,* pp. 67–94.

Chapter Thirteen

1. Shils, *Political Development in the New States,* pp. 25, 31.

2. Butler and Stokes, *Political Change in Britain,* pp. 24–27.

3. Campbell, *The American Voter,* p. 50.

4. Milbrath, *Political Participation,* pp. 16, 21; Verba and Nie, *Participation in America,* p. 32.

5. Verba and Nie, *Participation in America,* p. 2.

6. See for example, Frank Sorauf, *Party Politics in America* (Boston: Little, Brown & Co., 1968), chapter 4; Eldersveld, *Political Parties,* chapter 11, "Motivational Diversity in the Party Hierarchy"; Dwaine Marvick, "The Middlemen of Politics," in William Crotty, ed., *Approaches to the Study of Party Organization* (Boston: Allyn and Bacon, 1968), pp. 341–74.

7. Shils, *Political Development in the New States,* p. 29.

8. See Milbrath, *Political Participation,* p. 9, for a variety of distinctions among participatory acts.

9. In data about the U.S. public, we typically find that 70 to 80 percent of the electorate reports having read "something" about the presidential campaign in one of the printed media (Converse, "Information Flow and the Stability of

Partisan Attitudes,'' p. 149).

10. The India data came from our 1967 national election study, except where it is indicated that they are taken from the report by Verba et al., *The Modes of Democratic Participation*, p. 36. One should note particularly that these Indian data are for the male sample only. The data for the United States and United Kingdom are for the total samples, with male data in parentheses when available. The British data are taken from Butler and Stokes, *Political Change in Britain* (the 1963, 1964, and 1966 studies). The American data come from Campbell et al., *The American Voter* (1952 and 1956 studies) except where indicated. The ellipses in the table indicate that no data were available. Not all items are perfectly comparable. In the item ''Follow politics in mass media,'' the British study used the phrase ''mass media or personal conversation.'' In the item ''Met political candidates,'' the American figure is from Eldersveld, *Political Parties* (1956 election, Detroit only), p. 536; the British figure is from a question using the phrase ''seen in person'' (Butler and Stokes, p. 490).

For the item ''Political interest,'' a comparable figure is difficult to secure due to different code categories: ''very'' (United States), ''good deal'' (Britain), and ''great deal'' (India). The India figure is 34 percent for those who said a ''great deal'' or ''some.'' See the Detroit study by Eldersveld (*Political Parties*) for the American data, p. 458; British study, Butler and Stokes, p. 468. The American data on campaign interest came from Campbell et al., *The American Voter*, p. 84; the British data, from Butler and Stokes, *Political Change in Britain*, p. 482. The item ''Knowledge about politics'' is based on the ability to name their representatives. The American figure comes from the study by Verba and Nie, *Participation in America*, p. 369. The British figure would be higher if the 1964 results after the election are used—as high as 80 percent.

For the item ''Attending rallies'' the Verba figure for India is lower (14 percent) and refers to such activity over a three-year period. The Verba figure for the United States is higher (19 percent). The British figure is for 1964; in 1963 it was 4 percent.

For the item ''Belonging to parties'' the Verba figure is 6 percent for India and 8 percent for the United States. The British figure is reported to be 12 percent in 1963, but if trade union ''nominal'' affiliated party membership is included, the figure is 25 percent. The source for the item ''Ever worked for a party'' is the Verba study. British data are determined from a question as to whether the respondent has been ''active in parties,'' but this was asked in 1963 only of those who said they had paid their party dues. The item ''Work with community groups'' comes from the Verba study.

Voting turnout data from survey respondents are all probably inflated. The Indian actual percent was probably closer to 65 percent for men. Local turnout data for the United States and India are from the Verba study.

The item ''Active in campaign'' came from Campbell et al., *The American Voter* data for the United States, which varied for the two elections. It is the same level as reported by Milbrath, *Political Participation*. On ''Gave money in a campaign'' we used the Verba data. The percentages for the United States of Campbell et al. and Milbrath are 8 percent and 10 percent.

For the item "Elite contact" the figures used by Verba for India differ from ours. For India, party leader contact is 16 percent and government leader contact is 8 percent. For the United States the Verba figures are used. The only British data available come from a question as to whether or not the respondent had tried to influence Parliament members.

For the item "Potential involvement," though no strictly comparable American data are available, our 1956 Detroit study found 37 percent who said they would contribute to the parties if asked, and 18 percent were individuals who, on the basis of their predispositions toward parties, were in a state of "readiness" to be activated for party and campaign work.

11. See Ahmed, "Political Stratification of the Indian Electorate," p. 252, for the exact percentages for a variety of participations in 1967. In a forthcoming article by Kim, Nie, and Verba, data are presented on Indian participation with which our national surveys of 1967 and 1971 disagree. The article is "The Amount and Concentration of Political Participation," in which the authors present an "index of inequality," or of "concentration," of participation for six countries. The Indian proportions of participation used, based on a four-state study, do not accord with our findings. Their analysis relied on male and female data, while ours as presented here is based on men only. For example, the proportions attending political rallies were 26 percent in our study and 14 percent in Verba's. The proportion engaged in some political participation act beyond voting which Verba uses is 36 percent for India, but Ahmed's percentage, without even including several of the participatory opportunities Verba used, was 47 percent. See Ahmed, "Political Stratification of the Indian Electorate," p. 255. The relatively low ranking of India, therefore, in the Verba study may not be acceptable based on later and more national data. This 47 percent for India ranks close to Verba's earlier figure of 50 percent for the United States (Verba and Nie, *Participation in America*, pp. 79–80), although his later figure of 64 percent for the United States is higher (and the difference is not clearly explained).

12. See Butler and Stokes, *Political Change in Britain*, p. 25.

13. Milbrath, *Political Participation*, p. 20.

14. Milbrath was inclined to see only 5 to 7 percent as "gladiators" in the United States, but he cited the 1956 study, on the one hand, as indicating a figure of 14 percent. The Indian data are found in Ahmed, "Political Stratification of the Indian Electorate," pp. 255–56; the U.S. data in Verba and Nie, *Participation in America*, pp. 79–80.

15. Bashir Ahmed, as noted earlier, found 47 percent engaged in some kind of activity beyond voting. This, however, includes "attentive" and information-getting activities or exposures, such as attending political meetings.

Chapter Fourteen

1. Selig Harrison, *India: The Most Dangerous Decades* (Princeton, N.J.: Princeton University Press, 1960).

2. Kothari, *Politics in India*, pp. 95–6. Also relevant to this matter is another

presentation by Kothari at pages 253–54. His discussion of this question is extremely insightful and helpful.

3. Verba and Nie, *Participation in America,* p. 100.
4. Almond and Verba, *The Civic Culture,* pp. 380–81.
5. Milbrath, *Political Participation,* pp. 122–23.
6. See Verba and Nie, *Participation in America,* p. 96. As explained there, "the formal definition of the ratio of over and under-representation for any given social group within any given population is $PR = \frac{Xi - Yi}{Xi} \times 100$
where PR = ratio

   Xi = the percentage of the entire population in the social group
   Yi = the percentage of the same social group within a given category of participation."
7. Ibid., p. 125.
8. S. Rokkan and A. Campbell, "Citizen Participation in Political Life: Norway and the U.S.A.," *International Social Science Journal* 12 (1960): 9–39.
9. John Kautsky, *Political Change in Underdeveloped Countries: Nationalism and Communism* (New York: John Wiley & Sons, 1962), p. 10.

Chapter Fifteen
1. See Milbrath, *Political Participation,* chapter 3, for an early summary of such research.
2. See Verba et al., *The Modes of Democratic Participation,* pp. 75–79, for the specification of models using attitudes as antecedent to political participation.
3. Shils, *Political Development in the New States,* pp. 29, 31.
4. See the appendix for the description of this scale.
5. We used a series of questions about Congress leadership, with reference to the Congress party's leadership in dealing with prices, food distribution, and similar issues. The basic pattern is in every case the same as shown in table 15.5.
6. *The American Voter* used interest in the campaign, concern over the election outcome, sense of political efficacy, and sense of citizen duty, plus intensity of partisan preference. See the discussion therein on pages 101–7. Verba and Nie use an index composed of a set of items which one could question as strictly measuring psychological involvement, including reading magazines and watching news broadcasts on television. See Verba and Nie, *Participation in America,* appendix, pp. 367–69.
7. Campbell et al., *The Voter Decides,* pp. 187–94.
8. See Campbell et al., *The American Voter,* p. 481, for these American data; also Philip Converse, "Change in the American Electorate," in Angus Campbell et al., *The Human Meaning of Social Change* (New York: Russel Sage, 1972), p. 328.

Chapter Sixteen
1. Huntington, *Political Order in Changing Societies.*
2. Kothari, *Politics in India,* pp. 102, 107.
3. Among many, see, for example, the discussion of the French system by

Converse and Dupeux, "Politicization of the Electorate in France and the United States." Also, the discussion by Campbell and Valen, "Party Identification in Norway and the United States."

4. The most pertinent discussion is in Campbell et al., *The American Voter*, chapter 11.

5. See, among others, V.O. Key, *Southern Politics* (New York: Random House, 1949) and *Politics, Parties and Pressure Groups* (New York: Thomas Y. Crowell Co., 1964).

6. A summary of these studies can be found in William Crotty, "Party Effort and its Impact on the Vote," *American Political Science Review* 65 (1971): 439–50.

7. Milbrath, *Political Participation*, p. 100.

8. See Verba and Nie, *Participation in America*, p. 190.

9. D. Katz and S. Eldersveld, "The Impact of Local Party Activity upon the Electorate," *The Public Opinion Quarterly* 25 (Spring 1961): 1–24; Phillip Cutright and Peter Rossi, "Grass Roots Politicians and the Vote," *American Sociological Review* 23 (1958): 171–79. See also Crotty, "Party Effort and its Impact on the Vote," pp. 439–50.

10. See Katz and Valen, *Political Parties in Norway*, pp. 120–31.

11. Verba and Nie, *Participation in America*, p. 208.

12. M. Janowitz and D. Marvick, *Competitive Pressure and Democratic Consent* (Ann Arbor: Bureau of Government, Institute of Public Administration, University of Michigan, 1956), p. 80.

13. Eldersveld, *Political Parties*, p. 442.

14. Janowitz and Marvick, *Competitive Pressure and Democratic Consent*, p. 77.

Chapter Seventeen

1. See Verba and Nie, *Participation in America*, p. 133; and Verba et al., *The Modes of Democratic Participation*, pp. 44–47. The earlier and most significant article which operationalized these variables and pioneered this approach was Norman H. Nie, G. Bingham Powell, Jr., and Kenneth Prewitt, "Social Structure and Political Participation: Developmental Relationships: I and II," *American Political Science Review* 63 (1969): 361–78, 63 (1969): 808–32.

2. The correlations in this figure and in those which follow should be interpreted as follows: Education and Intervening Variables, simple *r;* Education and Campaign activity is the residual after the effects of the intervening variables are removed (the *r* in parenthesis is the simple product moment correlation); intervening variables and "campaign activity" correlations are residuals after the effects of other variables are removed.

3. See the appendix for the operationalization of these measures.

4. The Verba analysis combines four types of orientations into a general "civic attitudes" variable in the U.S. study, but treats "psychological involvement" (based on interest in politics, discussion of politics, reading magazines, newspapers, and watching television) separately along with "party affiliation" and "sense of contribution to the community" in the comparative analysis

presented earlier in Verba et al., *The Modes of Democratic Participation.*

5. The simple product moment correlations for these three variables do reveal some relationships. These are largely erased when our path model is employed, however. The product moment correlations for all variables used here with campaign activity are

Political interest	.34
Newspaper exposure	.27
Candidate awareness	.21
Caste awareness	.16
Political efficacy	.11
Party identification strength	.21

6. See Verba et al., *The Modes of Democratic Participation,* pp. 75–79.

7. The description in Verba is not completely clear, using "expressed interest" in politics and public affairs as well as frequency of discussion of politics. Our variable includes extent of general political interest and exposure to newspapers. See Verba et al., *The Modes of Democratic Participation,* p. 45. In the later description of this variable by Verba and his associates, it included reading of magazines, newspapers, and watching television, as well as discussion of politics and general political interest. It is not clear whether these components are included in the comparative models.

8. We considered the possibility that it might be the fact that our study was conducted with a predominantly (85 percent) male sample. But our product moment correlations for men and women are similar—.00 for men, .10 for women, .03 for all those in our sample in 1967.

9. The "elite contact" variable is operationalized as including the following types of data: personal acquaintance with candidates; meeting party organization leaders or caste leaders; evidence of having gone to a governmental official or party leader for help; evidence of having gone to a caste leader for advice on voting.

10. This is different from our "elite contact" variable which is based on personal acquaintance with political leaders and whether the respondent has gone to such leaders for help.

Chapter Eighteen

1. Kothari, *Politics in India,* pp. 150, 337.

2. Shils, *Political Development in the New States,* p. 38.

3. See, for example, S. N. Eisenstadt, *Comparative Perspectives on Social Change* (Boston: Little, Brown & Co., 1968), p. xxiv; also, David Lerner, *The Passing of Traditional Society: Modernizing the Middle East* (Glencoe, Ill.: Free Press, 1958), p. 401.

4. Verba and Nie, *Participation in America.*

5. Based on population estimates and voting turnout data. See Chandidas et al., *India Votes,* p. 256.

6. Verba and Nie, *Participation in America,* pp. 267–98.

7. Ibid., p. 276.

8. David Apter, *The Politics of Modernization* (Chicago: University of Chicago Press, 1965), p. 186.

Chapter Nineteen

1. We have again in 1971 for this analysis partitioned our adult sample (men only) into five groups: inactives (4 percent); irregular voters, no other activity (11 percent); regular voters, no other activity (68 percent); actives, engaged in party or campaign activity (14 percent); very actives, engaged in party *and* campaign activities besides voting regularly (4 percent).

2. D. L. Sheth, "Structure of Indian Radicalism," *Economic and Political Weekly* 10 (1975): 319–34.

3. The 1971 wording was the same but rather than presented as an agree-disagree item, it was preceded by the phrase "Would you say that . . ." and followed with "Or would you say that . . . (the opposite)."

4. This comparison may be a bit misleading although technically correct. If we consider those who in 1967 gave *any* efficacious response at all (the top *three* categories of our index, rather than the top *two*) we do find that the "very active" persons were 50 percent efficacious (compared to 29 percent of the nonvoters, for example). There was some indication, therefore, in 1967 that involvement was beginning to be associated with a sense of efficacy.

5. A direct comparison here with the 1967 question is difficult because this question was not asked of those who in 1967 did not know how their caste voted. Of those who did respond to this question, 89 percent said "important."

6. One might argue that the smaller proportion of identifiers in 1971 might suggest that a more difficult test of party identification was used leading naturally to higher correlations. This would be more plausible if the basic trends noticed here—of stronger correlations in 1971—were not also true for other measures for which we developed correlations, such as political efficacy and involvement. Since these correlations were also greater and more positive in 1971 than in 1967, that explanation is not completely tenable.

7. It is possible that a wording change in presenting the efficacy items in 1971 could have accounted for these stronger correlations. In 1967 we used the standard Michigan set and format. In 1971 the phrasing was, for example, "Would you say that people like you have no influence over what the government does or that you have some influence over what the government does?" Again, the patterns of all our findings on these trends suggests that this phrasing change was probably not critical, but one must reserve final judgment on this.

8. The "Psychological Involvement Index" used here was based on the following items in both years: care about election outcome, general interest in politics, campaign interest. In 1971, discussion of politics was also included but analysis revealed that this influenced the index very little.

9. A recent unpublished study (Shanto Iyengar, "Childhood Learning of Partisanship in a New Nation: The Case of Andhra Pradesh," 1973) of political socialization of high school students in Andhra Pradesh, an area which at the

time was subjected to considerable political agitation, found that 40 percent of those children could recall their father's party identification.

Chapter Twenty
1. Rajni Kothari, "Restoring the Political Process," *Seminar,* July 1976, p. 13.
2. Richard L. Park, "Political Crisis in India, 1975," *Asian Survey* 15 (1975): 996–1013.
3. Kothari, "Restoring the Political Process," p. 16.

Chapter Twenty-one
1. *The Statesman,* New Delhi, 29 March 1977.
2. The Centre for the Study of Developing Societies was able to conduct six village studies at the time of the 1977 election campaign. The results of these should be available soon.
3. For an extensive statement of the model explaining electoral outcomes in India and an early interpretation of the March 1977 results see "The Electorate" and "The Outcome" by Bashiruddin Ahmed, in *Seminar,* no. 212, April 1977, pp. 19–24, 25–29.

Appendix One
1. This description was prepared initially by Douglas Madsen and appears in "The Sense of Political Efficacy in India: An Exploration in Political Psychology" (Ph.D. diss., UCLA, 1973), chapter 2.
2. The 1971 study used similar procedures by the same research staff and, therefore, will not be separately discussed here.
3. Under then-existing political conditions, field work was impossible in the states of Assam, Nagaland, and Jammu and Kashmir; and for design and other practical reasons, the Union Territories were not included in the study either.

Appendix Three
1. The 1971 questionnaire was in its basic form very similar to this questionnaire. As indicated in the text, there were some additions. We will supply a copy of the 1971 questionnaire to interested scholars who request it.

Index

Activists: attitude profile of, 245, 262–63, 290; in campaigns (*see* Campaign activity); candidate awareness of, 256, 268; and caste conformity, 281–83; and caste consciousness, 203–7, 214–15; caste distinctions among, 257, 260, 264, 267–68, 270; cross-national comparisons of, 264–65, 267–68; distribution of, 50–51; and education, 214–15, 265–68, 270, 278; leadership role of, 45–46, 257, 280; liberalism of, 265–70, 280–81, 292; motivations for, 172–73; and nonactivists, contrasted, 201, 243–44, 255–57, 259–60, 265–68, 279–80; party distinctions among, 257–59, 268–69; party identification of, 256–57, 261, 269; policy preferences of, 264-67, 281; political sophistication of, 255–57; and regime antagonism, 259–64, 269–70; social diversity of, 270, 277, 292; socioeconomic profile of, 189–93, 195–98, 277–78; and system support, 268–69; theoretical roles of, 254-55. *See also* Cross-national comparisons, of political involvement; Political involvement; *and names of political parties*
Age: and party identification, 47, 83–87; and party spacing ability, 127; and political involvement, 194–95, 218–19; and political orientations, 47; and political socialization, 47
Ahmed, Bashirrudin, 166, 180, 185
Alienation, and political involvement, 214–16, 291
Almond, Gabriel, 34, 42, 139, 189, 253
Andhra Pradesh, 53–59, 299

Apter, David, 271
Authoritarian attitudes, 202–3

Barnes, Samuel, 80, 110, 120
Bihar, 52–59, 299
Brahmans, 227
Burma, 5
Butler, David, 38, 82, 86, 97, 110, 117, 138, 171

Campaign activity, 23–24, 178, 182–83, 195, 219–21, 273, 275–76, 284; cross-national comparisons of, 24, 233–36; path models of, 232–36, 241, 248–49
Campaign and political interest, 56, 58; of activists, 256, 268; despite alienation, 215; and campaign exposure, 61–63, 175; cross-national comparisons of, 140–42, 186–87; and party identification, 140–42, 275; and political involvement, 182, 207–9, 232–33, 236–37, 243, 246–47; by states, 55; and voting behavior, 185–87, 236–37
Campaign exposure: of activists, 256–57; and candidate awareness, 68; and education, 66; and efficacy, 68; index of, 62, 64, 66, 314; and mobilization potential, 227; and party identification, 135–37, 145, 150, 153–56, 284; and party spacing ability, 125–27, 132; and political involvement, 8, 10, 24, 61–63, 220–29, 240–42; in specific elections, 23–24; and system support, 64, 66–68, 152; and voting, 136, 150, 173, 222–24. *See also* Cross-national comparisons, of campaign exposure; Mobilization

343

Index

Indian political structure: accomplishments of, 5, 294; attitudes and orientations toward, 34–51, 57–59, 134–54, 243–47, 254, 268–69, 274, 291; dynamism of, 5; fragility of, 1948–67, 4–5; fragmentation of, 12, 20–22, 26–27, 75, 113; images of, 272; and Independence, 48–51, 61, 86, 138, 194–95, 200, 217–18; and Indian states, 52–60; masculine character of, 179; penetration of, 61, 161, 288; support for, 57–59, 243–47, 268–69, 274, 291. *See also* Competitive party system; Election system; Indian political development; Integration of Indian politics
Indian public: apathy of, 7, 10, 280, 287, 293; cognitive orientations of, 36–38, 44; conformism of, 43, 164; evaluative orientations of, 38–42; expressive orientations of, 42–43, 154–55; ideological character of, 98–100; integration of, questioned, 7; mass action by, 39–40, 184, 196–97; mobilization of (*see* Mobilization, of Indian public); and party space, 117, 119–20, 122; and party system support, 95; passivity of, 5, 164; pessimism of, 10, 41, 44, 47, 209–10, 275, 292; and political involvement, 181–84, 246–47; political socialization of, 3, 11, 49, 66–67, 75, 91, 218–19, 274, 287, 292; political sophistication of, 7, 27, 124, 288–89, 302; radicalization of, 277, 292; social character of, 9, 287; survey participation of, 13, 124–25; traditional character of, 214. *See also* Party identification; Political involvement; *and entries on voters and voting*
Integration of Indian politics, 5–6, 47, 50–51, 55, 58–60, 269–70; through elections, 74, 160; extent of, questioned, 7, 188; and Hindu tradition, 189; and party identification, 87–93, 134–35; and party spacing, 133

Issue congruence: definition of, 77; and party identification, 100–106, 108, 273, 276; and polity maturity, 105
Issue defection, 105–8
Issues: cross-national comparisons of, 98–101, 104 n, 108–9; and party spacing, 129. *See also* Cow slaughter issue; Economic controls issue; Fasting issue

Janata-CFD, 297–98, 301–2
Janowitz, Morris, 224–25
Jan Sangh party, 19–21, 26–27, 49–50; activist cadre of, 258–59, 261–64; attitudes of, 144; and cow slaughter ban, 103, 105–6, 266–67; and economic controls, 101–2, 104–5, 107, 266–67, 280; and efficacy, 143; and fasting, 103; identification with, 143, 151; and party spacing, 112–19, 121–22, 126–28
Jatti, B.D., 296
Jennings, M.K., 97
Johnson, Lyndon B., 25
"Joint pressures" model of political involvement, 250–52

Katz, Daniel, 97
Kautsky, John, 199
Kerala, special survey in, 82–83
Kim, Jae-on, 167, 171, 180, 184, 232–35, 237
Klingemann, Hans, 110 n4
Kothari, Rajni, 3 n1, 20–21, 35 n6, 46, 52, 73–74, 134–35, 152, 160–61, 164–65, 189, 253, 294
Krishna, Gopal, 74, 159, 164, 166
Kubota, Akira, 82

Lal, Bansi, 297
Lerner, David, 6
Liberalism, 265–70, 280–81, 292
Linberg, Leon, 94–96
Lok Sabha, 19–20, 26, 130, 144, 147, 150–51, 190, 195, 246, 298–300

McCrone, Donald, 94–96

347